Employment, Living Standards and Poverty in Contemporary Indonesia

The **Indonesia Project**, a major international centre for research on the Indonesian economy and society, is housed in the **Crawford School of Economics and Government**'s **Arndt-Corden Department of Economics**. The Crawford School is part of the **ANU College of Asia and the Pacific** at **The Australian National University (ANU).** Established in 1965, the Project is well known and respected in Indonesia and in other places where Indonesia attracts serious scholarly and official interest. Funded by the ANU and the Australian Agency for International Development (AusAID), the Indonesia Project monitors and analyses recent economic developments in Indonesia; informs Australian governments, business and the wider community about those developments and about future prospects; stimulates research on the Indonesian economy; and publishes the respected *Bulletin of Indonesian Economic Studies*.

The College's **Department of Political and Social Change (PSC)** focuses on domestic politics, social processes and state–society relationships in Asia and the Pacific, and has a long-established interest in Indonesia.

Together with PSC, the Project holds the annual Indonesia Update conference, which offers an overview of recent economic and political developments and devotes attention to a significant theme in Indonesia's development. The *Bulletin of Indonesian Economic Studies* publishes the conference's economic and political overviews, while the edited papers related to the conference theme are published in the Indonesia Update Series.

The **Institute of Southeast Asian Studies (ISEAS)** was established as an autonomous organization in 1968. It is a regional centre dedicated to the study of socio-political, security and economic trends and developments in Southeast Asia and its wider geostrategic and economic environment. The Institute's research programmes are the Regional Economic Studies (RES, including ASEAN and APEC), Regional Strategic and Political Studies (RSPS), and Regional Social and Cultural Studies (RSCS).

ISEAS Publishing, an established academic press, has issued more than 2,000 books and journals. It is the largest scholarly publisher of research about Southeast Asia from within the region. ISEAS Publishing works with many other academic and trade publishers and distributors to disseminate important research and analyses from and about Southeast Asia to the rest of the world.

Indonesia Update Series

Employment, Living Standards and Poverty in Contemporary Indonesia

Edited by
Chris Manning and **Sudarno Sumarto**

ISEAS

INSTITUTE OF SOUTHEAST ASIAN STUDIES
Singapore

First published in Singapore in 2011 by
ISEAS Publishing
Institute of Southeast Asian Studies
30 Heng Mui Keng Terrace
Pasir Panjang
Singapore 119614

E-mail: publish@iseas.edu.sg
Website: http://bookshop.iseas.edu.sg

The responsibility for facts and opinions in this publication rests exclusively with the authors and their interpretations do not necessarily reflect the views or the policy of the Institute or its supporters.

ISEAS Library Cataloguing-in-Publication Data

Employment, living standards and poverty in contemporary Indonesia / edited
  by Chris Manning and Sudarno Sumarto.
  (Indonesia Update series)
  1. Poverty — Indonesia — Congresses
  2. Poverty — Government policy — Indonesia — Congresses
  3. Indonesia — Economic conditions — 1966-1997 — Congresses
  4. Indonesia — Economic conditions — 1997- — Congresses
  5. Industrialization — Indonesia — Congresses
  6. Education — Indonesia — Congresses
  7. Public health — Indonesia — Congresses
  I. Manning, Chris, 1945-
  II. Sumarto, Sudarno, 1960-
DS644.4 I41 2010   2011

ISBN 978-981-4345-11-8 (soft cover)
ISBN 978-981-4345-12-5 (hard cover)
ISBN 978-981-4345-13-2 (E-book PDF)

Cover photo: A nurse weighs a young child at a local health clinic. The use of maternal and child health services is increasing as women become aware of the contribution they can make to their own and their children's health — or even survival. The government continues to implement programs to raise knowledge and awareness about such services, especially in rural areas.
Photo courtesy of Stella Hutagalung

Edited and typeset by Beth Thomson, Japan Online, Canberra
Indexed by Angela Grant, Sydney
Printed in Singapore by Markono Print Media Pte Ltd

CONTENTS

TABLES

FIGURES

CONTRIBUTORS

Vivi Alatas   Senior Economist and Team Leader, Poverty Group, World Bank, Jakarta

Haryo Aswicahyono   Researcher, Department of Economics, Centre for Strategic and International Studies (CSIS), Jakarta

Lisa Cameron   Professor of Economics, Department of Econometrics and Business Statistics; and Director, Development Research Unit, Monash University, Melbourne

Tadjuddin Noer Effendi   Professor, Sociology Department, Faculty of Social and Political Sciences, Gadjah Mada University, Yogyakarta

Lisa Hannigan   Social Protection Manager, Australian Agency for International Development (AusAID), Jakarta

Nida P. Harahap   Medical Professional; and Guest Lecturer, University of Padjajaran, Bandung

Adrian C. Hayes   Adjunct Associate Professor, Australian Demographic and Social Research Institute (ADSRI), Australian National University, Canberra

Hal Hill   H.W. Arndt Professor of Southeast Asian Economies, Arndt-Corden Department of Economics, Crawford School of Economics and Government, Australian National University, Canberra

Sherry Tao Kong   Research Fellow, Research School of Economics, College of Business and Economics, Australian National University, Canberra

Chris Manning   Associate Professor and staff of the Indonesia Project, Arndt-Corden Department of Economics, Crawford School of Economics and Government, Australian National University, Canberra

Deswanto Marbun   Researcher, SMERU Research Institute, Jakarta

John Maxwell   Independent Researcher, Canberra

Riyana Miranti   Research Fellow, National Centre for Social and Economic Modelling (NATSEM), University of Canberra, Canberra

Dionisius Narjoko   Researcher, Economic Research Institute for ASEAN and East Asia (ERIA), Jakarta

Susan Olivia   Post-doctoral Research Fellow, Department of Econometrics and Business Statistics, Monash University, Melbourne

Ari Perdana   Economist, Centre for Strategic and International Studies (CSIS), Jakarta; and Lecturer, Faculty of Economics, University of Indonesia, Jakarta

Risti Permani   Post-doctoral Fellow, University of Adelaide, Adelaide

Lant Pritchett   Professor of the Practice of International Development and Faculty Chair of the Master in Public Administration in International Development program, Harvard Kennedy School of Government, Cambridge MA

Ririn Purnamasari   Economist, Poverty Group, World Bank, Jakarta

Umbu Reku Raya   PhD Fellow, Arndt-Corden Department of Economics, Crawford School of Economics and Government, Australian National University, Canberra

Robert Sparrow   Lecturer, International Institute of Social Studies, Erasmus University Rotterdam, Rotterdam

Pungky Sumadi   Director of Social Protection and Welfare, National Development Planning Agency (Bappenas), Jakarta

Sudarno Sumarto   Policy Advisor, National Team for the Acceleration of Poverty Reduction (TNP2K), Office of the Vice President of the Republic of Indonesia, Jakarta

Daniel Suryadarma   Research Fellow, Indonesia Project, Arndt-Corden Department of Economics, Crawford School of Economics and Government, Australian National University, Canberra

Asep Suryahadi   Director, SMERU Research Institute, Jakarta

Matthew Wai-Poi   Economist, Poverty Group, World Bank, Jakarta

Peter Warr   John Crawford Professor of Agricultural Economics and Head, Arndt-Corden Department of Economics, and Director, Poverty Research Centre, Crawford School of Economics and Government, Australian National University, Canberra

Vivi Yulaswati   Deputy Director for Poverty Program Development, National Development Planning Agency (Bappenas), Jakarta

Athia Yumna   Researcher, SMERU Research Institute, Jakarta

ACKNOWLEDGMENTS

This book is based on papers given at the Indonesia Update conference, held at the Australian National University (ANU) on 24–25 September 2010. It derives its title from that event. Following the tradition of Indonesian Updates in recent years, this occasion enabled some of the best minds on a topical issue related to Indonesia to gather in Canberra to present papers and join in lively discussion. For the first time, the 2010 Update addressed issues of living standards and poverty, generating spirited debate. We are especially grateful to former Australian Ambassador to Indonesia, Bill Farmer, for setting the tone by giving an engaging opening address, and to Lant Pritchett for travelling from the east coast of the United States to give a stimulating keynote address that placed Indonesia in broader comparative perspective.

The book, however, is much more than a collection of conference papers presented at the Update. The papers were all revised for publication, some substantially so, based on comments from the editors and readers. Three chapters in the book were not presented at the conference, and we thank the authors – Adrian Hayes and Nida Harahap, Riyana Miranti and Peter Warr – for taking the time to contribute. We also thank Julia Tobias, Samuel Bazzi, Ross McLeod, Edward Aspinall and Terry Hull for giving their time to comment on draft chapters. We are very grateful to the authors for revising the papers quickly and in good spirit.

Many of the authors are professional economists or policy specialists. Our goal from the outset was to try to ensure that their presentations at the conference and the chapters in this book were accessible to an audience beyond the specialists. This meant relegating technical material to appendices or footnotes, or omitting it altogether. We hope that the revisions to the original papers have achieved a reasonable balance between rigorous, academic analysis and description.

Our thanks go to the many ANU staff and helpers who helped make the conference a success, and to those who played a part in producing what we hope will be a useful reference on this complex topic. First and foremost we thank the staff of the Indonesia Project – Cathy Haberle, Trish van der Hoek and Nurkemala Muliani – for working hard, efficiently and cheerfully to organise such a large and complex event. They were helped by Allison Ley and Thuy Thu Pham from the Department of Political and Social Change. Academic staff members in the Indonesia Project lent their support; Ross McLeod and Ed Aspinall in particular made special contributions to helping organise the event. Planning for each Update conference begins in earnest more than six months before the event, and a successful conference requires concentrated effort in the two months or so before the Update. We greatly appreciate everyone's endeavours.

The publication of the book in a timely fashion (within approximately nine months of the conference) was made possible mainly through the efforts of Beth Thomson, who has now edited and typeset nearly every Indonesia Update book since 1994. This is a remarkable record, not only for the quality and timeliness of Beth's work, but also for the rigorous editing out of logical errors and inconsistencies that are the rightful responsibility of the editors.

Beth was assisted by Nurkemala Muliani from the Indonesia Project, who helped manage the flow of documents. We would also like to thank Mona Sinthia from the SMERU Research Institute for helping us to obtain the photographs for the front cover. As usual, we are grateful for the cooperation of Rahilah Yusuf and Triena Ong from the Institute of Southeast Asian Studies (ISEAS) in ensuring that the publication is attractively presented, and ready in time for our regular 'Mini' Update and book launch in Jakarta. This productive collaboration with ISEAS in the publication of the Indonesia Update book is now in its seventeenth year.

As in previous years, the Update Conference and book was funded by the Australian Agency for International Development (AusAID) as part of a generous grant to the ANU and the Indonesia Project. We thank AusAID for its support. We recognise that the ANU is extremely privileged to receive this assistance for what is now regarded as the premier annual international conference on Indonesia. The Department of Political and Social Change also makes some funding available, with the ANU providing the facilities for holding the conference.

We sincerely hope that this book will contribute to a deeper understanding of the difficult and pressing challenges facing Indonesia in relation to employment, poverty and living standards, not just in Australia and internationally, but also back home – *di tanah air*.

Chris Manning and Sudarno Sumarto

Canberra and Jakarta
March 2011

GLOSSARY

Asabri	Asurasi Sosial Angkatan Bersenjata Republik Indonesia (Armed Forces Social Insurance Plan)
ASEAN	Association of Southeast Asian Nations
Askes	Asuransi Kesehatan (Health Insurance)
Askeskin	Asuransi Kesehatan Masyarakat Miskin (Health Insurance for the Poor)
AusAID	Australian Agency for International Development
Bappenas	Badan Perencanaan Pembangunan Nasional (National Development Planning Agency)
BBM	Bahan Bakar Minyak (petroleum-based fuel initative)
BKS	Bantuan Khusus Siswa (Special Assistance for Students)
BLT	Bantuan Langsung Tunai (Direct Cash Assistance), an unconditional cash transfer program
BOS	Bantuan Operasional Sekolah (Schools Operational Assistance), a program of block grants for schools
BP3	Badan Pembantu Penyelenggaraan Pendidikan (Educational Assistance Board)
BPS	Badan Pusat Statistik (Statistics Indonesia), the central statistics agency
Bulog	Badan Urusan Logistik (the national food logistics agency)
bupati	district head
CLTS	Community-led Total Sanitation
CPI	consumer price index
DAK	Dana Alokasi Khusus (Special Allocation Fund)
DAU	Dana Alokasi Umum (General Allocation Fund)
DI	Daerah Istimewa (Special Region)
DKI	Daerah Khusus Ibukota (Special Capital Region)

DPR	Dewan Perwakilan Rakyat (People's Representative Council), the national parliament
DPRD	Dewan Perwakilan Rakyat Daerah (Regional People's Representative Council), regional legislature
dukun	traditional birth attendant
dusun	village, neighbourhood
gotong royong	mutual community self-help program
Guided Democracy	period of enhanced presidential authority under Sukarno (1959–65)
HDI	human development index
Infrastruktur Pedesaan	village infrastructure program
Inpres	Instruksi Presiden (Presidential Instruction), a program of special grants from the central government
Inpres Desa Tertinggal	Neglected Villages Program, a special presidential program for poor villages
Jamkesmas	Jaminan Kesehatan Masyarakat (Health Security for the Poor), subsidised health insurance scheme
Jamsostek	Jaminan Social Tenaga Kerja (Workers Social Security Program), social security program for wage employees
JPS	Jaring Pengaman Sosial (Social Safety Net)
kecamatan	subdistrict
kelurahan	village administrative unit (below *kecamatan*)
LP3ES	Lembaga Penelitian, Pendidikan dan Penerangan Ekonomi dan Sosial (Institute of Economic and Social Research, Education and Information)
madrasah	Islamic school
madrasah aliyah	Islamic senior high school
madrasah ibtidaiyah	Islamic primary school
madrasah tsanawiyah	Islamic junior high school
musrenbang	*musyawarah perencanaan pembangunan* (consultative community meeting to assess development priorities)
New Order	the Suharto era (1965–98)
ODF	Open Defecation Free
OECD	Organisation for Economic Co-operation and Development
OPK	Operasi Pasar Khusus (Special Market Operations), a subsidised rice program
Padat Karya	labour-intensive public works program

Pamsimas	Program Penyediaan Air Minum dan Sanitasi Berbasis Masyarakat (National Strategy for Community-based Total Sanitation), a continuation of the WSLIC programs
PDM-DKE	Program Pemberdayaan Daerah Mengatasi Dampak Krisis Ekonomi (Regional Empowerment Program to Overcome the Impact of the Economic Crisis)
pesantren	Islamic boarding school
PKH	Program Keluarga Harapan (Family Hope Program), a conditional cash transfer program
PKS	Partai Keadilan Sejahtera (Prosperous Justice Party)
PNPM	Program Nasional Pemberdayaan Masyarakat (National Program for Community Empowerment), an umbrella program for community development
Podes	Potensi Desa (Village Potential), a BPS survey of village economic status)
PPP	purchasing power parity
puskesmas	*pusat kesehatan masyarakat* (community health centre)
Raskin	Beras untuk Keluarga Miskin (rice program for poor families)
reformasi	'reform', ferequently used to refer to the post-New Order period
Sakernas	Survei Angkatan Kerja Nasional (National Labour Force Survey)
Sekolah Dasar Inpres	Inpres for Primary Schools
SMERU	Social Monitoring and Early Response Unit (now the SMERU Research Institute)
SToPs	Sanitasi Total dan Pemasaran Sanitasi (Total Sanitation and Sanitation Marketing, or TSSM)
Susenas	Survei Sosio-Ekonomi Nasional (National Socio-Economic Survey)
TIMSS	Trends in International Mathematics and Science Study
TNP2K	Tim Nasional Percepatan Penanggulangan Kemiskinan (National Team for the Acceleration of Poverty Reduction)
TSSM	Total Sanitation and Sanitation Marketing
USAID	United States Agency for International Development
WSLIC	Water Supply and Sanitation for Low-income Communities

Currencies

$	US dollar
Rp	Indonesian rupiah

Map of Indonesia

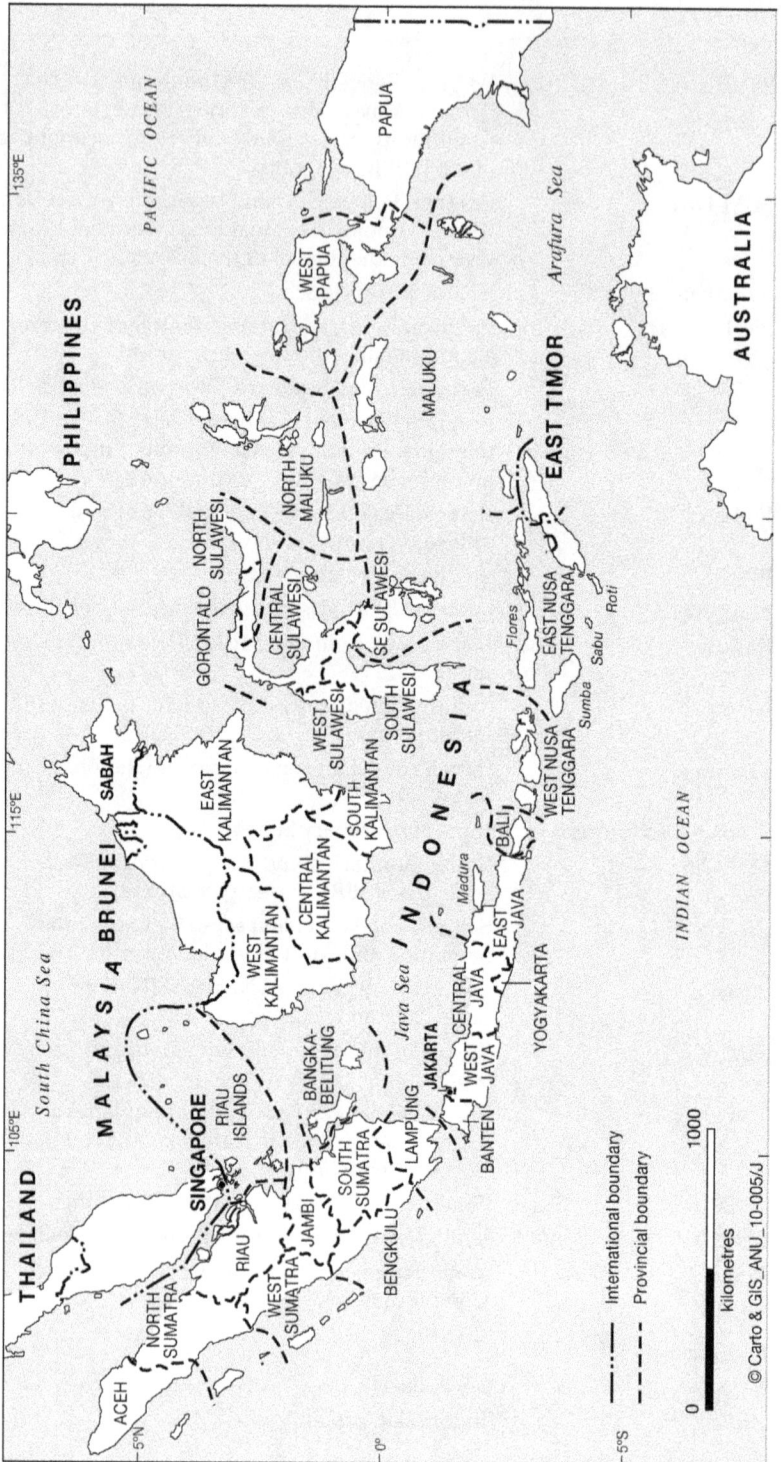

Map of Indonesia

THAILAND

MALAYSIA BRUNEI

PHILIPPINES

SINGAPORE

South China Sea

SABAH

PACIFIC OCEAN

ACEH

NORTH SUMATRA

RIAU ISLANDS

RIAU

WEST SUMATRA

JAMBI

SOUTH SUMATRA

BENGKULU

BANGKA-BELITUNG

LAMPUNG

WEST KALIMANTAN

CENTRAL KALIMANTAN

SOUTH KALIMANTAN

EAST KALIMANTAN

GORONTALO

NORTH SULAWESI

WEST SULAWESI

CENTRAL SULAWESI

SE SULAWESI

SOUTH SULAWESI

NORTH MALUKU

WEST PAPUA

PAPUA

MALUKU

Java Sea

JAKARTA

BANTEN

WEST JAVA

CENTRAL JAVA

YOGYAKARTA

EAST JAVA

Madura

BALI

WEST NUSA TENGGARA

EAST NUSA TENGGARA

Flores

Sumba

Sabu

Roti

EAST TIMOR

Arafura Sea

I N D O N E S I A

INDIAN OCEAN

AUSTRALIA

135°E

115°E

105°E

5°N

0°

5°S

International boundary

Provincial boundary

0

1000

kilometres

© Carto & GIS_ANU_10-005/J

xx

1 EMPLOYMENT, LIVING STANDARDS AND POVERTY: TRENDS, POLICIES AND INTERACTIONS

Chris Manning and Sudarno Sumarto

Job creation and poverty alleviation are important goals in themselves as well as instrumental in successful political development in a young democracy.
Professor Boediono, then Coordinating Minister of Economic Affairs,
Inter Parliamentary Union Assembly Meeting, Nusa Dua, Bali, 1 May 2007

By international standards, Indonesia has a credible record on poverty reduction and improvements in living standards in the first decade of the twenty-first century. This is particularly true with regard to the monetary measurement of poverty. Measured in this way, poverty has fallen significantly since the Asian financial crisis of 1997–98 despite only moderate rates of economic growth by regional standards. As the above comment by Boediono – now the vice president – suggests, the government takes poverty alleviation seriously, based not only on economic but also political considerations.

Nevertheless, unlike in the Suharto era, Indonesia can no longer rely on creating better jobs for workers in low-productivity agriculture and services to achieve significant declines in poverty and vulnerability. Nor is such a strategy a viable option politically. Post-*reformasi*, elected leaders now stand accountable for their record on poverty alleviation. This has encouraged governments to become more proactive in seeking to improve the living standards of the poor.

The more direct approach to poverty reduction has brought with it a myriad of problems and challenges. Many of the shortcomings in government policies have been the butt of criticism in the political arena, especially since Susilo Bambang Yudhoyono was elected president in 2004. Unemployment remains high, the quality of education has been

1

identified as a major problem, and many of the poor are unable to access free or subsided health care. While Indonesia is on track to meet several of its Millennium Development Goals by 2015, on current trends it is unlikely to meet others. These include reductions in child malnutrition and maternal mortality rates and improvements in access to clean water and sanitation. Reaching the poor through education and health programs, and through special cash grants, has been more difficult to achieve than most government office holders had anticipated.

This book sets out to provide a picture of Indonesia's progress in improving living standards, and to detail the government's policy approaches, successes and failures.[1] In this introductory chapter we provide an overview of these developments, indicating the contribution that the other chapters make to the subject. The organisation of the chapter follows that of the book. We start by looking briefly at Indonesia's performance in international perspective, and the mix of factors that have influenced poverty decline nationally and regionally. This is followed by discussions of the relationship between living standards and both employment and social investments. We then describe the evolution of policies directed at overcoming social disadvantage and poverty, before looking at specific areas of difficulty and achievement.

INDONESIA'S RECORD ON POVERTY REDUCTION

Viewed from a historical and comparative perspective, Indonesia's progress in improving living standards and eliminating poverty since the Asian financial crisis might be described as 'quite good, if patchy'. Of course, this conclusion depends partly on one's definitions of poverty and disadvantage. Following the literature, we rely here on three indicators of poverty incidence: the national poverty line set by the central statistics agency, Statistics Indonesia (currently just over Rp 200,000 per person per month, or slightly under $1.50 a day); the proportion of the population living below $1 (or $1.25) a day; and the proportion living below $2 a day. The latter two indicators are commonly used in international comparisons of poverty incidence.

To take the historical perspective first, the headcount rate of poverty (however measured) has fallen less rapidly in absolute terms over the past decade than in the decades before the Asian financial crisis; the total number of poor is estimated to have fallen by less than 10 million

---

1   One major gap in the coverage is the impact of natural disasters, which have both immediate and long-term effects on living standards and poverty. For an excellent treatment of this issue in relation to the Asian tsunami of December 2004, see Jayasuriya and McCawley (2010).

in 2000–2010, compared with over 20 million from 1980 through to the mid-1990s. The government has also fallen well short of the goal of halving poverty announced by Yudhoyono at the beginning of his first term of government in 2004. But it is not surprising to find that the pace of poverty decline has slowed since the fall of Suharto given the rapid and unequivocal shift towards a more democratic and decentralised polity.

Two factors have been at play. First, economic growth (at 4–6 per cent per annum) has been much slower than in the Suharto era, notwithstanding the fact that Indonesia is hardly a poor performer among countries experiencing such a big political transition (see Chapter 2 by Lant Pritchett). At the same time, poverty rates have become less responsive – or less 'elastic' – to economic progress.[2] Slower growth of employment in the more labour-intensive segments of manufacturing and services appears to have played a major part in this outcome. This in turn can be attributed to the less flexible environment for formal sector employment that now prevails.[3]

Despite the somewhat disappointing accomplishments in poverty reduction since the fall of Suharto, Indonesia has done better in terms of some key indicators of disadvantage. As pointed out earlier, it is on track to meet several of its Millennium Development Goals. The country no longer relies so heavily on macroeconomic growth and stability, and on (untargeted) public spending on social and physical infrastructure, as the main channels for achieving reductions in poverty.

From an international perspective, Indonesia's poverty rates are broadly in line with what would be expected for a lower middle-income country. As Figure 1.1 shows, in 2005 a much higher proportion of the population was living below the poverty line in Indonesia than in Malaysia and Thailand (and China), based on either of two internationally comparable poverty lines. The share of the poor was broadly on a par with the Philippines and Vietnam, and lower than in lower-income countries such as Cambodia (and India and Bangladesh).

Indonesia has also experienced intermediate rates of poverty *decline* since the crisis. Its rates of both poverty and poverty decline lie in between those attained by China and India.[4] Poverty has fallen less rapidly

---

2 This is perhaps to be expected given that a quite small proportion of the population (less than 15 per cent) is currently living below the national poverty line. As living standards improve, it becomes harder to move the 'hard core' of chronically poor people out of poverty.

3 See Chapter 6 by Haryo Aswicahyono, Hal Hill and Dionisius Narjoko for a discussion of these issues.

4 The World Bank computes data for urban and rural areas for these three countries through to 2005; of course, the definitions of urban and rural areas differ significantly among the three.

Figure 1.1   Poverty in Southeast Asia, 2005 (% of population below poverty line)

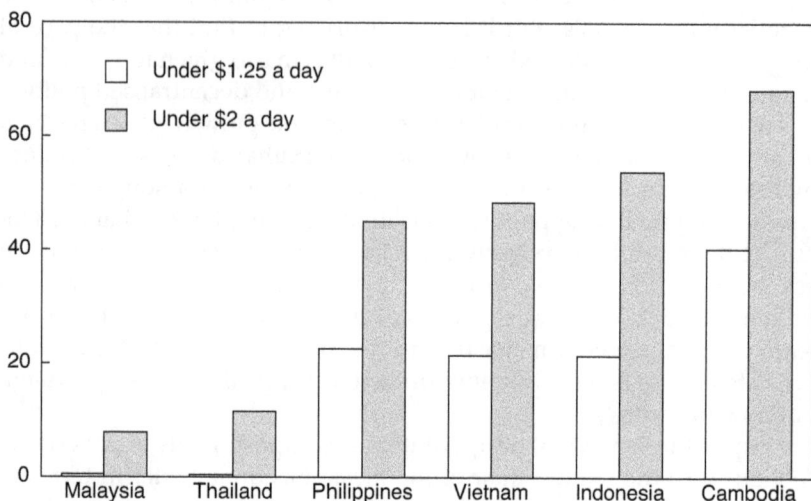

Source: World Bank.

in rural than in urban areas in all three countries. While the decline in urban poverty rates has been faster in Indonesia than in India, it has been much slower than in China where migration to the cities was tightly controlled until recently.

Lant Pritchett (Chapter 2) and Peter Warr (Chapter 3) both argue that Indonesia has performed well from a comparative perspective, despite the major political and administrative changes since 1998, including decentralisation. Indeed, Pritchett provides evidence that Indonesia has notched up much better economic growth than other countries that have experienced similar political transitions, even if that growth has not had the same impact on poverty as it did in the past. At the same time, both authors agree that slow economic growth combined with occasional price inflation remains an obstacle to improving living standards. This is especially relevant for the large numbers of people whose incomes are only just above the poverty line in Indonesia.

On non-monetary indicators of living standards, Indonesia again appears to be performing roughly on a par with its East Asian neighbours. General health indicators for the poor have improved less quickly than in China, Thailand and Vietnam, but more rapidly than in the Philippines and Cambodia (ESCAP 2010). Problems remain in a number of areas. The most recent data available point to a quarter of children below the age of five being malnourished; only 72 per cent of births being attended by a skilled birth attendant; 45 per cent of poor households having no access to sanitation; more than half having no access to safe drinking water; and around 20 per cent of children from poor households not proceeding to junior secondary school.

One approach to understanding poverty, and the policies to overcome it, is to identify key 'opportunities' and 'constraints'. This is done by Asep Suryahadi, Umbu Reku Raya, Deswanto Marbun and Athia Yumna (Chapter 4), who identify a strategy for accelerating poverty decline in Indonesia. The opportunities include making globalisation work for the poor, taking advantage of the demographic dividend, adopting a more participatory approach and galvanising support for the commitment to achieve the Millennium Development Goals. The constraints include insufficient productive opportunities, weak human capabilities and inadequate social protection.

Strategies for overcoming poverty also differ across regions. In Chapter 5, Riyana Miranti identifies three sets of factors: levels of and changes in income per capita, human capital and infrastructure. Dividing provinces into five groups based mainly on natural resources, geography and demography, she finds that the impact of economic growth, human capital and infrastructure can and often do work differently depending on the contrasting structural characteristics of groups of provinces. What works well in one group of provinces, she concludes, may not work well in others.[5]

During the early stages of a country's development, the main determinants of poverty decline are more jobs, better jobs, and improvements in education and health. To understand the crux of the relationship between economic activity, social investments, jobs and poverty alleviation, it is useful to think of a simple demand–supply framework. On the demand side, the acquisition of 'better' jobs (those that increase earnings and productivity) mainly occurs through increased investments and output by the private sector. Governments intervene to support the demand for labour and wages by ensuring macroeconomic stability and a competitive business environment at a national and regional level. As the share of wage workers grows, stable prices of key commodities are especially important for the protection of real incomes. Governments also undertake public investments in physical and social infrastructure to underpin this process. On the supply side, public and private invest-

---

5 Regression analysis by Miranti also confirms that where provinces lag on development indicators, both pro-poor growth (higher regional GDP per capita) and intervention through infrastructure or human capital investments are likely to be essential for any significant progress.

ments in education and health in particular contribute to the capacity of workers to undertake more intensive and higher-quality work.

While these are the main longer-term determinants of poverty decline, in the interim more comprehensive social security and safety nets are needed to help low-income and vulnerable households cope with poor living standards and poverty. They also help to prevent near-poor families from slipping into poverty, especially as a result of shocks to incomes and assets, at a household, regional, national or international level.

What has been Indonesia's experience in these matters? We look first at employment and migration, then at education and health, before turning to policies directly targeting poverty.

EMPLOYMENT AND MIGRATION

Job creation in the formal sector has been decidedly slower than in the pre-crisis period. After the initial recovery from the crisis, two broad periods can be distinguished: the first from around 2000 to 2005 when jobs were hard to come by, and the second through to the end of the decade when employment picked up and unemployment fell. During the first period, when economic growth fluctuated around 4–5 per cent, the record on formal sector employment was especially poor, with the index of regular wage employment declining through to the middle of the decade (Table 1.1). Unemployment rose from around 8 per cent in 2001 to 11 per cent in 2005 and real wages fell quite steeply, partly in response to high inflation at the beginning and in the middle of the decade. The movement of workers out of low-productivity agriculture stalled, and the informal sector (including casual wage employees) absorbed most of the increase in employment. This stood in stark contrast to the period before the crisis, when employment and wage increases in the formal sector outside agriculture had driven declines in poverty.

From around 2005, however, conditions improved, partly in response to higher economic growth rates of closer to 6 per cent per annum. Formal sector employment picked up and unemployment rates began to decline quite quickly, falling by the end of the decade to just below the rates recorded in 2001. While jobs growth in manufacturing continued to be sluggish, it rebounded in both trade and services. Nevertheless, the informal sector was still the main source of new jobs, and many of these were relatively low-wage casual jobs.[6] Poverty continued to be concen-

---

6   Casual wage jobs outside agriculture accounted for over one-third of all new jobs created in the period 2001–2009, almost double the share of regular wage jobs outside agriculture.

Table 1.1   Unemployment rate, index of employment by sector and employment status, and index of wages, 2001–2009

	Unem- ployment (%)	Index of employment (2001 = 100)				Index of wages[a]
		Total	Agricul- ture	Non-agriculture		
				Regular wage	Informal	
2001	8.1	100	100	100	100	
2002	9.1	101	102	95	104	
2003	9.5	100	106	89	100	100
2004	9.9	100	102	92	109	101
2005	11.2	102	104	98	107	93
2006	10.3	102	101	97	114	95
2007	9.1	106	104	102	122	97
2008	8.4	109	104	100	132	95
2009	7.9	111	105	107	138	105
Total (million)		**105**	**42**	**29**	**34**	

a   Index of real wages of regular male employees, 2003 prices (2003 = 100).
Source: National Labour Force Survey (Sakernas), various years.

trated in the agricultural sector where close to 40 per cent of the population still worked, and where productivity gains in the post-crisis period had been disappointing (World Bank 2006).

Overall, the explanations for these post-crisis patterns of employment include slower economic growth and lower rates of investment, especially in the more capital and skill-intensive sectors of the economy.[7] In Chapter 6, Haryo Aswicahyono, Hal Hill and Dionisius Narjoko find that employment growth in the manufacturing sector was also much slower after the Asian financial crisis. In addition, the composition of jobs had changed significantly, away from larger and more labour-intensive firms

---

7   A World Bank (2010a) survey of employment in Indonesia (the 'Indonesia Jobs Report') argues that slow service sector growth was an obstacle in the early years after the crisis. It also argues that employment growth in industry was more robust than has been suggested by commentators who have focused on 'jobless growth'. In the Indonesian case, growth of industry has largely been due to an expansion of jobs in construction (included as part of industry), rather than in manufacturing.

in industries such as garments and footwear. The authors suggest that the labour policies introduced in the early 2000s may be part of the explanation, although they also argue that Indonesia is not an outlier within Southeast Asia on industrial job creation. The country's high-wage policies appear to have discouraged labour-intensive investors at a critical time when the advantages of investing in China and Vietnam were becoming increasingly apparent. Once investments in industries such as footwear, garments and furniture had been made in other countries, it was hard to attract them back. The preference of employers to take on casual and contract workers rather than regular employees appears to be another consequence of Indonesia's labour policies, making any downsizing of the regular wage workforce costly.[8]

Finally, although small in relation to total employment, international migration has provided opportunities for poor, mainly rural Indonesians to work in neighbouring countries and the Middle East. With rural–urban migration now offering fewer opportunities than previously for social and economic advancement, international migration has expanded. While the remittances international migrants send home are substantial (estimated at around $7 billion in 2010), the high proportion of unskilled, mostly female, migrant workers and the poor governance arrangements for the protection of migrant workers have limited the benefits from the deployment of labour overseas. While internal migrants from rural to urban areas face their own difficulties in making the transition to city life, many of them (or their children) do 'make it' through migration. In Chapter 7, Sherry Tao Kong and Tadjuddin Noer Effendi show that occupational mobility among migrants to the city is related to higher levels of education, and especially to local (urban) educational experience.

EDUCATION AND HEALTH

Improvements to schooling and health, accompanied by more inclusive programs for the poor, are at the heart of immediate and longer-term efforts to overcome poverty. While much progress has been made in these areas since the Asian financial crisis, Indonesia still faces enormous challenges to provide services to the poor and lower middle-income groups.

Education

Education is an accepted route for lifting large numbers of people out of poverty, by increasing their capacity to earn a higher income. The main

---

8 See Manning and Roesad (2007) on the new labour policies.

challenges for Indonesia are to increase secondary school enrolments, improve the quality of schooling, and impart the vocational and other skills required by the labour market.

Indonesia has done much in this area, raising spending on education to close to 4 per cent of GDP. At just under 20 per cent, national expenditure on education is broadly in line with that in neighbouring countries such as Thailand, although still well behind Malaysia (del Granado et al. 2007). With most Indonesians now completing primary school, and a majority of poor household heads having a primary school education, the government has turned its attention to lifting junior secondary rates of enrolment and graduation. The junior secondary enrolment rate increased by 20 per cent, and the senior secondary rate by 25 per cent, between 1995 and 2005 (World Bank: 2010a: 120). By 2005, nearly two-thirds of all children of junior secondary school age, and 40 per cent of those of senior secondary school age, were enrolled in school. Senior secondary graduates can earn a significant wage premium over primary and junior secondary graduates in the workforce.

Programs focusing on the poor include new scholarship schemes for students and the Operational Assistance to Schools program (Bantuan Operasi Sekolah, or BOS). The new scholarship schemes serve more students than the program devised during the crisis to keep the children of the poor in school. According to Suharyo et al. (2006), nearly 20 per cent of primary school students and 26 per cent of junior secondary students received such scholarships in 2004. A condition of the schemes is that the money be spent on tuition, supplies, transport and living costs.

BOS is a comprehensive program of block grants to schools to improve the affordability and quality of schooling. It was introduced in mid-2005 to compensate for the steep rise in fuel prices resulting from the government's decision in March to cut fuel subsidies. The program directly addresses supply-side weaknesses by increasing the quality and quantity of educational resources available to students. However, it has been criticised for failing to ensure that recipient schools meet their obligation to give priority to poor students. Only 48 per cent of 43 schools surveyed in early 2006, for example, had used any of their BOS funding to assist these students (Suharyo et al. 2006: 18).

Despite the advances in education, Indonesian students continue to perform less well academically than their peers in comparable countries. In Chapter 8, Daniel Suryadarma finds that eighth grade students obtained lower scores in an international mathematics test than those in a group of countries with comparable economic and health conditions (Iran, Jordan, Tunisia and Romania), and far lower scores than those in a group of neighbouring countries (Malaysia, Singapore and Thailand). He discusses a range of factors that may have contributed to this situation, including course content and hours of instruction, teacher absence and qualifications, and an imbalance in the distribution of teachers across the country. Some of the initiatives introduced to improve the quality of schooling include a focus on community participation, a teacher certification program and a remote area allowance for teachers. So far, however, Suryadarma finds they have had only limited success.

Many of the problems in national education appear to be amplified in the Islamic education system. In Chapter 9, Risti Permani shows that the primary and secondary *madrasah* generally cater to lower-income families but have less access to funding than state schools. Under Indonesia's decentralised system of government, responsibility for *madrasah* funding rests with the under-resourced Ministry of Religious Affairs, whereas state school funding is supplied by the Ministry of Education (with the dispersal of funds increasingly the responsibility of district governments). Permani finds that problems of teacher quality in *madrasah* are particularly severe. Also, 30 per cent of class hours in the *madrasah* must be devoted to religious studies, tending to crowd out regular classes.

The cost of schooling is especially taxing for poor families. Tuition and other expenses are only partially covered by programs like BOS, and several studies suggest that it is difficult for the poor to pay for schooling, especially when their children reach secondary school.[9] Jobs are not assured, even after graduating. High rates of graduate unemployment are a particular problem for the poor, who tend to lack contacts and marketable skills.[10]

Health and sanitation

Indonesia has made significant gains in some areas of health care, although it continues to lag behind its neighbours in overall performance in this area. The number of public health facilities has expanded, contributing to significant gains in key indicators such as infant mortality (now below 30 deaths per 1,000 live births) and fertility decline. In place of the health card program set up during the crisis, poor households now receive cards entitling them to free services at public clinics and hospitals, although hospital use among the recipients of the card remains low.[11]

---

9   See Chapter 16 by Lisa Hannigan for case studies describing the high cost of transport to access services in rural areas, and the difficulties poor households face in funding their children through senior secondary school.

10 A major move towards more vocational schooling at the secondary level since 2005 should help, provided the curriculum can be adjusted quickly to meet changing demand (World Bank 2010a).

11 See Sparrow, Chapter 11, for details of some of the post-crisis health programs, and Arifianto et al. (2005a, 2005b, 2005c) for in-depth studies of the health card program in three provinces.

Nevertheless the public health care system faces many problems. These particularly affect the poor, among them the difficulty of accessing care in some areas, the inadequate supply of trained practitioners and the direct and indirect costs of care. In Chapter 10, Adrian C. Hayes and Nida P. Harahap argue that another reason for health system underperformance is the failure of the central government to exercise its authority effectively to improve governance in the sector. They are not optimistic about a major step forward even if universal health insurance coverage is achieved by 2014, as planned. Hayes and Harahap counsel a radical overhaul in the way the health system is organised.

Accumulated evidence suggests that the poor still underutilise health care, even though access and equity have improved considerably, and the reduced cost of public care has increased demand. In surveying the evidence on health care services, Robert Sparrow (Chapter 11) concludes that reducing the financial barriers will not be enough to achieve access for all, although the provision of universal social health insurance should help. It will be equally important to address other constraints. These include perceptions about the poor quality of care and lack of awareness and knowledge among the poor about services and programs. The indirect costs of injury or illness, such as loss of income, are also highlighted.

Greater public and private investment in sanitation is another major challenge: in 2009, more than 30 per cent of rural households in Indonesia did not have access to adequate sanitation. Lisa Cameron and Susan Olivia point out in Chapter 12 that preventable diseases resulting from a lack of sanitation and poor hygiene continue to impose a heavy disease burden on the poor, especially among infants. The authors argue that community-based programs have proven more effective than the initial top-down approach in improving sanitation and reducing the incidence of diarrhoea.[12]

POVERTY PROGRAMS AND POLICIES

Since the Asian financial crisis, Indonesia has joined many other developing nations in introducing more comprehensive social programs. These seek to provide better access to health, education, infrastructure and cash support for the poor, increasingly on a conditional basis. The success of such programs depends on political will and governance structures, as

---

12 Cameron and Olivia are are currently undertaking a 'randomised evaluation' of the Total Sanitation and Sanitation Marketing (TSSM) program in East Java to obtain a better understanding of what works, and what does not, in increasing the utilisation of sanitation.

well as institutional design, speed of response, success in targeting and efficiency of implementation. We look briefly at developments in these areas in Indonesia over the past several decades.

During the New Order period (1965–98), government policies focused on output, jobs and prices in general, with minimal efforts to target the poor directly. There was a major focus on rural development, through intensification of rice production and an expansion of rural infrastructure, especially roads, health centres and schools (Duflo 2001).[13] Although the New Order programs were hardly perfect (especially with regard to leakage of benefits to the non-poor), they did introduce several important themes of later programs, such as an element of community participation and an emphasis on human capital.

Subsequently, during the crisis of 1997–98, the government responded to steeply rising poverty by establishing a system of social safety nets (Jaring Pengaman Sosial, or JPS) for the poor.[14] The JPS programs covered food security, employment creation, education and health, some with an element of community empowerment. Indonesia embarked on a steep learning curve. Knowledge acquired covered a range of areas: the importance of defining objectives clearly; maintaining flexibility; targeting beneficiaries accurately; and developing different strategies for coping with major shocks, as opposed to core poverty (Sumarto and Pritchett 2001).

The latest phase has been one of consolidation and revision of programs to deal with poverty under more normal conditions. By 2005 Yudhoyono had amassed sufficient political capital to raise fuel prices (by 29 per cent in March and nearly 50 per cent in October), thereby easing the considerable burden on the budget of maintaining fuel subsidies.[15] To compensate for the effects on the economy in general and on household purchasing power, the government sought to reallocate resources swiftly to social programs. Some of the programs mounted during the Asian financial crisis were merged into the new compensation scheme to mitigate the impact of the price shock on welfare.

On 1 October 2005, the government launched its most ambitious social protection program to date, an unconditional cash transfer called

---

13 For example, more than 60,000 primary schools were built between 1973 and 1978 under a 1974 Presidential Instruction to build 'a primary school in every village'.

14 On the evolution of poverty during the crisis, see Suryahadi, Sumarto and Pritchett (2003).

15 The subsidy was first cut by 12 per cent in 2000, followed by further small reductions. By the time Yudhoyono raised fuel prices in 2005, spending on the subsidies had reached 2.9 per cent of GDP. To deal with the expected political fallout, the president promised to reallocate half the expected savings (Rp 11 trillion) for health, education and infrastructure programs.

Direct Cash Assistance (Bantuan Langsung Tunai, or BLT). Under the program, nearly a quarter of households received Rp 300,000 (approximately $30) every three months from October 2005 to September 2006.[16] By most accounts, BLT prevented a drastic increase in poverty and was reasonably well targeted to the poor, keeping many poor households from falling deeper into poverty. It also stopped near-poor and non-poor households from slipping into poverty, and promoted welfare improvements among poor households, pushing them to higher expenditure gradients (Sumarto, Bazzi and Suryahadi 2010).[17]

Much had to be done, however, to institutionalise and gain popular support for these programs, especially in the more open political environment that now prevailed. In Chapter 13, Ari Perdana and John Maxwell discuss the 'politics of poverty', with government achievements and approaches to poverty coming under close scrutiny from Indonesia's remarkably free press, civil society and parliaments. Local non-government activists have urged more deliberate consideration of poverty issues, while the critics of government programs have concentrated their attention on instances of corruption and leakages of program benefits. Democracy and openness provide various checks and balances, yet Perdana and Maxwell note that a more open political stage has also increased the risk that the government gives in to pressure for populist – but sometimes inequitable – solutions (such as higher fuel subsidies) advocated by politicians on both sides of parliament.

Partly in response to a national consensus that poverty alleviation is a high priority, substantial funds have been directed to key new programs in health and education. We now look briefly at two later schemes: a community development scheme and a conditional cash transfer scheme.

Community development

Funds gained through the removal of fuel price subsidies gave the government more room to move on a broad set of programs focusing on

---

16 Targeting was based on household welfare rankings derived from a 'proxy means test' that sought to distinguish poor from non-poor households using 14 qualitative variables as indicators of economic status.

17 In the absence of a cash compensation package, simulations based on data from the 2004 National Socio-Economic Survey suggest that the poverty rate would have risen quite dramatically (by around six percentage points). Perfect targeting would still have yielded an increase in poverty to nearly 18 per cent (an increase of less than two percentage points), which was remarkably close to actual poverty estimates for 2005/2006 (Statistics Indonesia circular, September 2006).

poverty alleviation through job creation and infrastructure improvement. Broadly subsumed under the National Program for Community Empowerment (Program Nasional Pemperdayaan Masyarakat, or PNPM), these programs delivered block grants to poor communities in both rural and urban areas, with funding to be allocated to specific projects through local decision-making processes. PNPM now covers every rural subdistrict (*kecamatan*) in Indonesia.[18] It is one of the world's largest community development programs, with a budget of close to $800 million in 2010.

Although it is still too early to make definitive judgements, empirical studies find that PNPM has had a positive effect on living standards in recipient areas. Vivi Yulaswati and Pungky Sumadi report on some of these results in Chapter 14. The poorest 20 per cent of households recorded gains in per capita consumption, employment and outpatient care, compared with households in control areas. Local participation in planning and implementation was quite high in PNPM areas, and rural infrastructure projects had high economic returns. Maintenance, however, was problematic. The authors stress that PNPM's long-term viability will depend on local governments taking greater responsibility for the planning, targeting and financing of pro-poor programs.

Cash transfers

Learning from experience with the unconditional cash transfer scheme (BLT), in 2007 the government introduced a conditional cash transfer scheme (Program Keluarga Harapan, or PKH). Payments were made conditional on poor households ensuring that their children attended school regularly and that children and pregnant women attended health clinics. By 2010 PKH was operating in 20 provinces, covering around 798,000 households. Whereas BLT was a short-term program intended to assist large numbers of poor and near-poor households during crises, PKH provides financial support to a narrowly targeted group of very poor households to build their longer-term human capital. Although quantifiable benefits will take some time to reveal themselves, Yulaswati and Sumadi (Chapter 14) find that after just one to two years the program seemed to have brought about small improvements in child and maternal health and education indicators, and had placed some pressure on local governments to provide well-functioning schools and health centres.

---

18 Each year, approximately 60,000 rural villages participate in PNPM's participatory planning exercise, resulting in disbursals of funds to over 50,000 projects (conversation with PNPM manager, 2011).

HURDLES, ACHIEVEMENTS AND CHALLENGES

The government's Medium Term Development Plan for 2010–2014 tries to sharpen the focus on the multidimensional and long-term nature of poverty, continuing the shift from universal subsidies to targeted social protection programs. Its goal is to reduce poverty from 14 per cent in 2009 to 8.0 per cent in 2014. Increasingly, all government departments are being encouraged to become involved in social protection programs ('mainstreaming'), with particular attention to pro-poor growth. The stated aim is to fulfil the national poverty goal, and targets associated with the Millennium Development Goals.

Achieving these goals will be no easy task, despite steady growth in public spending and more sustainable social protection. Many challenges will need to be addressed. Five will be discussed here: improving program targeting; protecting households from shocks; coordination across government departments and levels of government; managing 'voice' and 'noise'; and making decentralisation work.

Targeting

One of the main challenges in developing an effective social safety net has been to ensure that poor households are correctly identified and assisted, or targeted accurately in specific programs. Inadequate targeting is known to have limited the effectiveness of earlier social safety net programs.[19] In Chapter 15, Vivi Alatas, Ririn Purnamasari and Matthew Wai-Poi examine the effectiveness of social assistance and protection programs. The authors acknowledge the huge difficulties in accessing the poor in such a heterogeneous population, and show how targeting has improved since the blunt instruments applied during the Asian financial crisis. Nevertheless, rates of both inclusion error (the inclusion of non-poor in programs designed only for the poor) and exclusion error (the omission of the poor from such programs) remain quite large. The World Bank (2010b) has estimated rates of inclusion or exclusion error in some government programs at over 50 per cent.

Targeting the poor is particularly difficult in Indonesia for a number of reasons. First, a significant portion of the population is located close to the poverty line, making it difficult to find obvious characteristics that distinguish poor from near-poor households, and to deliver public programs to the 'transient' poor.

---

19 See, for example, Alatas et al. (2010), Bazzi, Sumarto and Suryahadi (2010) and Suryahadi et al. (2010).

Second, Indonesia's geographic diversity makes it difficult to identify and reach many households, as Alatas, Purnamasari and Wai-Poi make clear. Policies drawn up in Jakarta do not always have the intended consequences in diverse socio-economic environments. Some of these 'gaps' are discussed in the final chapter of this book by Lisa Hannigan. Drawing on case studies in very different regions, she finds that government social assistance priorities frequently do not align with the expressed needs of interviewed households. She discusses various types of undercoverage, including of risk and of specific household groups.

The potential benefits from well-targeted social expenditure aimed at the poorest households include increased effectiveness of programs, cost savings, and greater public support for such programs, due to perceptions of greater fairness. At the same time, the benefits of *narrow* targeting need to be weighed against the administrative costs of identifying, reaching and monitoring such a small proportion of the population.

Indonesia's conditional cash transfer (PKH), for example, narrowly targets the extreme poor (around 15 per cent of the population), while programs such as the unconditional cash transfer (BLT) and the health insurance program target both the poor and near-poor (all households up to 20 per cent above the poverty line, or closer to one-third of the total population). Raskin, the subsidised rice program, is supposed to target the poor, but in practice the benefits are often distributed equally among the community, resulting in considerable leakage to non-poor households (Hastuti et al. 2008).

One lesson learned from the experience so far is that transparency and gaining community support (that is, socialisation) are important to ensure the legitimacy of government programs and to avoid elite capture, where the benefits mainly go to the more established and powerful groups. Establishing a national targeting system for all household-level social programs is planned for 2011 as one step towards improving targeting outcomes.

Protecting households from shocks

Governments now use social protection programs widely to limit the potential effects of macroeconomic crises and fiscal cut-backs on the poor. They have also learned the lesson that real spending on formal social safety net programs needs to increase unambiguously at times of shock. One challenge in this area is to ensure that the data used to measure household welfare are comprehensive and up to date. Significant administrative resources are required to collect information on those hurt by a particular crisis. This is because the poverty criteria used to compile existing lists may not adequately capture the specific groups, sectors or regions affected. Additional institutional measures are needed to create an ongoing system of monitoring that can facilitate an early response to shocks. These would need to oversee a number of actions: better monitoring of vulnerabilities to poverty outside crisis periods; closer involvement of local governments in the collection, sharing, analysis and dissemination of data; and improved coordination between government agencies at the central and regional levels.

Coordination

Improved coordination between the various institutions involved in anti-poverty efforts – both across government departments and between the national and local levels of government – is crucial. At the same time, it is important to avoid overlapping responsibilities and to ensure clear lines of accountability. This is especially true as poverty programs become increasingly 'mainstreamed', involving many different central government departments.

The National Team for the Acceleration of Poverty Reduction (Tim Nasional Percepatan Penanggulangan Kemiskinan, or TNP2K) established in the office of the vice president under Presidential Regulation No. 15/2010 has been given the responsibility of overseeing the coordination of three clusters of poverty programs: household-based social assistance programs; community empowerment programs; and programs to expand economic opportunities for low-income households in areas such as micro credit.

Managing 'voice' and 'noise'

Indonesia's democratisation process now engages multiple voices in the decision-making processes that shape social programs (see Perdana and Maxwell, Chapter 13). But greater contestation in the political sphere and closer public scrutiny of government policies have also led to poverty issues being used as a political commodity, with some risk of driving policy in a more populist direction. The government is only slowly adjusting to the fact that opposition politicians inevitably focus on the negative aspects of poverty relief.

While it is difficult to communicate complex messages about the basis of poverty calculations in simple terms, it is nevertheless important for government leaders to explain the methodology in a way that the public can understand, and to ensure that poverty data are released in a timely and transparent manner. It would also help if leaders explained why contentious policies such as subsidy cuts and the associated plans for compensation are in the national interest. The welfare of the poor can be jeopardised by kneejerk public reactions that are not based on full knowledge of the facts.

Indonesia's experience with social safety net programs provides certain lessons relevant to managing 'voice' and 'noise' at both the central and local levels. First, it is critical that all relevant stakeholders receive clear messages about the purpose and design of programs, including how eligibility is determined. For example, the BLT program of cash transfers in 2005 was initially implemented very rapidly, leading to a rushed process of socialisation and targeting. This created negative perceptions about the fairness of the program and some community dissatisfaction, despite high levels of support overall. The subsequent PNPM strategy, in contrast, has been to conduct extensive village-level community consultation, which is considered to have boosted the sense of local ownership.

Second, information campaigns and responsive complaint mechanisms are critical to ensure community satisfaction and program transparency. If the implementation of programs is well managed, there need not necessarily be a trade-off between effective pro-poor policies and programs, and high levels of public support for those policies.

Making decentralisation work

The wide variation in poverty rates across districts (from 5–15 per cent in most of Java and Bali to 37 per cent in Papua) indicates that poverty alleviation strategies need to be tailored to local conditions.[20] Indonesia's decentralised system of government holds promise for strengthening poverty alleviation, although regional disparities in revenue are placing pressure on social welfare spending in some districts.

The national focus on poverty alleviation has created an increasingly important role for regional governments, bearing in mind that roughly 30 per cent of central government expenditure is now allocated to the regions as transfers. Whereas spending on health and education has increased at all levels of government, central government spending on physical infrastructure has decreased, and provincial and district-level spending has not risen enough to fill the resulting gap (see Perdana and Maxwell, Chapter 13). In cases where resources and responsibilities have been transferred relatively rapidly to regional governments, the quality of service provision has sometimes deteriorated. This is a particular problem in the new districts and provinces formed since decentralisation, which have tended to struggle in the early years to set up well-functioning systems.

---

20 See Miranti, Chapter 5, for a fuller discussion of regional disparities and their determinants.

In theory, regional governments are supposed to have better access to information about the needs of their areas, ensuring that poverty alleviation strategies are tailored specifically to local conditions and needs. Local initiatives that have worked well include community-based irrigation projects in Lumajang (East Java), city planning policies in Solo (Central Java) and e-government in Sragen (also in Central Java). At the same time, the central government retains an important role in disseminating information on poverty to the regions, to ensure a coordinated response, and to protect against the risk of greater regional inequality. The necessity to allocate the most resources to the poorest areas does not always align with the incentives facing politicians, however.

* * * * *

The remaining chapters in this book address the issues discussed above in greater detail. They also seek to answer some of the questions raised in our discussion of where Indonesia is at in terms of employment, living standards and poverty, one year into the second term of President Yudhoyono. Together, the 16 chapters in the book provide a wide-ranging treatment of varied outcomes and the features that underpin them, in the areas of welfare and poverty alleviation in Indonesia. Several chapters also offer a careful critique of some government programs. While the record is far from perfect, the chapters present data and arguments to suggest that a good deal of progress has been made since the fall of Soeharto, under the scrutiny of a more open and democratic polity.

REFERENCES

Alatas, V., A. Banerjee, R. Hanna, B. Olken and J. Tobias (2010) 'Targeting the poor: evidence from a field experiment in Indonesia', NBER Working Paper No. 19580, National Bureau of Economic Research, Cambridge MA, May.

Arifianto, A. et al. (2005a) 'Making services work for the poor in Indonesia: a report on health financing mechanisms in Kabupaten Purbalingga, Central Java, a case study' field report, SMERU Research Institute, Jakarta, September.

Arifianto, A. et al. (2005b) 'Making services work for the poor in Indonesia: a report on health financing mechanisms in Kabupaten Tabanan, Bali, a case study' field report, SMERU Research Institute, Jakarta, September.

Arifianto, A. et al. (2005c) 'Making services work for the poor in Indonesia: a report on health financing mechanisms in Kabupaten East Sumba, East Nusa Tenggara, a case study', field report, SMERU Research Institute, Jakarta, September.

Bazzi, S., S. Sumarto and A. Suryahadi (2010) 'Of safety nets and safety ropes: an evaluation of Indonesia's compensatory unconditional cash transfer program', paper presented to the Pacific Conference for Development Economics, University of Southern California, 13 March.

del Granado, F.J.A., W. Fengler, A. Ragatz and E. Yavuz (2007) 'Investing in Indonesia's education: allocation, equity and efficiency of public expenditures', Policy Research Working Paper No. 4329, World Bank, Washington DC, August.

Duflo, E. (2001) 'Schooling and labor market consequences of school construction in Indonesia', *American Economic Review*, 91(4): 795–813.

ESCAP (Economic and Social Commission for Asia and the Pacific) (2010) *Achieving the Millennium Development Goals in an Era of Global Uncertainty*, ESCAP, United Nations, Bangkok.

Hastuti et al. (2008) 'The effectiveness of the Raskin program', research report, SMERU Research Institute, Jakarta, February.

Jayasuriya, S. and P. McCawley (2010) *The Asian Tsunami: Aid and Reconstruction after a Disaster*, Asian Development Bank Institute and Edward Elgar, Cheltenham.

Manning, C. and K. Roesad (2007) 'The manpower law of 2003 and its implementing regulations: genesis, key articles and potential impact', *Bulletin of Indonesian Economic Studies*, 43(1): 39–86.

Suharyo, W.I. et al. (2006) 'A rapid appraisal of the PKPS-BBM education sector: School Operational Assistance (BOS)' research report, SMERU Research Institute, Jakarta, September.

Sumarto, S. and L. Pritchett (2001) 'Safety nets', *Nepali Times*, 14–20 September. Available at: http://himalaya.socanth.cam.ac.uk/collections/journals/nepalitimes/pdf/Nepali_Times_060.pdf.

Sumarto, S., S. Bazzi and A. Suryahadi (2010) 'Indonesia's social protection during and after the crisis', in A. Barrientos and D. Hulme (eds) *Social Protection for the Poor and Poorest: Concepts, Policies and Politics*, Palgrave Studies in Development, Palgrave Macmillan, Hampshire.

Suryahadi, A. S. Sumarto and L. Pritchett (2003) 'Evolution of poverty during the crisis in Indonesia', *Asian Economic Journal*, 17(3): 221–41.

Suryahadi, A. W. Widyanti, D. Suryadarma and S. Sumarto (2010) 'Targeting in social protection programmes: the experience of Indonesia', in S. Cook (ed.) *Social Protection as Development Policy: Asian Perspectives*, Routledge, New Delhi.

World Bank (2006) *Making the New Indonesia Work for the Poor*, World Bank, Jakarta.

World Bank (2010a) *Indonesia Jobs Report: Towards Better Jobs and Social Security for All*, World Bank, Washington DC.

World Bank (2010b) 'Targeting effectiveness of current social assistance programs in Indonesia', draft working paper, Targeting in Indonesia Policy Paper Series, Poverty Group, World Bank, Jakarta, July.

PART 1

Economic Transformation and Trends in Poverty: National and International Experience

2 HOW GOOD ARE GOOD TRANSITIONS FOR GROWTH AND POVERTY? INDONESIA SINCE SUHARTO, FOR INSTANCE?

Lant Pritchett

Benchmarking is an essential component of any performance assessment. While the world of high finance is hardly the place to draw positive lessons these days, the rewards to portfolio managers give a simple and clear example. Managers are typically assigned a particular asset class, and are rewarded based on how well their investments perform relative to the overall market return for that class. Although this compensation scheme has its problems, it provides clear benchmarks rather than assuming that all managers could make the same returns whether they are betting on risky or safe assets.

After the financial crisis of 1997–98 and the democratic transition in 1999, Indonesia did not return to the rapid rates of economic growth that had prevailed during the Suharto era. Growth in GDP per capita, which came in at 5.9 per cent per year from 1987 to 1997, fell to just 3.7 per cent in 1999–2008.[1] Hence growth was slower by roughly 2.2 per cent. Is that slower growth a 'disappointment'? Are the slower growth rates an indictment of the policies or economic management of Indonesia's democratic governments? I argue that past growth is not an appropriate benchmark for assessing the country's performance between 1999 and 2008 because it ignores two relevant facts about economic growth.

First, the literature has documented powerful regression to the mean in growth rates. Economies that have grown fast are expected to slow

---

1 All growth rates of output referred to in this chapter are in per capita terms, and calculated on an annual basis (unless specified otherwise).

down. If one benchmarks Indonesia's expected rate of growth based on cross-country estimates of the typical magnitude of regression to the mean, this factor alone places its growth performance right at the benchmark.

Second, it is plausible that a major political transition would affect a country's rate of economic growth through a variety of channels. To test this, I identify all national episodes of rapid democratisation and examine those countries' growth rates during the 10 years before and after the political transition. For countries that went into the transition with above-average growth rates, there appears to be a 'democratic transition' effect that slows post-transition growth by about two percentage points per capita per annum. Again, this effect alone would account fully for Indonesia's slower growth.

The combination of the two effects – regression to the mean and a large democratic transition – implies that if Indonesia's benchmark for growth in 1999–2008 were countries with rapid growth up to 1997 and a large democratising transition, then the expected deceleration of growth would be between 3.5 and 4.3 per cent. By this benchmark, Indonesia's actual post-transition deceleration of only 2.2 per cent (a slowing of growth from 5.9 per cent before the crisis to 3.7 per cent afterward) is substantially better performance than the benchmark. Of course, this conclusion applies only to the period up to 2008, so does not capture the effect of the global financial crisis. But I am not attempting to give an update on Indonesian GDP per capita, but rather to provide a retrospective on the decade immediately following the democratic transition.

In this chapter I also consider the effect of a large democratic transition on poverty. I find that Indonesia's headcount poverty rate has not declined nearly as fast as expected. On this there is less ability to tell, either from theory or empirics, what to expect from democracy.

DEMOCRATIC TRANSITIONS AND ECONOMIC GROWTH

'It is tough to make predictions, especially about the future.'
Yogi Berra (baseball player)

As the famous New York Yankee Yogi Berra has pointed out, it is much easier to predict the past than the future. I therefore start with the easy part, reviewing Indonesia's growth performance before, during and after the economic crisis and political transition of the late 1990s. The much trickier question is whether the growth performance since the crisis and political transition has been better or worse than expected. That requires some statement of what was 'expected'. Should we have expected Indonesia's growth to return to the same pace as before the crisis? Should

Figure 2.1   Five periods of growth in GDP per capita, 1960–2008 (in constant rupiah, 1997 = 1)

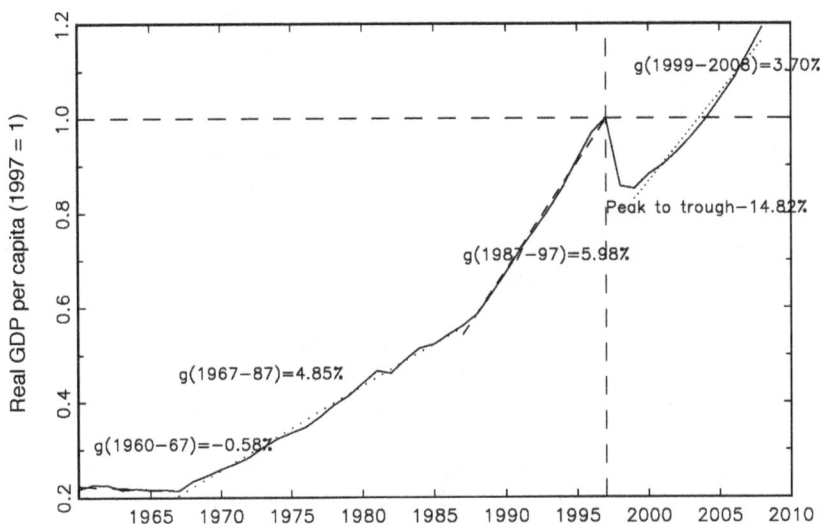

Source: Penn World Tables Version 6.3, http://pwt.econ.upenn.edu/php_site/pwt63/pwt63_form.php.

we have expected growth under democracy to *accelerate*, perhaps because democratic governments provide better or more stable economic policies? Or should we have expected growth to *decelerate*, because democracy cannot easily provide the impetus for rapid growth, given the conflicting pressures?

Indonesia's growth performance, in pictures

Figure 12.1 identifies five periods of growth in GDP per capita in Indonesia since 1960 (the year in which the standard data series begins). From 1960 to 1967 there was essentially zero growth, accompanied by other economic disruptions, including food shortages and rapid inflation. This weak performance is especially noteworthy because Indonesia in 1960 was an extremely poor country: the current GDP of even very poor countries today, such as Bangladesh and Nepal, is twice that of Indonesia's in 1960.

After the political chaos at the beginning of Suharto's New Order regime, the economy began to grow rapidly. Annualised GDP growth in 1967–87 was 4.9 per cent, placing Indonesia among the period's growth stars. From 1987 to 1997, growth accelerated further to nearly 6 per cent.

The East Asian financial crisis beginning in the middle of 1997 was particularly severe for Indonesia. The rupiah collapsed in late 1997, nearly the entire banking sector was illiquid and much of it insolvent, and new investment ground to a halt. This was followed by inflation, a rapid rise in rice prices and a huge increase in headcount poverty rates. Yet amazingly, the worst of the crisis was over by 1999, with the economy stabilising at a much lower level. The first post-New Order national elections on 7 June 1999 marked the progress of the democratic transition. Between 1999 and 2008, the economy grew at a pace of 3.7 per cent.[2]

Indonesia was slower than other East Asian countries to recover from the crisis. Its GDP per capita did not recover to its 1997 level until 2004, whereas South Korea regained its 1997 peak in 1999 after a severe but short jolt, and Thailand did so in 2002. By 2008, Korea's GDP per capita was 47 per cent above its 1997 level and Thailand's 26 per cent, while Indonesia's was only 19 per cent. In 2008, Indonesia's GDP per capita was almost exactly 40 per cent higher than at its lowest point during the crisis.

Whether this post-transition growth performance is below or above expectations depends on what those expectations are. Figure 2.2 illustrates a range of scenarios. A super-optimistic scenario would be a quick, V-shaped recovery, plus a resumption of the pre-crisis growth rate of 5.9 per cent. Under that scenario, output would have increased nearly 75 per cent in the 10 years from 1999 to 2008. Another scenario would be a return in 1999 to the rapid growth path of 1987–97, but without any particularly rapid recovery from the crisis. A third scenario would acknowledge the exceptional rapidity of Indonesia's 1987–97 growth rate and anticipate a return to the more moderate rate seen in 1967–87. Output under this scenario would exceed the actual, but not by much. In fact, in the four years from 2004 to 2008, growth was almost the same as in 1967–87 (4.5 per cent versus 4.8 per cent).

Two other scenarios can also be considered. One is that Indonesia would grow at the average rate for East Asia – which it did almost exactly, as the mean for the East Asian region was also 3.7 per cent.[3] The other scenario is that Indonesia would grow at the average rate for all countries in its income range, so Figure 2.2 also shows the median growth of

---

2 To facilitate the following discussion of comparative growth rates, I only use data for the period ending in 2008. More recent standardised data for other countries are often unavailable.

3 I define East Asia regionally, excluding China and South Korea but including Laos, Cambodia and Papua New Guinea. East Asia is often defined to mean just the high-performing East Asian countries, a category that grows fast by construction.

Figure 2.2   Four scenarios for the expected path of growth in GDP per capita, 1999–2008 (1999 = 1)

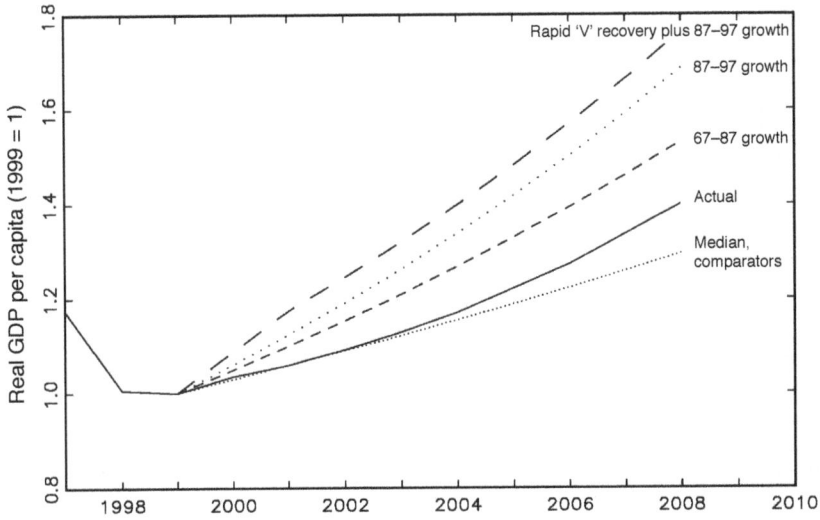

Source: Author's calculations.

GDP per capita for this group of countries.[4] By that standard Indonesia did well, growing well above the median rate of 2.9 per cent – but few countries strive to achieve merely 'ordinary' growth performance.

What is the expected outcome of a big and good political transition?

The scenarios in Figure 2.2 are mechanical and address only superficially the question of whether growth was 'as expected' or 'disappointing'. When *were* expectations about growth formed, and on the basis of what information? I lived in Indonesia from 1998 to 2000, when widely different political and social outcomes seemed possible, if not probable. Nearly all of them – military intervention, increased separatism and unrest, ethnic violence, unstable democracy, various stripes of populism – were scenarios with pessimistic growth expectations. The more tractable question is: knowing the actual political and social trajectories, what would our growth expectations have been? Suppose one had been told in 1998 by a visitor from the future that peaceful, free and fair national elections would take place in June 1999; that the party that had controlled

4   I calculated growth for all countries with purchasing power parity (PPP) GDP per capita between $2,000 and $10,000, giving a total of 84 countries.

Table 2.1   *Polity ratings for selected East Asian countries, 1996–2008*
(–10 = autocracy, +10 = democracy)

Country	Year	Polity rating
Indonesia	1996	–7
China	2008	–7
Vietnam	2008	–7
Singapore	2008	–2
Malaysia	2007	3
Philippines	2008	8
Indonesia	2008	8
Japan	2008	10

Source: Polity IV, http://www.systemicpeace.org/polity/polity4.htm.

Indonesia for 30 years would cede power peacefully to an elected government; that there would be an ordered democratic transition from June 1999 onward; and that mainstream political figures (not fringe figures) would be elected. What would our growth expectations have been *conditional* on knowing that the political transition from 30 years of authoritarian one-party rule would go so smoothly?

It might seem natural to expect that this good political transition to democracy would be accompanied by good outcomes on the economic front: that economic growth and poverty reduction would be at least as rapid as they were during the Suharto years. Viewed in this light, Indonesia's post-transition growth has been 'disappointing'. However, what do the growth experiences of, and data from, other countries with rapid transitions to democracy really lead us to expect? This is a question to which I can at least propose an empirically grounded answer.

One commonly used indicator of the degree of democracy is a measure called Polity, used to rate countries on a scale of 'autocracy' from zero to negative 10 and on a scale of 'democracy' from zero to positive 10.[5] The simple sum of these two indicators gives an empirical rating that ranges from –10 (completely autocratic) to +10 (completely democratic). Table 2.1 shows the Polity scores of selected East Asian countries. They reveal that the rating is about democracy, *not* economic performance (both

---

5   The Polity data series developed by the Center for Systemic Peace is widely used in political science research. The latest version (Polity IV) covers 163 countries with populations of 500,000 or more, classifying them according to the nature of their political systems. See http://www.systemicpeace.org/polity/polity4.htm.

Figure 2.3   Polity ratings for Indonesia, 1960–2008 (–10 = autocracy, +10 = democracy)

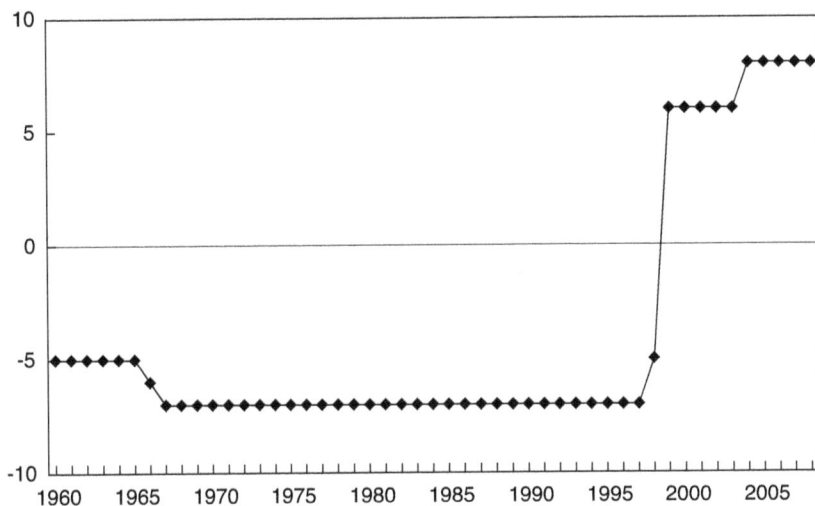

Source: Polity IV, http://www.systemicpeace.org/polity/polity4.htm.

China and Vietnam are rated –7) or even quality of governance in the sense of having the administrative capability to carry out governmental functions (highly capable Singapore and Malaysia are rated –2 and 3 respectively, while less capable Philippines is rated 8).

The Polity rating captures Indonesia's massive, rapid and sustained transition to democracy. Figure 2.3 shows the ratings for Indonesia from 1960 to 2008. They follow the known major events of Indonesia's political trajectory: the Sukarno era when Indonesia was rated –5; the entire Suharto period (1967–97) when it was rated –7; the June 1999 elections, which propelled its score to 6; and the election of Susilo Bambang Yudhoyono to the presidency in 2004, which raised its rating to 8.

Knowing that Indonesia has been a democracy since 1999 does little to delimit its expected growth rate. Figure 2.4 plots countries' average Polity scores over the 1998–2007 period against their growth rates (each country is identified with a three-letter code and Indonesia, or IDN, is inside the circle). The median growth rate for imperfect democracies (defined as countries with an average Polity score above 5 but less than 10) is 2.95 per cent, which puts Indonesia's growth rate of 3.3 per cent (in this data set) squarely in the middle of growth performance. But there is no strong association between growth and Polity score; the autocracies do slightly better, with average growth of 4.3 per cent, while the countries in between do worse, with average growth of 1.39 per cent. But it is evident

Growth in GDP per capita, 1999–2007

Average Polity rating, 1999–2008

Median, Polity<–5: 4.31%   Median, Middle: 1.39%   Median, 10>Polity>5: 2.95%

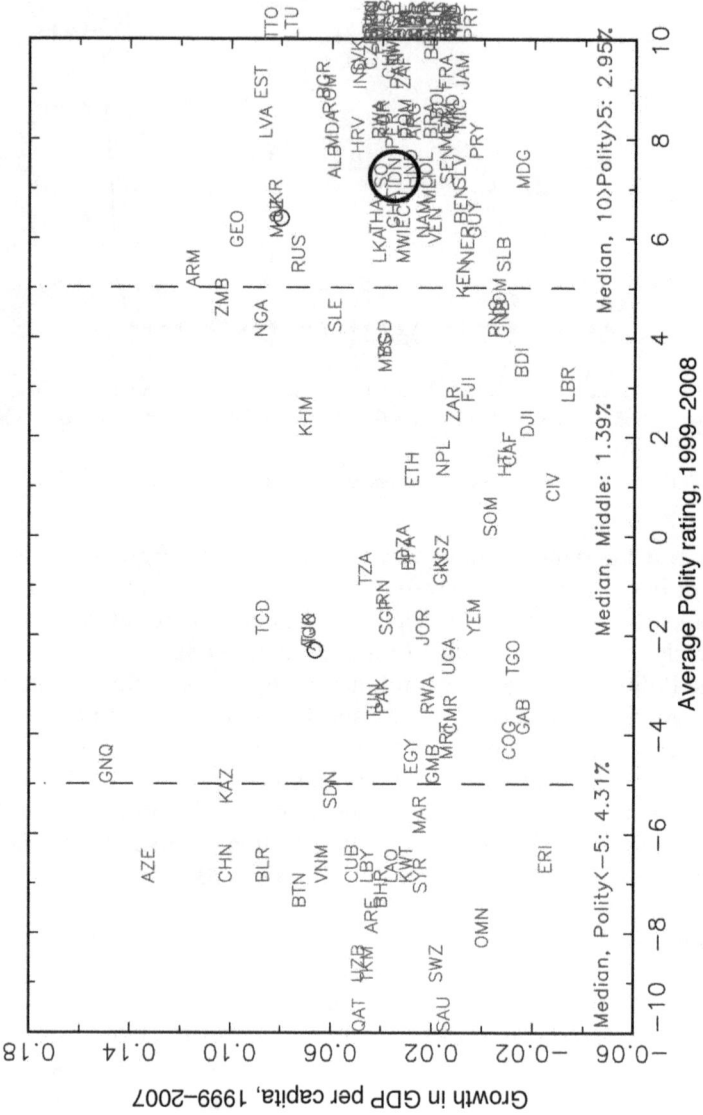

Source: Polity IV, http://www.systemicpeace.org/polity/polity4.htm; Penn World Tables Version 6.3, http://pwt.econ.upenn.edu/php_site/pwt63/pwt63_form.php.

that there are countries with a wide range of economic growth rates in each Polity category.[6]

A simple analysis of whether democracies grow faster or slower than non-democracies does not capture the possibility that large political transitions may themselves have impacts. In this case, while democracies may be capable of sustaining rapid growth in the long run, the transition period itself may create an adjustment period of slow growth. To examine this question, we need to compare countries' growth rates before and after large, rapid political transitions from autocracy to democracy. For this, we need to identify 'large' transitions.

First, I searched the Polity combined democracy indicator to identify all instances in which a country's index had increased by more than five units in a single year. These were the candidates for a 'large' democratic transition. I then used a decision tree to classify and date these potential transitions, addressing in particular the treatment of countries with multiple transitions (Table 2.2). This classification scheme resulted in 52 episodes of large democratic transition (see Table A.2.1 for a complete list).

Once large democratic transitions had been identified, the next step was to calculate growth rates before and after the transition.[7] Because I wanted to capture the medium term, I calculated the growth rate for the 10-year period ending three years before the transition and that for the 10-year period beginning one year after the transition (or, if 10 years of data were not available, until the data ended). In the case of Indonesia, the two 10-year periods would be 1986–96 (the period ending three years before the democratic transition in 1999) and 2000–2007 (the period beginning one year after the transition and ending in 2007, where the data in Version 6.3 of the Penn World Tables stop).[8]

---

6 There is a substantial literature by economists on whether democracies tend to have higher or lower economic growth rates than non-democracies (and what causes what). My reading of the current conventional wisdom is that there is very little connection between the average growth rates of democracies and non-democracies as distinct groups, but that there is much higher variance in growth rates among non-democracies, with some experiencing rapid growth (China, Vietnam, Indonesia under Suharto) but others experiencing very slow growth or even growth implosions. That said, one can find specifications in which being a democracy appears to matter (see, for instance, Persson and Tabellini 2006).

7 The comparative data on PPP-adjusted real GDP per capita are taken from Version 6.3 of the Penn World Tables, compiled by the Center for International Comparisons at the University of Pennsylvania. See http://pwt.econ.upenn.edu/php_site/pwt63/pwt63_form.php.

8 These timing assumptions are not innocuous. Often a political transition is preceded by a large fall in GDP per capita, sometimes as the result of the chaos surrounding the transition itself. If one then calculated the growth before the

Table 2.2   Classification of candidate countries with large democratic transitions (absolute change in Polity rating > 5, all years)

Number of episodes	Decision rule	Example
If country has only one candidate episode	Keep that episode with transition dated to year of new value	Indonesia: 1998 = –6, 1999 = 5, change = 11. Transition year is 1999.
If country has two episodes, and …		
Episodes are more than three years apart	Keep both episodes	Taiwan: 1986 = –7, 1987 = –1, 1991 = –1, 1992 = 7. Two transitions, in 1987 and 1992.
Episodes are less than three years apart and in the same direction	Classify as one episode, dated to the earlier period	Madagascar: 1990 = –6, 1991 = 2, 1992 = 9. One transition dated to 1992.
Episodes are less than three years apart and in the opposite direction	Do not keep as an episode	Armenia: 1995 = 3, 1996 = –6, 1997 = –6, 1998 = 5. No sustained democratic transition; brief cycle into autocracy.
If country has three or more episodes	Each episode is classified separately depending on the timing and direction of the change, in order to keep and date distinct episodes	(20 countries)

Source: Polity IV, http://www.systemicpeace.org/polity/polity4.htm.

The first result is that nearly every country that experienced a large democratic transition after a period of above-average growth (more than the cross-country average of 2 per cent) experienced a sharp deceleration in growth in the 10 years following (the year after) the transition

---

transition to include this fall (which could be the result of the transition itself), then it would look as though the political transition had accelerated growth. That is why I go back some years before the transition, so that the pure disruption effects are not counted as part of the pre-democratic period. Rodrik and Wacziarg (2005) obtain similar results overall: of the nine countries they identify with democratising transitions begun from above 2 per cent growth, the average deceleration is 3.53 per cent, which is exactly what we find in Table 2.3. But in some countries timing differences produce different results.

(Table 2.3). Thus, Indonesia's growth rate decelerated from 5.54 per cent in 1986–96 to just 3.28 per cent in 2000–2007. This is very close to the rate of deceleration observed earlier, where growth was found to be 2.2 per cent lower in the democratic, post-Suharto era than in the authoritarian period.

This analysis suggests that Indonesia has had less deceleration of economic growth than would have been expected based on the experience of other countries. First, of the 22 countries with episodes of large democratic transition from above-average growth, all but one (Korea in 1987 with an acceleration of only 0.22 per cent) experienced a growth deceleration. The combination of high initial growth and democratic transition seems to make some deceleration all but inevitable. Second, the magnitude of the decelerations was very large: the median deceleration across the 22 countries was 2.99 per cent and the average deceleration was 3.53 per cent. If Indonesia had experienced the typical (median) or average (mean) deceleration of this group of countries, its growth rate would have been either 2.55 per cent (5.54 less 2.99) or 2.01 per cent (5.54 less 3.53) rather than the 3.3 per cent growth it actually experienced. So, while one framing is that Indonesian growth has been 'disappointing' in the post-transition era, this is only relative to a completely arbitrary expectation – not consistent with any cross-country experience – that the country would maintain the same growth rate. There is no evidence to suggest that zero deceleration is a reasonable expectation for growth after a democratic transition.

The next step was to calculate the 10-year growth rates of countries that had not experienced a large democratising transition. The problem was to identify an appropriate year for the before and after comparisons of growth in 'no transition' countries; choosing an arbitrary year (say, 1999) for the calculation would be misleading, because the countries that had experienced political transitions had done so in many different years, and because the before and after growth rates for the 'no transition' countries could be affected by secular differences in growth rates. Instead, I picked a random year for each of the countries and calculated its growth rate in the same way as I had done for the countries with political transitions.[9] I then calculated the average for the countries with no political transition. Again, I found that countries with above-average growth experienced a deceleration in growth and those with below-zero growth experienced an acceleration in growth (Table 2.4). That is, there

---

9 Since I was choosing a 'break' point randomly, I iterated this procedure 25 times, so that in each iteration each country had a different year around which the growth difference was calculated. The results reported in Table 2.4 are the average over all iterations.

Table 2.3   Countries with large democratic transitions starting from above-average growth in GDP per capita[a]

Country		Year of transi-tion	Magni-tude of Polity increase	Growth in 10-year period ending 3 years before transition (%)	Growth in 10-year period be-ginning 1 year after transition (%)	Change in pre-/post-transition growth rates (%)
1	Greece	1975	7	7.19	0.02	−7.17
2	Iran	1979	10	7.11	0.11	−7.01
3	Portugal	1976	6	7.11	1.48	−5.63
4	Taiwan	1992	8	6.47	3.95	−2.52
5	Taiwan	1987	6	6.42	5.78	−0.64
6	Nigeria	1979	7	5.81	−2.44	−8.25
7	Ecuador	1979	14	5.69	−1.66	−7.36
8	Congo	1992	6	5.68	0.57	−5.11
9	**Indonesia**	**1999**	**11**	**5.54**	**3.28**	**−2.26**
10	Dominican Rep.	1978	9	5.50	1.35	−4.14
11	South Korea	1987	6	5.36	5.57	0.22
12	Thailand	1992	10	4.67	0.82	−3.85
13	Mongolia	1990	9	4.39	2.09	−2.30
14	Bulgaria	1990	15	4.02	−0.10	−4.12
15	Panama	1989	16	3.91	1.68	−2.23
16	Benin	1990	7	3.62	1.30	−2.32
17	Pakistan	1988	12	3.50	1.32	−2.18
18	Uruguay	1985	16	3.44	3.16	−0.27
19	Brazil	1985	10	3.31	−0.34	−3.65
20	Paraguay	1989	10	2.70	−0.75	−3.45
21	Bolivia	1982	15	2.37	0.27	−2.09
22	Romania	1989	6	2.14	0.85	−1.28
Median				5.01	1.08	−2.99
Average				4.82	1.29	−3.53

a   A large democratic transition is an increase in Polity rating of more than 5. Above-average growth in GDP per capita is growth at least 2 per cent above the cross-country average. Growth in the post-transition period is either for 10 years or until the data end.

Source: Author's calculations based on Polity IV, http://www.systemicpeace.org/polity/polity4.htm; and Penn World Tables Version 6.3, http://pwt.econ.upenn.edu/php_site/pwt63/pwt63_form.php.

Table 2.4 *Difference in growth rates of countries with, versus those without, a large democratic transition (%)*[a]

| Growth in 10-year period ending three years before transition | Growth rate in countries with a transition | | | Difference in before and after growth rates of countries with no transition | Difference in growth rates of countries with, versus those without, a transition ((3) – (4)) |
| | Before transition | After transition | Difference ((2) – (1)) | | |
	(1)	(2)	(3)	(4)	(5)
High (>2% above average)	4.8	1.3	–3.5	–1.8	–1.76
Medium (0–2% above average)	1.3	2.0	0.7	0.3	0.43
Negative (<0%)	–2.2	1.5	3.8	4.6	–0.87

a   A large democratic transition is an increase in Polity rating of more than 5.
Source: Author's calculations.

was regression to the mean even around some arbitrarily chosen year. The average deceleration was 1.8 per cent for the countries with growth above 2 per cent, returning them roughly to the cross-country average. The average acceleration for the countries with below-zero growth was larger, 4.6 per cent. In part this was because their growth rates were further from the cross-country average than those of the high-growth countries (being not just below the average, but below zero).

The deceleration of growth among countries that started with above-average growth and had a large democratising transition, of 3.5 per cent, is substantially larger than the counterfactual of deceleration among countries with no such transition, of 1.8 per cent (Table 2.4). That is, countries with large democratising transitions, on average, decelerated by 1.76 per cent more than countries with no political transition. So, about half the deceleration among rapidly growing economies following a large democratising transition seems to be due to 'natural' regression to the mean, and about half due to the large democratising episode itself.

Two final benchmark comparisons are simple regressions that associate the change in countries' growth rates with their previous growth rates (and income levels). For the first, we regress the change in growth rates between 1987–97 and 1999–2007 for all developing countries – those with GDP per capita below $10,000 in purchasing power parity (PPP) terms in 1987. Indonesia's predicted deceleration is 1.97 per cent, versus

Table 2.5   Summary of Indonesia's post-crisis, post-transition growth performance relative to benchmarks

Definition of benchmark	Predicted	Actual	Performance relative to benchmark
1 Indonesia's pre-crisis growth rate, 1987–97 to 1999–2008	5.98 (1999–2008)	3.70 (1999–2008)	−2.28
2 Median, all developing countries, 1999–2007	2.56 (1999–2007)	3.29 (1999–2007)	+0.72
3 Regression to the mean, predicting changes in growth in 1999–2007 versus 1987–97 in developing countries	3.47 (1999–2007)	3.29 (1999–2007)	−0.18
4 Countries with a large democratic transition starting from above-average growth (predicted = 5.54 – 3.53; see Table 2.3)	2.01 (2000–2007)	3.28 (2000–2007)	+1.27
5 Predicted value from regression among 52 countries with large democratising transitions	1.28 (2000–2007)	3.28 (2000–2007)	+2.0

Source: Author's calculations.

the actual deceleration of 2.15 per cent. That is, regression to the mean alone explains almost all of Indonesia's growth deceleration.

For the second comparison, we regress the change in growth rates for all 52 countries with large democratising transitions on their initial growth rates (and levels of income at the beginning of the post-transition period). This gives us the predicted deceleration for those countries that experienced democratic transitions. Indonesia's predicted deceleration from this regression (which combines mean reversion and a large democratising transition) is 4.26 per cent.

Summary of the post-transition growth performance

Table 2.5 brings together the main empirical results from benchmarking Indonesia's economic performance since the economic crisis of 1997–98 and the ensuing political transition. The naive expectation that growth would return to its previous high levels might imply disappointment with Indonesia's post-transition performance, as growth decelerated by 2.28 per cent compared with what would have been expected from the country's pre-crisis growth rate (first row in Table 2.5). However, Indonesia's growth rate of 3.29 per cent was actually better than the median rate for all developing countries in 1999–2007, of 2.56 per cent (second row in Table 2.5). A variety of other ways of setting an empirical benchmark for the performance of the economy also suggests that it has outperformed statistical expectations, given the presence of two forces associated with a deceleration in growth: regression to the mean and a large democratising transition.

The simplest possible regression of growth rates in 1999–2007 on countries' growth rates in 1987–97 predicts growth for Indonesia of 3.47 per cent versus the actual rate of 3.29 per cent (third row in Table 2.5); typical regression to the mean therefore fully explains Indonesia's growth deceleration.

But, the analysis of large democratising episodes suggests that countries that enter with above-average growth (nearly) always decelerate. The mean deceleration among the 22 countries in 2000–2007 was 3.53 per cent, so the prediction for Indonesia, if it experienced average deceleration, was growth of just 2.01 per cent; it therefore outperformed by 1.27 percentage points (fourth row in Table 2.5).

Finally, a simple regression of post-transition growth rates in all countries with large democratising transitions on their previous growth rates predicts Indonesia's growth to slow to 1.28 per cent, through the combined effects of regression to the mean and a democratic transition (last row in Table 2.5). By this measure Indonesia performed better by an average of 2 per cent. Its outperformance on this benchmark completely overturns the idea that democracy has been 'disappointing' for the country's growth performance. Relative to this benchmark, Indonesia has sustained much higher growth than other, reasonable, benchmarks would have predicted.

POVERTY REDUCTION AFTER A DEMOCRATIC TRANSITION

Some might expect that a democratic transition would accelerate poverty reduction: that a democratic government, motivated by elections and disciplined by democratic accountability, would be able to engineer larger poverty reductions than the previous authoritarian regime, even out of the same or less total economic growth. That is not so – nor, I would argue, is there any good reason to expect it to be so on either empirical or theoretical grounds.

Figure 2.5 shows the evolution of Indonesia's headcount poverty rate – the proportion of the population below an absolute threshold of household per capita consumption expenditure. The series breaks in

Figure 2.5   Headcount poverty rate, 1976–2010 (%)[a]

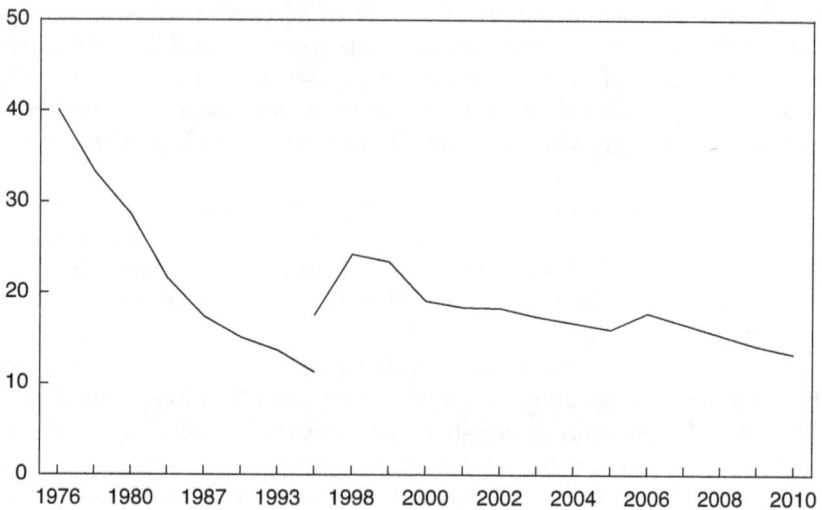

a   The break in the series in 1996 is due to a change in the poverty line.

Source: World Development Indicators, http://data.worldbank.org/data-catalog/world-development-indicators.

1996 when the poverty line was changed, so the first and second series are internally consistent but not comparable to each other. Poverty fell extremely rapidly between 1976 and 1996 – from 40 per cent of the population to just 11.6 per cent in only 20 years. This was one of the most rapid reductions – if not *the* most rapid reduction – in mass destitution in history. The downward trend was interrupted by the crisis, when poverty increased dramatically. It then resumed, but less rapidly than before the crisis and with a reversal in 2005–2006.

The question is whether the downward trend in the headcount poverty rate is 'good enough' or 'disappointing' – which again depends upon one's expectations. Here there are insufficient comparable cross-country, time-series data on poverty headcount rates to do the episodic analysis of democratising episodes that are possible for growth and governance indicators. Instead, I discuss two scenarios that suggest that part of the puzzle is not just that growth has been slower in the democratic period, but also that the responsiveness of poverty reduction to growth, or the poverty elasticity, appears to have fallen.

Figure 2.6 shows the actual evolution of the headcount poverty rate during the period 2000–2008 and what it would have been under two alternative scenarios. The first asks what the evolution of the poverty rate

Figure 2.6   *Headcount poverty rate and two scenarios for the expected path of poverty reduction, 2000–2008 (%)*

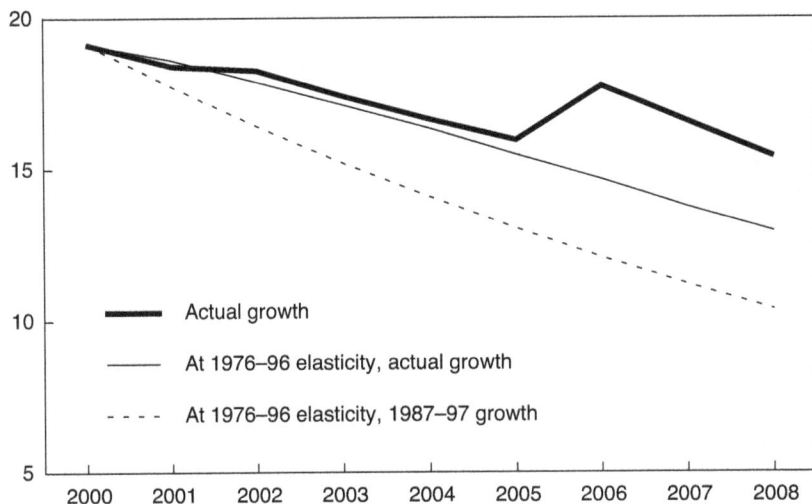

Legend:
- **——** Actual growth
- —— At 1976–96 elasticity, actual growth
- - - - - At 1976–96 elasticity, 1987–97 growth

Source: Author's calculations.

would have been had poverty had the same elasticity as in the 1976–96 period. Table 2.6 shows the calculation of the poverty elasticity of growth – the ratio of the percentage reduction in the poverty headcount rate to the percentage increase in GDP per capita. The average elasticity for the period 1976–96 was –1.15 and the median elasticity was –1.24.

Table 2.7 shows the same calculation for 2000–2008. During this period the simple overall ('arc') elasticity of poverty reduction with respect to growth declined to –0.55. But as Table 2.7 and Figure 2.6 illustrate, this was mainly the result of the anomalous increase in poverty – despite an increase in GDP per capita – during 2005–2006; the median year-to-year elasticity was similar to that in 1976–96.[10]

The second scenario shows what would have happened if the elasticity of poverty with respect to growth had been the same as in the 1976–96 period *and* the faster growth rate of 1987–97 had prevailed. In this instance poverty would have been five percentage points lower in 2008 than it actually was.

Actual poverty declined over the entire period by less than would have been expected in either scenario – even given the lower overall economic growth rate – though nearly all of this was because of the sudden

---

10   See Chapter 3 by Warr for further discussion of the 2005–2006 episode.

Table 2.6   Poverty, economic growth and implied elasticity, 1976–96

Year	Headcount poverty rate (%) (1)	Change in headcount poverty rate (%) (2)	GDP per capita (1976 = 100) (3)	Change in GDP per capita (%) (4)	Implied growth elasticity ((2)/(4)) (5)
1976	40.1		100.0		
1978	33.3	−17.0	113.6	13.6	−1.25
1980	28.6	−14.1	126.5	11.4	−1.24
1984	21.6	−24.5	147.9	17.0	−1.44
1987	17.4	−19.4	161.5	9.2	−2.12
1990	15.1	−13.2	194.0	20.1	−0.66
1993	13.7	−9.3	231.9	19.5	−0.48
1996	11.3	−17.5	278.5	20.1	−0.87
Average					−1.15
Median					−1.24

Source: Author's calculations.

Table 2.7   Poverty, economic growth and implied elasticity, 2000–2008

Year	Headcount poverty rate (%) (1)	Change in headcount poverty rate (%) (2)	GDP per capita (2000 = 100) (3)	Change in GDP per capita (%) (4)	Implied growth elasticity ((2)/(4)) (5)
2000	19.1		100.0		
2001	18.4	−3.8	102.2	2.2	−1.70
2002	18.3	−0.8	105.5	3.2	−0.26
2003	17.4	−4.6	109.1	3.4	−1.35
2004	16.7	−4.4	113.1	3.6	−1.20
2005	16.0	−4.1	117.9	4.3	−0.97
2006	17.8	11.1	122.9	4.2	2.64
2007	16.6	−6.6	129.1	5.1	−1.30
2008	15.4	−7.0	135.2	4.7	−1.48
Average					−0.70
Median					−1.25
End to end, 2000–2008		−19.4		35.2	−0.55

Source: Author's calculations.

rise in poverty in 2005–2006. This brings us back to the same question: is there any reason to expect that Indonesia's democratic transition would have led to faster poverty reduction?

We first need to ask whether Indonesia's poverty was particularly unresponsive to growth in either the pre- or post-transition period. There are two answers to this, one empirical and one arithmetic.[11] The empirical answer uses cross-country differences in GDP per capita and headcount poverty rates to estimate a simple bivariate relationship.[12] Using two different data sets, one providing comprehensive information on levels of poverty (the World Bank's World Development Indicators) and the other focusing on poverty changes or spells (Kraay 2006), it can be seen that the elasticity of 'dollar a day' headcount poverty to GDP per capita, averaged across low and middle-income countries, ranges from about –1.12 to –1.82 depending on the sample and specification (Table 2.8).

The question, though, is whether the transition to democracy has itself been disappointing, in that one might have expected more pro-poor growth from a democratic government. Yet there is no theoretical or empirical reason to expect a democratic government to produce more pro-poor growth.

In spite of the huge popularity of the terms 'pro-poor growth', 'inclusive growth' and 'broad-based growth', there is no empirically based guidance as to which governmental policies produce such growth. Since income distribution is a general equilibrium outcome in an economy involving the investment, production and consumption decisions of millions of firms and individuals, it is unlikely that any simple formula exists. In this context, well-meaning but naive actions by the government may have counterproductive results. For instance, since the main asset of the poor is (unskilled) labour, policies to 'strengthen' labour protection might seem pro-poor. But if the measures to protect labour are only effective in the formal sector, where wages are already high, they may reduce demand for labour in this sector, expanding the supply of labour in the informal sector. This may reduce the relative wages in the informal sector, leading to an actual increase in poverty, as Aswicahyono, Hill and Narjoko suggest has occurred in Indonesia (see Chapter 4 of this volume).

---

11 The arithmetic point is overly technical to discuss, but the poverty elasticity can be calculated exactly and these calculations suggest Indonesia's growth elasticity should be more like 3 than 1. See Bourguignon (2002) and Lopez and Serven (2006) for details.

12 In technical language, the equation estimates a reduced-form and non-structural elasticity.

Table 2.8   Cross-country estimates of the elasticity of 'dollar a day' headcount poverty to GDP per capita

Source of poverty data and sample	N	Specification	Poverty elasticity (standard error)
World Development Indicators			
All low & middle-income countries, all observations	331	Log level of headcount poverty on log level of GDP per capita	−1.23 (0.04)
All low & middle-income countries, first observation for each country	79	As above	−1.15 (0.10)
All low & middle-income countries, last observation for each country	79	As above	−1.13 (0.09)
Kraay (2006) dataset			
Poverty spells	59	Change over time in log headcount poverty on change in log GDP per capita	−1.82 (0.50)
Poverty spells (high-quality sample)	41	As above	−1.12 (0.42)

Source: World Development Indicators, http://data.worldbank.org/data-catalog/world-development-indicators; Kraay (2006).

It is possible that a democracy would experience faster poverty reduction if it pursued policies that involved more pro-poor public expenditures, such as larger or better-targeted social transfer programs, but this is not grounded in solid theory. This might occur if poverty were defined broadly, but it is not clear why a democracy would target a small, 'impoverished' fraction that comprised only 15 per cent or so of the population. Theoretical papers on targeting (for example, Gelbach and Pritchett 2002) show that voters prefer less sharp targeting than the poverty-minimising allocation; in a simple setting with three income groups (poor, middle and rich), sharp pro-poor targeting emerges only when the rich are disproportionately powerful. When the middle group has a political weight equal to its population share, then uniform targeting is the strongest targeting that is politically feasible. A recent field experiment by Alatas et al. (2010) also suggests that voters in Indonesia are dissatisfied with sharp proxy means tests without community engagement with the beneficiaries. So, while one might naively associate democracy with pro-poor policies, there is no theoretical or empirical justification for that when 'poor' is construed on narrow consumption expenditure definitions.

Finally, empirical examination of the data on headcount poverty, GDP per capita and a measure of democracy (such as Polity) does not reveal any relationship between democracy and the level of headcount poverty for countries with equivalent output. In fact, in most specifications it appears that democracy is associated with slightly *higher* levels of poverty. Moreover, several of the outstanding examples of rapid reductions in mass poverty have been in authoritarian countries – Indonesia in 1967–96, China post-1978, Vietnam since 1986 – demonstrating that it is possible for non-democracies to produce rapid progress on poverty.

CONCLUSION

Looking at the simple GDP per capita numbers presented in Figure 2.1, it might seem reasonable to ask what Indonesia's democratic government has done wrong to cause such poor growth performance. But this assumes that a 'natural' prediction of growth for a country is its own past performance; it ignores regression to the mean. After one's best round of golf ever, the next round will probably be worse.

Moreover, there are reasons to believe, and an analysis of democratic episodes suggests, that large political transitions create at least short to medium-term slowdowns in growth. This chapter estimates that countries that begin an episode of large, rapid democratisation with above-average growth can expect a deceleration of growth of 2.2 percentage points. Perhaps the right question to ask, then, is: what was it about the democratising transition in Indonesia that made growth decelerate so little?

Finally, I was not able to compare measures of poverty reduction with and without a democratic transition. But it does appear that Indonesia made less progress on consumption expenditure measures of headcount poverty than could be accounted for by the lower growth rate in the democratic era. However, there is no theoretical or empirical reason to expect democracy to be particularly pro-poor – especially when poverty is construed at penurious levels that include only a small fraction of the population (Pritchett 2006).

REFERENCES

Alatas, V., A. Banerjee, R. Hanna, B. Olken and J. Tobias (2010) 'Targeting the poor: evidence from a field experiment in Indonesia', NBER Working Paper No. 15980, National Bureau of Economic Research, Cambridge MA, May.

Bourguignon, F. (2002) 'The growth elasticity of poverty reduction: explaining heterogeneity across countries and time periods', DELTA Working Paper Series 2002-03, Département et Laboratoire d'Economie Théorique et Appliquée, Paris, February.

Gelbach, J. and L. Pritchett (2002) 'Is more for the poor less for the poor? The politics of means-tested targeting', *Topics in Economic Analysis and Policy*, 2(1). Available at: http://www.bepress.com/bejeap/topics/vol2/iss1/art6.

Kraay, A. (2006) 'When is growth pro-poor? Evidence from a panel of countries', *Journal of Development Economics*, 80(1): 197–227.

Lopez, H. and L. Serven (2006) 'A normal relationship? Poverty, inequality and growth', Policy Research Working Paper No. 3814, World Bank, Washington DC, January.

Persson, T. and G. Tabellini (2006) 'Democracy and development: the devil in the details', NBER Working Paper No. 11993, National Bureau of Economic Research, Cambridge MA, February.

Pritchett, L. (2006) 'Who is *not* poor? Dreaming of a world truly free of poverty', *World Bank Research Observer*, 21(1): 1–23.

Rodrik, D. and R. Wacziarg (2005) 'Do democratic transitions produce bad outcomes?', *American Economic Review Papers and Proceedings*, 95(2): 50–56.

Table A2.1   All countries with large democratic transitions[a]

Country		Year of transi- tion	Magni- tude of Polity increase	Growth in 10-year period ending 3 years before transition (%)	Growth in 10-year period beginning 1 year after transition (%)	Change in pre-/post- transition growth rates (%)
1	Nigeria	1979	7	5.8	-2.4	-8.2
2	Ecuador	1979	14	5.7	-1.7	-7.4
3	Greece	1975	7	7.2	0.0	-7.2
4	Iran	1979	10	7.1	0.1	-7.0
5	Zaire (now Democratic Republic of Congo)	1992	8	-1.1	-7.2	-6.1
6	Portugal	1976	6	7.1	1.5	-5.6
7	Nicaragua	1979	8	1.3	-4.0	-5.3
8	Congo	1992	6	5.7	0.6	-5.1
9	Dominican Republic	1978	9	5.5	1.4	-4.1
10	Bulgaria	1990	15	4.0	-0.1	-4.1
11	Thailand	1992	10	4.7	0.8	-3.9
12	Brazil	1985	10	3.3	-0.3	-3.7
13	Paraguay	1989	10	2.7	-0.7	-3.4
14	Madagascar	1991	8	1.5	-1.4	-3.0
15	Taiwan	1992	8	6.5	4.0	-2.5
16	Benin	1990	7	3.6	1.3	-2.3
17	Mongolia	1990	9	4.4	2.1	-2.3
18	Indonesia	1999	11	5.5	3.3	-2.3
19	Panama	1989	16	3.9	1.7	-2.2
20	Pakistan	1988	12	3.5	1.3	-2.2
21	Bolivia	1982	15	2.4	0.3	-2.1
22	Algeria	1989	7	1.7	0.1	-1.6
23	Romania	1989	6	2.1	0.9	-1.3
24	Philippines	1987	7	1.5	0.8	-0.8
25	Taiwan	1987	6	6.4	5.8	-0.6
26	Argentina	1983	16	1.0	0.4	-0.6
27	Uruguay	1985	16	3.4	3.2	-0.3
28	South Korea	1987	6	5.4	5.6	0.2

continued

Table A2.1 (continued)

Country		Year of transition	Magnitude of Polity increase	Growth in 10-year period ending 3 years before transition (%)	Growth in 10-year period beginning 1 year after transition (%)	Change in pre-/post-transition growth rates (%)
29	Cyprus	1968	7	1.4	2.0	0.6
30	Nepal	1990	7	1.3	1.9	0.6
31	Mali	1991	7	1.9	2.5	0.6
32	Bangladesh	1991	11	0.9	1.6	0.7
33	Central African Republic	1993	11	−1.4	−0.6	0.8
34	Zambia	1991	15	−2.6	−1.5	1.1
35	Hungary	1989	6	1.6	2.8	1.2
36	Nepal	1981	7	0.7	2.0	1.3
37	Iran	1997	9	1.9	3.5	1.7
38	Malawi	1994	14	−0.8	1.0	1.8
39	Fiji	1990	8	−0.6	1.4	2.0
40	Nicaragua	1990	7	−1.3	1.0	2.3
41	Guatemala	1966	8	1.4	3.8	2.4
42	Djibouti	1999	8	−4.9	−2.3	2.6
43	Albania	1990	10	0.6	4.3	3.7
44	Ethiopia	1991	8	−2.1	1.9	4.1
45	Chile	1989	9	0.4	5.3	4.9
46	Ecuador	1968	6	1.3	6.8	5.4
47	Poland	1989	11	−1.1	4.7	5.8
48	Sierra Leone	1996	11	−1.6	4.6	6.2
49	Guyana	1992	13	−5.4	1.1	6.4
50	Mozambique	1994	12	−1.0	6.6	7.5
51	Croatia	1999	6	−3.2	5.1	8.3
52	Liberia	1990	6	−4.0	5.7	9.7

a   A large democratic transition is an increase in Polity rating of more than 5. Growth in the post-transition period is either for 10 years or until the data end. The dating of democratising episodes is described in Table 2.2. Some countries have multiple episodes of transition.

Source: Author's calculations based on Polity IV, http://www.systemicpeace.org/polity/polity4.htm; and Penn World Tables Version 6.3, http://pwt.econ.upenn.edu/php_site/pwt63/pwt63_form.php.

3 POVERTY, FOOD PRICES AND ECONOMIC GROWTH IN SOUTHEAST ASIAN PERSPECTIVE

*Peter Warr**

Viewed in long-term perspective, Indonesia's record of sustained poverty reduction is remarkable. Over the two decades ending in 1996, the proportion of the population with expenditure below the government's poverty line declined from almost two-thirds to less than one-fifth. Poverty incidence declined dramatically in both rural and urban areas and in all provinces. The principal driver was economic growth (Figure 3.1).[1] Since 1996 the rate of poverty reduction has been more moderate but there were just two periods during which poverty incidence did not fall (Figure 3.2). The first was the Asian financial crisis of 1997–98. A massive economic contraction occurred during which GDP declined by 13 per cent in a single year. It is hardly surprising that poverty incidence temporarily increased (by 5.7 per cent). The second period was 2005–2006. Explaining this episode is more difficult, because poverty incidence rose (from 16 per cent in 2005 to 17.8 per cent in 2006) despite GDP growth exceeding 5 per cent.[2]

---

* Excellent research assistance from Ramesh Paudel and Razib Tuhin is gratefully acknowledged.

1 See Chapter 2 of this volume, where Pritchett examines the relationship between growth and poverty reduction in Indonesia before and after the Asian financial crisis.

2 A consequence of these two episodes of increased poverty incidence was that by 2009 the proportion of the Indonesian population that was poor (14.1 per cent) was lower than in 1996 (17.7 per cent), but the absolute number of Indonesians living below the poverty line (34 million) was almost the same.

Figure 3.1   *Annual real GDP growth rates, Indonesia, Thailand, the*
Philippines and Malaysia, 1980–2009

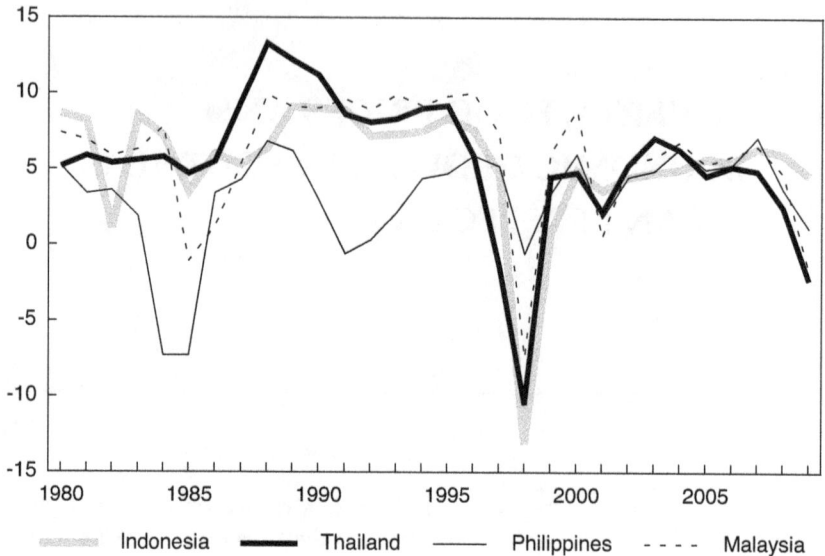

Source: World Bank (various years).

Viewed in regional perspective, the experiences of Indonesia and its neighbours share some key features. First, other rapidly growing economies, such as Thailand and Malaysia, also achieved dramatic long-term reductions in poverty incidence. Even the Philippines, while recording lower growth rates than the other three, nevertheless experienced significant long-term reductions in poverty incidence. Second, in all four countries poverty incidence rose during the recessions accompanying the Asian financial crisis. Third, Thailand and the Philippines, like Indonesia, experienced a mysterious increase in poverty incidence around 2006, of a similar magnitude to Indonesia's.[3] In all three countries, poverty incidence rose despite continued GDP growth above 5 per cent. This chapter looks at this puzzling increase, focusing on Indonesia.

In the next section, I review some of the empirical and analytical issues arising from the measurement of poverty incidence and comparisons over time and across countries. I then examine the long-term data on changes in poverty incidence in the above four Southeast Asian coun-

---

3 The Malaysian data do not make it possible to say whether such an increase occurred at this time.

Figure 3.2   Poverty incidence, Indonesia, 1976–2009 (%)[a]

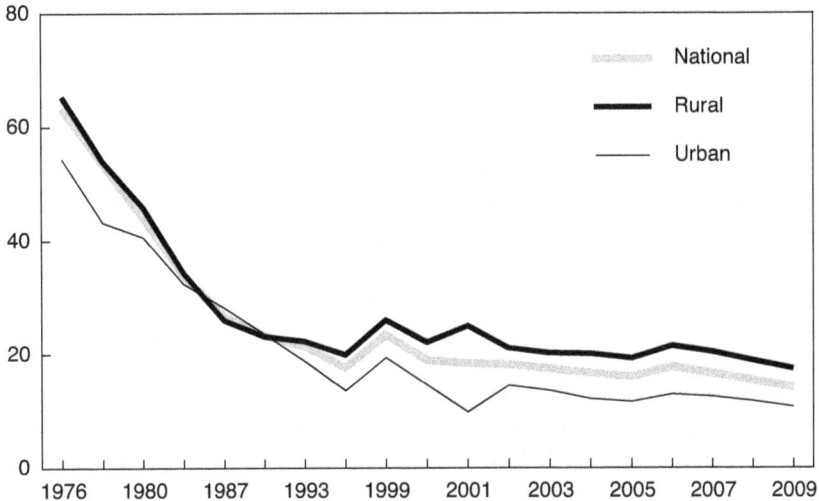

a   National poverty is the share of the total population with income below a national poverty line held constant over time in real terms; rural poverty is the share of the rural
population with income below a rural poverty line held constant over time in real terms;
and urban poverty is the share of the urban population with income below an urban
poverty line held constant over time in real terms. The number of poor at the national
level is the sum of the number of rural and urban poor, which means that national poverty incidence must always lie between the rates of rural and urban poverty incidence.

Source: Statistics Indonesia (various years), based on household expenditure data collected
in the Susenas survey.

tries. The analysis then focuses on the 2006 increase in measured poverty
incidence in Indonesia. I show that a projection of changes in poverty
incidence based on the econometrically estimated relationship between
changes in poverty incidence and the rate and sectoral composition of
economic growth predicts a significant reduction in poverty incidence
between 2005 and 2006, rather than the increase that actually occurred.

Some analysts have attempted to explain this outcome in terms of
the 'jobless growth' that is said to have occurred during the period (see,
for example, Chapter 4 of this book by Aswicahyono, Hill and Narjoko).
Changes in the nature of economic growth during this period could have
had an impact on poverty incidence, but this chapter advances the alternative hypothesis that the explanation lies primarily in the behaviour
of consumer prices, rather than the nature of the economic growth that
occurred. In particular, I argue that the policy-induced increases in rice
prices, relative to other consumer prices, arising from Indonesia's post-

2004 policy to protect domestic rice growers, explains most of the otherwise unexplained increase in poverty incidence.[4]

MEASURING POVERTY

Before we can analyse the causes of or determinants of changes in poverty, we must first quantify it. By *poverty incidence,* we mean here the headcount index – the proportion of the population whose expenditure or income falls below a fixed threshold, the poverty line, the monetary value of which is adjusted over time to maintain a constant real purchasing power. Before turning to the more technical aspects of poverty measurement, I will make four observations about the broader dimensions of poverty measurement (see also Ravallion 2002 and World Bank 2000).

First, although poverty entails more than just a low level of income or expenditure, the various dimensions of poverty do tend to be highly correlated (World Bank 2000). People who are poor by one measure tend, generally speaking, to be poor by another. This means that measuring poverty accurately by narrow measures such as real income or real expenditure may be useful even though it does not capture all of the elements of poverty that may reasonably be considered relevant.

Second, it is important for users of poverty measures to be able to compare poverty incidence over time. This means that when government statistical agencies make changes in the way poverty is measured, those changes should take the form of *adding* to the set of measures already in place, rather than *replacing* them. That is, poverty incidence using 'old' measures should continue to be published on an ongoing basis even when new and possibly superior measures are introduced.

Third, objective quantification is important. As far as possible, poverty measures need to avoid personal opinion affecting the measures, because such opinions differ among individuals and can change over time. Subjectivity can enter at the level of primary data collection or at the level of analysis.

Fourth, poverty estimates are controversial and can have political consequences. The statistical organisations responsible for compiling the household survey data on which poverty estimates are based, and for the subsequent analysis of those data, are generally government agencies. In some countries the politicisation of poverty measures has caused the informed public to lose confidence in the integrity of the government

---

4 See also the papers in the special issue of the *Bulletin of Indonesian Economic Studies* of April 2008 (Volume 44, Issue 1) devoted to rice policy in Indonesia.

agencies responsible for producing the poverty estimates.[5] The continued openness of this process is the means by which public confidence in the reliability of the estimates can be maintained.

Several issues are involved in quantitative measurement of poverty incidence over time. First, are we discussing *absolute* or *relative* poverty? Measures of absolute poverty relate to that part of the population whose incomes (or expenditures) fall below a given level (the poverty line) whose value is held fixed in real purchasing power over time and across social groups. Relative poverty means *inequality*, and to avoid confusion it is probably better to call it that. Measures of inequality compare the incomes (or expenditures) of the poor with those of the rich, or some other reference group. The concept of absolute poverty is quite different, because it reflects the overall size of the economic pie as well as its distribution. For example, suppose the real incomes (or expenditures) of all households doubled. Inequality would not change but absolute poverty would decline dramatically. Not surprisingly, when the overall size of the economic pie is changing significantly, measures of absolute poverty and inequality do not necessarily move together and may not even change in the same direction. This chapter is concerned with absolute poverty incidence.

Second, what *variable* is used for the calculation of poverty incidence? In Thailand, Malaysia and the Philippines, the official statistics are based on *household income* per household member, adjusted for the gender and age distribution of the household. In most other countries, including Indonesia and several other Southeast Asian countries, such as Vietnam, Cambodia and Laos, household expenditure is used. The use of household expenditure to measure poverty is more consistent with economic theory, in that expenditure is more directly related to household welfare than income. In addition, the measurement of income is problematic in rural areas where much of the return to labour is non-monetary. The distinction between income-based and expenditure-based measures of poverty is especially important when we are considering the impact on poverty of a short-term change in income.

Third, what is the *poverty measure*? Most studies of poverty focus on the headcount measure of absolute poverty incidence, which means the proportion of the population whose income falls below a given threshold, held constant in real terms over time and across regions. At a conceptual

---

5 To some extent, this has happened in Indonesia. In 2008 demonstrators outside the Statistics Indonesia offices in Jakarta claimed that the poverty data had been 'manipulated' and did not relate to the true situation of the poor. See, for example, 'Indonesia's poor protest manipulation of poverty statistics', Action in Solidarity with Asia and the Pacific, 15 August 2008, http://www. asia-pacific-action.org/node/142.

level, this measure has the disadvantage that changes in the headcount poverty rate are normally due mainly to changes in the living conditions of members of the population with income or expenditure close to the poverty line. Other measures of absolute poverty incidence lacking this disadvantage have been calculated from time to time, such as the poverty gap and the poverty gap squared, but, as noted above, these measures are normally highly correlated with the headcount measure.

Fourth, what *data source* is used for the calculation? Household-level survey data are essential, but the statistical design and frequency of these surveys vary between countries. In Indonesia, the National Socio-Economic Survey (Survei Sosio-Ekonomi Nasional, or Susenas) conducted by the central statistics agency, Statistics Indonesia, is the source of the raw data. In Thailand, the periodic Socio-Economic Surveys carried out by the government's National Statistical Office provide virtually the sole source of reliable information at the household level that can be compared over time (Krongkaew 1993; Warr 2005). In the Philippines, the corresponding survey is the Family Income and Expenditure Survey conducted by the National Statistical Coordination Board. In Malaysia, the poverty data are assembled by the Economic Planning Unit in the Prime Minister's Office, based on the National Family Income and Expenditure Survey.

Fifth, how is the *base level of the poverty line* determined? Some concept of the minimum level of income or expenditure per person must be established for a household to be classified as non-poor. Although studies of poverty measurement often give great attention to this matter, drawing on studies of minimum nutritional requirements, setting the level of the poverty line necessarily involves a large element of arbitrariness (see also Ravallion 1998).

Sixth, what is the *poverty line deflator*? A poverty line deflator is used to adjust the current monetary value of the poverty line over time to keep its real purchasing power constant. Although this may seem a minor technical matter, it is a central issue for poverty measurement over time and across regions where consumer prices vary. Empirical studies of poverty incidence differ in their handling of this issue. The ideal deflator uses the actual expenditure pattern of the poor to weight price changes at the commodity level. This deflator may, at times, behave differently from the overall consumer price index (CPI), which reflects 'average' expenditure patterns. In particular, when the prices of food items move relative to the prices of other consumer goods, the two series may diverge significantly because the share of food in the poverty line basket is higher than its share in the CPI basket.

The final issue relates to the *timing* of the publication of poverty estimates. To be useful as a monitoring tool for policy purposes, estimates of poverty incidence need to be published as frequently as possible and with minimum delay from the time of collection of the survey data. Most countries have moved towards more frequent household income and expenditure surveys, despite the cost. Indonesia and Thailand now produce poverty incidence estimates annually while Malaysia normally publishes them every two years and the Philippines every three years. In Indonesia the Susenas is conducted annually, but the specialised 'consumption module', which provides the most reliable source of data for poverty estimation based on household expenditure, is conducted only every three years. Most countries have also reduced the delay between collection of the survey data and publication of the resulting poverty estimates. For example, in early 2011 poverty estimates were available for 2009 in the cases of Indonesia, Thailand and the Philippines, while the most recent estimates available for Malaysia related to 2007.

POVERTY REDUCTION IN REGIONAL PERSPECTIVE

Over the last four decades, measured poverty incidence has declined dramatically throughout most of Southeast Asia. At the same time, long-term economic growth has been impressive throughout most of the region, despite temporary setbacks such as the financial crisis of 1997–98. The available data on poverty incidence in Thailand, the Philippines and Malaysia are summarised in Figures 3.3–3.5 and may be compared with the trends for Indonesia shown in Figure 3.2. These are the four Southeast Asian countries for which national poverty incidence data are available for a period longer than a decade. The data are based on official statistics reporting the headcount measure of absolute poverty incidence published by the respective national statistical agencies. Over the periods shown, national poverty incidence declined substantially in each of these four countries, in both rural and urban areas.

Two important sources of difference between the poverty estimates for these countries should be emphasised. First, the poverty incidence data for Thailand, Malaysia and the Philippines are based on comparisons of household *income* with an official poverty line adjusted over time to hold real purchasing power constant. However, the data for Indonesia are based on a comparison of household *expenditure* with such a poverty line. This difference could introduce some inconsistencies between Indonesia and the other three countries in the short-run behaviour of the resulting poverty estimates. During periods when incomes rise unexpectedly, income should rise faster than expenditure and poverty incidence estimates based on income should decline faster. When incomes fall unexpectedly (as happened during the Asian financial crisis, for example),

Figure 3.3   Poverty incidence, Thailand, 1969–2009 (%)

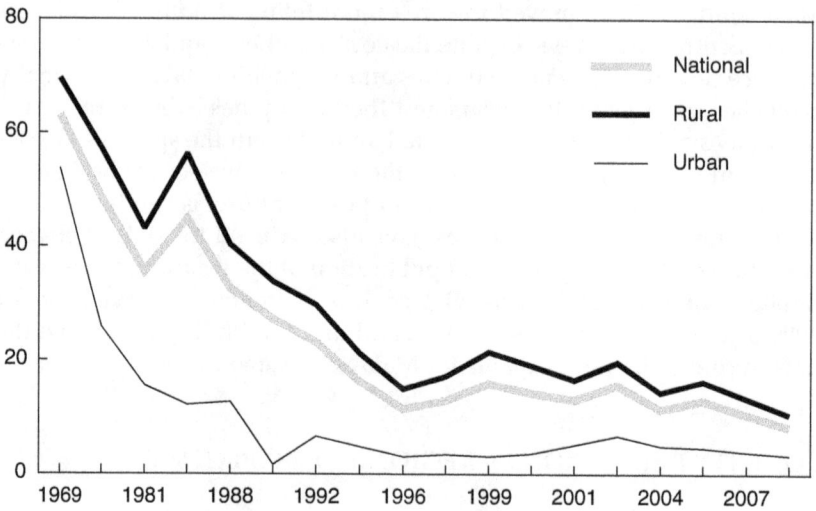

Source: National Economic and Social Development Board, Bangkok, based on household income data collected in the Socio-economic Survey conducted by the National Statistical Office.

Figure 3.4   Poverty incidence, Philippines, 1971–2009 (%)

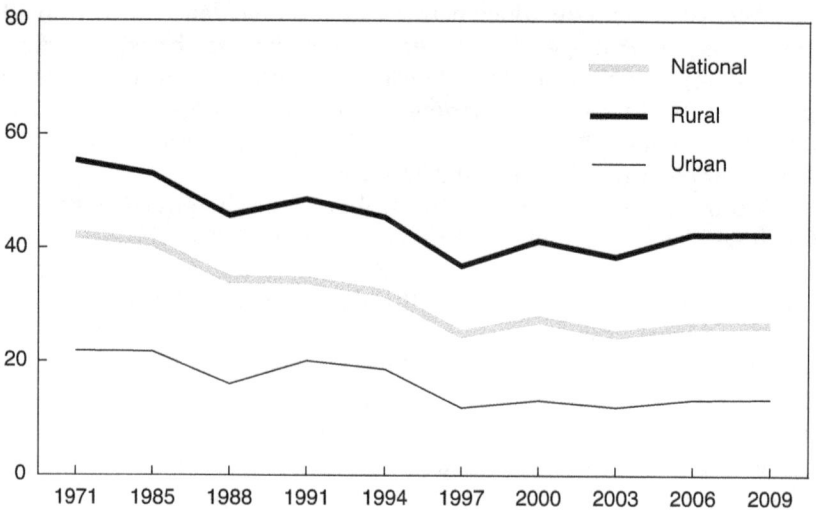

Source: National Statistical Coordination Board, based on household data collected in the Family Income and Expenditure Survey conducted by the National Statistics Office.

Figure 3.5   Poverty incidence, Malaysia, 1970–2007 (%)

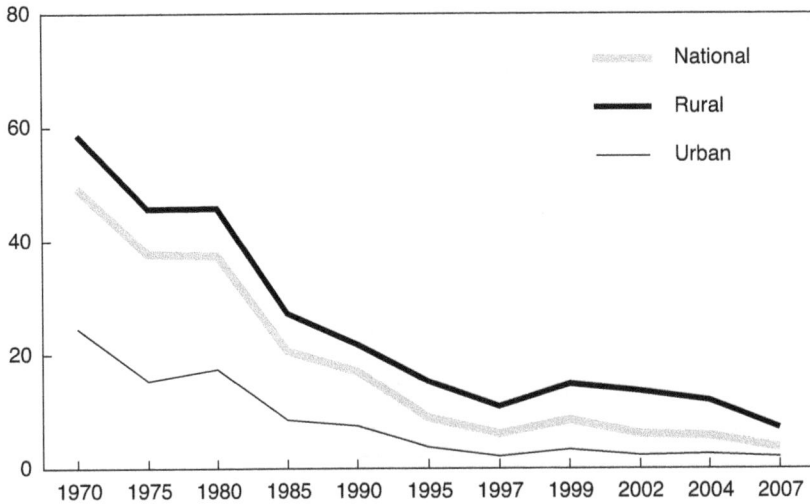

Source: Economic Planning Unit, Prime Minister's Office, based on data from the National Family Income and Expenditure Survey.

the reverse should occur; poverty estimates based on income should rise more than estimates based on expenditure.

Second, the real purchasing power of the poverty line used in each of the countries is different. Even if the shape of the distribution of real income (expenditure) was exactly the same in all four countries – which it is not – each country's poverty line would still relate to a different point on the income or expenditure distribution.

The data for the four countries are summarised in Table 3.1, which shows the mean values of the annual rates of change in national, rural and urban poverty incidence and also the contribution of rural-to-urban migration. The mathematical relationships between these aggregates are set out in Appendix A3.1.

The upper half of Table 3.1 shows the results of this decomposition. All results are evaluated at the mean values of the data set. For example, the mean annual change in the aggregate level of poverty incidence for Indonesia is –1.385 percentage points per year, representing an average annual reduction from, let's say, 20 per cent to 18.615 per cent.[6] The mathematical discussion in Appendix A3.1 shows that this mean aggregate

---

6 Equation (A3.2) in the appendix is an identity and must apply at all points in the data set. It must therefore apply at the means of the data.

Table 3.1   *Data decomposition: annual rate of change in poverty incidence*[a]

	Indonesia	Thailand	Philippines	Malaysia
Actual				
National[b]	–1.385	–1.231	–0.630	–0.996
Rural[c]	–0.844	–1.049	–0.305	–0.715
Urban[d]	–0.448	–0.171	–0.169	–0.187
Migration[e]	–0.092	–0.011	–0.156	–0.094
Normalised (national = 100)				
National[b]	100.00	100.00	100.00	100.00
Rural[c]	60.94	85.28	48.45	71.76
Urban[d]	32.38	13.86	26.79	18.77
Migration[e]	6.68	0.86	24.77	9.47

a   The decomposition relates to the terms of equation (A3.2). National = rural + urban + migration.
b   Mean annual value of dP, the year-on-year change in national poverty incidence.
c   Mean annual value of $a^R dP^R$, the year-on-year change in rural poverty incidence weighted by population share.
d   Mean annual value of $a^U dP^U$, the year-on-year change in urban poverty incidence weighted by population share.
e   Mean annual value of $(P^R - P^U)da^R$, the year-on-year change in poverty incidence induced by migration.

Source: Author's calculations based on equation (A3.2).

change in poverty incidence can be decomposed into three components: average poverty reduction in urban areas; average poverty reduction in rural areas; and the movement of population between these two areas, calculated as a residual in Table 3.1.

The lower half of the table normalises the decomposition by dividing all values by the mean change in aggregate poverty (–1.231 for Thailand, for example) and multiplying by 100. For Indonesia, reduced rural poverty accounted for 61 per cent of the overall fall in poverty, reduced urban poverty for 32 per cent and migration for 7 per cent.

For each of these four countries, poverty reduction in rural areas was the most important single contributor to the decline in poverty at the national level. But rural-to-urban migration was also important (with the partial exception of Thailand), as was the reduction of poverty in urban areas. A lesson from the data is therefore that even though poverty *incidence* is indeed heavily concentrated in rural areas, poverty *reduction* over time is not just a matter of reducing poverty incidence in these areas. Poverty can be, and is, reduced by attracting people away from rural areas to urban areas where economic conditions are more favourable and by reducing poverty in urban areas themselves.

The above calculations are, of course, merely descriptions of the data. We wish to know what caused these observed changes in poverty incidence and what caused the differences between countries. Poverty incidence and the changes in incidence over time obviously depend on many factors. Economic variables are only part of the story, and among those variables, many issues aside from simply the overall rate of growth will be relevant.

The growth of real GDP per person has followed a similar pattern to poverty incidence. From fastest to slowest, the ranking of the four countries by annual rate of change in poverty incidence is: Indonesia, Thailand, Malaysia and the Philippines.[7] The ranking by rate of real GDP growth per person is similar but not identical to this. At the level of individual economies as well, a relationship between the rate of poverty reduction over time and the rate of growth over time seems possible. For example, in Thailand poverty incidence fell throughout the period shown in Figure 3.3, except during the recession of the early 1980s and the Asian financial crisis of the late 1990s. In all four cases, the crisis of 1997–98 produced negative growth rates of real GDP per person, temporarily reversing the long-term pattern of sustained poverty reduction.

THE NEXUS BETWEEN POVERTY INCIDENCE AND ECONOMIC GROWTH

The presumption that economic growth can normally be expected to reduce poverty is uncontroversial among economists, although non-economists tend to be more sceptical.[8] The economist's expectation that growth will reduce absolute poverty over the long term is based on the statistical definition of absolute poverty incidence and two empirical observations. Absolute poverty incidence is defined as the proportion of the population whose income or expenditure falls below a given threshold, the 'poverty line', a level of income or expenditure whose nominal value is adjusted over time to hold its real purchasing power constant. The level of real income represented by this threshold is essentially arbitrary, but once it is determined, poverty incidence depends simply on the size of the economic pie and its distribution.

---

7 See Balisacan (2002) for an insightful analysis of the lagging performance of the Philippines.

8 This lack of consensus often derives from a failure to distinguish properly between the concepts of absolute poverty and relative inequality.

The two empirical observations are: (1) whereas the size of the pie (real national income per person) can change considerably over time, the degree of inequality generally changes only slowly; and (2) the changes in inequality that do occur are not systematically related to the rate of growth. Changes in poverty incidence must therefore normally be related statistically to changes in the size of the pie – through economic growth or its reversal (Dollar and Kraay 2002). Exceptions are possible, but they are rare.

According to this view, in the long term, economic growth is a necessary condition for large-scale poverty reduction, because no amount of redistribution could turn a poor country into a rich one. It will also be a sufficient condition, even in the short term, provided inequality does not increase 'too much'.

The available empirical evidence supports this expectation: on average, the faster the growth, the greater the reduction in absolute poverty. Nevertheless, while differences in aggregate rates of growth explain much of the observed difference in rates of poverty reduction, they do not explain *all* of it. It is obvious that poverty incidence can be affected by factors other than just the growth rate. These factors may include redistributive policies targeted towards (or away from) poor people (which would include most poverty alleviation programs), technological change, movements in commodity prices due to fluctuating production conditions and changes in the international economic environment. The relative importance of these factors and the efficacy of policy interventions directed to reducing poverty are important matters for quantitative research.

But the emphasis on the aggregate rate of growth may be overly simplistic for another reason. The nature of the growth may also be important – and is itself influenced by the policy environment in place. The literature on economic development has emphasised the sectoral composition of growth as a possible determinant of its distributional effects, although this emphasis has usually been based primarily on *a priori* theorising rather than empirical analysis. In most poor countries, a majority of the poor live in rural areas and are employed in agriculture. From this it has seemed probable that growth of agriculture is more important for poverty reduction than growth of industry or services. Many authors in the development economics field have taken this view, but the conclusion does not necessarily follow.

In an earlier paper (Warr 2006), I systematically examined the relationship between poverty reduction and economic growth in the four countries discussed above. Because data on poverty incidence were available for a period of at least two decades for all four countries, I pooled the data for Indonesia, Thailand, the Philippines and Malaysia. However, the intervals between the available data points were often several years long, which meant that the total number of data points available for any one country was still small. Statistical analysis of the relationship between poverty incidence and economic growth is highly problematic for any one of these countries, taken separately. But this kind of analysis becomes feasible when the data are appropriately pooled across countries. In addition, the number of data points makes it possible to study the way in which the sectoral composition of growth influences the rate of poverty reduction and not simply the overall rate of GDP growth.

There are reasons for thinking that pooling data for this particular group of four countries is reasonable. First, these countries have roughly similar economic structures. All four are market-oriented economies with agricultural sectors which consist primarily of small farming units and which dominate total employment, but not national output. In all four, industrial production has combined export-oriented production with limited protected production for domestic markets. All four have large service sectors. In all four, the rural population dominates the total number of poor people, but rural-to-urban migration has been a prominent feature of the long-term development process. These facts suggest that the underlying relationship between sectoral growth and poverty reduction may be similar among these four countries, whereas this may not be the case for groups of countries whose structural features differ widely.

Second, despite their structural similarities these countries have somewhat different economic histories. Three of the four experienced growth rates above their long-term historical norms during the boom decade from the mid-1980s to the mid-1990s, during which aggregate poverty incidence declined, followed by deep recessions from 1997 onward, during which poverty incidence increased. But these similarities aside, their experiences have been quite different. Thailand has grown more rapidly in all three sectors (agriculture, industry and services) than the other three countries and the Philippines the least rapidly. The rates at which agriculture has contracted as a share of GDP during the process of long-term economic growth have differed, along with rates of industrialisation. The above facts suggest that these countries provide four different sets of empirical experience around a similar underlying structure, comprising the circumstances in which the pooling of data is most likely to be appropriate.

The statistical analysis estimated the equation

$$dP = a^1 + b_a^1 H_a y_a + b_i^1 H_i y_i + b_s^1 H_s y_s + c^1 n, \tag{3.1}$$

where dP is the annual rate of change in poverty incidence over a particular period; y_a, y_i and y_s are the growth rates of value added in agriculture, industry and services respectively; H_a, H_i and H_s are the corresponding GDP shares of these three sectors; and the other terms are estimated parameters. Similar equations are estimated for rural and urban poverty reduction. The econometric results are summarised in Table A3.1 in the appendix.

We now wish to use these results to project poverty incidence in Indonesia, based on the estimated relationship between poverty reduction and economic growth. In particular, we wish to project the change between 2005 and 2006, based on the statistical evidence summarised in Table A3.1. Real value added in agriculture, industry and services increased by 2.72, 4.69 and 8.13 per cent respectively between 2005 and 2006. Population growth was 1.28 per cent. Substituting these data into the estimated equation gives a projected change in poverty incidence of –0.72 per cent. That is, we project a *reduction* in poverty of 0.7 per cent of the population, rather than the *increase* of 1.8 per cent that actually occurred. The difference to be explained is therefore a 2.5 per cent increase in poverty incidence, relative to what would otherwise have occurred.

FOOD PRICES AND POVERTY IN INDONESIA

In 2004 the Indonesian government introduced a ban on imports of the country's staple food, rice. Government officials said that the import restriction was motivated by the wish to protect poor rice farmers from the effects of cheap imports of rice, thereby reducing poverty incidence. It is significant that the import restriction was accompanied by a ban on rice exports, intended to protect consumers from the possibility of large increases in the world price of rice.

The ban has been only partially effective, in that some imports still enter the country and imported rice can still be found within the Jakarta retail market. In effect, the ban is more like an import quota where the quantity of imports permitted is about one-tenth the previous level. The permitted quantity of imports is apparently variable and has changed with market conditions.

Indonesian rice prices rose relative to international prices after the ban on imports was introduced. The behaviour of rice prices is summarised in Figure 3.6. Rice prices also increased relative to the CPI, as shown in Figure 3.7. There were two components to this real price increase in the years after 2004.

First, the import quota initially had a protective effect, increasing domestic rice prices relative to international prices, especially during 2005–2007. This protective effect reversed during the period of high international rice prices from 2008 to 2009. The import quota had the effect of

Figure 3.6   Indonesian and world prices of rice, 1985–2010 (Rp/kg)

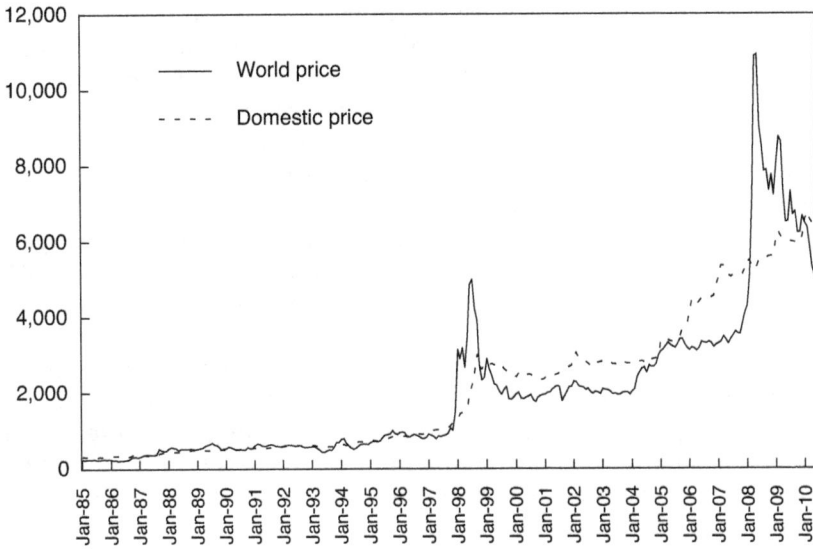

Source: Rice prices: Bulog, Jakarta; exchange rates: Statistics Indonesia, Jakarta.

Figure 3.7   Real price of rice, Indonesia, 1985–2010

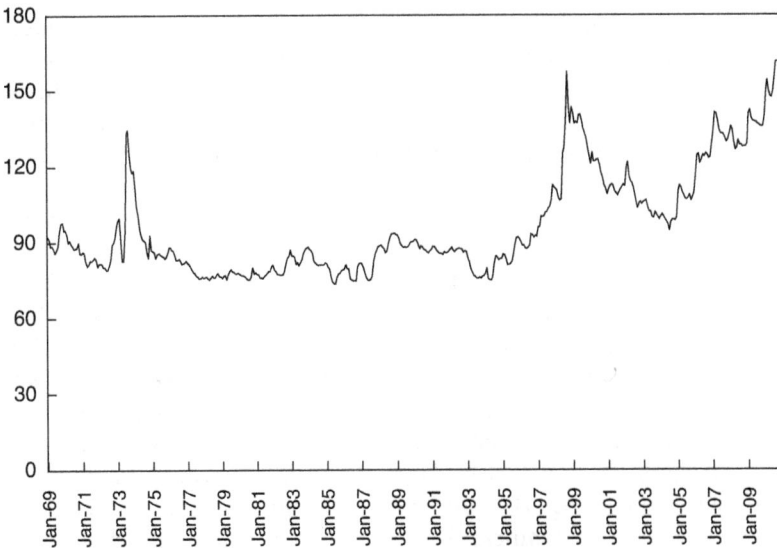

Source: Rice prices: Bulog, Jakarta; CPI: Statistics Indonesia, Jakarta.

reducing the rents associated with the quota and domestic rice prices did not increase as much as they would have under free trading conditions.

Second, the quota converted rice from a traded good whose domestic price was driven by international prices to a non-traded good whose domestic price was determined by domestic supply and demand conditions. The fiscal stimulus implemented in response to the global financial crisis of 2007–2009 increased domestic demand, and thereby increased domestic rice prices, but this occurred well after the 2005–2006 increase in poverty incidence that we wish to explain.

During the period of interest to us, the important story with regard to rice prices is the protective effect of the import quota. From mid-2005 to mid-2006, the ratio of domestic rice prices to international prices, expressed in rupiah, increased by 28 per cent (Figure 3.7). In an earlier paper (Warr 2005), I argued on the basis of a general equilibrium model of the Indonesian economy that the rice import policy had the opposite effect of the poverty reduction that was said to be its goal. Before the ban Indonesia had been a large importer of rice. Net sellers of rice benefited from the restrictions on imports but net buyers were harmed. There were many more poor Indonesians in the second category than the first. The main beneficiaries of the ban were not poor rice producers but the largest producers. Most Indonesians residing in rural areas were net buyers of rice. This included all landless labourers and a surprisingly large number of small farmers, who produced some rice but sold other commodities to purchase additional rice for their own consumption.

Warr (2005) estimated that an import restriction that raised the real domestic price of milled rice by 9 per cent would raise poverty incidence in Indonesia by 0.72 per cent; this increase in poverty incidence would occur in both rural and urban areas but would be larger in the former than the latter. As estimated above, rice prices actually increased by 28 per cent, implying a projected increase in poverty incidence of 2.24 per cent. The increase in poverty incidence we wish to explain is 2.5 per cent of the population. The restriction on rice imports therefore explains most (90 per cent) of the otherwise unexplained increase in poverty incidence.

International prices for food increased dramatically in 2008–2009, but these price increases were not transmitted to the domestic market. Rice is the most important case. Indonesia's near-ban on rice imports insulated the domestic rice market from the international price rises. The effect of the international price increases was to reduce the economic rent obtainable from those limited imports that were permitted. The international price increases were in fact so large that exports would have become profitable; if such exports had been possible, domestic prices would have increased very significantly. The rice protection policy therefore insulated the Indonesian market from the temporarily high international rice prices of 2008–2009. However, it did so at the expense of increasing the domestic price of rice relative to the world market price, thereby making the incidence of poverty higher than it would otherwise have been. There can be no guarantee that international price spikes like those in 2008–2009 will not recur, but events of this kind are temporary. On the other hand, the domestic price increase induced by protection is not temporary. It persists as long as the import restrictions remain in place.

CONCLUSIONS

The four Southeast Asian countries studied in this chapter – Indonesia, Thailand, the Philippines and Malaysia – have each achieved significant reductions in poverty incidence in recent decades. According to statistical analysis of this experience, the achievement of poverty reduction was mainly attributable to the aggregate rate of economic growth, although changes in the sectoral composition of the growth had an effect as well. Changes in poverty incidence are generally well explained by changes in the rate and composition of economic growth. A puzzling exception to this pattern was the increase in poverty incidence observed between 2005 and 2006 in at least three of the four countries: Indonesia, Thailand and the Philippines. During that period, poverty incidence increased in all three despite real GDP growth in excess of 5 per cent. This chapter has attempted to explain this paradoxical outcome, focusing on Indonesia.

Poverty incidence changes when the real expenditure of households close to the poverty line rises or falls, causing the level of some households' per capita real expenditure to cross the threshold of the poverty line. This can occur for two reasons, one on the income side and the other on the expenditure side. First, absolute real incomes can change. This is the principal effect of economic growth, in that it increases the real returns to the factors of production owned by the poor. Second, and less obviously, relative consumer prices can change, particularly the prices of staple food items relative to other items. The reason for the second effect is that the share of staple foods in the consumer basket of the poor (about 65 per cent) is much higher than it is for the general population (about 35 per cent), and thus much larger in the deflator used to adjust the poverty line over time than its share in in the basket of goods and services whose prices are used to calculate the CPI or to deflate GDP.

In Indonesia, poverty incidence increased by 1.8 per cent from 2005 to 2006. On the basis of the observed historical relationship between poverty incidence and economic growth, a 0.7 per cent reduction in poverty incidence would have been expected from the growth that occurred, taking into account its sectoral composition. The unexplained difference between the observed and counterfactual rates of poverty reduction was therefore 2.5 per cent of the population. This chapter has argued that the increase in domestic rice prices that followed the implementation of restrictions on rice imports after 2004 explains most of this otherwise mysterious increase in poverty incidence.[9]

Rising poverty incidence as a result of policy-induced increases in staple food prices should not really be surprising. Moreover, quantitative research that predicted this outcome was available to the Indonesian government at the time of its decision to restrict rice imports, and subsequently. Examples include Ikhsan (2005), Warr (2005), World Bank (2006), McCulloch (2008) and McCulloch and Timmer (2008). Ikhsan (2005) conducted a quantitative analysis based on Susenas data, focusing on the negative effects that rice price increases have on poor consumers. Originally prepared for the United States Agency for International Development (USAID), this paper was first circulated in working paper form in 2003. Warr (2005) prepared a multi-sector, multi-household general equilibrium analysis for the World Bank and circulated it in working paper form in late 2003. The World Bank's (2006) assessment of poverty in Indonesia emphasised the potential for rice price increases to increase poverty incidence.

All of these studies pointed out that rice industry protection could be expected to have negative effects on poverty incidence. The fact that the government chose to implement and maintain the policy despite this evidence reveals that the political benefits expected to accrue from protecting the rice industry outweighed the projected negative effects on the poor.

REFERENCES

Anand, S. and S.M.R. Kanbur (1985) 'Poverty under the Kuznets process', *Economic Journal*, 95: 42–50.
Balisacan, A. (2002) 'Poverty and inequality', in A. Balisacan and H. Hill (eds) *The Philippine Economy: Development, Policies and Challenges*, Oxford University Press, Oxford.
Dollar, D. and A. Kraay (2002) 'Growth is good for the poor', draft report, World Bank, Washington DC, March. Available at: http://siteresources.worldbank.org/DEC/Resources/22015_Growth_is_Good_for_Poor.pdf
Ikhsan, M. (2005) 'Rice price adjustment and its impact on the poor', *Economics and Finance in Indonesia*, 53: 61–96.

---

9   The explanation for increased poverty incidence in Thailand and the Philippines remains to be studied systematically. It may or may not prove to be similar to the Indonesian story analysed in this chapter.

Krongkaew, M. (1993) 'Income distribution and poverty', in P. Warr (ed.) *The Thai Economy in Transition*, Cambridge University Press, Cambridge.

McCulloch, N. (2008) 'Rice prices and poverty in Indonesia', *Bulletin of Indonesian Economic Studies*, 44(1): 45–63.

McCulloch, N. and C.P. Timmer (2008) 'Rice policy in Indonesia: a special issue', *Bulletin of Indonesian Economic Studies*, 44(1): 33–44.

Ravallion, M. (1998) 'Poverty lines in theory and practice', LSMS Working Paper No. 133, World Bank, Washington DC, June.

Ravallion, M. (2002) *Poverty Comparisons*, Taylor & Francis, London.

Statistics Indonesia (various years), *Statistical Yearbook of Indonesia*, Statistics Indonesia, Jakarta.

Warr, P. (2005) 'Food policy and poverty in Indonesia: a general equilibrium analysis', *Australian Journal of Agricultural and Resource Economics*, 49(4): 429–51.

Warr, P. (2006) 'Poverty and growth in Southeast Asia', *ASEAN Economic Bulletin*, 23(3): 279–302.

World Bank (2000), *World Development Report 2000/2001: Attacking Poverty*, World Bank, Washington DC.

World Bank (2006) *Making the New Indonesia Work for the Poor*, World Bank, Jakarta, November.

World Bank (various years) *World Development Indicators*, World Bank, Washington DC.

APPENDIX A3.1   RURAL, URBAN AND NATIONAL POVERTY INCIDENCE

We write N, N^R and N^U for the national, rural and urban populations respectively, where $N = N^R + N^U$. We write $a^R = N^R/N$ and $a^U = N^U/N$ for the rural and urban shares of the national population respectively, where $a^R + a^U = 1$. The total number of people in poverty is given by $N_p = N_p^R + N_p^U$, where N_p^R and N_p^U denote the number of people in poverty in rural and urban areas respectively. National poverty incidence is given by

$$P = N_p/N = (N_p^R + N_p^U)/N = a^R P^R + a^U P^U, \qquad (A3.1)$$

where $P^R = N_p^R/N^R$ denotes the proportion of the rural population that is in poverty and $P^U = N_p^U/N^U$ the corresponding incidence of poverty in urban areas. Now, differentiating (A3.1), we obtain a key relationship,

$$dP = a^R dP^R + a^U dP^U + (P^R - P^U)da^R. \qquad (A3.2)$$

Equation (A3.2) states that the change in poverty incidence may be decomposed into three parts: the change in rural poverty incidence weighted by the share of the rural population; the change in urban poverty incidence weighted by the share of the urban population; and the movement of population from rural to urban areas weighted by the difference in poverty incidence between these two areas.

The last of these terms is described by Anand and Kanbur (1985) as the 'Kuznets effect'. As the population moves from rural to urban areas, a change in aggregate poverty incidence will occur even at constant levels of rural and urban poverty incidence, provided that the levels of poverty incidence in the two sectors are different. In growing economies, we expect to find the share of the rural population falling $(da^R > 0)$ and the incidence of poverty in rural areas exceeding that in urban areas $((P^R - P^U) > 0)$. Thus, the expected sign of $(P^R - P^U)da^R$ is negative. How important the Kuznets effect is as a determinant of overall poverty reduction is, of course, an empirical matter.

Table A3.1 Regression results: Thailand, Indonesia, the Philippines and Malaysia

Variable	Change in total poverty		Change in rural poverty		Change in urban poverty	
	Coeffi-cient	*t*-statistic	Coeffi-cient	*t*-statistic	Coeffi-cient	*t*-statistic
Constant	1.589	4.226	2.006	5.860	0.150	0.996
Agriculture growth	-0.543	-2.283	-0.729	-3.369	-0.174	-1.826
Industry growth	0.058	0.476	0.006	0.057	-0.053	-1.078
Services growth	-1.186	-8.621	-1.094	-8.376	-0.120	-2.167
Population growth	-0.071	-0.631	-0.036	-0.353	-0.0367	-0.815
Intercept dummy, Indonesia	0.412	1.355	0.666	2.408	0.239	1.968
Intercept, dummy Thailand	1.050	3.627	0.885	2.408	0.232	1.997
Intercept dummy, Malaysia	0.629	1.956	0.712	2.431	0.3376	2.618
R-squared	0.672		0.708		0.2554	
Adjusted R-squared	0.652		0.691		0.2112	
F-statistic	34.5		40.9		5.8	

Source: Author's calculations based on estimation of equation (3.1). Details of the estimation are in Warr (2006).

4 ACCELERATING POVERTY AND VULNERABILITY REDUCTION: TRENDS, OPPORTUNITIES AND CONSTRAINTS

*Asep Suryahadi, Umbu Reku Raya, Deswanto Marbun and Athia Yumna**

Before the onset of the Asian financial crisis in 1997, the Indonesian economy was growing quickly; as a result, poverty fell significantly. Other welfare indicators, such as the infant mortality rate, the school enrolment rate and life expectancy at birth, were also showing improvements. The economic crisis that engulfed Indonesia in 1997–98 reversed these trends, resulting in a large increase in poverty in 1999.

To alleviate the effects of the economic crisis, in mid-1998 the government introduced a social safety net for the poor (Jaring Pengaman Sosial, or JPS) covering food, education, health and employment. Some components of the JPS continue today with some changes to their design and targeting. Together with general economic growth and sectoral development, these programs have contributed to a resumption in the downward trend in poverty. The poverty rate fell from a peak of 23.4 per cent in 1999 to 13.3 per cent in 2010.

Poverty rates tell only part of the story, however, and the number of poor people would more than double if people who are not officially counted as poor, but are nevertheless vulnerable to poverty, were taken

* Part of the research for this paper was conducted while the authors were working on a report for the Asian Development Bank (RETA No. TA 6397 (REG): 'Strengthening country diagnosis and analysis of binding development constraints for selected developing member countries'). The authors thank Armand Sim for assistance with poverty profiles.

into account. Because these near-poor have per capita household expenditure that is only slightly above the poverty line, they are easily pushed into poverty when negative shocks occur.

The numbers of such people are substantial. In 2008, for example, 15.4 per cent of Indonesians were living below the national poverty line, but a much larger 42.6 per cent were living below the international poverty line of $2.00 per capita per day in purchasing power parity (PPP) terms. This meant that 27.2 per cent of Indonesians were living above the national poverty line but below the international poverty line.

These people are likely to fall below the poverty line if they experience a 'shock' that adversely affects their income, such as job loss, business bankruptcy, crop failure, illness, accident, natural disaster or social conflict. Social protection in the form of security of access to basic services such as food, education and health is therefore needed to reduce the risk that these people will fall into poverty.

Another distinct feature of poverty in Indonesia is that the country lags behind its neighbours in reducing *non-monetary* poverty at the same time as it has made significant progress in reducing monetary poverty. Compared with countries such as Singapore, Brunei Darussalam, Malaysia, Thailand, Vietnam and the Philippines, for instance, Indonesia performs poorly on education and health indicators. Over 50 per cent of the labour force has only a primary school education or less, and the country has high rates of infant and maternal mortality.

The distribution of poverty across population groups and regions is also unequal. Seven of the 10 provinces with the highest incidences of monetary poverty are located in eastern Indonesia – although, in terms of absolute numbers, most of the poor still reside in Java and several provinces in Sumatra. Similarly, there is unequal access to education, health, clean water and sanitation across population groups and regions, indicating the existence of a welfare gap.

The chief objective of this chapter is to analyse the profile of poverty in Indonesia and identify some ways of reducing it further. First, we discuss trends in the monetary and non-monetary dimensions of poverty. Next, we identify the opportunities that are available to reduce poverty. We then analyse the constraints to poverty reduction, and offer some solutions to those constraints, before providing some conclusions.

POVERTY PROFILE AND TRENDS

Indonesia recorded its lowest ever rate of monetary poverty before the Asian financial crisis, of 11.3 per cent in 1996. High and stable economic growth over the previous 20 years had contributed to a significant decrease in the headcount poverty rate, of 1.4 percentage points per year on

Figure 4.1   Monetary poverty rate and number of poor people, 1976–2010[a]

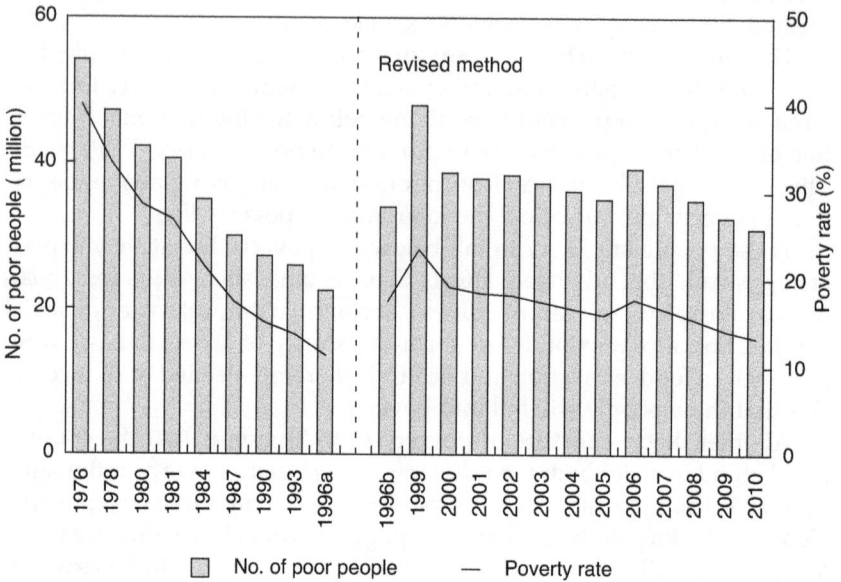

a   The method for calculating the poverty rate was revised in 1998 and applied to the data
     for 1996.
Source: Statistics Indonesia (various years).

average between 1976 and 1996. In the decade after the crisis (1999–2009),
the annual decrease in the headcount poverty rate fell to 1.0 percentage
point per year. Based on the revised method of calculating the official
poverty rate implemented since 1998 (and backdated to 1996), the headcount poverty rate was 13.3 per cent in 2010 (Figure 4.1).

   Although the total incidence of poverty has fallen over the past four
decades, the gap in poverty incidence between urban and rural areas has
widened. The higher poverty rate in rural areas reflects in part the cumulative effect of the longstanding push for national industrial development, which has given greater emphasis to manufacturing and services
at the expense of agricultural development (Booth 2000; Thee 2010). In
1987, manufacturing overtook agriculture as the main contributor to exports, and it has continued to consolidate its position as the major source
of economic growth and employment since then. Because the rural poor
rely mainly on agriculture, which has weak linkages with manufacturing, they have benefited much less from the expansion of the manufacturing sector (ADB, ILO and IDB 2010).

   Although the incidence of monetary poverty is higher in rural areas,
the share of the urban poor has also increased significantly over the past

Table 4.1 Rural–urban gap for various dimensions of poverty and deprivation, 2009

Indicator	Definition	Rural areas (%)	Urban areas (%)	Gap (percentage points)
Under-5 mortality rate (in 2007)	Number of deaths per 1,000 live births among children aged 0–5	60.1	37.8	22.3
Lack of sanitation (toilet)	Percentage of population living in a house without a proper toilet	50.4	15.1	35.4
Poorly educated household head	Percentage of population living in a household in which the household head has not completed nine years of basic education	83.7	50.5	33.2
Lack of access to clean water	Percentage of population living in a household without access to a clean and protected source of drinking water	56.5	30.6	26.0
Poorly educated youth	Percentage of population living in a household in which members aged 18–24 years have not completed nine years of basic education	40.7	16.0	24.7
Unhygienic floor	Percentage of population living in a house with an earth floor	15.8	5.0	10.8
Monetary poverty	**Percentage of population below the official poverty line**	**17.4**	**10.7**	**6.6**

Source: Authors' calculations based on Susenas, 2009 (Consumption Module); under-5 mortality rates are from Measure DHS (Demographic and Health Surveys) database, http://www.measuredhs.com (accessed 16 August 2010).

two decades as Indonesians have flocked to the cities, from 18.5 per cent in 1976 to 36.6 per cent in 2009. Taking into account the exclusion from the official data of children in orphanages, street children, beggars and the homeless, most of whom reside in urban areas, it seems likely that the share of urban poverty is higher than the official estimate.

It is clear from Table 4.1 that the rural–urban differences in poverty extend well beyond monetary poverty: while the rural–urban gap in

Figure 4.2   *Trends in the poverty rate, human development index (HDI) and gender-related development index (GDI), 2000–2007*

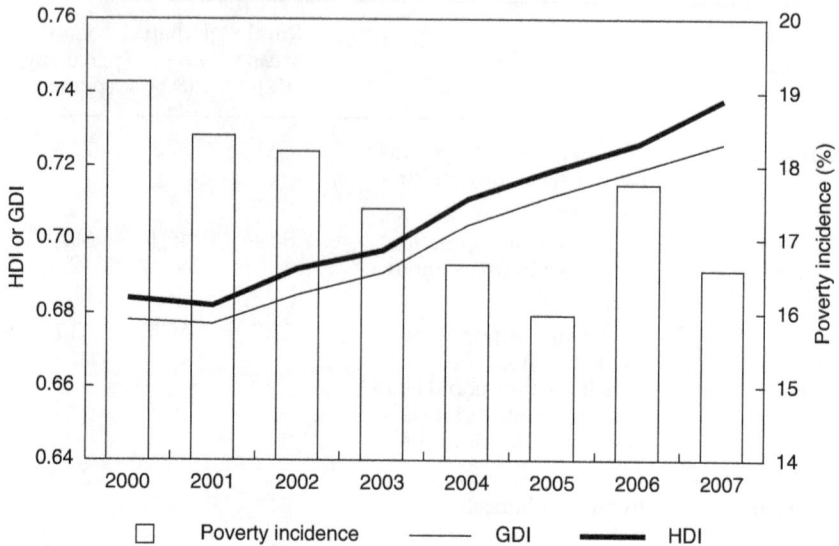

☐   Poverty incidence   ——— GDI   ▬▬▬ HDI

Source: Menkokesra (2009); UNDP (2003, 2008, 2009).

monetary poverty is 6.6 percentage points, the gaps for the other measures of poverty are two to five times higher. This indicates that the reduction in monetary poverty has not translated sufficiently into improvements in other social indicators. Moreover, despite having a higher per capita income, Indonesia lags behind other Southeast Asian countries such as Vietnam when it comes to social indicators such as the mortality rate among children under five.[1]

While the reductions in monetary poverty have translated into improvements in human development, it appears that men have benefited more than women. This is apparent in Figure 4.2, which shows poverty incidence in 2000–2007 as well as trends in Indonesia's rankings on the human development index (HDI) and the gender-related development index (GDI). It indicates that women have lagged slightly behind men when purchasing power and human development capabilities are taken into account.

---

1   In 2008, Indonesia had a per capita gross national income (GNI) of $2,010 and an under-5 mortality rate of 41. Vietnam had a lower per capita GNI of $890 but a far better under-5 mortality rate of 14. See the country comparisons at http://www.unicef.org/.

Table 4.2   Monetary welfare indicators by gender of household head,
2007 and 2009

Indicator	Female household head	Male household head	Total
Share in national poor (%)			
2007	50.2	49.8	100.0
2009	50.1	49.9	100.0
Share in total Susenas sample (%)			
2007	49.9	50.1	100.0
2009	49.9	50.1	100.0
Mean per capita consumption (Rp)			
2007	349,385	345,204	345,615
2009	444,459	424,420	426,520
Median per capita consumption (Rp)			
2007	258,029	256,140	256,366
2009	330,289	322,091	322,901

Source: Authors' calculations based on Susenas, 2007 and 2009 (Consumption Module).

The monetary poverty indicator does not provide any evidence of a feminisation of poverty, however. Table 4.2 shows that male and female household heads have similar incidences of poverty, and that the difference in mean (and median) per capita expenditure between the two groups of households has been increasing in favour of women. Thus, the difference in the mean increased from Rp 4,181 in 2007 to Rp 20,039 in 2009. This suggests that we need to look beyond the monetary poverty dimension to explain the inequality between men and women revealed by the GDI – to examine, for instance, women's participation in the labour force, the incidence of poverty among women who are working, and households' human capital investments in girls versus boys.

While women still have far lower labour force participation rates than men, the good news is that they are joining the workforce in increasing numbers. The female participation rate grew at a rate of 1.7 per cent per annum on average in 2003–2009, two percentage points higher than the rate for men (–0.3 per cent) (Table 4.3). Similarly, while the incidence of unemployment and underemployment remains significantly higher among women, rates of both have been falling faster among women than among men.

Table 4.3   Employment indicators by gender, 2003–2009

Indicator	2003	2004	2005	2006	2007	2008	2009	Average change (% p.a.)
Labour force participation rate (%)								
Total	65.7	65.7	65.7	66.2	67.0	67.2	67.2	0.4
Female	46.3	46.3	46.3	48.1	50.2	51.1	51.0	1.7
Male	85.3	85.3	85.3	84.2	83.7	83.5	83.7	-0.3
Unemployment rate (%)								
Total	9.5	9.9	11.2	10.3	9.1	8.4	7.9	-0.6
Female	13.0	12.9	14.7	13.4	10.8	9.7	8.5	-3.2
Male	7.6	8.1	9.3	8.5	8.1	7.6	7.5	1.6
Underemploy-ment rate (%)								
Total	28.4	26.9	27.3	27.4	27.6	27.8	27.7	-0.6
Female	38.5	36.8	36.9	36.0	36.9	36.2	36.6	-3.2
Male	22.8	21.2	21.9	22.4	22.1	22.6	22.3	1.6

Source: National Labour Force Survey (Sakernas), 2003–2009.

Data from the 2009 National Socio-Economic Survey (Survei Sosio-Ekonomi Nasional, or Susenas) reveal that more households are reporting a gender-neutral position in education (78.8 per cent), paid work (64.8 per cent) and domestic work (49.3 per cent), but that there is still a tendency for female children to be given less preference in education (pro-male 14.8 per cent versus pro-female 6.5 per cent) and paid work (pro-male 32.4 per cent versus pro-female 2.8 per cent) and more preference in doing domestic work (pro-male 2.3 per cent versus pro-female 48.4 per cent) (see Table 4.4).

A worrying characteristic of poverty in Indonesia is that movements out of poverty tend to coincide with simultaneous movements into poverty, resulting in a relatively slow rate of poverty reduction being observed in recent years. For example, Table 4.5 shows that 53.3 per cent of people who were classed as poor in 2008 moved out of poverty in 2009, while at the same time almost half of the people who were classified as poor in 2009 had not been poor in 2008. This provides strong support for the argument that it is important not only to empower the poor to move

Table 4.4   *Priority given to gender in education, the labour market and household domestic work, 2009 (% of households)*

Area of priority	Priority to males	Priority to females	Priority to neither
Education			
Indonesia	14.8	6.5	78.8
Quintile 1 (poorest)	15.5	6.3	78.2
Quintile 5 (richest)	13.2	6.2	80.6
Rural	13.6	6.1	80.4
Urban	15.4	6.7	78.0
Labour market			
Indonesia	32.4	2.8	64.8
Quintile 1 (poorest)	33.8	2.9	63.4
Quintile 5 (richest)	27.9	2.9	69.2
Rural	27.7	2.7	69.5
Urban	35.0	2.8	62.2
Household work			
Indonesia	2.3	48.4	49.3
Quintile 1 (poorest)	2.5	49.8	47.7
Quintile 5 (richest)	2.2	44.2	53.7
Rural	2.0	43.9	54.1
Urban	2.4	50.9	46.7

Source: Authors' analysis based on Susenas, 2009 (Socio-cultural and Education Module).

out of poverty, but also to strengthen the capacity of the near-poor to avoid falling into poverty.

OPPORTUNITIES FOR POVERTY REDUCTION

Several factors make the outlook for poverty reduction more promising. The opportunities available to reduce poverty include: (1) the current economic expansion due to globalisation; (2) the realisation of a demographic dividend due to the high proportion of the population of working age; (3) better identification of the problems faced by the poor, and of their solutions, through the adoption of a participatory development approach; and (4) greater international support for the Millennium Development Goals.

Table 4.5   Poverty transition matrix, 2008–2009

		2009			Row total
		Poor	Near-poor[a]	Non-poor	
2008	Poor	46.7 / 51.0	20.3 / 26.8	33.0 / 6.5	100.0
	Near-poor[a]	22.3 / 20.2	21.5 / 23.6	56.2 / 9.2	100.0
	Non-poor	5.4 / 28.8	7.7 / 49.7	87.0 / 84.3	100.0
Column total		100.0	100.0	100.0	

a The line for the near-poor is equal to 120 per cent of the poverty line.
Source: Authors' analysis based on Susenas, 2008, 2009 (Consumption Module).

Economic expansion due to globalisation

Over the long run, exposure to globalisation in the form of trade liberalisation, capital inflows, foreign direct investment (FDI) and global production networks is good for developing countries. It brings about rapid economic growth and an accompanying decline in poverty.[2] For centuries, global trade has been creating jobs, reducing prices, increasing the variety of goods available to consumers and providing a route for countries to acquire new technologies. It is also evident that the flow of FDI into developing countries has contributed to faster economic growth, transfers of technology and increases in domestic investment.[3]

The capacity of trade liberalisation to reduce poverty is stronger, however, when complementary policies are in place (Harrison 2006; Harrison

2 See, for example, Dollar and Kraay (2001), Winters (2001) and Henderson (2005). Owing to space limitations, we focus here on trade and FDI. Nonetheless, it is important to note that other inherent features of economic globalisation make a major contribution, directly or indirectly, to poverty alleviation. In addition to the ones mentioned in the text, they include international flows of low-skilled labour and the availability of low-cost information through the spread of information and communications technology.
3 See, for example, Borensztein, De Gregorio and Lee (1998), Bosworth and Collins (1999) and Kis-Katos and Sparrow (2009).

and McMillan 2007). Such policies would include flexible labour laws, investments in human capital and infrastructure, the establishment of channels to ensure adequate access to credit and the provision of technical assistance. Similarly, the capacity of FDI to reduce poverty is dependent on several factors, such as the quality of host country policies and institutions, the quality of the investment, the nature of the regulatory framework and the flexibility of labour markets (Mayne 1997). In the Indonesian context, we look at two different periods, the pre- and post-crisis eras, to establish the relevance of this line of argument.

Before the crisis, strategic economic policies directed at promoting the export-oriented manufacturing sector were put in place as the oil boom of the 1970s came to an end. These policies took the form of tariff reductions, liberalisation of export and import procedures, incentives to attract FDI, reductions in labour market distortions, devaluations of the exchange rate and widespread deregulation of the domestic economy.[4] They were accompanied by large public investments in education, health, family planning and infrastructure, helping to pull the bulk of the poor out of poverty.[5]

In the post-crisis era, Indonesian engagement with the global economy has slowed. Since 1997, Indonesia has been the only crisis-affected economy to register negative flows of FDI. Exports have grown, but this growth has mainly come from favourable world prices rather than an expansion of volumes (Athukorala 2006). A non-conducive investment climate, unfriendly labour market regulations and political and policy uncertainty are among the factors identified as having contributed to this situation.[6]

Surprisingly given this unfavourable enabling environment, Indonesian poverty rates have continued to decline in the post-crisis period, albeit moderately compared with the pre-crisis era. Much of the credit for this can be attributed to the government's nationwide social protection programs initiated at the onset of the crisis and now formally included in the Medium Term Development Plan for 2010–2014 (Suryahadi et al. 2010). Nevertheless, Indonesia's own past experience clearly shows that it is through strategic exposure to economic globalisation coupled with complementary social development policies that pervasive poverty is most effectively tackled.

---

4 See, for example, Fane (1996), Fane and Condon (1996), Hill (1996), Suryahadi (2001), Suryahadi et al. (2003) and Thee (1991).
5 See Duflo (2001), Lucas and Timmer (2005) and World Bank (2006).
6 See, for example, Suryahadi et al. (2003), Tambunan (2005) and Aswicahyono, Bird and Hill (2009).

Demographic dividend

Indonesia is currently benefiting from a demographic dividend that is likely to continue for the next two decades. This can be briefly explained as follows. In the 1950s to 1970s, Indonesia experienced a baby boom as high fertility rates coincided with lower mortality rates. Many couples who had postponed marriage in the 1940s as the country recovered from the chaos caused by the fight for independence were now having children. And with the increased use of antibiotics, many more of these children were surviving to adulthood (Adioetomo 2005).

Under the intensive family planning program implemented in the 1970s to 1990s, the fertility rate dropped, resulting in a decrease in the proportion of the population aged under 15 years. With the fall in the share of this age group, the increase in the share of the working-age population and the slow increase in the share of the elderly, Indonesia faces a demographic transition where the age dependency ratio (the proportion of the population not in the labour force to the proportion in the labour force) has declined steadily. As a result, Indonesia is benefiting from a demographic dividend, where the working-age population is roughly twice the size of the population aged under 15. Adioetomo (2005) predicts that the age dependency ratio will hit a low point of 44/100 between 2020 and 2030, after falling steadily from 86/100 in 1970 to 54/100 in 2000.

With such a large number of people of working age now in or entering the labour market, this is an opportune time to accelerate efforts to utilise the country's workforce to its full capacity to reduce poverty. Moreover, the falling age dependency ratio should leave scope for higher rates of saving, with households likely to have income in excess of their consumption requirements. If these savings are invested in children's education, the quality of Indonesia's human capital will rise, lifting more people out of poverty.

Adoption of a participatory development approach

The changing political landscape since the fall of Suharto in 1998 has opened new avenues for the government to address poverty. Democratisation and decentralisation have allowed more participatory development planning processes to flourish, in particular through the multi-stakeholder consultation forums known as *musyawarah perencanaan pembangunan* (*musrenbang*). These forums involve both state and non-state actors and provide a formal avenue for communities to voice their aspirations and produce development programs that are in accordance with their needs.

Law 25/2004 on National Development Planning institutionalises *musrenbang* at all levels of government (village, subdistrict, district/

municipal, provincial and national) over different timeframes (short term, medium term and long term). In addition, a joint ministerial decree of Bappenas and the Ministry of Home Affairs (0008/M.PPN/01/2007) states that development planning recommendations made at the village level must be accommodated by higher levels of government, to ensure a bottom-up development planning process.

Despite the laudable intentions behind the creation of the *musrenbang* mechanism, at least two factors are hampering the effectiveness of this type of participatory development planning. First, there is a risk of elite capture at the village level, which reduces the effectiveness of the *musrenbang* as a voice-channelling mechanism.[7] This results in the needs of the poor being neglected and those of the elite groups dominating. Second, there tends to be an absence of local government commitment and willingness to support the process of participatory development. This leads to poor-quality or insufficient information being provided to participants. The limited acceptance of the *musrenbang* process is caused by a narrow understanding of the role and importance of public participation, a failure to appreciate the long-term benefits of good governance for sustainable development, and a general inability to distinguish between political and public participation.

A study by the United States Agency for International Development and the Local Governance Support Program confirms this assessment of the effectiveness of the *musrenbang* mechanism (USAID and LGSP 2008). It finds that the forums can be a useful way of determining needs-based project interventions and an effective tool in participatory budgeting. However, they also suffer from a lack of political support from local government and from the limited role of civil society in the development planning process. In short, there is an urgent need to improve the *musrenbang* process.

The *musrenbang* are, of course, not the only channel through which the poor can participate in development programs; the Indonesian government also operates one of the biggest community-driven development programs in the world, the National Program for Community Empowerment (Program Nasional Pemberdayaan Masyarakat, or PNPM). Covering all districts and cities across the country, it considerably increases the opportunities available to the poor to take an active role in local, and by extension national, development (see Chapter 14 by Yulaswati and Sumadi for details).

---

7 See, for example, Platteau and Gaspart (2003), Bebbington et al. (2004) and Fritzen (2007).

Global commitment to poverty reduction

Indonesia is receiving increasing support from the international community for its efforts to deliver development and reduce poverty. In 2008, the OECD's Development Assistance Committee allocated a total of $119.8 billion, representing 0.3 per cent of member countries' combined gross national income, in net official development assistance (ODA), the highest amount ever. Even in the midst of the global financial crisis, the international community managed to maintain its commitment to ODA, which declined only slightly to $119.6 billion in 2009.

For Indonesia alone, net ODA and official aid increased by 34 per cent between 2007 and 2008, from $391 million to $593 million.[8] The level of aid reached its highest point in 2005, when $2.2 billion was allocated to Indonesia, mainly to support the rehabilitation and reconstruction of Aceh after the devastating tsunami of 26 December 2004. Of all members of the Development Assistance Committee, Australia is the single biggest contributor of ODA to Indonesia, particularly grant disbursements, followed by Japan, the United States, Germany and the Netherlands.

It is important to note, however, that Indonesia is not an aid-dependent country. Aid represents less than 1 per cent of Indonesian GDP. The country receives approximately $11 of ODA per capita, compared with $23 for Vietnam and $38 for Cambodia. Moreover, in 2005 Indonesia was classified as a middle-income country for the purposes of the Development Assistance Committee's reporting of ODA. This means that it is considered to have sufficient fiscal resources to finance much of its own expenditure on poverty reduction and the achievement of its Millennium Development Goals.

CONSTRAINTS TO ACCELERATING POVERTY REDUCTION

The slower rates of poverty reduction recorded in Indonesia over the past decade have been the subject of several analyses. These studies have identified several constraints that would need to be addressed to accelerate the pace of poverty reduction. Based on the growth diagnostic framework developed by Hausmann, Rodrik and Velasco (2005), in Figure 4.3 we identify three critical constraints to poverty reduction: insufficient productive opportunities for the poor and near-poor; weak human capabilities among this group; and inadequate social protection for the poor and near-poor.

---

8   See http://data.worldbank.org/indicator/DT.ODA.ALLD.CD?cid=GPD_54.

Figure 4.3   Diagnostic framework explaining slow rates of reduction in poverty and vulnerability to poverty

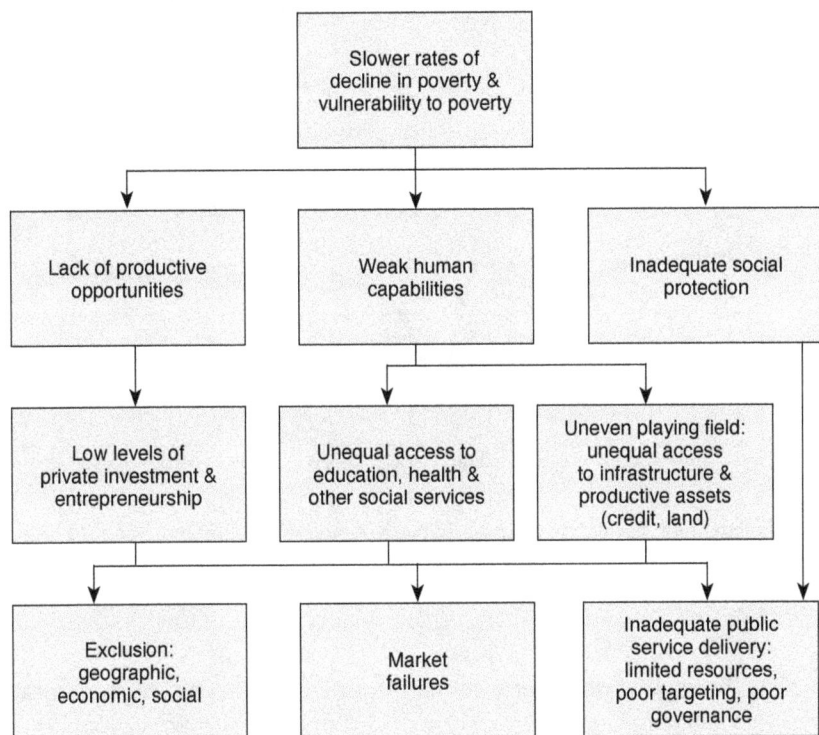

Source: Based on the framework developed by Hausmann, Rodrik and Velasco (2005).

Insufficient productive opportunities

Several underlying factors account for the lack of productive opportunities for the poor and near-poor. The first one is the relatively low level of economic growth in Indonesia. Before the onset of the Asian financial crisis, the country's high and sustained rates of economic growth had brought about rapid reductions in poverty. Between 1976 and 1996, the economy grew at around 7.5 per cent annually, bringing the poverty rate down from 40.1 per cent in 1976 to 11.3 per cent in 1996 (Figure 4.4). Between 2002 and 2009, on the other hand, economic growth moderated to 5.2 per cent annually, or around 70 per cent of the average growth rate during the pre-crisis period, resulting in a slower pace of poverty reduction. The poverty rate fell from 18.2 per cent in 2002 to 14.2 per cent

Figure 4.4   GDP growth rate and poverty rate, 1976–2009 (%)

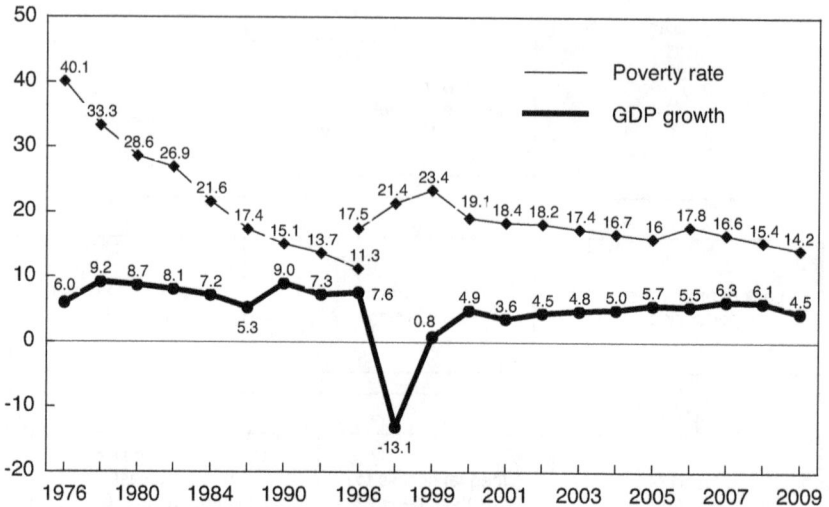

a   The method for calculating the poverty rate was revised in 1998 and reapplied to the data for 1996.

Source: GDP growth rate: World Development Indicators; poverty rate: Statistics Indonesia (various years).

in 2009. The speed of poverty reduction was just 40 per cent that in the pre-crisis period.

The slower pace of poverty decline in the post-crisis period is clearly related to the lower rates of economic growth. In addition, each percentage point of economic growth now has less power to reduce poverty; that is, the growth elasticity of poverty is lower. One of the reasons for this lower elasticity lies in the changing composition of growth. The share of the industrial sector in GDP doubled from 20 per cent in the early 1970s to around 40 per cent in the 1980s, and has remained relatively constant since then. The share of the agricultural sector, meanwhile, dropped from 45 per cent in the early 1970s to 25 per cent in 1980 and further still to 17 per cent in 1995, and has stayed constant at around 15 per cent since then. That is, the agricultural sector – the main source of income for the majority of the poor – has shrunk by a massive 30 percentage points during the last four decades. The services sector experienced a relatively small increase in its share of GDP over the same period, from 35 per cent in the early 1970s to 46 per cent in 2008 (Suryahadi, Suryadarma and Sumarto 2009; Statistics Indonesia, various years). It is clear from these numbers that the agricultural sector, which absorbs the majority of the poor, has lagged behind the other sectors, reducing its capacity to contribute to further reductions in poverty.

Labour market distortions are another reason for the lack of productive opportunities for the poor and near-poor. These distortions are caused by excessive regulation of minimum wages, hiring and firing mechanisms, contract work, severance pay and outsourcing, as set out in Law 13/2003 on Labour. Employers now have less discretion over the size and composition of their workforces, severely reducing labour market flexibility (Manning 2004). As the labour market becomes more rigid, labour-intensive investments are likely to become less attractive to employers, inducing them to adopt more capital and skill-intensive technologies. This in turn will reduce the demand for unskilled workers, who constitute the majority of the poor.

Weak human capabilities

A lack of education and skills, combined with poor living conditions, put the poor and near-poor at a disadvantage when competing with the non-poor in the labour market. It is difficult for the poor to move out of poverty, and easy for the near-poor to fall into poverty, when they are deprived of basic services such as education, health, nutrition, sanitation and clean water. Only 55 per cent of 16–18 year olds from the poorest 20 per cent of households by income have completed junior secondary school. This low level of education not only prevents them from gaining the skills and access to information they need to move out of poverty, but it reduces the likelihood that the next generation will be able to do so (World Bank 2006).

The limited access of the poor and near-poor to education and health services is due to both supply-side constraints (which mainly affect rural areas) and demand-side constraints (more common in urban areas). Both types of constraint are equally important, but in different ways. In the case of education, the supply-side constraints include poor infrastructure and the insufficient quantity and poor quality of teachers. Half of the areas where most of the poor dwell do not have a senior secondary school. On the demand side, lack of financial capacity is the main reason for poor households not to enrol their children in school. It has to be remembered that the opportunity cost of sending children to school, rather than sending them out into the workforce, is higher for the poor.

Similarly, in the case of health services, the main supply-side constraint is the limited availability of health facilities and health workers. In rural areas, where most of the poor dwell, such facilities are likely to be scarce or even nonexistent. The most widely available health facility in the poorest villages is the village maternity centre (*pondok bersalin desa*),

staffed by village midwives (*bidan di desa*) who usually provide only pre-
natal, delivery and neonatal care. It is difficult in such circumstances for
the poor to receive adequate medical treatment, let alone preventative
health care. The main demand-side constraint is cost. To receive proper
medical treatment by a doctor or nurse in a health facility, a poor person
would need to travel to a subdistrict community health centre (*puskesmas*) or to a district public hospital. In addition to the cost of the medical
examination and medicine, the person would need to pay for transport
to and from the facility and take time off work, thereby missing out on
much needed income.

The poor also face severe problems of lack of access to sanitation and
clean water. Indonesia's sewerage network reaches only 1.3 per cent of
the population, and 80 per cent of the rural poor and 59 per cent of the
urban poor do not have access to either plumbed sewerage or a septic
system. Many poor people do not have access to clean water, particularly
in rural areas. According to the 2009 Susenas, only 48 per cent of the
poorest 20 per cent of households have access to safe water in rural areas,
compared with 78 per cent in urban areas.

Inadequate social protection

No matter how good the government's policy in creating a conducive environment for the poor to participate in the process of economic growth,
there will always be some groups that are left out. It is therefore important to develop a social protection system that is able to maintain people's standard of living above the socially agreed minimum level. This
includes guaranteed access to basic services such as education, health
care, clean water and sanitation.

The 1997–98 economic crisis caused almost 15 million people to become poor (Figure 4.1). Poverty again rose significantly in 2006 following
the government's decision to reduce fuel subsidies in the last quarter of
2005. This led to higher transport costs, leading in turn to increases in
the prices of staple goods such as rice. The World Bank (2006) points out
that the increase in the rice price between February 2005 and March 2006
was particularly hard on the poor because rice is one of the largest components of their expenditure. This provides a salient lesson: that poverty
reduction efforts should be aimed not only at reducing the number of
people living below the poverty line, but also at reducing the number of
people who are vulnerable to poverty.

Another lesson learned from past experience is that there is a need
for integrated rather than ad hoc social protection programs. When programs are scattered across different institutions, the result is uneven
outcomes, poor targeting and problems of undercoverage and leakage.

The quality and extent of monitoring and evaluation, too, tend to vary across programs. The newer programs apparently have better monitoring and evaluation procedures, but effective methods for evaluating the overall impact of programs are still generally lacking. Two programs that do incorporate monitoring and evaluation as part of their design are the community-driven PNPM program mentioned earlier and the Family of Hope conditional cash transfer program (Program Keluarga Harapan, or PKH). Both are discussed in more detail by Yulaswati and Sumadi in Chapter 14 of this volume.

Efforts to integrate the plethora of anti-poverty programs into a national social protection system face significant challenges, including, not least, a general lack of administrative and fiscal capacity. Indeed, Cook (2009) points out that countries across East Asia have had great difficulty coming to terms with the institutional arrangements needed to integrate their fragmented social protection systems. This fragmentation extends to both government agencies and service providers. In Indonesia, several ministries are responsible for managing the country's conditional and unconditional cash transfer programs, and social insurance is delivered through four programs for four different groups: civil servants, the military, private sector employees and the poor. The same story applies in China, where an estimated 17 government agencies are responsible for different social protection programs, often competing for resources and funding (Cook 2009).

A critical issue in ensuring the effectiveness of social protection programs is the accurate targeting of beneficiaries. Since the potential benefits of effective targeting are considerable, it always features prominently in the design of such programs. The targeting performance of Indonesia's various social safety net and poverty reduction programs is generally poor, however, with a large portion of the benefits being received by the near-poor or non-poor. Both the exclusion error (the proportion of the poor not included in the program) and the inclusion error (the proportion of beneficiaries who are non-poor) are high. Improving the effectiveness of targeting is therefore a crucial issue (see Alatas, Purnamasari and Wai-Poi, Chapter 15, for more details).

The results of evaluations of various social assistance programs suggest that their implementation suffers from a number of weaknesses: they are too narrowly focused on a single sector, so tend to miss opportunities for cross-sector synergies; there is a lack of coordination across programs; and there is a high degree of leakage and undercoverage. This has resulted in some sections of the poor being only partially covered or not covered at all by such programs. Moreover, most of the programs seem to be fairly ineffectual in lifting the poor out of poverty and increasing the welfare levels of the near-poor.

CONCLUSION

Indonesia has made considerable progress in reducing poverty over the last four decades. Despite this, poverty remains a significant problem in Indonesia today and will continue to do so in the future. There are at least three reasons for this. First, no matter how fast the economy is growing, there will always be some groups in society that are left behind and are unable to reap the benefits of growth. Second, as the economy develops and becomes more modernised, the causes of poverty become more complex and more difficult to untangle, making poverty ever more difficult to resolve. Third, as the economy grows and standards of living increase, people's expectations also rise, pushing up the threshold that separates the poor from the non-poor.

Nevertheless, there are opportunities to accelerate the pace of poverty reduction. These opportunities are provided by the current economic expansion due to globalisation; the realisation of a demographic dividend owing to the favourable age dependency ratio; better identification of the problems faced by the poor, and better solutions, following the adoption of a more participatory approach to development; and international support for the Millennium Development Goals. The realisation of these opportunities naturally depends on the ability to capitalise on them.

There are also, of course, factors that tend to hamper the effectiveness of Indonesia's poverty reduction strategies. The critical constraints are insufficient productive opportunities for the poor and near-poor, weak human capabilities among the poor and near-poor, and inadequate social protection for the poor and near-poor. To be successful, strategies to address these constraints will need to be formulated carefully and implemented effectively. This will require cooperation among the various actors involved in poverty reduction, including central and local governments, civil society, the private sector, international aid agencies and, not least, poor communities themselves.

Expanding productive opportunities for the poor and near-poor will necessitate the reform of labour laws, the provision of critical economic infrastructure to support the development of micro and small enterprises, and other initiatives to promote the growth of labour-intensive industries as well as micro, small and medium-sized enterprises.

Strengthening the human capabilities of the poor and near-poor will require investments in social infrastructure, careful and gradual expansion of the conditional cash transfer program (PKH) and the development of an incentive mechanism to encourage service providers to improve the quality of their services.

Finally, to strengthen social protection for the poor and near-poor, the government must improve the targeting of social assistance programs to ensure that the poor are properly included. It needs to commit to allocating a portion of the state budget to food, education, and health subsidies for the poor, and to persuade local governments to become more actively involved in the implementation of social protection programs.

REFERENCES

ADB, ILO and IDB (Asian Development Bank, International Labour Organization and Islamic Development Bank) (2010) 'Indonesia: critical development constraints', Country Diagnostics Studies, ADB, ILO and IDB, Manila.

Adioetomo, M. (2005) 'Bonus demografi: menjelaskan hubungan antara pertumbuhan penduduk dengan pertumbuhan ekonomi' [Demographic bonus: explaining the relationship between population growth and economic growth], Population Economics Professorial Inaugural Speech, Faculty of Economics, University of Indonesia, Jakarta.

Aswicahyono, H., K. Bird and H. Hill (2009) 'Making economic policy in weak, democratic, post-crisis states: an Indonesian case study', *World Development*, 37(2): 354–70.

Athukorala, P. (2006) 'Post-crisis export performance: the Indonesian experience in regional perspective', *Bulletin of Indonesian Economic Studies*, 42(2): 177–211.

Bebbington, A., L. Dharmawan, E. Fahmi and S. Guggeheim (2004) 'Village politics, culture, and community-driven development: insights from Indonesia', *Progress in Development Studies*, 4(3): 187–205.

Booth, A. (2000) 'Poverty and inequality in the Suharto era: an assessment', *Bulletin of Indonesian Economic Studies*, 36(1): 73–104.

Borensztein, E., J. De Gregorio and J.-W. Lee (1998) 'How does foreign direct investment affect economic growth?', *Journal of International Economics*, 45(1): 115–35.

Bosworth, B.P. and S.M. Collins (1999) 'Capital flows to developing economies: implications for saving and investment', *Brookings Papers on Economic Activity*, 30(1): 143–80.

Cook, S. (2009) *Social Protection in East and South East Asia: A Regional Review*, Institute of Development Studies, Sussex.

Dollar, D. and A. Kraay (2001) 'Trade, growth, and poverty', Policy Research Working Paper No. 2615, World Bank, Washington DC, June.

Duflo, E. (2001) 'Schooling and labor market consequences of school construction in Indonesia: evidence from an unusual policy experiment', *American Economic Review*, 91(4): 795–813.

Fane, G. (1996) 'Deregulation in Indonesia: two steps forward, one step back', *Agenda*, 3(3): 341–50.

Fane, G. and T. Condon (1996) 'Trade reform in Indonesia, 1987–95', *Bulletin of Indonesian Economic Studies*, 32(3): 33–54.

Fritzen, S.A. (2007) 'Can the design of community-driven development reduce the risk of elite capture? evidence from Indonesia', *World Development*, 35(8): 1,359–75.

Harrison, A. (2006) 'Globalization and poverty', NBER Working Paper No. 12347, National Bureau of Economic Research, Cambridge MA, July.

Harrison, A. and M. McMillan (2007) 'On the links between globalization and poverty', *Journal of Economic Inequality*, 5(1): 123–34.

Hausmann, R., D. Rodrik and A. Velasco (2005) 'Growth diagnostics', John F. Kennedy School of Government, Harvard University, Cambridge MA.

Henderson, J. (2005) 'Global production networks, competition, regulation, and poverty reduction: policy implications', paper presented at the Centre for Regulation and Competition Workshop, University of Manchester, Manchester, 22–24 June.

Hill, H. (1996) *The Indonesian Economy since 1996: Southeast Asia's Emerging Giant,* Cambridge University Press, Cambridge.

Kis-Katos, K. and R. Sparrow (2009) 'Child labor and trade liberalization in Indonesia', IZA Discussion Paper No. 4376, Institute for the Study of Labor (IZA), Bonn.

Lucas, S. and P. Timmer (2005) 'Connecting the poor to economic growth: eight key questions', CGD Brief, Center for Global Development, Washington DC, April.

Manning, C. (2004) 'Labour regulation: poverty alleviation or poverty creation?', in A.S. Alisjahbana and B.P.S. Brodjonegoro (eds) *Regional Development in the Era of Decentralization,* Unpad Press, Bandung.

Mayne, K. (1997) 'The OECD Multilateral Agreement on Investment (MAI)', Oxfam UK/I.

Menkokesra (2009) '*UNHDR 2009: HDI dan GDI Indonesia 2007 Membaik*' [UN-HDR 2009: Indonesia's 2007 HDI and GDI is improving]. Available at: http://data.menkokesra.go.id/content/unhdr-2009-hdi-dan-gdi-indonesia-2007-membaik.

Platteau, P.J. and F. Gaspart (2003) 'The "elite capture" problem in participatory development', Centre for Research on the Economics of Development (CRED), Namur.

Statistics Indonesia (2010) *Labor Force Situation in Indonesia, August 2009,* Statistics Indonesia, Jakarta.

Statistics Indonesia (various years) *Statistics Indonesia* [Statistical Yearbook of Indonesia], Statistics Indonesia, Jakarta.

Suryahadi, A. (2001) 'International economic integration and labor markets: the case of Indonesia', Economics Study Area Working Paper No. 22, East-West Center, Honolulu.

Suryahadi, A., D. Suryadarma and S. Sumarto (2009) 'The effects of location and sectoral components of economic growth on poverty: evidence from Indonesia', *Journal of Development Economics,* 89(1): 109–17.

Suryahadi, A., W. Widyanti, D. Perwira and S. Sumarto (2003) 'Minimum wage policy and its impact on employment in the urban formal sector', *Bulletin of Indonesian Economic Studies,* 39(1): 29–50.

Suryahadi, A., A. Yumna, U. Raya and D. Marbun (2010) 'Binding constraint to poverty reduction in Indonesia', working paper, SMERU Research Institute, Jakarta.

Tambunan, T. (2005) 'The impact of foreign direct investment on poverty reduction: a survey of literature and a temporary finding from Indonesia', paper presented at the consultative meeting on Foreign Direct Investment and Policy Changes: Areas for New Research, United Nations Conference Centre, Bangkok, 12–13 March.

Thee, K.W. (1991) 'The surge of Asian NIC investment into Indonesia', *Bulletin of Indonesian Economic Studies,* 27(3): 55–8.

Thee, K.W. (2010) 'A brief overview of growth and poverty in Indonesia during the New Order and after the Asian economic crisis', in J. Hardjono,

N. Akhmadi and S. Sumarto (eds) *Poverty and Social Protection in Indonesia*, Institute for Southeast Asian Studies and SMERU Research Institute, Singapore.

UNDP (United Nations Development Programme) (2003) *Human Development Report 2003. Millennium Development Goals: A Compact among Nations to End Human Poverty*, UNDP, New York NY.

UNDP United Nations Development Programme (2008) *Human Development Report 2007/2008. Fighting Climate Change: Human Solidarity in a Divided World*, UNDP, New York NY.

UNDP United Nations Development Programme (2009) *Human Development Report 2009. Overcoming Barriers: Human Mobility and Development*, UNDP, New York NY.

USAID and LGSP (United States Agency for International Development and Local Governance Support Program) (2007) 'Musrenbang as a key driver in effective participatory budgeting: key issues and perspective for improvements', Good Governance Brief, USAID and LGSP, Jakarta, July.

Winters, L.A. (2001) 'Trade, trade policy, and poverty: what are the links?', Working Paper No. 2382, Centre for Economic Policy Research, London.

World Bank (2006) *Making the New Indonesia Work for the Poor*, World Bank, Jakarta.

5 REGIONAL PATTERNS OF POVERTY: WHY DO SOME PROVINCES PERFORM BETTER THAN OTHERS?

*Riyana Miranti**

Indonesia's falling absolute poverty rates have been very impressive, particularly in the period before the Asian financial crisis in 1997–98. There was a significant reduction in the proportion of the population below the poverty line, from 40.1 per cent in 1976 to 11.3 per cent just before the crisis in 1996. This dramatic decline occurred in both urban and rural areas. But although the record has been impressive nationally, the regional statistics reveal a more varied picture of stubbornly high poverty rates in some areas but low rates in others. In 2009, for example, the poverty rate for the national capital, Jakarta, was about one-eighth that in Papua and one-sixth that in East Nusa Tenggara. The gap between South Kalimantan and Bali, both low-poverty provinces, and Papua, Aceh, and East and West Nusa Tenggara, all high-poverty provinces, was almost as large.

What determines the differences in both levels of poverty and rates of change in poverty across the archipelago? We would expect poverty rates to be closely related to levels of regional development, given the differences in resource endowments across regions and the persistence of socio-economic differences over time (Hill 1989). But at the same time, we would expect a tendency towards convergence in poverty rates over time as capital moves into and labour out of the poorer, low-wage provinces and districts.

* The author thanks Chris Manning, Hal Hill and Budy Resosudarmo for valuable guidance with the research on which this article is based.

This chapter discusses regional disparities in poverty rates and attempts to link them with socio-economic or development indicators known to be associated with poverty. It relies heavily on the regional poverty data for 1984–2002 presented in Miranti (2007). Most of the data discussed in this study therefore relate to the period before decentralisation was implemented in 2001. The development indicators used in the chapter are income, human capital and infrastructure. Knowing which indicators matter most for poverty in particular regions should help policy makers propose more suitable poverty alleviation strategies.

In discussing the relationship between regional poverty rates and development indicators, initial conditions in each region can be expected to play an important role. In addition to discussing those initial conditions – in this case, referring to the situation in 1984 – this chapter describes the state of development in 2002 and, briefly, in 2009. The 2009 data show that decentralisation has advanced development in most provinces since 2002, the end year of the analysis in Miranti (2007). However, the main determinants of poverty identified in this chapter are unlikely to have changed much since then, because the structural characteristics of provinces remain much the same. It is striking that the correlation coefficient between provincial poverty rates in 2002 and 2009 is very high at 0.97.

The chapter is organised as follows. The first section provides an overview of regional poverty patterns and classifies provinces according to their structural characteristics. The second section introduces the development indicators used in the analysis. The third examines levels and trends in poverty and the persistence of poverty over time, and the fourth discusses some regression findings drawn from Miranti (2007). The final section contains some policy implications and caveats.

AN OVERVIEW OF REGIONAL POVERTY AND PROVINCIAL GROUPINGS

Figure 5.1 shows the distribution of poverty rates by province in 2009 relative to the national average of 14.2 per cent. As can be seen, there are marked differences between the best and worst performing provinces. The high-poverty provinces include several relatively remote provinces (Bengkulu, Southeast Sulawesi, Maluku) and some densely populated provinces (Lampung, Yogyakarta, Central Java, East Java). The low-poverty provinces, on the other hand, include several resource-rich provinces (East Kalimantan, Riau) and others with agriculturally productive or more diversified economies (South Kalimantan, Jambi, North Sumatra, West Java). That is, provinces that have similar patterns of poverty also seem to have broadly similar regional characteristics. The region with

Figure 5.1   Headcount poverty rate by province, 2009 (%)[a]

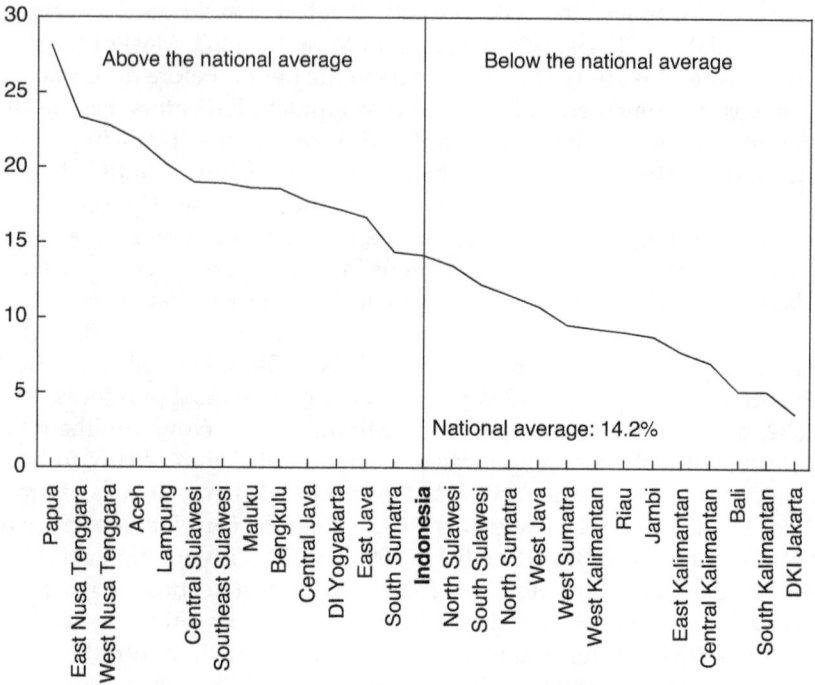

a   The data cover 26 provinces. For simplicity, the data for the provinces formed since 2001 have been combined with the data for the provinces they separated from: Bangka Belitung with South Sumatra, Banten with West Java, Gorontalo with North Sulawesi, North Maluku with Maluku, Riau Islands with Riau, West Sulawesi with South Sulawesi, and West Papua with Papua.

Source: Author's calculations.

the lowest poverty rate in 2009 (3.6 per cent) was the national capital, Jakarta, followed closely by South Kalimantan and Bali.

What does the literature tell us about the determinants of regional and spatial differences in poverty and rates of poverty decline? It is generally accepted by economists that economic growth is a necessary condition for poverty reduction. Most cross-country studies put more emphasis on the growth elasticity of poverty, that is, the impact of economic growth (changes in income) on poverty. The seminal paper on the relationship between economic growth and poverty reduction is that by Dollar and Kraay (2002). While arguing that growth-enhancing policies should be at the centre of any effective poverty reduction strategy, the authors stress that a high elasticity does not mean that growth is all that is needed to improve the lives of the poor. Other cross-country studies have also tried to identify the factors that make growth pro-poor, and to connect rates of poverty reduction to the determinants of pro-poor economic growth. The variables found to be most strongly associated with economic growth and poverty reduction are human capital, infrastructure, natural resource abundance, openness and governance.

Similarly, most studies on regional poverty in Indonesia find that economic growth has contributed to a decline in poverty and to some extent helps explain regional differences. Friedman (2005), for example, observes that growth has been pro-poor nationally but not always regionally, and that its impact has differed across regions. Miranti and Resosudarmo (2005) find that growth has had less impact on poverty in eastern Indonesia than in western Indonesia, with the former region continuing to lag on many development indicators. The puzzle is why absolute poverty measures are high in some regions even though their regional economies have grown, and why they are low in other regions even though they have recorded below-average performance on several development indicators.

It is common in the economics literature to classify countries according to their key characteristics in order to facilitate comparison. Many countries in the Middle East and Latin America, for instance, are classified as natural resource-abundant countries. Despite the intuitive expectation that the presence of natural resources would increase national wealth, many of these countries have experienced lower growth than their resource-poor neighbours – the natural resource 'curse' described by Sachs and Warner (1995, 2001). Roemer and Gugerty (1997) point out that in mineral-rich countries the country's wealth tends to be in the hands of the few, and advise measures to channel mining revenue to the poor and develop other sectors. Gallup, Sachs and Mellinger (1999) classify countries according to their geographical characteristics in order to explore the links between geography and income growth. They find that location and climate have a large impact on income. This in turn may have an impact on poverty rates.

A similar classification can be carried out for provinces or regions within a country. Hill (1989) pioneered this type of classification for Indonesia, grouping provinces according to their geographical location, natural resource endowment and population density. Miranti (2007) updates Hill's classification to 2002 to reflect subsequent structural changes; the original classification relied on data from the 1980s. The revised classification is shown in Table 5.1. It sorts the Indonesian provinces into five categories: resource-rich provinces, densely populated provinces, isolated provinces, settled Outer Island provinces and sparsely populated provinces.

Table 5.1   Revised Hill provincial grouping

Resource-rich provinces		Settled Outer Island provinces	
1	Aceh	14	North Sumatra
2	Riau	15	West Sumatra
3	East Kalimantan	16	South Sumatra
4	Papua	17	South Kalimantan
		18	North Sulawesi
Densely populated provinces		19	South Sulawesi
5	Lampung		
6	DKI Jakarta		
7	West Java	**Sparsely populated provinces**	
8	Central Java	20	Jambi[a]
9	DI Yogyakarta	21	Bengkulu[b]
10	East Java	22	West Kalimantan
11	Bali	23	Central Kalimantan
		24	Central Sulawesi
Isolated provinces		25	Southeast Sulawesi
12	West Nusa Tenggara	26	Maluku
13	East Nusa Tenggara		

a   Jambi is classified as a resource-rich province in the Hill provincial grouping.
b   Bengkulu is not classified in the Hill provincial grouping.
Source: Hill (1989); Miranti (2007).

Resource-rich provinces

The resource-rich provinces – Aceh, Riau, East Kalimantan and Papua – are endowed with abundant mineral, oil and gas reserves. These provinces have high levels of regional GDP (RGDP) per capita. However, they consume much less than they produce, indicating that their populations do not benefit greatly from the income generated by their regions' natural resources. At least until decentralisation, most of the revenue from mining went to the central government, not to the people living in the areas where the resources were located. Opportunities for mining sector employment in these provinces are limited, with most residents continuing to depend on agriculture.

Densely populated provinces

The densely populated provinces are Lampung, Bali and all of the provinces in Java (including Jakarta and Yogyakarta). They tend to have higher levels of economic development than elsewhere: higher RGDP per capita, better performance on human capital indicators and more developed infrastructure. The more advanced state of these provinces supports Bloom, Canning and Malaney's (1999) contention that more densely populated regions have higher per capita income if there are chances for specialisation and economies of scale. Historically, specialisation in trade benefits the densely populated coastal regions, which tend to have lower transport costs, better infrastructure and more opportunities for division of labour (Gallup, Sachs and Mellinger 1999).

Isolated provinces

The two isolated provinces, West and East Nusa Tenggara, are located far from the rest of Indonesia, not to mention Jakarta, the main centre of economic activity. They have poor transport networks and inadequate infrastructure. Like the landlocked economies described by Gallup, Sachs and Mellinger (1999), they are disadvantaged both by their distance from the main centres of economic activity and by inadequate infrastructure. The isolated provinces are poor in resources and rely mainly on agriculture.

Settled Outer Island provinces

The settled Outer Island provinces – North, West and South Sumatra, North and South Sulawesi, and South Kalimantan – have in common a long-established economic identity due to their historical trading links with other parts of Indonesia and with other countries (Hill and Weidemann 1989). These provinces have high scores on at least one development indicator.

Sparsely populated provinces

The sparsely populated provinces – West and Central Kalimantan, Central and Southeast Sulawesi, and Jambi, Bengkulu and Maluku – perform worse than all except the isolated provinces on nearly every development indicator. These provinces are disadvantaged both by their distance from Jakarta and other centres of economic activity and possibly by the sparseness of their populations.

DEVELOPMENT INDICATORS ASSOCIATED WITH REGIONAL POVERTY

Following the literature, we expect some of the variation in regional poverty rates to be explained by regional variations in development indicators. The indicators used in this study to analyse differences in regional poverty are income, human capital and infrastructure.

Income and economic growth

The study looks at the initial income of each province in 1984 and its rate of economic growth during the period 1984–2002. We know that economic growth is important for poverty reduction. But initial income also matters because it indicates the level of development from which the region started.

Provincial income is expressed in per capita terms (in constant 1983 rupiah) to reflect what each province produces per person. The proxy of income is non-oil and gas RGDP; income from oil and gas is excluded from the calculation to avoid the problem noted earlier of resource-rich provinces having high income per capita but a very uneven distribution of income across the population. Non-oil and gas income is considered to be a more reliable way of comparing income across provinces.

Human capital

Romer (1996) defines human capital as the process of enlarging people's choices by expanding human capabilities and functioning. It refers to the abilities, skills and knowledge that people can develop by invest-ing in themselves. Education and training are among the most impor-tant investments that people can make to increase their lifetime earnings (Becker 1993). This has important implications for poverty alleviation given that human capital is the main asset of the poor (World Bank 2000). Most studies focus on the role of education in increasing the stock of hu-man capital, but health is another significant component.

The indicators used in this chapter as proxies of human capital are net enrolments in junior secondary school as a percentage of the relevant age group, and the number of people who have completed junior sec-ondary school as a percentage of the population aged 10 or above. The study focuses on secondary schooling because there is very little varia-tion in primary schooling indicators (especially enrolment ratios) across provinces. Schooling increases the ability to learn and also productivity (Garcia Garcia and Soelistianingsih 1998).

Infrastructure

The poor are usually concentrated in remote areas situated far from do-mestic and international markets. The problem is compounded by poor infrastructure, which prevents the poor from taking advantage of op-portunities created by the growth process.[1] Paved roads, for example,

---

1   See, for example, Ali and Pernia (2003), Yao (2003) and Kwon (2006).

are essential to give remote communities access to markets, employment opportunities and the means to increase both agricultural and non-agricultural productivity (Hayami and Kawagoe 1993). They also make it possible for people living in remote regions to reach health and education facilities, thereby improving their physical wellbeing and future prospects.[2] The length of paved roads directly affects the cost of transport and so may be considered a form of basic infrastructure. Good roads are important for everyone, not just the poor. The indicator selected in this chapter as a proxy of infrastructure is the density of paved roads (kilometres of paved roads per 1,000 square kilometres).

LEVELS OF REGIONAL POVERTY AND TRENDS

Table 5.2 shows provincial poverty rates in 1984 and 2002, and rates of change over that period. Table 5.3 describes the performance of provinces on the selected development indicators – income per capita, junior secondary school enrolment and attainment ratios, and the density of paved roads – over the same period. Based on the 2002 data shown in Tables 5.2 and 5.3, provinces can be classified into three groups: those that have high poverty rates and have performed poorly on most development indicators; those that have low poverty rates and have performed well on most development indicators; and the 'anomalies' – those where the picture is mixed. The first two groups of provinces tend to confirm the expected relationship between poverty and development, while the anomalies suggest a more complicated relationship.

Among the poor performers are East and West Nusa Tenggara, with higher than average poverty rates and lower than average RGDP per capita. East Nusa Tenggara's income per capita was only around half the national average in 2002, and West Nusa Tenggara's slightly higher at around two-thirds the national average. These two provinces' junior secondary enrolment and attainment ratios also lag behind the national average.

Prominent among the high performers is Jakarta, with the country's lowest poverty rate, highest RGDP per capita (around three times the national average in 2002), highest junior secondary attainment ratio and highest density of paved roads. Bali also has above-average income and performs well on all development indicators.

Some provinces – the anomalies – cannot easily be classified as either low or high performers. Papua, for instance, would appear to be a

---

2 These relationships are discussed by Jalilian and Weiss (2006), Warr (2006) and Kwon (2006).

Table 5.2   *Headcount poverty rates by province and change in poverty over time, 1984–2002*

No.	Province	1984	2002	Change (%)	Annualised change (% p.a.)
	Resource-rich provinces	**25.1**	**22.7**	**–9.5**	**–0.6**
1	Aceh	14.3	29.8	108.6	4.2
2	Riau	29.1	13.6	–53.3	–4.1
3	East Kalimantan	37.7	12.2	–67.6	–6.1
4	Papua	27.2	41.8	54.0	2.4
	Densely populated provinces	**16.7**	**17.7**	**5.8**	**0.3**
5	Lampung	54.5	24.1	–55.9	–4.5
6	DKI Jakarta	13.7	3.4	–75.0	–7.4
7	West Java	19.4	12.9	–33.4	–2.2
8	Central Java	37.9	23.1	–39.1	–2.7
9	DI Yogyakarta	30.1	20.1	–33.2	–2.2
10	East Java	29.1	21.9	–24.8	–1.6
11	Bali	34.4	6.9	–80.0	–8.5
	Isolated provinces	**52.9**	**29.2**	**–44.8**	**–3.3**
12	West Nusa Tenggara	53.8	27.8	–48.4	–3.6
13	East Nusa Tenggara	52.9	30.7	–41.9	–3.0
	Settled Outer Island provinces	**26.7**	**16.1**	**–39.5**	**–2.8**
14	North Sumatra	22.6	15.8	–29.8	–2.0
15	West Sumatra	23.8	11.6	–51.4	–3.9
16	South Sumatra	34.1	21.3	–37.7	–2.6
17	South Kalimantan	22.4	8.5	–62.0	–5.2
18	North Sulawesi	26.7	17.5	–34.3	–2.3
19	South Sulawesi	24.7	15.9	–35.6	–2.4
	Sparsely populated provinces	**37.9**	**18.2**	**–52.1**	**–4.0**
20	Jambi	27.7	13.2	–52.4	–4.0
21	Bengkulu	16.7	22.7	35.8	1.7
22	West Kalimantan	47.0	15.5	–67.1	–6.0
23	Central Kalimantan	29.4	11.9	–59.6	–4.9
24	Central Sulawesi	45.7	24.9	–45.6	–3.3
25	Southeast Sulawesi	29.1	24.2	–16.8	–1.0
26	Maluku	31.7	19.3	–39.2	–2.7
	National average	**29.5**	**18.2**	**–38.3**	**–2.7**

Source: Author's calculations based on Susenas, various years.

rich province based solely on its RGDP per capita, and it has a high net enrolment ratio in junior secondary school (although the latter may be affected by measurement error in the enrolment variable). However, its junior secondary attainment ratio is below the national average and it has the lowest density of paved roads among all provinces. Despite its per capita wealth, Papua also suffers from high rates of poverty.

What about the trends in poverty rates over time? As is clear from Table 5.2, there is a very big difference between the annual rate of poverty change in the best performing province, Bali (where poverty fell by 8.5 per cent per annum) and that in the worst performing province, Aceh (which actually experienced an increase in poverty of 4.2 per cent per year). Of the six provinces with the fastest rates of poverty reduction (Bali, Jakarta, and East, South, West and Central Kalimantan), three (Jakarta, South Kalimantan and Central Kalimantan) already had headcount poverty rates in 1984 that were below the national average.

So, why do some provinces experience rapid poverty decline while others lag? Part of the explanation may lie in the regional characteristics known to be associated with poverty. To shed light on this issue, we compare the aggregated poverty rates for the five groups of provinces in 1984–2002 (Table 5.2) with their aggregated performance on income, human capital and infrastructure indicators (Table 5.4).

The poverty rates for each group of provinces shown in Table 5.2 indicate that there has been some degree of convergence in rates over time. The sparsely populated provinces recorded the fastest annual rate of poverty decline between 1984 and 2002, of 4 per cent, starting from the highest rate of poverty in 1984, of 38.0 per cent. This group also experienced rapid improvements in human capital indicators, with annualised changes in both attainment and enrolment ratios that exceeded the national average (Table 5.4).

On the other hand, the densely populated provinces actually experienced an increase in poverty between 1984 and 2002, of 0.3 per cent per annum, although they started out with, and continue to have, relatively low poverty. These provinces also experienced stagnant performance on income and development indicators: their RGDP per capita grew by only 0.8 per cent per annum, slightly below the national average of 0.9 per cent, and their junior secondary attainment and enrolment ratios improved at a slower rate than the national average. That is, since this group started out with higher income and better development indicators than the other groups of provinces, it has experienced diminishing returns in terms of poverty reduction.

Among the remaining three groups, the isolated provinces rank second best in terms of poverty decline, with the poverty rate falling by 3.3 per cent per annum between 1984 and 2002 (Table 5.2). This group of

Table 5.3   Provincial performance on selected development indicators, 1984–2002

Province	RGDP per capita, excluding oil & gas (in 1983 rupiah)			Junior secondary school attainment ratio[a]		
	1984	2002	Change (% p.a.)	1985	2000	Change (% p.a.)
Resource-rich provinces						
1 Aceh	599,733	720,321	1.0	21.6	38.0	3.2
2 Riau	578,500	735,641	1.3	17.8	37.2	4.2
3 E. Kalimantan	1,418,109	1,962,944	1.8	24.2	40.5	2.9
4 Papua	736,945	1,085,330	2.2	24.2	26.7	0.6
Densely populated provinces						
5 Lampung	369,236	496,709	1.7	12.7	27.6	4.4
6 DKI Jakarta	1,938,535	2,544,383	1.5	41.4	60.1	2.1
7 West Java	484,065	480,224	-0.0	14.8	28.8	3.8
8 C. Java	437,279	529,407	1.1	13.2	24.9	3.6
9 DI Yogyakarta	429,799	542,287	1.3	24.5	43.6	3.3
10 E. Java	584,649	719,326	1.2	13.1	27.7	4.3
11 Bali	686,698	901,738	1.5	15.6	34.8	4.6
Isolated provinces						
12 W. Nusa Tenggara	296,885	472,412	2.6	11.7	21.2	3.3
13 E. Nusa Tenggara	263,181	357,667	1.7	8.5	18.3	4.3
Settled Outer Island provinces						
14 N. Sumatra	654,690	866,935	1.6	23.6	40.0	3.0
15 W. Sumatra	538,205	718,939	1.6	20.4	34.8	3.0
16 S. Sumatra	646,016	653,261	0.1	16.2	28.8	3.3
17 S. Kalimantan	625,593	845,581	1.7	14.6	28.2	3.7
18 N. Sulawesi	456,884	277,578	-2.7	24.2	35.7	2.2
19 S. Sulawesi	469,985	629,106	1.6	24.2	28.3	0.9
Sparsely populated provinces						
20 Jambi	436,316	539,166	1.2	15.0	29.7	3.9
21 Bengkulu	404,867	459,404	0.7	14.9	32.8	4.5
22 W. Kalimantan	549,907	682,611	1.2	11.3	23.7	4.2
23 C. Kalimantan	619,456	706,025	0.7	14.8	30.1	4.0
24 C. Sulawesi	383,670	496,254	1.4	24.2	27.6	0.7
25 S.E. Sulawesi	415,535	503,235	1.1	24.2	28.5	0.9
26 Maluku	467,878	274,690	-2.9	24.2	32.7	1.7
National average	**586,035**	**693,816**	**0.9**	**16.5**	**31.9**	**3.7**

n.a. = not available.
a   The calculation is based on data from the 1985 intercensal population survey and 2000 population census because data for 1984 and 2002 were not available.

Table 5.3 (continued)

Province	Junior secondary school net enrolment ratio			Density of paved roads (km per 1,000 km^2)		
	1984	2002	Change (% p.a.)	1984	2002	Change (% p.a.)
Resource-rich provinces						
1 Aceh	43.0	80.2	2.5	37.6	103.1	5.8
2 Riau	36.2	63.6	2.3	13.6	34.6	5.3
3 E. Kalimantan	50.7	62.6	0.9	4.6	8.1	3.1
4 Papua	40.7	82.7	2.9	1.8	5.9	6.8
Densely populated provinces						
5 Lampung	33.9	62.8	2.5	73.2	127.4	3.1
6 DKI Jakarta	68.0	77.5	0.5	n.a.	7,605.4	n.a.
7 West Java	35.0	60.8	2.2	220.4	348.4	2.6
8 C. Java	38.0	64.7	2.2	325.3	499.1	2.4
9 DI Yogyakarta	62.0	76.6	0.9	466.1	1621.5	7.2
10 E. Java	44.0	63.7	1.5	258.6	426.6	2.8
11 Bali	56.1	68.4	0.8	257.2	753.4	6.2
Isolated provinces						
12 W. Nusa Tenggara	37.4	57.9	1.8	92.1	123.7	1.7
13 E. Nusa Tenggara	20.0	38.6	2.7	41.9	119.4	6.0
Settled Outer Island provinces						
14 N. Sumatra	56.0	69.0	0.8	89.8	128.0	2.0
15 W. Sumatra	50.4	66.0	1.1	89.4	236.6	5.6
16 S. Sumatra	40.1	49.4	0.8	35.1	29.1	–1.0
17 S. Kalimantan	33.0	55.9	2.1	37.3	113.3	6.4
18 N. Sulawesi	46.0	66.7	1.5	70.3	184.5	5.5
19 S. Sulawesi	39.0	53.3	1.3	122.2	360.7	6.2
Sparsely populated provinces						
20 Jambi	34.1	61.0	2.4	10.3	75.5	11.7
21 Bengkulu	43.1	59.1	1.3	52.6	90.0	3.0
22 W. Kalimantan	22.0	45.2	2.9	11.2	16.7	2.2
23 C. Kalimantan	39.0	52.6	1.2	3.4	8.1	5.0
24 C. Sulawesi	43.1	51.3	0.7	19.0	37.6	3.9
25 S.E. Sulawesi	40.0	50.4	0.9	16.7	28.8	3.1
26 Maluku	41.0	72.6	2.3	16.3	15.7	–0.2
National average	**41.1**	**61.7**	**1.6**	**39.9**	**79.3**	**3.9**

Source: Intercensal population survey, 1985; population census, 2000; regional accounts, 1984 and 2002; Susenas, 1984 and 2002; Statistics Indonesia's Division of Transportation and Statistics, 2005; Miranti (2007).

Table 5.4 Selected development indicators of the Hill provincial grouping

Group of provinces	RGDP per capita, excluding oil & gas (in 1983 rupiah)			Junior secondary school attainment ratio[a]			Junior secondary school net enrolment ratio			Density of paved roads (km per 1,000 km²)		
	1984	2002	Change (% p.a.)	1985	2000	Change (% p.a.)	1984	2002	Change (% p.a.)	1984	2002	Change (% p.a.)
Resource-rich provinces	763,371	1,009,606	1.6	19.6	35.6	3.4	42.6	72.3	2.1	6.5	16.8	5.4
Densely populated provinces	602,158	699,326	0.8	20.4	35.4	3.1	50.5	68.6	1.2	267.4	419.5	2.5
Isolated provinces	280,066	416,374	2.2	13.0	19.7	2.3	39.0	48.3	0.9	46.0	120.7	5.5
Settled Outer Island provinces	579,531	680,909	0.9	19.3	32.6	3.0	45.1	60.1	1.2	60.5	139.5	4.8
Sparsely populated provinces	477,599	545,617	0.7	14.5	29.3	4.0	35.8	55.2	1.7	10.5	25.9	5.1
National average	**586,035**	**693,816**	**0.9**	**16.5**	**31.9**	**3.7**	**41.1**	**61.7**	**1.6**	**39.9**	**79.3**	**3.9**

a The calculation is based on data from the 1985 intercensal population survey and 2000 population census because data for 1984 and 2002 were not available.

Source: Intercensal population survey, 1985; population census, 2000; regional accounts, 1984 and 2002; Susenas, 1984 and 2002; Statistics Indonesia's Division of Transportation and Statistics, 2005; Miranti (2007).

provinces also experienced the highest growth in RGDP per capita during the period, of 2.2 per cent per year, and the highest rate of improvement in the density of paved roads, of 5.5 per cent per annum (Table 5.4). These statistics again indicate convergence of income and poverty rates, and the potential for the isolated provinces to gradually catch up with the richer provinces. In fact, as Hill (1992) points out, the growth rate of the isolated provinces has never lagged far behind that of the rich provinces, and they have sometimes grown faster. This story of convergence is confirmed by Garcia Garcia and Soelistianingsih (1998), who found slow convergence of regional income between low-income provinces and middle and high-income ones during the period 1975–93.

The settled Outer Island provinces recorded a rate of poverty reduction of 2.8 per cent per annum (just above the average), starting from below-average poverty of 26.7 per cent in 1984 (Table 5.2). This group also started out with good basic endowments of income, human capital and infrastructure. Between 1984 and 2002, income per capita grew at the national average, and infrastructure above the average.

Finally, the resource-rich provinces recorded an annual reduction in poverty of only 0.6 per cent, despite experiencing a high rate of increase in RGDP per capita and performing well on the net enrolment and infrastructure indicators. This supports the earlier argument that the resource-rich provinces do not benefit greatly from what they produce.

Persistence of poverty

To examine the persistence of poverty over time, Figure 5.2 plots the poverty rate for each province relative to the national average in 1984 (point 1 on the horizontal axis) against its rate in 2002 (point 1 on the vertical axis). Thus, a province situated at point 1.5, 2 would have a poverty rate that was one and half times the national average in 1984 and twice the national average in 2002. The four quadrants formed by the intersection of the two lines (the national averages in 1984 and 2002, or point 1, 1) then tell us whether a province had a low poverty rate in 1984 and a high poverty rate in 2002 (quadrant 1); a high poverty rate in both 1984 and 2002 – that is, persistently high poverty (quadrant 2); a low poverty rate in both 1984 and 2002 (quadrant 3); or a high poverty rate in 1984 and a low poverty rate in 2002 (quadrant 4). An examination of initial conditions in these provinces, and changes over time, may help explain why some did better than others between 1984 and 2002.

Five of Indonesia's 26 provinces are found in quadrant 1: Aceh, Papua, Bengkulu, Southeast Sulawesi and East Java. These provinces had higher relative poverty rates in 2002 than in 1984. Aceh and Papua are both resource-rich provinces that have experienced considerable social

Figure 5.2   Persistence of provincial poverty rates, 1984–2002[a]

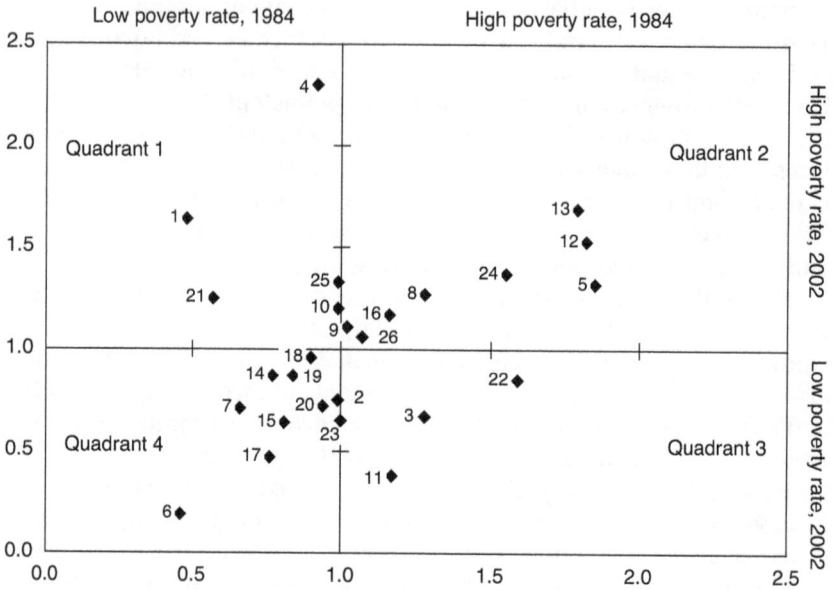

a   Refer to Table 5.1 for the names of the individual provinces and their classification. Each
    point in the graph represents a combination of the ratio of a province's poverty rate to
    the national average in 1984 (horizontal axis) and its ratio in 2002 (vertical axis).
Source: Author's calculations.

and political unrest over long periods. Despite good initial conditions –
better than average RGDP per capita and human capital ratios – this social
unrest may have hampered development in both provinces, increasing
their poverty rates. Bengkulu and Southeast Sulawesi are sparsely populated provinces that suffer from limited connectivity with Jakarta. Both
had below-average income in 1984 and have performed poorly on several development indicators. The final province in quadrant 1, densely
populated East Java, had a below-average attainment ratio in 1984 but
in other respects was around or above the national average. Its presence
in quadrant 1 is surprising given the region's good initial conditions and
extensive links with the rest of Indonesia.

Eight provinces are found in quadrant 2: Lampung, Central Java and
Yogyakarta (all densely populated provinces); West Nusa Tenggara and
East Nusa Tenggara (the isolated provinces); South Sumatra (a settled
Outer Island province); and Central Sulawesi and Maluku (sparsely pop-
ulated provinces). These provinces had persistently high poverty, that is,
higher than average poverty rates in both 1984 and 2002. Most also per-

formed below the national average on one or more development indicators in both years, although there is no clear pattern in terms of changes over time. South Sumatra had lower than average human capital and infrastructure ratios in both 1984 and 2002 (but above-average income in 1984), while the other seven provinces had lower than average RGDP per capita in both years.

Just three provinces are found in quadrant 3: Bali, West Kalimantan and East Kalimantan. These provinces had higher than average poverty rates in 1984 but lower than average rates in 2002. Bali and East Kalimantan performed above the national average on one or more indicators in 1984, but this was not the case for West Kalimantan. Nevertheless, all three achieved rapid progress on at least one indicator, which may then have contributed to an improvement in the poverty rate. Bali, for example, experienced rapid growth in RGDP per capita of 1.5 per cent per year and impressive improvements in junior secondary school attainment (4.6 per cent per year) and infrastructure (6.2 per cent per year). This province also benefited from the decision to allow direct flights from other countries to Bali from 1985 (Jayasuria and Nehen 1989), which helped to expand labour-intensive activities in the tourism and related sectors. East Kalimantan continues to enjoy a resources boom that started in the 1980s. It experienced rapid growth in RGDP per capita of 1.8 per cent per annum and recorded the country's second highest level of income in 2002 (after Jakarta). The gains in West Kalimantan are more difficult to understand. It experienced rapid improvements in human capital (both attainment and enrolments) and may have benefited from greater connectivity with Malaysia, Brunei and Singapore.

Ten provinces are found in quadrant 4: resource-rich Riau; densely populated Jakarta and West Java; the settled Outer Island provinces of North Sumatra, West Sumatra, South Kalimantan, North Sulawesi and South Sulawesi (that is, all provinces in this group except South Sumatra); and sparsely populated Jambi and Central Kalimantan. These provinces had low rates of poverty in both 1984 and 2002. In contrast to the provinces in quadrant 2, which had high poverty rates and lower than average development ratios in both years, this group recorded better than average performance on one or more development indicators in both 1984 and 2002 (although no clear pattern can be observed in terms of the annualised changes). Jakarta has performed well above average on all indicators. West Java has benefited greatly from its proximity to the capital, with many of those who work in the capital living in cities in West Java such as Bogor, Tangerang and Bekasi. Like most provinces in Java, Jakarta and West Java have benefited from good infrastructure and a high concentration of modern industries (Garcia Garcia and Soelistianingsih 1998).

Finally, we look briefly at the period since 2002, when the new decentralisation arrangements might be expected to have had a considerable impact on poverty. In most provinces, poverty continued to fall between 2002 and 2009 (see Figure 5.1 and Table 5.2), although Jakarta experienced a slight increase in its poverty rate of 0.2 percentage points (from 3.4 per cent in 2002 to 3.6 per cent in 2009). In Papua, Aceh, Southeast Sulawesi, West Nusa Tenggara and East Nusa Tenggara, poverty remained persistently high (higher than the national average in both 2002 and 2009), while in Jakarta, Bali, South Kalimantan, West Java and West Sumatra it remained persistently low (lower than the national average in both years). This suggests that the patterns of persistence and change observed for 1984–2002 are still valid in the current setting, bearing in mind the very high correlation between rates of regional poverty in 2002 and 2009 noted in the introductory section of this chapter. It also suggests that the relative ranking of provinces on development indicators may not have changed much.

REGIONAL DETERMINANTS OF POVERTY: SOME FINDINGS FROM REGRESSION ANALYSIS

This section discusses some findings on the determinants of poverty reduction and what works well in particular regions. The discussion draws on Miranti (2007), which used regression analysis to investigate this issue for the period spanning 1984–2002.[3] Some of the main findings are discussed below, particularly those that are relevant to the previous discussion of the relationship between poverty and development indicators.

First, Miranti (2007) found that economic growth was a significant determinant of poverty reduction. Using mean consumption per capita from the National Socio-Economic Survey (Survei Sosio-Ekonomi Nasional, or Susenas) as the proxy of income, the study estimated Indonesia's growth elasticity of poverty to be around –2.5 over the 18 years from 1984 to 2002. That is, a 10 per cent increase in real mean consumption per capita reduced the absolute poverty headcount rate by 25 per cent.

In the resource-rich provinces, however, the results showed that the impact of growth on poverty reduction was low. This strengthens the

---

3 The analysis relied on a panel data set with both cross-sectional (across provinces) and time series (across years) dimensions (see Miranti 2007: Chs 6–7). Panel data analysis was applied not only to incorporate unobserved heterogeneity across provinces but also to control for bias in the omitted time variables that was captured in the year dummies. Two types of panel data estimation were used: fixed effects to estimate the poverty equation; and the Arellano-Bond generalised method of moment to estimate the growth equation.

earlier contention that growth based on oil and gas is less effective in reducing poverty because it is likely to be less labour intensive. It should be noted, however, that most of the revenue produced by this group of provinces went to the central government rather than the producing province, a situation that has changed since decentralisation was implemented in 2001.

Second, the availability of good basic development indicators (human capital or infrastructure) combined with growth to reduce poverty. Thus, using average years of schooling as a proxy of human capital, Miranti (2007) found that human capital reduced poverty in the settled Outer Islands. This finding is plausible given that the settled Outer Island provinces of North Sulawesi, North Sumatra and West Sumatra are generally considered to have the most advanced levels of human capital outside Java and Bali. But surprisingly, improvements in human capital seemed to have the reverse effect of increasing poverty rates in the isolated and remote provinces. Moreover, Miranti found that the impact of human capital on poverty in the densely populated provinces was not significant. Presumably this was because the stock of human capital in this group of provinces had remained steady and high, leaving little room for big improvements. This is the phenomenon of diminishing returns described earlier.

Infrastructure also mattered for poverty reduction, supporting the empirical observation that the availability of good infrastructure is critical to give the poor access to employment, trade, education and other opportunities. However, across the provincial groupings, infrastructure significantly reduced poverty only in the settled Outer Island provinces, where at least one development indicator was already above the national average.

Third, Miranti (2007) examined the role of interprovincial migration (both in-migration and out-migration) on poverty.[4] The results indicated that regional differences in poverty were explained by regional differences in interprovincial migration. Using Hill's (1989) provincial grouping as a tool for the analysis, Miranti found that in-migration worked well in reducing poverty in the sparsely populated provinces, perhaps because of their low levels of unemployment. On the other hand, out-migration had the reverse effect of increasing poverty in the settled Outer Islands, possibly due to the loss of highly educated individuals. Many of these provinces recorded negative net migration rates (higher rates of out-migration than in-migration) between 1984 and 2002. Of course, ethnic groups such as the Minangkabau in West Sumatra, the Batak in North Sumatra, the Minahasa in North Sulawesi and the Buginese and

---

4 This subject is not discussed earlier in the chapter due to space limitations.

Makarese in South Sulawesi are well known for undertaking migration for social or cultural reasons.

CONCLUSION, POLICY IMPLICATIONS AND LIMITATIONS

This chapter has discussed the significant differences in poverty rates among the Indonesian provinces and offered some explanations for the variations. So why do some provinces perform better than others? At least four conclusions can be drawn from this study.

First, performing well on one or more development indicators (income per capita, human capital or infrastructure) is generally associated with a lower poverty rate. But at the same time, better than average performance on a single indicator is *not* a sufficient condition for a low level of poverty or a low rate of poverty decline. For example, the resource-rich provinces as a group have high income but also high poverty.

Second, rapid changes in poverty rates are associated with rapid changes in one or more development indicators. Provinces that initially had very high development indicators, such as the densely populated provinces, have had sluggish rates of poverty reduction, as one would expect from the various studies of convergence in the economic growth literature. On the other hand, some provinces with lagging development indicators have been able to catch up (reduce poverty) by achieving rapid improvements in one or more development indicators.[5]

Third, the analysis across groups of provinces shows that poverty alleviation strategies can and often do work differently. This seems to depend on the differing structural characteristics of groups of provinces, and how those characteristics interact with development interventions. What works well for one group of provinces may not work well for others. One interesting finding from the regression analysis is substitution or interplay between growth in income per capita and the other development indicators, except in the resource-rich and isolated provinces.

The results for the densely populated provinces provide evidence of substitution, with their higher initial development indicators contributing to a higher growth elasticity of poverty. Substitution between growth and other development indicators is also found in the other groups of provinces that have relatively high scores on some development indicators, such as the settled Outer Islands.

---

5   This does not necessarily mean that their poverty rates fell below the national average; in some cases the declines in poverty were offset by other factors that contributed to the persistence of poverty.

Finally, the regression analysis confirms that for the groups of provinces where development indicators have generally lagged, both pro-poor growth to increase RGDP per capita and interventions to improve other development indicators are likely to be essential for any significant progress in poverty alleviation. The isolated provinces are a case in point. In these provinces, absolute levels of poverty remain high despite their better than average rates of income growth, indicating that growth has failed to effect the improvements in basic development indicators seen in, for instance, the settled Outer Islands. In the case of the resource-rich provinces, special treatment to return a higher share of the revenue generated by natural resources to the producing region would seem necessary to accelerate poverty decline. This has actually occurred with the implementation of the decentralisation policy since 2001.

It is worth mentioning two limitations of the analysis. One caveat concerns the data and the units of analysis. To be able to access a consistent time series, the data refer to provincial averages, not individual households. Second, most of the data relate to the Suharto era and the period before decentralisation, when institutional arrangements were different to those that apply today. However, as discussed earlier, relative poverty levels across provinces have not changed much since 2002, suggesting that many of the development challenges now facing Indonesia are likely to be similar to those of previous decades.

REFERENCES

Ali, I. and E.M. Pernia (2003) 'Infrastructure and poverty reduction: what is the connection?', ERD Policy Brief Series No. 13, Asian Development Bank, Manila, January.

Becker, G.S. (1993) *Human Capital: A Theoretical and Empirical Analysis, with Special Reference to Education*, third edition, University of Chicago Press, Chicago IL.

Bloom, Canning and Malaney (1999) 'Demographic change and economic growth in Asia', CID Working Paper No. 15, Center for International Development, Harvard University, Cambridge MA, May.

Dollar, D. and A. Kraay (2002) 'Growth is good for the poor', *Journal of Economic Growth*, 7: 195–225.

Friedman, J. (2005) 'How responsive is poverty to growth? A regional analysis of poverty, inequality and growth in Indonesia, 1984–99', in R. Kanbur and A.J. Venables (eds) *Spatial Inequality and Development*, Oxford University Press, New York, NY.

Gallup, J.L, J.D. Sachs and A. Mellinger (1999) 'Geography and economic development', CID Working Paper No. 1, Center for International Development, Harvard University, Cambridge MA, March.

Garcia Garcia, J. and L. Soelistianingsih (1998) 'Why do differences in provincial incomes persist in Indonesia?', *Bulletin of Indonesian Economic Studies*, 34(1): 95–120.

Hayami, Y and T. Kawagoe (1993) *The Agrarian Origins of Commerce and Industry: A Study of Peasant Marketing in Indonesia*, St Martin's Press, New York, NY.

Hill, H. (ed.) (1989) *Unity and Diversity: Regional Economic Development in Indonesia since 1970*, Oxford University Press, Singapore.

Hill, H. (1992) 'Regional development in a boom and bust petroleum economy: Indonesia since 1970', *Journal of Economic Development and Cultural Change*, 40(2): 351–79.

Hill, H. and A. Weidemann (1989) 'Regional development in Indonesia: patterns and issues', in H. Hill (ed.) *Unity and Diversity: Regional Economic Development in Indonesia since 1970*, Oxford University Press, Singapore.

Jalilian, H. and J. Weiss (2006) 'Infrastructure and poverty: cross-country evidence', in J. Weiss (ed.) *Poverty Strategies in Asia: A Growth Plus Approach*, Edward Elgar, Cheltenham.

Jayasuria and Nelson (1989) 'Bali: economic growth and tourism', in H. Hill (ed.) *Unity and Diversity: Regional Economic Development in Indonesia since 1970*, Oxford University Press, Singapore.

Kwon, E. (2006) 'Infrastructure, growth and poverty reduction in Indonesia: a cross-sectional analysis', paper presented at a workshop on Transport Infrastructure and Poverty Reduction, Asian Development Bank Institute, Tokyo, 7 March.

Miranti, R. (2007) 'The determinants of regional poverty in Indonesia: 1984–2002', PhD dissertation, Australian National University, Canberra.

Miranti, R. and B.P. Resosudarmo (2005) 'Understanding regional poverty in Indonesia: is poverty worse in the east than in the west?', *Australasian Journal of Regional Studies*, 11(2): 141–54.

Roemer, M. and M.K. Gugerty (1997) 'Does economic growth reduce poverty?', CAER II Discussion Paper 4, Harvard Institute for International Development, Cambridge MA. Available at: http://pdf.usaid.gov/pdf_docs/PNACA656.pdf.

Romer, D. (1996) *Advanced Macroeconomics*, McGraw-Hill, Singapore.

Sachs, J.D. and A.M. Warner (1995) 'Natural resource abundance and economic growth', NBER Working Paper No. 5398, National Bureau of Economic Research, Cambridge MA, December.

Sachs, J.D. and A.M. Warner (2001) 'The curse of natural resources', *European Economic Review*, 45: 827–38.

Warr, P. (2006) 'Roads and poverty reduction in Lao PDR', in J. Weiss (ed.) *Poverty Strategies in Asia: A Growth Plus Approach*, Edward Elgar, Cheltenham.

World Bank (2000) *The Quality of Growth*, World Bank, Washington DC.

Yao, X. (2003) 'Infrastructure and poverty reduction: making markets work for the poor', ERD Policy Brief Series No. 14, Asian Development Bank, Manila, May.

PART 2

Employment and Migration

6   INDONESIAN INDUSTRIALISATION: JOBLESS GROWTH?

Haryo Aswicahyono, Hal Hill and Dionisius Narjoko

East Asia is notable for its historically rapid rates of both industriali-sation and poverty alleviation. These two trends are not unconnected. The region led the way among developing countries in its emphasis on labour-intensive, export-oriented industrialisation, commencing with Ja-pan and the newly industrialising economies (NIEs), then spreading to the larger Southeast Asian economies, China and later South Asia (Athu-korala 2010). The early emphasis was on products employing standard-ised technology, such as garments, footwear, toys and sporting goods. As the vertically integrated operations of multinational corporations began to spread – a process that came to be known as the 'slicing up' or fragmentation of the production process (Athukorala 2006; Kimura 2006) – the range of manufactures expanded and became increasingly techno-logically sophisticated. This phenomenon had transformative effects on labour markets and therefore living standards. It accelerated the process of structural transformation from agriculture to industry.

The international orientation of this type of industrialisation – in con-trast to the traditional import-substituting model – resulted in countries specialising in activities in which they had a comparative advantage, that is, labour-intensive industries. The very rapid growth in employ-ment, at wage levels which, while low, were above those prevailing in agriculture and the informal sector, offered a path out of poverty while absorbing the large pools of surplus labour. In Japan, the NIEs and later Malaysia, it provided the major demand-side explanation for the transi-tion to tighter labour markets and higher wages. On the supply side, the main factors were the expansion of education and the process of technol-ogy acquisition.

Indonesia was a relative latecomer to this process of export-oriented, labour-intensive industrialisation. It lagged behind both the NIEs and its more advanced ASEAN neighbours, Malaysia and Thailand, principally because it was slower to adopt a comprehensive outward-looking strategy. In addition, its industrialisation experience was more recent and, for the decade from 1973, the oil boom had pushed the country's comparative advantage more towards the natural resource-based sectors. From the mid-1980s, however, Indonesia became increasingly 'East Asia like' in its industrialisation patterns. A sharp decline in oil prices boosted the competitiveness of non-oil tradables, and prompted the government to undertake a comprehensive reform program that embraced trade liberalisation, exchange rate depreciation, deregulation and more open policies towards foreign investment. For a country long dominated by 'elasticity pessimism' – the view that exports won't respond to an exchange rate depreciation – the economy responded in an orthodox fashion to a largely orthodox policy package. For the first time, Indonesia became a major industrial exporter, of garments, textiles, footwear, furniture and other products (Hill 1997). The labour market implications of this industrialisation were profound: for the decade from the mid-1980s, manufacturing became the fastest-growing sector and the largest incremental contributor to employment growth (Manning 1998).

The Asian financial crisis of 1997–98 interrupted this process in two ways. First, the crisis resulted in a sharp economic contraction. Even when growth resumed, it was on a lower trajectory, both for the economy as a whole as well as for manufacturing. Second, increased labour market regulation in a slower-growing economy resulted in even slower industrial employment, prompting some observers to refer to the phenomenon as 'jobless growth', and in turn to link this outcome to weaker poverty reduction. We have provided a broad examination of Indonesia's post-crisis industrialisation in an earlier paper (Aswicahyono, Hill and Narjoko 2010).

In this chapter, we focus on the nexus between industrial output and employment growth since the reforms of the mid-1980s. This task is facilitated by the availability of three industrial censuses, for the years 1986, 1996 and 2006. The first intercensal period (1986–1996) coincides with the 'reform decade' of rapid growth; the second (1996–2006) covers the crisis and the return to (slower) growth, accompanied by an apparently less responsive labour market. An additional advantage of the censuses is that they enumerate not only enterprises with at least 20 employees, like the annual *Statistik Industri* surveys, but also those with 5–19 employees. They therefore allow us to obtain a deeper picture of labour force dynamics. The more comprehensive data allow us to examine, for example, the hypothesis that tighter regulation of the labour market mainly affected formal sector enterprises, thereby restricting employment growth in these firms and pushing workers into the less regulated smaller enterprises.

The chapter is organised as follows. The next section provides an overview of industrial output and employment growth in Indonesia. The analysis is undertaken with reference to the pre- and post-crisis periods. We compare the results for different sectors of the Indonesian economy, then for the industrial sectors of Indonesia and other East Asian economies. The third section examines Indonesia's industrial output and employment growth in more detail, disaggregating by major sector and firm size for the two time periods. The focus is on the relationship between employment and output, and in particular the impact of output growth and a range of other factors (including labour regulation) on the growth in jobs. In this section we also briefly examine the effect of wage changes on employment, as one proxy measure of a more or less flexible labour market. Our principal conclusions are summarised in the final section of the chapter.

INDUSTRIAL GROWTH: THE AGGREGATE PICTURE

Employment growth is the outcome of a simple identity; it is the product of output growth and the elasticity of employment growth with respect to output growth. That is:

$$\Delta N = \Delta Y (\Delta N / \Delta Y). \tag{6.1}$$

To understand employment growth, the variable on the left-hand side of the equation, we therefore need data on the two variables on the right. The analysis commences with the aggregate picture for the major sectors in Indonesia before and after the crisis, followed by a comparison of the industrial sectors of Indonesia and several neighbouring economies. Since we are focusing on longer-term trends, and the crisis years are so atypical, we present data for two subperiods, 1990–96, corresponding to the later years of the long Asia-wide boom, and 2000–2008, by which time the immediate effects of the crisis had been resolved and economic growth had resumed, but before the global financial crisis had had any major impact.[1]

---

1 In the next section of the chapter, which examines the industrial census data in more detail, we work with the economic census years, 1986, 1996 and 2006. However, for the broad pre- and post-crisis stories, the two periods chosen here can provide an adequate illustration of the trends.

The aggregate picture for Indonesia

Table 6.1 shows output and employment growth for 1990–96 and 2000–2008 by sector, together with the implied output elasticities.[2] It also shows the changes in growth rates between the two periods, and ranks the sectors on the basis of these differences.

It is apparent that aggregate output growth was considerably slower in the second period, at about two-thirds that in 1990–96. However, the slowdown was not uniform across sectors. In fact, the data point to major changes in the drivers of Indonesian economic dynamism before and after the crisis. Two sectors actually grew faster: agriculture, reflecting generally buoyant commodity prices and competitive exchange rates; and transport and communications, driven by technological change and substantial deregulation.

However, there was a major slowdown in three sectors – mining and utilities, manufacturing and construction – with growth rates in the second period less than half those in the first. The explanations for these outcomes are both sector specific and economy wide. Construction growth had reached unsustainable levels before the crisis and was particularly hard hit. Growth since then has been subdued, owing in part to financing constraints and reduced public sector investment. The latter factors also explain the slower growth in utilities, while growth in mining has been affected by the uncertain exploration and taxation environment, notwithstanding historically high commodity prices.

The contraction in manufacturing growth, from well above the economy-wide average to just below it, is the most puzzling result. As a tradable goods sector it benefited, like agriculture, from the competitive boost of a depreciating exchange rate in the wake of the crisis. Moreover, the sector did not face any significant demand-side constraints until the recent global financial crisis. Global manufacturing growth was rapid, industry continued to relocate to developing economies, and there were no major external trade barriers to manufacturing, unlike in agriculture.

Employment growth also slowed, but not as quickly as output. Employment growth in the second period was about three-quarters that in the first, in a context where aggregate labour supply was in any case gradually beginning to decline. Here too there was considerable variation across sectors. Of particular note is the turnaround in agriculture, from a contraction in 1990–96 to slightly positive growth in 2000–2008, and the collapse in manufacturing growth. Employment growth slowed in all other sectors, in some cases by a significant margin. In some sectors this reflected a continuation of significant labour-saving technological

---

2 Henceforth, for convenience we will refer to output–employment elasticities as 'output elasticities' and wage–employment elasticities as 'wage elasticities'.

Table 6.1   Output and employment growth by sector, 1990–2008

	1990–96	2000–2008	Change	Ranking
GDP growth (% p.a.)				
Agriculture	3.1	3.9	0.8	2
Mining & utilities	5.3	1.5	–3.8	5
Manufacturing	11.2	5.2	–6.0	6
Construction	13.7	6.5	–7.3	7
Wholesale trade	8.9	5.8	–3.0	4
Transport & communications	8.2	10.1	1.9	1
Other	6.4	5.8	–0.7	3
Total	**7.9**	**5.3**	**–2.6**	
Employment growth (% p.a.)				
Agriculture	–1.7	0.2	1.9	1
Mining & utilities	6.0	3.7	–2.3	3
Manufacturing	6.0	0.9	–5.0	5
Construction	10.8	5.7	–5.1	6
Wholesale trade	6.5	1.7	–4.8	4
Transport & communications	9.4	3.9	–5.5	7
Other	4.6	3.6	–1.0	2
Total	**2.3**	**1.7**	**–0.6**	
Implied output elasticities				
Agriculture	–0.56	0.05	0.61	2
Mining & utilities	1.14	2.56	1.42	1
Manufacturing	0.53	0.18	–0.35	5
Construction	0.78	0.88	0.10	3
Wholesale trade	0.74	0.30	–0.44	6
Transport & communications	1.14	0.38	–0.76	7
Other activities	0.71	0.62	–0.09	4
Total	**0.29**	**0.32**	**0.03**	

Source: ADB Statistical Database System, https://sdbs.adb.org/sdbs/index.jsp.

change, such as the major transformation in trade patterns from traditional petty trade to modern malls and retail outlets, the revolution in cellular telecommunications technology and the rapid growth of civil aviation and motorised land transport.

The bottom panel of Table 6.1 presents the implied output elasticities. They indicate whether the slowdown in non-agricultural employment was due mainly to slower output growth or to less employment-elastic output growth. The aggregate picture is that output elasticity rose slightly. However, the increase was due almost entirely to the change in agriculture, from labour shedding to slightly positive growth. With the exception of mining and utilities, which employ few workers, and a slight increase in construction, the general picture points to less elastic employment growth. In particular, the elasticities fell sharply for three major employers of labour: manufacturing, trade, and transport and communications. The explanation in the case of the latter two sectors is clear: there was a major change in the 'technology' through which the service was provided, that is, modern shopping malls in the case of trade and a rapid expansion of civil aviation, cellular technology and so on in the case of transport and communications. Even in a low-wage economy such as Indonesia, these activities are much more capital intensive than the services they replace. However, no such exogenous labour-displacing technology was sweeping through manufacturing. The explanation for the declining output–employment elasticities in manufacturing must therefore lie elsewhere, in the commercial environment and the factors affecting the willingness of employers to hire labour.

To sum up, employment growth in aggregate was marginally slower after the crisis. But this conceals major sectoral differences. Agriculture returned to positive growth, reflecting Indonesia's diverse natural re-source advantages in the context of high commodity prices. Construction employment growth fell sharply, but this was entirely due to lower output growth. Employment growth slowed significantly in some of the service sectors experiencing rapid technological change, even though output growth was strong. Manufacturing was unique in that it was the only major sector to experience more than a halving of both its output growth and its output elasticity. This was a major turnaround for a sector that had consistently led economic growth in Indonesia for a quarter of a century, and that had been the largest source of employment growth since the mid-1980s. This trend of apparent 'jobless industrialisation' is the focus of the remainder of the chapter.

Indonesia in comparative perspective

Before examining the industrialisation data in more detail, it may be use-ful to briefly survey outcomes in neighbouring developing economies, to ascertain whether any similar trends are evident. Four countries were selected for the comparison: Malaysia, the Philippines, Thailand and South Korea. Malaysia, the Philippines and Thailand are the most ob-vious comparators in Southeast Asia in terms of stage of development and economic structure; Indonesians also often measure their country against more industrialised Korea in tracing their country's development performance. Again we conduct the analysis for the pre- and post-crisis

Table 6.2   *Output and employment growth in manufacturing, Indonesia and comparison countries, 1990–2008*

	1990–96	2000–2008	Change	Reverse ranking
GDP growth (% p.a.)				
Indonesia	11.2	4.7	–6.4	2
Malaysia	12.7	4.3	–8.4	1
Philippines	2.6	4.2	1.6	5
Thailand	11.2	6.0	–5.1	3
South Korea	7.9	6.3	–1.6	4
Employment growth (% p.a.)				
Indonesia	5.8	0.9	–4.8	3
Malaysia	6.2	–1.4	–7.6	1
Philippines	3.2	0.7	–2.5	4
Thailand	6.8	2.0	–4.8	2
South Korea	–0.6	–1.0	–0.4	5
Implied output elasticities				
Indonesia	0.52	0.20	–0.32	4
Malaysia	0.49	–0.32	–0.81	1
Philippines	1.22	0.17	–1.05	2
Thailand	0.61	0.33	–0.28	3
South Korea	–0.08	–0.16	–0.08	5

Source: ADB Statistical Database System, https://sdbs.adb.org/sdbs/index.jsp.

periods, with respect to output and employment growth, and estimate the implied elasticities. Table 6.2 presents the results.

In the pre-crisis period, the pace of industrialisation in Indonesia was similar to that in its rapidly industrialising neighbours, Malaysia and Thailand, and much faster than in South Korea and the Philippines. Industrial growth in the three Southeast Asian growth economies – Indonesia, Malaysia and Thailand – slowed sharply after the crisis, most of all in Malaysia and least in Thailand. The Philippine growth rate accelerated slightly, from a weak base, while Korean growth slowed somewhat. Thus, from a growth perspective, Indonesia is well within Southeast Asian norms.

The employment picture is broadly similar. The three Southeast Asian economies experienced very sharp slowdowns in growth. Manufacturing employment in Malaysia actually shrank, reflecting the fact that this higher-wage economy had progressively been shedding its labour-intensive segments. Employment growth in Thailand was slightly stronger, but the absolute decline in growth was sharper than in Indonesia. Korean and Philippine employment growth was anaemic throughout, contracting in the former case since 2000. Thus, here also Indonesia does not emerge as a regional outlier.

The output elasticities declined significantly in all five economies. As noted, they turned negative for South Korea and Malaysia. The rates of decline are broadly similar for Indonesia, the Philippines and Thailand. In fact, although Thailand's output elasticity remains the highest of the five, the rate of decline in Indonesia is the lowest among the Southeast Asian sample.

To sum up the analysis so far, on the basis of the aggregated sectoral data, it is apparent that Indonesia has experienced a pronounced slowdown in industrial employment growth since the Asian financial crisis. Manufacturing was the only sector to experience both a marked deceleration in output growth and a major decline in output elasticity. This suggests that sector-specific factors were at work in the country's industrial labour market. However, in comparative East Asian terms, the Indonesian industrial record is not an outlier. Other fast-industrialising, middle-income developing countries have registered similar declines in both output growth and output elasticities. Among the four comparison countries, Thailand's experience is arguably the most relevant. South Korea has clearly moved out of the labour-intensive phase of industrialisation, while Malaysia is in transition. In both cases, very low or even negative employment–output elasticities are not surprising. Growth in the Philippines has been slower throughout.

The widespread presumption in Indonesia is that the tighter labour market regulation since 2000 provides the principal explanation for the sharp drop in the country's output elasticity. Yet, although Thailand's output and employment growth remain somewhat higher, its output elasticity has fallen just as fast. This is in spite of the fact that the Thai labour market is not as heavily regulated as Indonesia's, and has not been subject to regulatory tightening since the crisis. In other words, more general factors affecting the patterns of Southeast Asian industrialisation and employment seem to be at work, in addition to labour market policies. We now turn to the more disaggregated Indonesian industrial census data to shed light on these issues.

THE RECORD IN DETAIL

The Indonesian government publishes two main series of industrial statistics, the annual survey of establishments with at least 20 employees, known as *Statistik Industri*, and the decennial economic census of all industrial establishments conducted since 1986, *Sensus Ekonomi*. In this section we work with both series. *Sensus Ekonomi* has the advantage that its enumeration is presumed to be more complete, whereas *Statistik Industri* suffers from underenumeration in some years. It is also more comprehensive in scope in that it includes the smaller establishments, down to five or more employees.[3] However, *Sensus Ekonomi* has the drawback that the census is conducted only once a decade, and the data on small firms for 1986 are incomplete. One shortcoming of the *Sensus Ekonomi* data for the period 1996–2006, in particular, is that we are unable to distinguish the impact of the Asian financial crisis in 1997–98 from the effect of subsequent moderate growth, uncertainty and new regulations that may have affected industrial structure and employment in the recovery period through to 2006. We therefore employ the *Statistik Industri* series to obtain a more detailed picture, including for the non-census years.

The *Sensus Ekonomi* censuses were conducted in 1986, 1996 and 2006, neatly coinciding with the two major subperiods of interest here. The first subperiod, 1986–96, was a decade of reform and rapid growth (but noting the limitation above of the 1986 *Sensus Ekonomi* data). The second, 1996–2006, encompassed the crisis and the return to (slower) growth.

The impact of output growth on employment

To investigate the impact of output growth on employment across firms of different sizes, we classify establishments into three (arbitrary) groups: large (those with 100 or more employees), medium (20–99 employees) and small (5–19 employees). Alternative size classifications do not affect the results. The disaggregation by size is relevant because we conjecture that scale may influence firms' responses to economic events and regulations. For example, smaller firms may be more resilient to adverse economic shocks,[4] and they may fall outside the regulatory net. We further combine firms into broader groupings according to the factor intensity of the industry in which they operate: labour intensive, resource based and capital intensive. See Appendix A6.1 for a brief description of the basis of these classifications.

---

3 *Sensus Ekonomi* also includes household enterprises with 1–4 employees. However, we exclude this group from the analysis because the employment data are less reliable. There are problems associated with estimating full-time-equivalent employment, the seasonality of employment in these enterprises and data accuracy.

4 Elsewhere, we have shown that this does not appear to have been the case for the 1997–98 economic crisis. See Narjoko (2006) and Aswicahyono, Hill and Narjoko (2010).

Table 6.3   Manufacturing sector employment by firm size, 1986–2006

	Large firms	Medium-sized firms	Small firms	Total
No. of employees (thousand)				
1986	1,331	345	770	2,446
1996	3,545	609	2,273	6,427
2006	3,921	823	5,297	10,041
Share of total employment (%)				
1986	54	14	32	100
1996	55	10	35	100
2006	39	8	53	100
Growth in employment (% p.a.)				
1986–96	10.3	5.8	11.4	10.1
1996–2006	1.0	3.1	8.8	4.6
1986–2006	5.6	4.4	10.1	7.3

Source: Sensus Ekonomi.

First, it will be useful to look at the raw data on manufacturing employment. Table 6.3 summarises the results from the three *Sensus Ekonomi* censuses by size group. Employment grew quite rapidly over the whole period, 1986–2006, by 7.3 per cent per annum. However, there was a marked slowdown between the two subperiods, with growth declining from 10.1 per cent in the first to just 4.6 per cent in the second. There were also some significant compositional shifts. In both 1986 and 1996, large firms accounted for just over half of all employment, whereas by 2006 the small firms had become the dominant employer. The share of medium-sized firms declined throughout the period. Employment in both large and small firms grew rapidly in the first decade, by 10.3 per cent and 11.4 per cent respectively. But from 1996 to 2006, large firm employment barely increased, at just 1 per cent per annum, whereas small firm employment continued to expand quickly, by 8.8 per cent. Employment growth in medium-sized firms also declined, but not to the same extent as in the large firms. We return to the interpretation of these results below.[5]

5   One caveat to be attached to these results is that the employment data are all headcount estimates. We do not have data on the intensity of work – that is, hours worked – by firm size. While the estimates for large and medium-sized

Unlike the above analysis, which rests on implied elasticities, this section computes the elasticities more precisely, based on firm-level output, employment and wage data. Specifically, the output and wage elasticities are the estimated coefficients (a_1 and a_2 respectively) from the regression equation (see Appendix A6.1 for details).

The regressions are undertaken at the establishment level, and thus draw on an extremely large and rich database. For the large and medium-sized firms, the years of observation are 1986, 1990 and 1996 (both pre-crisis), 2000 (immediate post-crisis) and 2006. For small firms (5–19 employees), we are restricted to two observation points: 1996 and 2006. Dummy variables are used in the regression equation to control for differences across establishments, and also for differences across industries.

The results below differ from those in section 2 in three respects. First, the data, and therefore the results, are more comprehensive. Second, we are able to provide both output and wage elasticities (that is, the extent of the changes in employment in response to unit changes in output and unit changes in wages).[6] The latter may be interpreted analogously to the former – that is, how responsive employment is to wage changes, all other things being equal. This has the advantage that it enables us to assess more directly the effect of changes in the labour regulatory regime, as reflected in total labour costs. Third, the elasticities are generated as coefficients from the equation, and therefore consist of a series of 'point' estimates. We proceed first with the large and medium-sized firms, then identify changes within each of the two groups separately. The final step is to include the small firms. In each case, we focus primarily on what we refer to here as output elasticities. The results for the wage elasticities generally accord with *a priori* expectations and are therefore not presented in detail here.

We have two *a priori* expectations. First, as discussed in Aswicahyono, Hill and Narjoko (2010), we would expect the major effects on employment to be felt in the labour-intensive activities, particularly the large textiles, clothing and footwear group (corresponding to International Standard Industrial Classification (ISIC) 32). These export-oriented industries are characterised by fierce international competition and low profit margins. Rising wage levels, combined with other cost disadvantages – notably an appreciating exchange rate since around 2004 and complexities in import–export procedures – are likely to have taken a toll

---

firms are likely to closely resemble some full-time-equivalent employment figure, the estimate for the small firms could well be lower, owing to seasonality factors and more variable output and work patterns. Hence, it is possible – but not certain – that the rising share for small firms is an overstatement.

6 In the literature, the changes in employment in response to unit changes in output are often referred to as employment elasticities.

Table 6.4   Output elasticities for large and medium-sized manufacturing firms, 1986–2006

ISIC code and industry	1986	1996	2006
All large & medium-sized manufacturing firms	**0.56**	**0.59**	**0.49**
Labour-intensive	0.56	0.65	0.57
32 Textiles & garments	0.55	0.68	0.58
33 Wood products	0.58	0.61	0.55
39 Other manufacturing	0.65	0.57	0.45
Resource-intensive	0.57	0.55	0.43
31 Food & beverages	0.57	0.54	0.42
34 Paper products	0.58	0.57	0.43
35 Chemical, rubber & plastic products	0.57	0.56	0.43
Capital-intensive	0.56	0.54	0.49
36 Non-metallic mineral products	0.54	0.52	0.46
37 Basic metal industries	0.36	0.45	0.55
38 Machinery & transport equipment	0.58	0.55	0.50

ISIC = International Standard Industrial Classification.
Source: Sensus Ekonomi; Statistik Industri.

on employment levels. Firms that had large stocks of permanent work-ers with lengthy employment experience would have had to put aside significant reserves to insure against the possibility of large severance payments in the event of declining output. In contrast, in the more capi-tal and resource-intensive activities where labour is a relatively small proportion of total costs, the labour market regulatory regime is unlikely to have had much impact on employment levels.

Second, we expect there to be differential impacts across firm-size groups, as is evident from our first inspection of the data in Table 6.3. Small firms may fall outside the regulatory net, and larger firms may seek to avoid labour restrictions by subcontracting their operations to these firms. Larger firms may be better able to adapt to the labour regula-tions than medium-sized firms, or at least have the political and bureau-cratic connections to manage the new provisions.[7]

Table 6.4 presents the output elasticities for large and medium-sized manufacturing firms for 1986, 1996 and 2006. Overall, the major change

---

7 See Narjoko and Jotzo (2007: 155–8) for further discussion of these points.

Table 6.5   Change in output elasticities for large and medium-sized manufacturing firms, 1986–96 and 1996–2006 (%)

ISIC code and industry	Large firms		Medium-sized firms	
	1986–96	1996–2006	1986–96	1996–2006
All large & medium-sized manufacturing firms	**18**	**–22**	**4**	**–31**
Labour-intensive	33	–15	26	–31
32 Textiles & garments	43	–13	41	–32
33 Wood products	19	–14	13	–22
39 Other manufacturing	34	–36	–43	–39
Resource-intensive	13	–33	–4	–38
31 Food & beverages	13	–38	0	–33
34 Paper products	–6	–20	–13	–42
35 Chemical, rubber & plastic products	23	–24	0	–44
Capital-intensive	11	–5	–10	–22
36 Non-metallic mineral products	18	5	–15	–21
37 Basic metal industries	36	11	n.a.	20
38 Machinery & transport equipment	5	–10	0	–26

ISIC = International Standard Industrial Classification. n.a. = not available.
Source: Sensus Ekonomi; Statistik Industri.

reported in the previous section for all manufacturing is not evident. There is a slight increase in the elasticity over the reform period, after which it declines substantially. Broadly similar trends are observed for most of the major industry groups. The biggest variation occurs in the largest labour-intensive group, textiles, clothing and footwear. Its elasticity increased during the reform period but by 2006 had fallen back to the 1986 level. The coefficients for the three resource-based groups also declined noticeably after 1996. There is no clear trend for the capital-intensive group, consistent with the notion that employment coefficients – that is, the technologies in use – are less flexible.

Table 6.5 presents the changes in elasticities separately for large and medium-sized firms. We report only the percentage changes in the elasticities for the two periods for each size group and each industry group. (The raw data are available on request.) Here we find a more varied and complex picture, with the main results as follows. First, overall there is, as expected, a sizeable increase in the elasticities in the reform period, followed by a larger decline in the subsequent decade. For both size groups, the decline is larger than the increase, marginally so for large firms and by a substantial margin for medium-sized firms. The latter were already generally more labour intensive at the beginning of the reform period, so a pronounced increase in employment elasticities would not be expected.

Among the major industry groups, a very large change occurs, as expected, in the labour-intensive group. It is dominated by textiles, clothing and footwear, where employment growth was highly (positively) output elastic in 1986–96, but much less so in 1996–2006, especially for medium-sized firms. The results for the capital-intensive industries are also as predicted, with declining employment elasticities in the second decade (and a swing from positive to negative changes for the large firms), but much less change in the elasticities. The response of the resource-intensive industries is closer to the labour-intensive group. Both large and medium-sized firms exhibit declining elasticities in the second period, and either positive or negligible trends in elasticities in 1986–96. As the largest sector in the group, food and beverages dominates these results.

This is the story for firms with at least 20 employees. With regard to small firms, as noted reliable data are available only for the period 1996–2006. These are reported in Table 6.6. Here, too, output has become less employment elastic, but the declines are concentrated in just a few sectors, mainly wood products and the capital-intensive activities. Moreover, the overall decline is less than that for the larger firms, and for some key sectors – textiles, clothing and footwear, and food and beverages – there is virtually no change. These results suggest that smaller firms, especially in the labour-intensive sectors, have behaved differently. That is, there is no pronounced trend towards lower labour intensity, suggesting a 'wedge' between these firms and the larger units. Whether the difference arises from the uneven impact of the labour regulatory environment between enterprises in the formal and informal sectors, as is commonly hypothesised, or simply reflects the different rates of technological change across firm sizes, remains to be seen, and is beyond the scope of this chapter.

Employment response to wage changes

Thus far we have examined the responsiveness of employment to output changes. We now examine the relationship between wages and employment, a more direct measure of the effect of any changes in the labour market environment. The wage data refer to the total labour costs divided by the total workforce for each firm. In principle, therefore, they

Table 6.6 *Output elasticities for small manufacturing firms, 1996–2006*

ISIC code and industry	1996	2006
All small manufacturing firms	**0.26**	**0.21**
Labour-intensive	0.26	0.21
32 Textiles & garments	0.25	0.24
33 Wood products	0.31	0.19
39 Other manufacturing	0.20	0.21
Resource-intensive	0.22	0.21
31 Food & beverages	0.21	0.21
34 Paper products	0.24	0.21
35 Chemical, rubber & plastic products	0.23	0.21
Capital-intensive	0.34	0.20
36 Non-metallic mineral products	0.36	0.21
37 Basic metal industries	0.30	0.18
38 Machinery & transport equipment	0.30	0.18

ISIC = International Standard Industrial Classification.
Source: Sensus Ekonomi; Statistik Industri.

should include all costs of employing workers, extending to any separation costs incurred by firms.[8] As with the approach above, the results are derived from the coefficients in the regression equation (see Appendix A6.1). Owing to space limitations the data are not presented here, but are available from the authors on request.

The key finding for the wage elasticities for large and medium-sized firms over the three census years is a stable coefficient during the reform period, 1986–96, followed by a sharp decline in the second period, 1996–2006. That is, in the first decade, characterised by rapid output, export and employment growth, and with a minimally regulated labour market, employment was quite responsive to wage changes, controlling for other variables as in the output equation.. However, in the second decade, characterised by slower growth and more regulation, employment became less sensitive to wage changes, with the elasticity falling by 28 per cent. We interpret these data as indicating that employers have

---

8 The labour cost data probably understate the effect of the labour market regulatory changes, to the extent that they do not capture the increased uncertainty associated with the new measures.

been reluctant to change employment levels in response to any change in wages. That is, in the face of higher minimum wages or much higher severance pay regulated in Law 13/2003 on Labour, labour has increasingly come to be seen as a quasi-fixed cost, with the result that employment decisions are less sensitive to wage changes.

Among the major industry groups, there is no clear pattern. The wage elasticity rose through to 1996 for the large textiles, clothing and footwear sector, but had declined to its previous levels by 2006. That is, employment was increasingly responsive to wage changes in the first decade, but less so in the second. We interpret this as an indication of labour market flexibility and employment growth before the crisis as employers sought to recruit workers by pushing up wages in a dynamic job market, in contrast to the much slower growth since the late 1990s. Employment elasticities have fallen sharply in some other major sectors, notably food and beverages. However, for the more capital-intensive machinery and equipment industries, the changes seem to have had very little effect, reflecting the fact that labour costs are relatively unimportant in their calculations.

When the changes in wage elasticities are disaggregated by firm size, period and major industry group, unlike in the case of the output elasticities there is no clear trend, and the results do not always accord with *a priori* expectations. For both large and medium-sized firms, there was a small increase in the elasticities in 1986–96, followed by a larger decrease in 1996–2006. That is, in the first period employment became slightly more responsive to wage changes, while in the second it became substantially less responsive. But there is considerable variation across and within the major groups.[9]

SUMMING UP

There has clearly been a sharp slowdown in industrial employment growth in Indonesia since the Asian financial crisis, especially when compared with the 'reform decade' of 1986–96. This has occurred because of the country's slower industrial growth, and most particularly because of the much slower response of employment to growth in production, or what we have referred to as the output–employment elasticity. We

---

9 For labour-intensive industries, there was a sizeable decrease in the elasticities in the second period for both large and medium-sized firms. But in the first decade, the elasticity fell slightly for large firms, while there was a major increase for medium-sized firms. For textiles, clothing and footwear, the elasticities of both groups of firms declined in the second period but rose in the first, especially for medium-sized firms.

have also noted less response of employment to wage changes. Among the sectors, manufacturing is unusual in this respect, in that there has been both slower output growth and lower employment elasticity. This slowdown appears to have occurred across all major manufacturing sectors. There have also been significant compositional shifts since the Asian financial crisis, with almost all industrial employment growth coming from small firms. Firms in the 'factory' sector with 20 or more workers seem to have virtually stopped hiring during this period.

It is beyond the scope of this chapter to examine in detail the reasons for this slowdown, but the general factors are well known and have been explored elsewhere (Aswicahyono, Hill and Narjoko 2010). In the immediate aftermath of the crisis, there was a major boost to competitiveness from the rapidly depreciating nominal exchange rate. But this did not translate into employment growth, since much of the formal sector of the economy was incapacitated by corporate debt workouts, the exodus of foreign investors and the freezing up of financial markets. Also, regulatory and policy uncertainty increased following the transition from authoritarian to democratic rule, and the major decentralisation initiative of 2001. The latter especially affected access to natural resources, on which several Indonesian manufacturing activities depend. Intensified labour market regulation and infrastructure constraints emerged as serious problems after 2000. From about 2003, rising commodity prices and the return of foreign capital began to put pressure on the exchange rate, with a significant real appreciation commencing from around 2005. By then, all the earlier competitiveness advantages from the exchange rate depreciation had been eroded. These events occurred in the context of intensified international competition, particularly from China, but also from other lower-wage competitors, notably Vietnam.

These factors operated as economy-wide influences, in addition to sector-specific effects. For example, we would contend that tighter labour market regulation had an adverse effect on the traditional labour-intensive sectors, especially textiles, clothing and footwear, on top of the breakdown in the formerly effective operation of the import drawback facility for export-oriented firms. The more cumbersome export–import procedures and a less inviting foreign investment regime made Indonesia a relatively minor participant in the rapidly expanding global production networks centred on 'fragmentation trade'. Natural resource-based activities were affected by interruptions to reliable raw material supplies.

Does this slower growth of manufacturing employment matter? The answer to this question depends on the explanation for the slower growth. It is of concern to the extent that a major link in the transmission mechanism from growth to poverty alleviation has been weakened, especially given the strength of the relationship in the pre-crisis decade.

That is, fewer workers are now drawn into the relatively better-paid jobs in the manufacturing sector. Moreover, most of the industrial jobs now being created are in small firms, where employment conditions are likely to be inferior to those in the larger enterprises, especially to the extent that smaller firms are able to evade labour protection measures. As argued above, the much slower jobs growth is principally the result of Indonesia's declining international competitiveness, underlining again the crucial link between macro-level economic reform and poverty alleviation.

Nevertheless, it is important not to overstate the problems, for at least three reasons. First, Indonesia's record is not so different from that of its neighbours, including the traditionally dynamic Thai economy where intensified labour market regulation has not occurred. This suggests that the changes observed in this chapter are part of a generalised regional phenomenon, in which rising competition from China and the demise of very labour-intensive segments are important factors explaining the slower employment growth.

Second, we have shown that more jobs are being created in other sectors. The fastest growth has occurred in several service sectors, reflecting technological advance, deregulation and, at the margin, the switch to non-tradables as a result of an appreciating real exchange rate since around 2005. While a slowdown in the movement of labour out of low-productivity agriculture is of concern, this sector has reversed its earlier decline, reflecting buoyant commodity prices, and reminding us of Indonesia's resource-based economic diversity. It is an overstatement to assert – as some have done – that Indonesia is experiencing premature deindustrialisation, but an industrial deceleration is certainly evident, and seems to have become a permanent feature of the economy. Is this structural shift in employment patterns a cause for concern? Industrial fundamentalists would assert that it is, on the grounds that there are greater externalities associated with industrialisation, such as interindustry linkage creation and skill formation. But such views may be of dubious validity, at least in the later stages of development, as shown by the existence of many high-income service and resource-based economies around the world.

Finally, in addition to the data limitations noted above, three additional caveats need to be attached to the discussion. First, our analysis is confined to the period through to 2006, by which time Indonesia had accomplished the transition to political normality. Since then, growth rates and the business environment have become more secure, apart from the relatively brief interruption caused by the global financial crisis. Thus, it might be expected that firms would now have more confidence in hiring new workers. Analysis of employment trends in the second half of the decade does indeed suggest a somewhat more robust labour market, albeit with manufacturing continuing to be a laggard (Manning 2010).

Second, we have not taken account of major supply-side factors in this analysis. Over the past quarter-century there have been two major supply-side developments in Indonesia's labour market. One is slower labour force growth, the result of both declining population growth and delayed age of entry into the labour force as post-primary education participation rates increase. While underutilisation of labour remains a serious problem, this trend does begin to alleviate the pressure for employment creation. The other development concerns how the rising rates of participation in education translate into labour market behaviour and preferences. As is well documented, the least educated tend to exhibit the lowest rates of unemployment, reflecting their limited job options. As education levels rise, new job entrants are likely to become more selective and to shun the more menial job offerings, if necessary choosing temporary unemployment while continuing the search for more attractive work. Combined with rising mechanisation and slower labour force growth, economic growth is therefore by definition likely to become less labour elastic.

The third caveat is that our analysis has not considered the regional dimensions of these changes, always an important dimension of Indonesian development dynamics. Here the general picture is well known. Most of the rapid growth in industrial employment in 1986–96 occurred in Java, together with a small number of other locations that possessed region-specific advantages. The most important of these were Batam, with its Singapore-linked manufactured exports, the wood-processing (mostly plywood) activities in Kalimantan and the tourism-linked exports of garments and handicrafts in Bali. Java's rapid industrialisation transformed its labour market, and was central to the rapid decline in poverty there. The slower industrial employment growth since 1996 could be one explanation for Java's less poverty-responsive employment growth over the past decade. However, a mitigating factor has been that many of the emerging high-growth service sectors have also been based in Java, so the net loss of employment opportunities has been contained.

REFERENCES

Aswicahyono, H., H. Hill and D. Narjoko (2010) 'Industrialisation after a deep economic crisis: Indonesia', *Journal of Development Studies*, 46(6): 1,084–108.
Athukorala, P. (2006) 'Product fragmentation and trade patterns in East Asia', *Asian Economic Papers*, 4(3): 1–27.
Athukorala, P. (ed.) (2010) *The Rise of Asia: Trade and Investment in Global Perspective*, Routledge, London.

Hill, H. (1997) *Indonesia's Industrial Transformation*, Institute of Southeast Asian Studies, Singapore.

Kimura, F. (2006) 'International production and distribution networks in East Asia: eighteen facts, mechanics, and policy implications', *Asian Economic Policy Review*, 1: 346–7.

Manning, C. (1998) *Indonesian Labour in Transition: An East Asian Success Story?* Cambridge University Press, Cambridge.

Manning, C. (2010) 'A turnaround in employment: what's going on?', paper presented to Indonesia Study Group seminar, Australian National University, Canberra, 1 December.

Narjoko, D.A. (2006) 'Indonesian manufacturing and the economic crisis of 1997–98', PhD dissertation, Australian National University, Canberra.

Narjoko, D. and F. Jotzo (2007) 'Survey of recent developments', *Bulletin of Indonesian Economic Studies*, 43(2): 143–69.

APPENDIX A6.1 CLASSIFICATION OF INDUSTRIES, AND THE REGRESSION EQUATION

In classifying manufacturing industries into three groups, we use the International Standard Industrial Classification (ISIC). Labour-intensive industries are the two-digit ISIC codes 32, 33 and 39; resource-based industries are ISIC codes 31, 34 and 35; and capital-intensive industries are ISIC codes 36, 37 and 38. The labour-intensive industries are textiles, garments and footwear; wood products and furniture; and miscellaneous manufactures. The resource-based industries are food and related products; paper products; and chemical, rubber and plastic products. The capital-intensive industries are non-metallic minerals; steel products; and metal and machine goods, electronics and autos.

More elaborate classifications could be employed but they are unlikely to affect the results significantly. If Indonesia were a major participant in global electronic production networks, then strictly speaking the components assembly industry should be classified as labour intensive. But it is not a major participant. Moreover, Indonesia's electronics output is relatively small, accounting for only 22 per cent of output in ISIC group 38 and 5 per cent in all manufacturing.

To obtain the elasticity of employment with respect to output changes, we estimate the following regression equation:

$$\ln(L)_{i,t} = \alpha_0 + \alpha_1 \ln(Q)_{i,t} + \alpha_2 \ln(w)_{i,t} + \alpha_3 DFor_{i,t} + \alpha_4 DExp_{i,t}$$
$$+ \sum_{\alpha_5}^{\alpha_k} DIndustry_{i,j,t} + \varepsilon_{i,t} \qquad (A6.1)$$

where:
i = firm/plant i;
j = industry j, defined at the ISIC three-digit level;
L = employment, defined as the total (headcount) labour force;
w = wage per labour, defined as labour expenditure per employee;
Q = output, defined as real value added;
$DFor$ = dummy variable for foreign ownership (equal to 1 if firm i has any foreign ownership share, and 0 otherwise);
$DExp$ = dummy variable for firms engaged in exporting (equal to 1 if firm i exports any of its output, and 0 otherwise); and
$DIndustry$ = dummy variable for industries, defined at the ISIC three-digit level.

The dummy variables $DFor$ and $DExp$ are introduced to control for differences across establishments; the dummy variable $DIndustry$ is used to control for differences across (ISIC) three-digit industries.

7 OCCUPATIONAL CHOICE AND MOBILITY AMONG MIGRANTS TO FOUR CITIES

Sherry Tao Kong and Tadjuddin Noer Effendi

Over the past four decades, Indonesia has experienced a series of major social and economic changes against a background of almost uninterrupted economic growth. Two of the more important features of socio-economic development during this period have been the surge in rural–urban migration and the spread of mass education. The continuing flow of rural migrants to the cities, attracted by job opportunities and the prospect of higher earnings, has contributed to a marked reduction of poverty in Indonesia.

The process of rural–urban migration is likely to have important implications for social and economic mobility. Specifically, occupational mobility can serve as an effective channel for achieving improvements in income and reductions in poverty and inequality because of its close association with career progression and earnings. Few studies, however, have looked into issues related to occupational mobility in Indonesia, especially among rural–urban migrants.[1] This chapter attempts to shed light on this topic by investigating migrants' choice of first occupation in the city, patterns of subsequent occupational mobility and the determinants of stability or change, in the context of economic and social changes over the past few decades.

In studying the experiences of migrants to developed countries, especially the United States, the economics literature finds strong evidence of downgrading of occupational status when immigrants first arrive in a country. But is this phenomenon exclusive to international migration? And how do migrants – both domestic and international – fare over time? In many respects rural–urban and international migrants face a similar set of challenges and risks in the destination labour market, despite the differences between those who choose to migrate internation-

---

1 Two exceptions are Steele's (1980) study of occupational mobility among migrants to Surabaya, and Alisjahbana and Manning's (2010) study of recent and long-term migrants in the urban labour market.

ally and those who choose to relocate internally. These risks include the possibility that one's qualifications may be discounted or not recognised, a lack of job networks and knowledge about the local labour market, credit constraints and a general lack of social support.

This chapter focuses on occupational choice and mobility among internal migrants living in four Indonesian cities. Using data from the 2008 and 2009 waves of the Rural–Urban Migration in China and Indonesia (RUMiCI) project (http://rumici.anu.edu.au), we examine the choice of first occupation in the city, and compare it with the occupation in 2009. We investigate the underlying determinants of the choice of first occupation, taking into account the main activities of migrants before moving to the city, and examine the factors that may contribute to any subsequent occupational mobility.

The rest of the chapter is organised as follows. The first section briefly reviews the relevant literature on rural–urban migration and occupational choice and mobility. The second outlines the main features of rural–urban migration in Indonesia over the past few decades and describes each of the four cities' idiosyncratic characteristics. The third section explains our econometric strategy. It introduces the data set and presents summary statistics on the migrant and local resident samples, with special reference to occupational distribution. The fourth section presents the analytical results on migrants' choice of first occupation in the city. It also examines occupational mobility among migrants by comparing the first and current occupations. The concluding section discusses future research directions.

LITERATURE REVIEW

The experience of international migration in the host country is of great relevance for the study of rural–urban migration. In the international migration context, much research has focused on occupational choice and mobility among immigrants. Several studies find evidence of downgrading of occupation on arrival in the host country, induced by factors such as previous work experience, race and gender.

Akresh (2006), for example, finds strong evidence of downgrading of occupation when immigrants first arrive in the United States, with highly skilled individuals from Latin America and the Caribbean especially likely to experience labour market discrimination. Similarly, Constant and Massey (2003) find that immigrants to Germany encounter a high degree of downgrading of the initial occupation, and experience little occupational mobility over time. Chiswick and Miller (2007: 2) find a negative relationship between pre-immigration experience and occupational status among migrants to the United States; they attribute this to 'less-than-perfect international transferability of human capital skills'. Schmidt and Strauss (1975) also find evidence of occupational downgrading among migrants to the United States, due to racial and gender discrimination.

Similar issues of occupational mobility are of interest in the context of rural–urban migration, particularly for researchers looking at urbanisation (modernisation) and its effect on the wellbeing of rural–urban migrants in developing countries. Moreover, from a development perspective, it is important to investigate the extent to which migration serves as a source of social and economic mobility, as one of the main channels for improving the incomes and welfare of surplus rural labour.

Two main schools of thought can be identified in the literature. The first, the theory of occupational segmentation, is based on the concept of a dualistic urban labour market. It describes the urban labour market as consisting of two sectors: a slower-growing, higher-wage formal sector and a faster-growing, lower-wage informal sector. The theory predicts that entry into the formal sector will be restricted by a combination of economic and institutional factors. Most new labour force entrants, including rural–urban migrants, will therefore be forced to seek avenues of self-employment in the informal sector, where entry is relatively easy but transition to the formal sector difficult (Mazumdar 1994: 96).

The second school of thought emphasises the idea of fragmented urban labour markets, challenging the concept of duality. Such studies argue conceptually and demonstrate empirically that the concept of bipolar formal and informal sectors tends to oversimplify actual conditions in the urban labour market, particularly in developing countries. The fragmented labour market hypothesis emphasises the heterogeneity of the informal sector, arguing that it does not take the single, exclusive form of self-employment but is shared by wage earners in certain parts of services, trade and industry.

Breman (1976) argues that access to employment takes place at many different levels and is dependent on a range of factors, such as socio-economic background, education, presence or absence of urban contacts, and ethnicity. Under conditions of surplus labour, occupational stability or lateral movement between jobs of the same status is more common than occupational mobility. Based on a study of lifetime migrants to the city of Surabaya in East Java, Steele (1980) also concludes that informal sector employment is far more multifaceted than the urban dualism model would suggest. 'A model such as the urban dualism model based solely on sector of employment', he says, 'is too coarse and mechanistic to substantially contribute to an understanding of occupational mobility' (Steele 1980: 462). Using longitudinal data to compare occupation on first arrival with later occupation, he too finds evidence that occupational stability occurs more frequently than occupational mobility (Steele 1980: 456).

Three other areas of theory and research are also relevant to issues of migration and occupational mobility. First, the human capital theory argues that human capital is a major source of heterogeneity in labour markets, through its effect on the productivity of the individual and hence labour market outcomes (Becker 1975). In an occupational choice context, this implies that an individual will be likely to choose the occupation that offers the highest discounted present value of potential future earnings. To apply this to the context of migration, when migrants move from the countryside to the city, they will endeavour to find better jobs and convert their human capital into occupations that maximise their returns. As a result, human capital affects current occupation and associated labour market performance, through its impact on both the initial status of the first job and directly on the current occupation. A large number of empirical studies have demonstrated that occupational allocation and sorting are significantly affected by human capital characteristics (Velling 1995; Muller, Steinmann and Ell 1998; Kalter and Granato 2002).

The second relevant research area is the occupational choice literature, which studies the choice of a particular occupation given the characteristics of the individual. Using discrete choice models, this body of literature provides a basis for examining the determinants of occupation (Schmidt and Strauss 1975; Constant and Zimmermann 2003).

Third, related to both occupational choice and human capital theory are the theoretical and empirical studies examining the influence of parents on the behaviour, skills and abilities of the individual. This literature places particular emphasis on the influence of parental education – both father's and mother's – on occupational outcomes among their children. Heckman and Hotz (1986), for example, find that parents' education positively affects the earnings of Panamanian men, while Gang and Zimmermann (1999) find that a father's education is more important than a mother's in explaining educational attainment among German children.[2]

THE FOUR CITIES AND MIGRATION IN INDONESIA

Over the past four decades, Indonesia has experienced increasing urbanisation as rural migrants have flocked to the cities in search of a better

---

2 Robertson and Symons (1990), Bradley (1991) and Tsukahara (2007) also include parental variables in their analyses of occupational choice. See also Boskin (1974), Mazumder (2005) and Akerlof (1997).

life (Forbes 1979; Hugo 1978; Manning 1987). Three distinct time periods can be distinguished: pre-1986, 1986–96 and 1997–2009. The first was a period of intensive rural–urban migration during the early Suharto period when most of those moving to the cities found work in the informal sector. The second was a shorter period of rapid export-oriented growth during the last decade of Suharto's New Order regime when many migrants moved into wage employment. The third was a period of slower economic growth after the Asian financial crisis when the pace of rural–urban migration declined. We summarise the main developments in each period below.[3]

The underlying forces encouraging rural–urban migration before 1986 were pull factors related to economic growth and investment and push factors related to high levels of poverty, landlessness and surplus labour in rural areas, especially in Java. The high incidence of rural poverty pushed many people into urban areas in search of alternative activities offering higher wages (Temple 1974; Suharso and LEKN 1976; Hugo 1978). Many ended up in the informal sector where they worked as construction workers, street vendors, peddlers, food stall vendors and the like, in cities such as Jakarta (Hugo 1978), Surabaya (Steele 1980) and Makassar (Forbes 1979). While their incomes may have been higher than in the countryside, they were still low. Many migrants left their families behind, renting small huts (*pondok*) in the cities or squatting in temporary dwellings in slum areas (Jellinek 1978). The remittances they sent home to support their families were an important source of rural household income, contributing to a reduction in poverty in rural areas (Hugo 1978: 267–73). The incidence of rural poverty fell steeply during this period as rural residents continued to relocate to urban areas, where poverty was lower, and as conditions in rural areas improved (Manning 1998).

In the second period, 1986–96, urban wage employment expanded as manufacturing employment took off, especially in cities in the vicinity of Jakarta such as Tangerang, Bogor and Bekasi, in other Javanese cities such as Surabaya, and in off-Java centres such as Medan. However, as in the previous period, rural–urban migrants faced numerous difficulties in adjusting to city life (Pelly 1994). While the central government's stance on migration was relatively liberal, some of the larger cities introduced regulations and policies that discriminated against migrants, slowing the rate of assimilation.[4]

---

3 See Effendi et al. (2010) for further details on the demographic, social and employment characteristics of the four cities.

4 Migrants, especially street vendors, hawkers and peddlers, were often blamed for the growth of slums and the spread of illegally erected dwellings along riverbanks or next to the railway tracks, and were linked in the public mind

The third, most recent, period (1997–2009) was characterised by slower economic growth accompanied by a decline in rural–urban migration. During and after the Asian financial crisis, many migrants returned to their villages, and rural people looking for new jobs began to seek employment overseas. Political and social unrest within Indonesia provided an additional incentive for Indonesians to seek work abroad rather than in a nearby city, leading to a significant increase in the number of international migrants. During the period 1999–2004, the number of Indonesians officially working overseas rose above 2 million, to which must be added the large number of undocumented workers. Much research has focused on the welfare of these international migrants. It is equally important, however, to ask how more recent rural–urban migrants have fared in the urban labour market.

While the Indonesian economy did not experience a major downturn during the global financial crisis of 2007–2009, the export-oriented manufacturing sector nevertheless suffered a negative shock. Although it would be of interest to observe whether patterns of occupational mobility among the most recent migrants to the city changed during this period, a comprehensive evaluation of the impact of the latest crisis on employment is beyond the scope of this study.

The present study looks at rural–urban migrants in four Indonesian cities: two 'younger' cities (Tangerang in the province of Banten near Jakarta, and Samarinda in East Kalimantan); and two 'older' cities (Medan in North Sumatra and Makassar in South Sulawesi).[5] In total, these four cities hosted around one-third of all short-term and long-term rural–urban migrants in 2005. The former two cities have become major urban settlements only in the past 20 years; the two more established cities have been major urban centres since the colonial period.

Tangerang is an industrial city on the outskirts of Jakarta with a population of around 1.5 million. It has the second-largest population of migrant workers in the manufacturing sector, after Batam in the Riau Islands. The city grew rapidly in the 1980s through mid-1990s, with migrants finding ready employment in its factories making textiles, garments, shoes, electronic goods, ceramics and other products (Warouw 2006). Tangerang remained an attractive destination for migrants throughout the 1990s; the city's intercensal population growth rate for 1990–2000 was 4.1 per

---

to criminal activity, traffic jams and disturbances to public order. In many cities migrants were required to carry identity cards stating that they had been granted residence in the city, or face eviction. Authorities also often destroyed the food stalls (*warung*) and temporary dwellings built by migrants.

5 The reasons for the choice of the four cities are discussed in Resosudarmo, Yamauchi and Effendi (2010).

cent per annum, well above the national average of 1.4 per cent (Statistics Indonesia 2000). The other younger city, Samarinda, is a medium-sized city in the resource-rich province of East Kalimantan with a population of around 600,000. Like Tangerang, it has experienced rapid inflows of migrants and above-average population growth rates. Timber and later mining have underpinned regional growth and migration in Samarinda.

The two more established cities, Medan and Makassar, have grown at a more steady pace. With a population of over 2 million, Medan is the largest city in the agriculturally rich province of North Sumatra. It has been a trading centre since colonial times and was an important manufacturing hub until the Asian financial crisis. During the last decade, Medan has experienced a reduction in the inflow of rural–urban migrants, partly due to the slowdown in manufacturing after the crisis and partly because of the increased demand for palm oil, a major product of the region, which has driven up the opportunity cost of rural–urban migration. Makassar has a population of around 1 million. As the largest city in eastern Indonesia, it has historically been the main destination for regional migrants (Forbes 1979). More recently, the city has become a major centre for (tertiary) education, attracting large numbers of students from the surrounding districts and elsewhere in eastern Indonesia.

METHODOLOGY

Data

This study uses data from the 2008 and 2009 waves of the Rural–Urban Migration in China and Indonesia (RUMiCI) project. We rely primarily on the cross-sectional occupational information collected in 2009 and on the information about early occupational status collected in both 2008 and 2009. In the RUMiCI survey, rural–urban migrants are defined as people who lived continuously in a rural area for at least five years before the age of 12, and currently reside in an urban area. Unlike the conventional birthplace definition, the RUMiCI definition emphasises the rural background of a migrant. Conversely, non-migrants (or local urban residents) are people who did not spend at least five years consecutively in a rural area before the age of 12. By definition, this category may include people who have migrated from one urban area to another. In this study, we are mainly interested in how rural–urban migrants have fared in the urban labour market; the urban resident sample is therefore used only occasionally as a reference point. For simplicity, we focus mainly on the characteristics of household heads as the basis for the analysis.

The RUMiCI survey sample covers migrants and local urban residents in the four cities. Exactly 2,052 households were interviewed in both

Table 7.1   Distribution of migrant sample by period of first arrival and city of destination, 2009[a]

Cohort	Younger cities		Older cities		Total
	Tangerang	Samarinda	Medan	Makassar	
Pre- 1986					
Number	81	78	189	81	429
Share (%)	23.0	34.1	60.4	27.5	36.1
1986–98					
Number	122	74	81	62	339
Share (%)	34.7	32.3	25.9	21.0	28.5
1999–2009					
Number	149	77	43	152	421
Share (%)	42.3	33.6	13.7	51.5	35.4
Total					
Number	352	229	313	295	1,189
Share of city observations (%)	100	100	100	100	100
Share of all observations (%)	29.6	19.3	26.3	24.8	100.0

a   Seven respondents were excluded because information on the year of first arrival in the city was missing.
Source: RUMiCI survey, 2008 and 2009.

2008 and 2009. About 60 per cent were migrants (including both recent and lifetime migrants) and the rest were non-migrant urban residents.[6] To highlight the experiences of rural–urban migrants during different phases of migration, we divide the migrant sample into three cohorts by year of arrival: before 1986, 1986–98 and 1999–2009. Information on the migrant sample distribution is presented in Table 7.1. Table 7.2 describes the basic characteristics of both the migrant and non-migrant samples.

---

6   The migrant sample was divided into 'lifetime' migrants (those who had migrated more than five years before the 2008 survey) and 'recent' migrants (those who had migrated less than five years before the survey), based on the status of the household head. About 68 per cent of the migrant households surveyed in 2009 were lifetime migrants and 32 per cent recent migrants. For a detailed description of the RUMiCI survey's sampling methodology, see Reso-sudarmo, Yamauchi and Effendi (2010).

Table 7.2 Descriptive statistics on migrants by period of first arrival in the city[a]

	Before 1986	1986–98	1999–2009	All migrants	Urban residents	Total
Age when first migrated to city	18.8	22.1	22.2	20.7		
Age in 2009	54.3	38.9	27.8	43.0	45.6	44.3
Share of female household heads (%)	17.2	7.0	32.3	17.0	13.2	15.1
Education (years of schooling)	9.5	10.1	12.6	10.4	9.2	9.8
Main activity before migration (%)						
Farmer	36.1	31.7	17.5	30.4		
Agricultural worker	3.0	6.2	1.3	3.7		
Self-employed non-agricultural worker	4.2	5.2	2.9	4.2		
Non-agricultural wage worker	3.9	7.2	4.6	5.2		
Student	35.3	26.4	52.8	36.1		
Not working	14.1	21.7	19.1	17.9		
Other	3.5	1.7	1.9	2.5		
Total	100.0	100.0	100.0	100.0		
Reason to migrate (%)						
Family or social reasons	15.2	8.0	4.3	10.2		
Employment	63.2	82.6	47.2	66.4		
Education	16.2	8.6	47.3	20.5		
Other	5.4	0.9	1.2	2.9		
Total	100.0	100.0	100.0	100.0		
No. of observations	429	339	421	1,196	856	2,052

142

	Before 1986	1986–98	1999–2009	All migrants	Urban residents	Total
Occupational category of first job (%)[b]						
Professional/managerial	18.2	10.1	9.2	13.6	14.6	14.1
White collar	13.7	9.5	14.3	12.1	14.9	13.5
Craft	8.9	9.5	10.1	9.4	7.49	8.3
Blue collar	18.3	23.2	13.5	19.5	17.82	18.7
Menial	40.9	47.7	53.0	45.5	45.17	45.4
Total	100.0	100.0	100.0	100.0	100.0	100.0
Industry of first job (%)[b]						
Agriculture/mining	8.3	4.0	8.4	6.7	7.6	7.2
Manufacturing	20.0	32.9	36.7	27.7	24.2	25.9
Construction	6.8	11.1	6.1	8.3	10.3	9.4
Trade	20.4	21.1	20.3	20.7	21.5	21.1
Transport	12.0	12.9	10.2	12.0	11.6	11.8
Services	32.5	18.0	18.4	24.6	24.8	24.7
Total	100.0	100.0	100.0	100.0	100.0	100.0
No. of observations	395	334	305	1,034	821	1,855
Share of total observations (%)				55.7	44.3	100.0

a   Seven respondents were excluded from the data because information on the year of first arrival in the city was missing.
b   Information on first job was available for 821 urban residents and 1,034 migrants. Of the other respondents, 31 urban residents and 132 migrants were excluded because they had never worked (including students), and the remainder because information on the first job or year of migration was missing.

Source: RUMiCI survey, 2008 and 2009.

As one would expect, more recent migrants predominate in the younger city of Tangerang. The other younger city, Samarinda, has roughly equal proportions of migrants in each cohort (Table 7.1). In contrast, the established city of Medan has experienced a distinct decline in migrant inflows over time, particularly in the most recent decade. The other established city, Makassar, has by far the highest proportion of migrants in 1999–2009 (52 per cent). Rather than being in the workforce, however, around three-quarters of them came to the city to further their education.

Table 7.2 describes the demographic characteristics of migrants (by cohort) and non-migrants, in addition to providing information on occupation before and after arriving in the city.[7] The average age of migrants when they first arrive in the cities has increased from 19 for the pre-1986 cohort to 22 for the most recent cohort. The trend to delay migration probably reflects both an increase in high school completion rates (more time in school) and the less favourable economic prospects in the cities in the aftermath of the Asian financial crisis. Consistent with this speculation, the educational attainment of migrants, measured by years of formal schooling, has increased steadily over time. Moreover, the pursuit of an education has itself become a major reason for migration; close to half of the migrants who arrived in a city between 1999 and 2009 gave this as their reason for migrating.

Many migrants were not working before they came to the city. On average, 36 per cent were students and another 18 per cent were not working for other reasons. The share of farmers and other agricultural workers fell from around 40 per cent in the pre-1986 period to just 20 per cent in the most recent period. In contrast, the share of migrants who were students prior to migration surged from 35 per cent to 53 per cent. Nearly all of the remaining migrants in the 1999–2009 cohort were either not working (19 per cent) or working in the non-agricultural sector (8 per cent).

Table 7.2 also provides information on the first job in the city for both migrants and local urban residents. Following other studies on occupational choice and mobility (Schmidt and Strauss 1975; Constant and Zimmermann 2003), we classify jobs into five occupational categories: professional, white collar, craft, blue collar and menial.[8] We departed from the simple skilled versus unskilled dichotomy and chose to use five

---

7   We apply sample weights in calculating the summary statistics (except frequency) to provide a comparable picture across the four cities. The weights are derived based on sampling methods described in Resosudarmo, Yamauchi and Effendi (2010).

8   The codes and the content of each category are shown in appendix Table A7.1.

occupational categories for two reasons. First, we wanted to characterise occupations in such a way as to capture a distinctive ranking that would reflect the economic returns to and social prestige of different types of jobs. Second, we wanted to be able to investigate the five categories separately, to uncover any movement between the more finely defined categories that might be obscured by a broader categorisation.

Based on the five-category classification, we find that, on average, 45 per cent of both migrants and locals had a first job in the city that fell into the menial category (Table 7.2). Turning to the three migrant cohorts, it is clear that there has been a decline in the share of professional jobs over time, met by a steady increase in the share of menial jobs. In particular, there is a noticeable reduction in the shares of both the professional and white collar categories for the 1986–98 cohort, offset by an expansion in the blue collar and menial categories. This probably reflects the high demand for workers in the production sector during this period of rapid economic growth.

In terms of sector of first occupation, we observe a remarkable increase in the share of manufacturing from 20 per cent for the pre-1986 cohort to 33 per cent for the 1986–98 cohort and almost 37 per cent for the 1999–2009 cohort.[9] This is generally consistent with the export boom since the mid-1980s and the fact that trade has become an increasingly important part of the Indonesian economy. The propensity to enter the manufacturing sector upon arrival in the city also accords with the generally low level of skills of newly arrived migrants.

As the share of the manufacturing sector has risen, so has the share of the services sector fallen. Around one-third of migrants in the pre-1986 cohort, but less than 20 per cent in the 1986–98 and 1999–2009 cohorts, found their first job in the services sector.

Econometric strategy

We employ a standard multinomial logit model as the main tool to investigate occupational choice and mobility among migrants. The multinomial framework allows us to analyse the five occupational categories

---

9 Note that the RUMiCI sample is not nationally representative: the national share of manufacturing sector employment is only around 12 per cent. The difference between the national industrial distribution and the one presented here is probably driven by the inclusion of Tangerang in the sample. As a major manufacturing centre, Tangerang has a much higher share of manufacturing sector workers. Moreover, as a younger city, it attracts a large number of recent migrants: 42.3 per cent of migrants in the 1999–2009 cohort were sampled in Tangerang. The high concentration of manufacturing workers in Tangerang is therefore more pronounced in the summary statistics for the overall sample.

separately as dependent variables. We include a number of independent variables to explore the underlying factors affecting occupational outcomes as well as occupational mobility over time. These variables enter the model as covariates.[10]

In our investigation of migrants' choice of first occupation in the city, the dependent variable is the occupational category of the first job obtained in the urban labour market. There are three sets of control variables: individual demographic characteristics and cohort effects; individual human capital variables; and parental background variables.

The individual demographic characteristics and cohort effects are:[11]

- *Gender*, where being female takes a value of 1 and being male takes a value of 0. Many previous studies have demonstrated that, for many reasons, gender can lead to significant differences in the odds of occupational matching and mobility.
- *Age* of migrant when he or she first migrated to the city, and age squared. To some extent age measures experience, which may have a non-linear effect on an individual's choice of occupation.
- *Cohort effects*. The division of rural–urban migrants into three cohorts according to year of arrival in the city (before 1986, 1986–98 or 1999–2009) should reflect the overall development strategy of the country and economic performance during each period. It may also capture other generational variation in the unobserved characteristics.

The individual human capital variables are:

- *Education*, measured in number of years of formal schooling. Human capital theory and a large number of empirical studies suggest that

---

10 As explained in Long and Freese (2006), we can specify the predicted choice probability, given the covariates, as follows:

$$\Pr(y = m \mid X) = \frac{\exp(X\beta_{m\backslash b})}{\sum_{j=1}^{J} \exp(X\beta_{j\backslash b})}$$

where b is the comparison group and X is a vector of control variables. The log-odds ratio that an individual chooses occupation m with respect to the base outcome b is given by

$$\ln\Omega_{m\backslash b}(X) = \ln \frac{\Pr(y = m \mid X)}{\Pr(y = b \mid X)} = X\beta_{m\backslash b} \text{ for } m = 1 \text{ to } J.$$

11 Marital status and number of children are often included as control variables in an occupational choice equation. They could not be included in our analysis because no such information was available in our dataset for migrants at the time of first migration.

education is a key predictor of occupational choice. The multinomial approach allows us to compare the relative contribution of education to the choice of different occupations.

- *Local educational experience,* where pre-migration study in a city takes a value of 1, and 0 otherwise. Individuals who have studied in a city before taking their first job are considered to have local educational experience and therefore a better chance of obtaining a good job in the city.
- *Previous experience.* An individual's occupational category before migration may imply advantage or disadvantage in a subsequent occupation, and hence affect occupational choice.

The parental background variables are:

- *Parents' level of education,* measured in number of years of formal schooling. The educational attainment of parents reflects their knowledge and skills, which in turn may have an impact on their children's unobserved attitudes, abilities, skills and job networks.
- *Parents' occupational background.* It is often hypothesised in the occupational choice literature that parental occupation influences a child's choice of occupation – in particular, that it increases the probability that a child will choose the same or a similar occupation to the parents, everything else held constant.

To investigate occupational mobility, we compare the first and current occupational categories for each individual. The comparison can have three possible outcomes: the person's occupational status improves, remains the same or declines. Using the second outcome (remains unchanged) as the reference group, we investigate the factors that affect migrants' occupational mobility between the time they first obtain a job in the city and the present.

Table 7.3 presents the distribution of the three possible outcomes for the three migrant cohorts and for migrants versus non-migrants. On average, we see that around two-thirds of respondents have experienced a downward change in occupational category since taking their first job. Those who have experienced upward mobility constitute 21 per cent of the total sample, while the remaining 14 per cent have remained in the same occupational category. There is relatively little variation in the shares of those experiencing upward mobility across cohorts of migrants, or between migrants versus non-migrants. However, migrants in the oldest (pre-1986) cohort are less likely to experience downward mobility than the other two groups, and the 1986–98 cohort noticeably more likely to do so.

Table 7.3 *Incidence of occupational mobility between first and current occupation in the city (%)*

	Before 1986	1986– 98	1999– 2009	Migrant	Non- migrant	Total
Up	22.5	19.8	21.3	21.1	20.1	20.5
Unchanged	18.5	7.6	13.5	13.0	14.2	13.7
Down	59.1	72.6	65.2	66.0	65.7	65.8

Source: Authors' estimation based on RUMiCI survey, 2008 and 2009.

Table 7.4 sets out a transition matrix for transfers between occupational categories. It suggests two main sources of occupational mobility: downward mobility among individuals in the higher categories into menial jobs over time; and upward mobility among individuals from high-end to higher-end jobs. Thus, 33 per cent of migrants who started out as white collar workers had become menial workers by 2009, while another 25 per cent had moved into higher-end professional jobs.

Three general observations can be made at this point. First, while the five-category classification is able to capture finer distinctions between occupations, it does not capture mobility within each category. Second, because the 2009 survey was carried out immediately after the global financial crisis when high-paying jobs had become relatively scarce, downward movement in occupation could be over-represented in our

Table 7.4 *Transition matrix of occupational mobility between first and current occupation in the city (%)*

	Occupational category in 2009					Total
	Profes- sional	White collar	Craft	Blue collar	Menial	
Category of first job						
Professional	58.4	19.7	0.0	4.5	17.4	**100.0**
White collar	25.5	31.6	2.6	7.2	33.1	**100.0**
Craft	7.5	5.9	36.2	12.4	38.0	**100.0**
Blue collar	7.6	13.1	4.2	38.7	36.4	**100.0**
Menial	7.2	10.0	8.5	12.9	61.5	**100.0**
Total	**16.3**	**14.1**	**8.2**	**16.2**	**45.1**	**100.0**

Source: Authors' estimation based on RUMiCI survey, 2008 and 2009.

results. Third, we note that changing occupational categories can be difficult: there are skill and knowledge barriers to moving into higher-end occupations, and (naturally) general resistance to moving downward into lower-end occupations.

The same three sets of variables are used to investigate the issue of mobility, again using the category of first occupation as the control variable. We also include the number of years since first job in the city to capture the duration of migration. This allows us to see whether the effect of migration duration on occupational mobility is non-linear. In the beginning migrants accumulate information and build networks, increasing the probability of occupational mobility. But such effects diminish over time, so that moving to a new or better occupation becomes increasingly difficult.

In all regressions, we use sample weights to address the issue of samples from different cities having a different probability of being sampled. In addition, we specify clusters at the city level in the estimators to calculate the standard errors.[12]

Finally, a number of caveats should be made with respect to the multinomial logit model. First, it is not possible to control for all factors. For example, we do not know when migrants first arrived in the city, what kinds of networks they had or what kinds of credit constraints they faced (or the value of their assets). Second, while we are not relying on migration duration to predict occupational mobility, nevertheless like other researchers we are obliged to confront issues such as (dynamic) sorting and self-selection. Fundamentally, we observe only those migrants who have 'made it' in the city; therefore, we are likely to overestimate the effect of migration duration on occupational mobility. In the absence of a complete employment history for each individual, we cannot take occupational evolution between the year of first arrival and the survey year into account. At this stage, we can only control for the years that have elapsed between the year of the first job in the city and 2009.

EMPIRICAL FINDINGS

Migrants' choice of first job in the city

We first discuss the multinomial logit results for migrants' choice of first job in the city. The results are given in Table 7.5, which shows the average

---

12 This is to take account of the fact that the observations may not be completely independent within each cluster, and hence their errors are correlated. Both sample weights and clustering improve the accuracy of the standard errors.

Table 7.5 Migrants' choice of first job in the city

	Profes-sional	White collar	Craft	Blue collar	Menial
Female	0.051***	0.043	0.020	−0.168***	0.053
Age	0.007	−0.004	−0.009***	0.014	−0.008
Age squared	0.000	0.000	0.000***	0.000	0.000
Education (years of schooling)	0.022***	0.008**	0.005	−0.016***	−0.020***
Local education	0.028***	0.015	−0.011	−0.011	−0.021
Pre-migration occupation					
Agricultural worker	0.080**	−0.062	0.023	−0.029	−0.012
Self-employed	−0.273***	0.132***	0.005	−0.005	0.142***
Non-agricultural worker	0.428***	−1.565***	0.174	0.189	0.773***
Civil servant	−0.040	0.020	0.052	0.251***	−0.282**
Student	0.047*	0.056**	−0.030	0.030	−0.103***
Not working	−0.003	0.072**	−0.010	0.013	−0.072**
Other	0.129*	0.320***	−1.299***	0.311***	0.539***
Father's education (years of schooling)	0.011**	0.004	−0.009***	0.002	−0.007
Mother's education (years of schooling)	−0.003***	0.001	0.006***	−0.005**	0.001
Father's occupation					
Agricultural worker	0.040	−0.103**	0.001	0.040	0.022
Civil servant	0.010	−0.035	−0.016	0.058	−0.018
Business owner/ self-employed	−0.008	−0.145***	0.029	0.143	−0.018
Private sector employee or unpaid domestic worker	0.006	0.063	−0.070	0.075	−0.073
Not working	−1.504***	0.448***	−0.045	0.347	0.754***
Other	0.131***	0.161***	−1.326***	0.290***	0.744***
Mother's occupation					
Agricultural worker	−0.080	0.105	−0.104**	−0.054	0.134
Civil servant	−0.079*	0.063***	−0.084	0.040	0.060
Business owner/ self-employed	0.000	0.023	0.001	−0.012	−0.013
Private sector employee or unpaid domestic worker	0.035	0.067	0.171**	−0.315*	0.042
Not working	−0.050**	0.013	0.028	−0.016	0.025
Other	0.020	0.055	0.009	0.163***	−0.248***
City					
Tangerang	−0.052***	0.012	0.108***	−0.095***	0.026***
Samarinda	0.034**	−0.037	0.058***	0.016	−0.072***
Makassar	0.062***	−0.003	−0.051**	0.087***	−0.094***
Cohort					
Pre-1986	0.045	−0.021	0.022***	0.038	−0.084*
1986–99	0.037*	−0.027	0.015	0.073	−0.098***

*** = $p<0.01$; ** = $p<0.05$; * = $p<0.1$. The omitted category for pre-migration experience is 'farmer/fisherman/plantation worker'. The omitted category for parental occupation is 'farmer'.
Source: Authors' estimation based on RUMiCI survey, 2008 and 2009.

marginal effects of various control variables on the five occupational categories. To allow a more intuitive interpretation of the results, instead of log-odds ratios, we derive the mean of the marginal effects of each independent variable on the dependent variable. Statistically significant effects are shown in the table.

Being female seems to be important to one's chance of obtaining a job in the professional category, but it is also (unsurprisingly) a barrier to obtaining a job in the blue collar category. Age, which probably implies some degree of experience and an established job network, is positively but insignificantly related to the probability of obtaining a skilled job in the professional category. However, it is negatively related to the probability of obtaining a white collar or craft job, suggesting that younger age provides an advantage for workers seeking jobs in these categories. Our results do not suggest the presence of non-linearity of age effects.

More years of education is a significant predictor of the choice of a professional or white collar job, and reduces the probability of entering a blue collar or menial occupation. Another human capital variable, local educational experience (that is, being educated in a city), is consistently positive and significant for the professional category. This indicates the benefit – in addition to years of education – accruing to local educational experience, which might include contacts and networks in the job market. The main activity prior to migration also has an impact on occupational category. For example, a person who was engaged in non-agricultural work before migration has a significantly greater chance of obtaining a white collar job than someone who was a farmer (the omitted category).

The educational background of parents also affects the choice of first occupation in the city, but the influence of mother and father work in somewhat different ways. Specifically, a father's education matters more for an individual's chance of getting a top (professional) job, while a mother's education matters more for avoiding falling into a less desirable (blue collar) job. Parents' employment background also has some impact on occupational outcomes. Migrants whose parents are not working (as opposed to the omitted variable, being a farmer) have a significantly reduced probability of obtaining a professional first job.

City effects are generally significant in terms of the probability of a migrant obtaining a job in the professional, craft and menial categories. In line with our earlier discussion, younger cities such as Samarinda seem to present better opportunities for migrants to find semi-skilled jobs in the craft and menial categories, while more established cities such as Makassar present more opportunities for entry into professional occupations. For instance, controlling for the above-mentioned variables, migrants to Tangerang or Samarinda (rather than Medan) have a significantly greater chance of getting a craft (as opposed to menial) job.

Finally, cohort effects also play a role in shaping the first occupation. Migrants who arrived in the city earlier (that is, before 1999) are more likely to have found a first job as a professional and significantly less likely to have been engaged in a menial occupation. This is consistent with the slower pace of economic growth since the Asian financial crisis, which has made it more difficult for recent migrants to find high-end jobs.

Occupational mobility between first and current job

As we saw earlier (see Table 7.3), there is a great deal of occupational mobility between the first and current jobs held by rural–urban migrants. Using the case where occupational category remains unchanged as a benchmark, and adopting a multinomial logit model, we analyse the factors that contribute to upward mobility, downward mobility or immobility between the first and current occupations.

Table 7.6 reports the average marginal effects of various factors on occupational mobility. As gender seems to be an important predictor of mobility, we estimate the multinomial models separately for men and women. For women, more years of education increases the probability of an upward change and reduces the chance of a downward change in occupational category. While the impact is not statistically significant for either upward or downward mobility, a higher level of education does significantly reduce a woman's probability of standing still.[13] For men, however, the impact of education is less helpful: more education is not associated with upward mobility.

It is easy to think of a number of channels through which education should affect occupational mobility. The finding here that there is no statistically significant link between education and occupational mobility could be due to the presence of what are known as 'floor–ceiling effects' – that is, a ceiling on upward mobility among those who are already in the highest occupational category (which prevents them from moving any higher no matter how good their education) and a floor on those who are in the lowest occupational category (which prevents them from moving lower no matter how poor their education). Floor–ceiling effects typically appear at the top and bottom of a transition matrix. Our econometric results may therefore tend to overstate the degree of occupational immobility at the top and bottom of the occupational ladder.

---

13 Moreover, the squared term for education in most cases has the opposite sign to the first-order term, indicating a diminishing marginal effect of more years of schooling.

The occupational background of father and mother seems to be very important for both male and female occupational mobility. In particular, a female migrant with a father employed in agriculture has a significantly reduced probability of upward mobility and a significantly increased probability of downward mobility, while a male migrant with a mother employed in agriculture has a significantly increased chance of downward mobility.

Using Medan as the omitted case, all of the other three cities, particularly Makassar and Tangerang, seem to play a positive role in encouraging upward mobility. As the slowest-growing city, Medan would appear to offer only limited scope for rural–urban migrants to progress occupationally in the city's labour market.

Finally, cohort effects are generally insignificant, with the most recent cohort being the omitted group.

DISCUSSION AND CONCLUSION

In this chapter, we have employed data from the 2008 and 2009 waves of the RUMiCI survey to investigate occupational choice and mobility among Indonesian rural–urban migrants over the past four decades. Using multinomial models, we have demonstrated that age, education, parents' education and some aspects of parents' occupational background have a significant impact on migrants' choice of first occupation in the city. Our results show that, in addition to years of schooling, the experience of studying in a city increases the probability that a migrant will obtain a skilled job. This is the case for both rural–urban and international migrants, although for somewhat differing reasons. In the case of international migrants, a local education is likely to be particularly important for gaining recognition of one's skills and qualifications, whereas for rural–urban migrants, it is probably more important for the accumulation of local knowledge and the building of social networks.

Looking at the changes in occupation across the three cohorts (pre-1986, 1986–99 and 1999–2009), we observe that the share of migrants experiencing occupational mobility (either upward or downward) fluctuates but remains large over time. While the degree of mobility may depend in part on the classification of occupational categories, the observed movement nevertheless indicates that occupational mobility is an important feature of Indonesia's urban labour market. Our results provide consistent and strong support for the human capital hypothesis. The analysis points in particular to the central role of education. More education is closely associated with upward occupational mobility, which in turn is a predictor of higher earnings. The association between human

Table 7.6   Occupational mobility of migrants between first and current job

	Upward	Unchanged	Downward
Male migrants			
Age	0.020	−0.001	−0.019
Age squared	0.000	0.000	0.000
Education			
Years of schooling	−0.016	−0.002	0.018
Years of schooling squared	0.002*	0.001	−0.003***
Father's occupation			
Agricultural worker	0.000	0.046	−0.045
Civil servant	−0.057	−0.048	0.105**
Business owner/self-employed	0.054*	0.059	−0.113*
Private sector employee or unpaid domestic worker	0.001	−0.009	0.007
Not working	0.215*	−0.169	−0.046
Other	0.149***	−0.102***	−0.047
Mother's occupation			
Agricultural worker	−0.044	−0.078	0.122*
Civil servant	0.048	0.028	−0.076
Business owner/self-employed	−0.475***	−0.001	0.476***
Private sector employee or unpaid domestic worker	−0.008	0.037	−0.028
Not working	−0.052	0.008	0.044
Other	0.012	0.007	−0.019
Father's education (years of schooling)	0.009	0.011***	−0.020**
Mother's education (years of schooling)	−0.005	−0.009***	0.014**
City			
Tangerang	0.126***	−0.015*	−0.111***
Samarinda	0.008	−0.006	−0.002
Makassar	0.112***	0.075***	−0.188***
Cohort			
Pre-1986	−0.043	0.075	−0.032
1986–99	−0.049	−0.010	0.060

*** = $p<0.01$; ** = $p<0.05$; * = $p<0.1$. The omitted category for parental occupation is 'farmer'.

Table 7.6 (continued)

	Upward	Unchanged	Downward
Female migrants			
Age	–0.018	0.001	0.017
Age squared	0.000	0.000	0.000
Education			
Years of schooling	0.085	–0.057***	–0.028
Years of schooling squared	–0.003	0.004***	–0.001
Father's occupation			
Agricultural worker	–1.226***	–0.651**	1.877***
Civil servant	–0.073	0.159***	–0.086
Business owner/self-employed	–0.258	0.137	0.121
Private sector employee or unpaid domestic worker	–1.579***	0.508***	1.071
Not working	–1.263***	–0.415	1.678***
Other	–0.074	0.166**	–0.092
Mother's occupation			
Agricultural worker	–0.936***	–0.594***	1.530
Civil servant	0.262	0.009	–0.271
Business owner/self-employed	–1.195***	–0.771**	1.965***
Private sector employee or unpaid domestic worker	–0.723**	0.074	0.649
Not working	0.020	–0.280***	0.259***
Other	0.504**	–0.385***	–0.119
Father's education (years of schooling)	0.012	0.021***	–0.033
Mother's education (years of schooling)	–0.016	–0.021	0.037
City			
Tangerang	0.193*	–0.169	–0.023
Samarinda	0.057	–0.147	0.090
Makassar	0.186	0.126	–0.312***
Cohort			
Pre-1986	0.449*	–0.104	–0.344
1986–99	0.038	–0.081	0.043

Source: Authors' estimation based on RUMiCI survey, 2008 and 2009.

capital (especially education) and upward occupational mobility extends to the parents. Father's education is one factor that affects occupational choice, although (surprisingly) mother's education seems to influence occupational mobility only weakly. Clearly human capital can play an important role in contributing to occupational and social mobility.

The analysis has also highlighted differences between the four cities and between the different migrant cohorts. In terms of migrants' choice of first job, relative to Medan, Tangerang and Samarinda provide more employment opportunities in the semi-skilled craft category, while well-established Makassar is better at providing more prestigious professional jobs. Compared with the older generations of migrant workers, the most recent migrants arrive in the city with a higher human capital endowment, and many have local (urban) educational experience. Among the three cohorts, it is the generation that arrived in the city between 1986 and 1999 that has experienced the least upward occupational mobility. Overall, there is a high degree of occupational mobility among migrant workers in the four cities. It is sobering to observe, however, that most of this movement has been downward. How each city can foster upward occupational mobility is therefore an important project for future research.

REFERENCES

Akerlof, G. (1997) 'Social distance and social decisions', *Econometrica*, 65(5): 1,005–28.

Akresh, I.R. (2006) *Occupational Mobility among Legal Immigrants to the United States*, University of Illinois, Urbana IL.

Alisjahbana, A. and C. Manning (2010) 'Making it in the city: recent and long-term migrants in the urban labour market', in X. Meng and C. Manning (eds) *The Great Migration: Rural–Urban Migration in China and Indonesia*, Edward Elgar, Cheltenham.

Becker, G.S. (1975) 'Investment in human capital: effects on earnings', in G.S. Becker, *Human Capital: A Theoretical and Empirical Analysis with Special Reference to Education*, second edition, National Bureau of Economic Research, New York NY.

Boskin, M.J. (1974) 'A conditional logit model of occupational choice', *Journal of Political Economy*, 82(2): 389–98.

Bradley, S. (1991) 'An empirical analysis of occupational expectations', *Applied Economics*, 23(7): 1,159–73.

Breman, J. (1976) 'A dualistic labour system? A critique of the informal sector concept', *Economic and Political Weekly*, 11(48): 1,870–76; 11(49): 1,905–8; 11(50): 1,939–44.

Chiswick, B.R. and P.W. Miller (2007) 'Modeling immigrants' language skills', IZA Discussion Paper No. 2974, Institute for the Study of Labor (IZA), Bonn.

Constant, A. and D.S. Massey (2003) 'Labor market segmentation and the earnings of German guestworkers', IZA Discussion Paper No. 774, Institute for the Study of Labor (IZA), Bonn.

Constant, A. and K.F. Zimmermann (2003) 'Occupational choice across generations', IZA Discussion Paper No. 975, Institute for the Study of Labor (IZA),
Bonn.

Effendi, T.N, Mujiyani, F. Itriyati, D.A. Darmawan and D.S. Widhyarto (2010)
'Assessing the welfare of migrant and non-migrant households in four Indo-
nesian cities: some demographic, social and employment characteristics', in
X. Meng and C. Manning (eds) *The Great Migration: Rural–Urban Migration in
China and Indonesia*, Edward Elgar, Cheltenham.

Forbes, D. (1979) 'The peddlers of Ujung Pandang', Working Paper No. 17, Centre of Southeast Asian Studies, Monash University, Melbourne.

Gang, I.N. and K.F. Zimmermann (1999) 'Is child like parent? Educational attainment and ethnic origin', IZA Discussion Paper No. 57, Institute for the Study
of Labor (IZA), Bonn.

Heckman, J.J. and V.J. Hotz (1986) 'An investigation of the labor market earnings
of Panamanian males evaluating the sources of inequality', *Journal of Human
Resources*, 21(4): 507–42.

Hugo, G.J. (1978) *Population Mobility in West Java*, Gadjah Mada University Press,
Yogyakarta.

Jellinek, L. (1978) 'Circular migration and the "pondok" dwelling system: a case
study of ice cream traders in Jakarta', in P.J. Rimmer, D.W. Drakakis-Smith
and T.G. McGee (eds) *Food, Shelter and Transport in Southeast Asia and the
Pacific*, Australian National University, Canberra.

Kalter, F. and N. Granato (2002) 'Ethnic minorities education and occupational
attainment: the case of Germany', paper presented at the meeting of Research
Committee 28 of the International Sociological Association, Oxford, 10–13
April.

Long, J.S. and J. Freese (2006) *Regression Models for Categorical Dependent Variables
Using Stata*, second edition, Stata Press, College Station TX.

Manning, C. (1987) 'Rural economic change and labour mobility: a case study
from West Java', *Bulletin of Indonesian Economic Studies*, 23(2): 52–79.

Manning, C. (1998) *Indonesian Labour in Transition: An East Asian Success Story?*
Cambridge University Press, Melbourne.

Mazumdar, D. (1994) 'Urban poverty and labour markets', in E.M. Pernia (ed.)
Urban Poverty in Asia: A Survey of Critical Issues, Oxford University Press, Oxford.

Mazumder, B. (2005) 'Fortunate sons: new estimates of intergenerational mobility in the United States using social security earnings data', *Review of Economics and Statistics*, 87(2): 235–55.

Muller, W., S. Steinmann and R. Ell (1998) 'Education and labour-market entry in
Germany', in Y. Shavit and W. Muller (eds) *From School to Work: A Comparative Study of Educational Qualifications and Occupational Destinations*, Claren-
don Press, New York NY.

Pelly, U. (1994) *Urbanisasi dan Adaptasi: Peranan Misi Budaya Minangkabau dan
Mandailing di Medan, Sumatera Utara* [Urbanisation and Adaptation: A Case
Study of Minangkabau and Mandailing Migrants in Medan, North Sumatra],
LP3ES, Jakarta.

Resosudarmo, B.P, C. Yamauchi and T.N Effendi (2010) 'Rural–urban migration
in Indonesia: survey design and implementation, in X. Meng and C. Manning (eds) *The Great Migration: Rural–Urban Migration in China and Indonesia*,
Edward Elgar, Cheltenham.

Robertson, D. and J. Symons (1990) 'The occupational choice of British children',
Economic Journal, 100(402): 828–41.

Schmidt, P. and R.P. Strauss (1975) 'The prediction of occupation using multiple logit models', *International Economic Review*, 16(2): 471–86.

Statistics Indonesia (2000) *The Population of Indonesia: Results of the 2000 Census*, Series S2, Statistics Indonesia, Jakarta.

Steele, R. (1980) 'Origin and occupational mobility of lifetime migrants to Surabaya and East Java', PhD dissertation, Australian National University, Canberra.

Suharso and LEKN (Lembaga Ekonomi dan Kemasyarakatan Nasional) (1976) *Rural–Urban Migration: Indonesia*, National Institute of Economic and Social Research, Indonesian Institute of Sciences, Jakarta.

Temple, G. (1974) 'Migration to Jakarta: empirical search for theory', PhD dissertation, University of Wisconsin, Madison WI.

Tsukahara, I. (2007) 'The effect of family background on occupational choice', *Labour*, 21(4–5): 871–90.

Velling, J. (1995) 'Wage discrimination and occupational segregation of foreign male workers in Germany', ZEW Discussion Paper No. 95-04, Zentrum für Europäische Wirtschaftsforschung/Center for European Economic Research (ZEW), Mannheim.

Warouw, N. (2006) 'Community-based agencies as the entrepreneur's instruments of control in post-Soeharto's Indonesia', *Asia Pacific Business Review*, 12(2): 193–207.

Table A7.1   Content and codes of occupational categories

	Professional	White collar	Craft	Blue collar	Menial
Content	Professional Semi-professional Manager Upper or executive-level civil servant	Semi-skilled white collar worker Low or middle-level civil servant	Foreman, Self-employed farmer or Master craftsman	Skilled or semi-skilled blue collar worker	Un-skilled worker
Three-digit code	111–139 211–255 331–339 591–599	311–329 341–399 511 611–632	141 711–729 411–421	431–499 731–799	811–831 911–999

Source: Statistics Indonesia, Indonesian Standard Occupational Classification (Kode Klasifikasi Baku Jenis Pekerjaan Indonesia), 2000.

PART 3

Education and Health

8 THE QUALITY OF EDUCATION: INTERNATIONAL STANDING AND ATTEMPTS AT IMPROVEMENT

Daniel Suryadarma

Indonesia achieved virtually universal primary school enrolment in 1988, and is currently well on the way to achieving universal secondary school enrolment. The net enrolment rate in secondary school increased from 56 per cent in 2003 to 68 per cent in 2008. As access to education continues to improve, policy makers are shifting their focus from lifting enrolment rates to improving the quality of the education students receive while at school.

There are two main reasons for this paradigm shift. The first is that enrolment rates are not in themselves an accurate indicator of the performance of a country's education sector. In a sense, the level of schooling that an individual has completed (primary, secondary or tertiary) merely reflects the amount of resources invested in the individual. In other words, it measures the input into an individual's human capital. Given sufficient investment, most individuals would be able to attain a particular level of education. Behrman and Birdsall (1983) argue that not taking quality into account is likely to bias the estimates of returns to schooling upward, because the weight given to an expansion of student numbers is likely to mask less impressive improvements in indicators of educational quality, such as the number of years of teacher training.

The second reason for the increased emphasis on educational quality – usually measured in terms of how students perform on standardised tests – is that it has a positive and causal relationship with economic growth and living standards (Hanushek and Woessmann 2008). This makes perfect sense. A high-quality education produces highly skilled individuals.[1] Highly skilled individuals are able to earn higher levels of income over their lifetimes. In a review of several studies of the relationship between standardised test performance and earnings, Suryadarma (2010) finds that the relationship is positive, large and statistically significant in both developing and developed countries.

In an era of globalisation, firms that require highly skilled workforces – usually in capital-intensive industries – tend to invest in countries that can provide such workers. Countries that have higher-quality schools, and thus higher shares of highly skilled individuals, are therefore in a better position to attract such capital-intensive investments. This in turn translates into higher rates of economic growth for the country. The benefits of a high-performing economy include lower poverty rates (Suryahadi, Suryadarma and Sumarto 2009), higher levels of support for democracy (Barro 1999; Dee 2004) and healthier populations (Jamison, Jamison and Hanushek 2007).

The aim of this chapter is provide an overview of educational quality in Indonesia, measured by the performance of students on an international standardised mathematics test. The choice to focus on mathematics is a pragmatic one. While there are international standardised tests in reading, literacy and science, knowledge of mathematics is arguably the most important skill a student can acquire, as it is used in virtually every aspect of life. In addition, mathematical skills are generally learned at school, unlike reading or literacy skills, which can also be learned at home. While I admit that focusing on just one skill may be unsatisfactory, it does bring tractability to the analysis.

In the following sections, I describe the main challenges that policy makers face in their attempts to improve the quality of education in Indonesia. These challenges include problems with the curriculum, teacher absenteeism, teacher qualifications, teacher distribution, school facilities and community participation. I also discuss some of the solutions to those problems, including a number of collaborations between researchers and policy makers specifically designed to address some of the shortcomings that have been identified in the education system.

THE QUALITY OF EDUCATION IN INDONESIA

This chapter uses student performance on an international standardised mathematics test, the Trends in International Mathematics and Science

---

1 Although conditions at home and parental support for learning are also undeniably important in determining an individual's level of skills, this chapter abstracts away from those factors to focus only on school-based factors.

Study (TIMSS), to measure the quality of education in Indonesia.[2] TIMSS measures competence in mathematics and science at the fourth and eighth grades, and can be used to identify promising instructional practices from all parts of the world. The TIMSS tests were administered in 1995, 1999, 2003 and 2007, with planning under way for 2011.

Indonesia has been a TIMSS participant since 1999, although only the eighth grade test has been administered in the country. Indonesia's test scores may be compared with those of two groups of countries: countries at a similar stage of economic and social (in this case health) development; and countries situated in the same region. Measured in terms of gross national income per capita, Indonesia's closest peers are Armenia, Egypt, Georgia, Ghana, Jordan, Mongolia, Syria and Yemen. Measured in terms of health performance – proxied by the infant mortality rate – Indonesia's closest peers are Algeria, Colombia, El Salvador, Iran, Kazakhstan, Lebanon, Morocco, Palestine, Qatar, Romania, Saudi Arabia, Tunisia and Turkey.

This chapter focuses on the results of the 2007 TIMSS, with the results for 1999 and 2003 provided in some instances to show trends. In total, 241,613 eighth grade students from 50 countries and seven benchmarking cities, states or provinces (in Canada, Spain, the United States and the United Arab Emirates) participated in 2007. More than 4,000 students took the test in Indonesia.

The mathematics component of TIMSS attempts to assess two important areas: knowledge of content, that is, students' understanding of specific mathematical topics; and cognitive ability, that is, students' ability to apply mathematical processes. For eighth grade participants, the four areas tested within the content domain are number, algebra, geometry, and data and chance. The three areas tested within the cognitive domain are knowing, applying and reasoning, with heavier emphasis on the first two.

In total, eighth grade students taking the mathematics test in 2007 could be tested on 215 items to achieve a total possible score of 238, where half of the items required constructed responses and the rest were multiple choice questions. The results were then scaled in a way that took account of the differences in the difficulty of the various subsets, and that allowed for the fact that different students may have been administered different items in the test. The mean of the scale across countries was set at 500, with a standard deviation of 100. The tests were conducted in the national language of each country.

---

2 Information on TIMSS and the data used in this section are taken from Mullis et al. (2008).

Indonesia's performance on TIMSS

I begin my examination of the quality of schooling in Indonesia by comparing the achievement of Indonesian eighth grade students on the 2007 TIMSS test with that of students in a group of countries with comparable economic and health conditions, and in a group of countries in the same region. From the list of comparable countries given above, only Iran, Jordan, Tunisia and Romania participated in all three TIMSS between 1999 and 2007. These four countries therefore constitute the group of comparable countries referred to throughout this study. In addition, I describe the performance of students in three nearby Southeast Asian countries: Malaysia, Singapore and Thailand.[3]

Figure 8.1 shows the mean TIMSS scores in mathematics in 1999, 2003 and 2007. It shows that Indonesia performed significantly worse than its Southeast Asian neighbours and its peers throughout the period, although the gap between Indonesia and its peers was much narrower than the gap between it and its neighbours. The gap between Indonesia and its neighbours narrowed in 2007, although most of the change was driven by a sharp drop in performance among the three neighbouring countries. Indonesia's performance also deteriorated in 2007, but only slightly.

Indonesia's score in all three TIMSS tests conducted between 1999 and 2007 was below 500 – the average score. Its performance was worst in 2007, when it did not even manage to attain a mean score of 400. A mean score of less than 400 puts Indonesia below the lowest benchmark of achievement recognised by TIMSS (see below). The low average score in 2007 implies that the quality of education in Indonesia actually declined between 2003 and 2007. If one includes 1999 in the observation, the trend shows that the gains made to educational quality between 1999 and 2003 had completely disappeared by 2007.[4]

Although it is true that educational quality also declined in neighbouring countries between 2003 and 2007, the decline in Indonesia can be considered more serious given the low scores of Indonesian students

---

3   I include Singapore even though it has vastly better economic and health outcomes than Indonesia, and is one of the strongest TIMSS performers. Its inclusion reflects the disparity between the current state of educational quality in Indonesia and the improvements the country would need to achieve to be able to compete with its near neighbour, Singapore.

4   Not all Indonesian secondary school students take the TIMSS test. The selection of a sample of students to sit the test raises the question of possible bias in the selection process, the presence of which would cast doubt on the trend shown in Figure 8.1. However, the selection process is not likely to have changed over such a short time period. If this assumption holds, then the trend shown in the figure should be accurate.

Figure 8.1   *Score on mathematics component of TIMSS, Indonesia and comparison countries, 1999–2007*

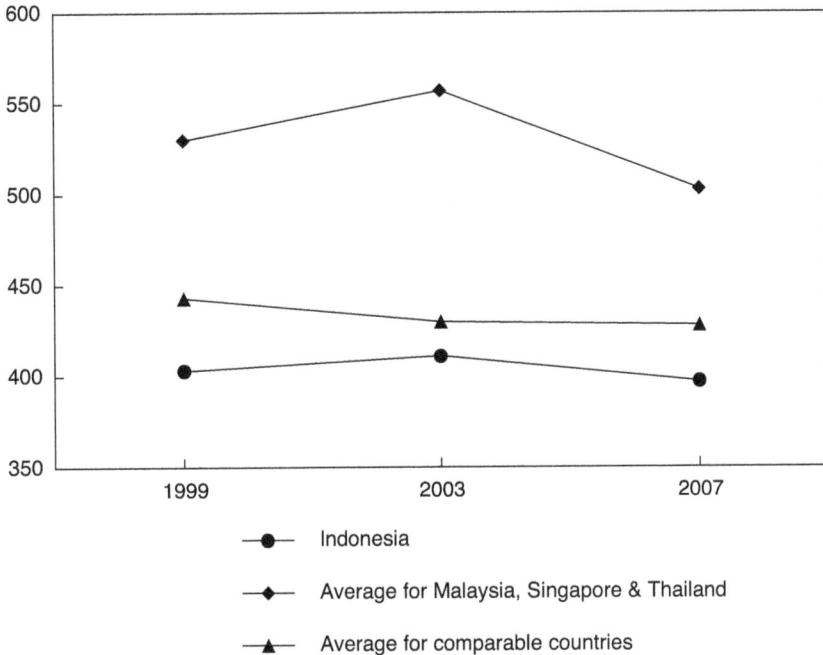

—●— Indonesia

—◆— Average for Malaysia, Singapore & Thailand

—▲— Average for comparable countries

Source: Author's calculations based on Mullis et al. (2008).

in 1999 and 2003. Individually, Singapore, Malaysia and Thailand scored 593, 474 and 441 respectively in the 2007 test. Indonesia therefore lags its neighbours by between 0.4 and 1.9 standard deviations. If a successful educational intervention to improve quality increased Indonesia's test score by about 0.3 standard deviations (Pradhan et al. 2010), implementation of one such intervention would bring Indonesia up to Thailand's level. For Indonesia to be on a par with Singapore, there would have to be about six such interventions. Currently, no single educational intervention in Indonesia has been able to improve learning by more than 0.3 standard deviations.

TIMSS sets four international benchmarks of achievement in mathematics: advanced, high, intermediate and low. Students reaching the advanced benchmark – a score of 625 or more on the test – can organise and draw conclusions from information, make generalisations and solve non-routine problems. Students reaching the high benchmark – a score of 550 – can apply their understanding and knowledge in a variety of relatively complex situations. Students attaining the intermediate

Figure 8.2   Attainment on mathematics component of TIMSS, Indonesia and comparison countries, 2007 (%)

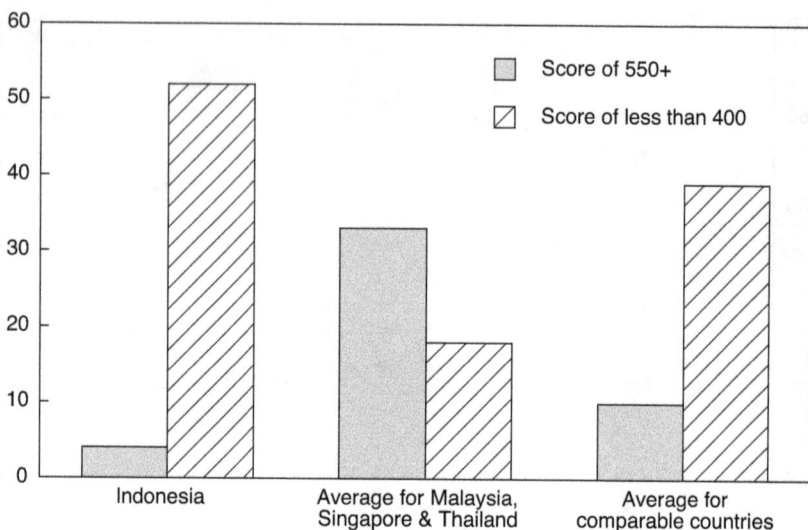

Source: Author's calculations based on Mullis et al. (2008).

benchmark – a score of 475 – can apply basic mathematical knowledge in straightforward situations. And students reaching the low benchmark – a score of 400 – have some knowledge of whole numbers and decimals, operations and basic graphs.

Figure 8.2 shows the proportion of students that attained a score of 550 or more, and the proportion that failed to achieve a score of at least 400, in the 2007 TIMSS. Around 52 per cent of Indonesian students did not manage to attain a score of 400. The proportion falling into the same bracket was around 20 per cent in the three neighbouring countries, and 40 per cent in the group of comparable countries. At the other end of the spectrum, only 4 per cent of Indonesian students managed to attain a score of 550, compared with one-third of students in the three neighbouring countries. This is a staggeringly poor result for Indonesia.

Indonesia's performance by domain and gender

As mentioned earlier, TIMSS tests two main areas of mathematical knowledge: content and cognition. An examination of the performance of Indonesian students within each domain should shed light on the areas where students are performing particularly well or poorly. In addi-

Figure 8.3 Score on mathematics component of TIMSS by domain and gender, Indonesia, 2007

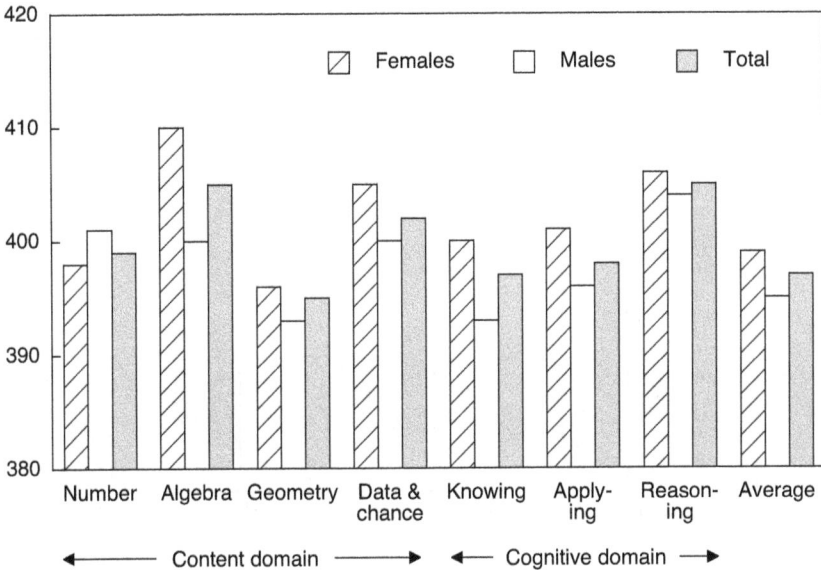

Source: Mullis et al. (2008).

tion to examining each component separately, I disaggregate the scores by gender.

Figure 8.3 provides the average scores for all seven components, for all students, male students and female students. Indonesian students appear to perform particularly well in algebra, data and chance, and reasoning, with average scores above 400. The average scores for the other components are below 400, with geometry garnering the lowest score.

Male students outperform female students in just one area, number. It is important to note, however, that the gaps are not statistically significant except in the case of algebra. That is, with the exception of algebra, there is no clear gender difference in the mathematical ability of Indonesian students.

WHAT ARE THE FACTORS THAT AFFECT EDUCATIONAL QUALITY?

In this section, I discuss a number of factors that may affect educational quality in Indonesia. Weaknesses in some of these areas have been linked

Figure 8.4   Hours of total instruction per week, share of mathematics in total instruction, and hours of mathematics instruction per month, Indonesia and comparison countries, 2007 (%)

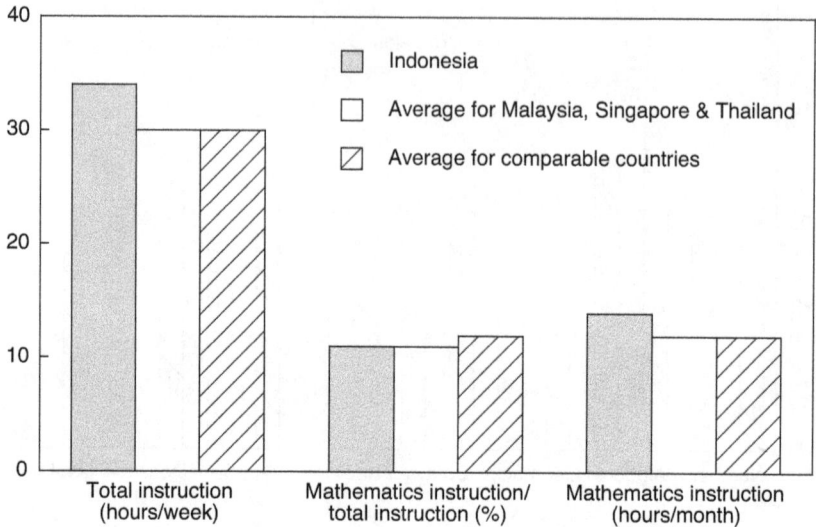

Source: Author's calculations based on Mullis et al. 2008.

to poorer educational outcomes in other developing countries. Although the following list is by no means exhaustive, the government may need to consider these factors as the first step to improving the quality of schooling in Indonesia.

Hours of instruction and course content

I first examine factors related to the school curriculum, namely the number of hours of instruction and the content of mathematics courses. I again compare Indonesia with the same two groups of countries, to provide some context for the findings.

Figure 8.4 shows the average number of hours of instruction per week, the share of those hours spent on mathematics, and the average number of hours of mathematics instruction per month. This information is recorded as part of the surveys that accompany the TIMSS tests. Compared with their counterparts in neighbouring and peer countries, Indonesian students receive about four more hours of instruction per week.[5] With

---

5   The differences reported for Figures 8.4–8.6 are statistically significant. Hence, I do not report the data on standard errors.

Figure 8.5   Number of TIMSS mathematics topics taught to students,
Indonesia and comparison countries, 2007

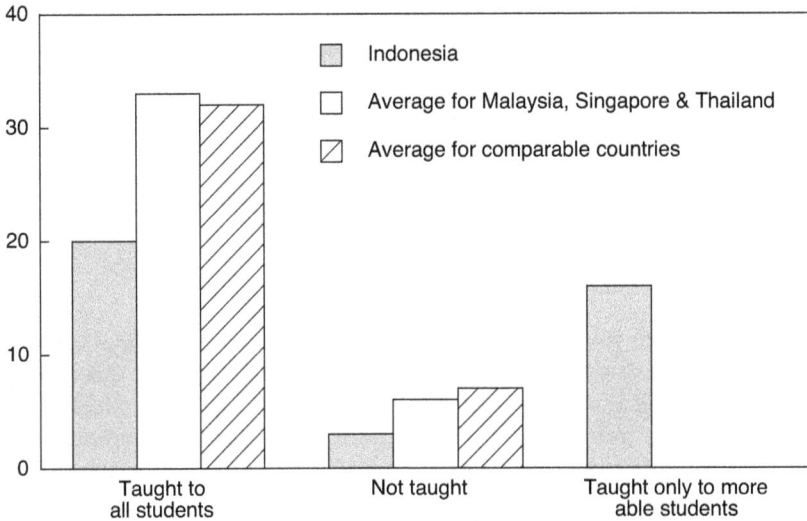

Source: Author's calculations based on Mullis et al. 2008.

similar shares of those hours spent on mathematics, it would appear that Indonesian students receive about two additional hours of mathematics instruction per month. Based on this information alone, one might conclude that the quality of mathematics instruction is poorer in Indonesia, because the students in the other countries significantly outperform Indonesian students even though the latter are exposed to more hours of tuition.

This conclusion would be justified if every other aspect of the curriculum were the same. This is not the case, however. As shown in Figure 8.5, of the 39 mathematics topics that were tested in the 2007 TIMSS, only 20 were taught to all Indonesian students. In contrast, on average, 33 and 32 topics respectively were taught in the neighbouring and peer countries.

The small number of mathematics topics taught in Indonesia is not because those topics are missing from the curriculum. In fact, only three are excluded from the curriculum, far fewer than in the other two groups of countries. Rather, the main reason for the small number of topics taught to most Indonesian students is that a large number – 16 topics – are reserved for more able students. Virtually no mathematics topic is reserved for a select group of students in the comparison countries.

In summary, although Indonesian students are exposed to more hours of mathematics in school, the majority study only a few mathematics topics. Indonesia is unique among its neighbours and peers in reserving a large number of topics for more able students. But although the small number of topics covered in Indonesian schools may be one reason for Indonesia's poor performance in TIMSS, it cannot be the only or even the main reason. If it were, then one would expect Indonesia to perform very well on the topics that *are* taught, as students would have spent more time on them than students in other countries. However, Indonesian students actually perform uniformly worse than students in neighbouring and peer countries across all mathematics topics. The evidence therefore points to other factors also being responsible for Indonesia's poor results.

Teacher absenteeism

The second factor that is understood to significantly affect school quality, as measured by student performance, is teacher absenteeism. According to Suryadarma et al. (2006), teacher absenteeism is negatively and significantly related to Indonesian students' performance in mathematics. The study finds that a 1 per cent increase in teacher absenteeism is associated with a 0.1 per cent reduction in students' scores in mathematics tests. In contrast, they find no relationship between teacher absenteeism and students' performance in Indonesian-language dictation tests. The differing effects of teacher absenteeism on mathematics and language performance make sense, as students have many opportunities to practise their language skills outside the classroom, whereas mathematics instruction is mainly provided at school.

Indonesia has high rates of teacher absenteeism relative to other developing countries. In a survey of six developing countries conducted in 2003, Chaudhury et al. (2006) found that Indonesia had the third-highest rate of teacher absenteeism, of 19 per cent. Uganda and India had higher rates and Bangladesh, Ecuador and Peru had lower rates. Five years on, the rates for Indonesia had shown no sign of decreasing (Toyamah et al. 2009). Teacher absenteeism is clearly a pressing issue that must be addressed urgently.

Teacher qualifications

The Indonesian government has been aware of the need to improve the standard of teacher qualifications for several decades. In the 1980s, primary school teachers were required to have a two-year diploma of education, although this was sometimes waived for teachers working in remote areas due to teacher shortages. The requirement was increased to a four-year diploma of education under Law 14/2005 on Teachers and Lecturers. For secondary school teachers, a four-year teaching degree – equivalent to a bachelor's of education – is generally required.

Figure 8.6   *Share of teachers with a university degree and share of mathematics teachers who have majored in mathematics, Indonesia and comparison countries, 2007 (%)*

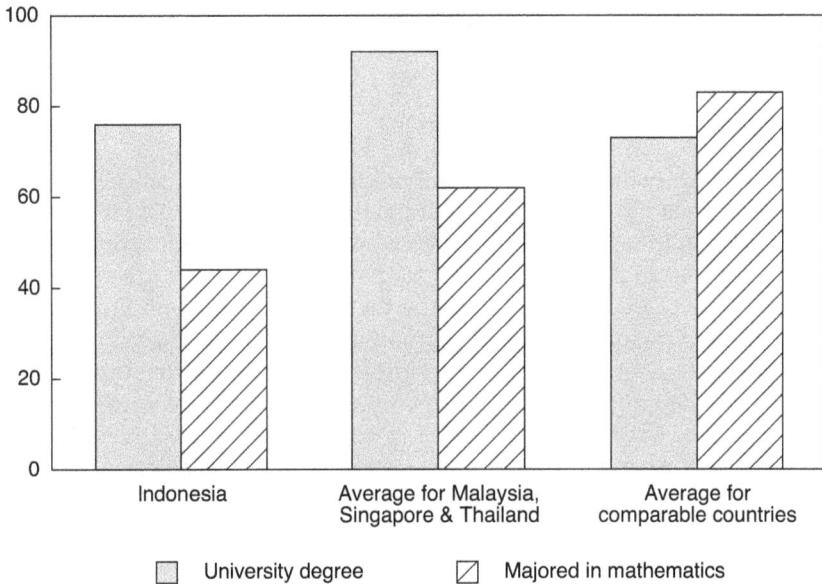

Source: Author's calculations based on Mullis et al. 2008.

Despite the focus on qualifications, very few studies have investigated the relationship between teacher qualifications and student performance in Indonesia. Suryadarma et al. (2006) examined the relationship at the primary level, but found no significant correlation between teachers' qualifications and students' performance on mathematics and dictation tests.

Figure 8.6 presents information collected by the TIMSS team on teacher qualifications in Indonesia and the two comparison groups of countries. The first measure of qualifications is the share of teachers with at least a university degree. On this measure, the level of qualifications in Indonesia is about the same as that in the group of countries with comparable economic and health performance, but significantly lower than that in the three neighbouring countries. The second measure is more specific. It compares the proportions of mathematics teachers who have majored in mathematics at university. Whereas only 44 per cent of mathematics teachers in Indonesia have majored in mathematics, 83 per cent of those in comparable countries and 62 per cent of those in neighbouring countries have done so.

Assuming that teacher qualifications matter, a comparison of the gap in qualifications and the gap in TIMSS scores between Indonesia and the peer and neighbouring countries indicates that having a university degree matters more than the actual choice of major.[6] Therefore, it may be the case that Indonesian schools simply need to attract more teachers with tertiary degrees.

Class size and teacher distribution

The student/teacher ratio, a commonly used measure of teacher availability, has been the focus of much of the research on school quality. Internationally, Indonesia has one of the lower student/teacher ratios. Figure 8.7 shows that in 2008, Indonesia had a student/teacher ratio at the secondary level of 12. This was similar to the ratios of Japan and France, and lower than those of Germany, Singapore and the United States.

Although theory predicts that a lower ratio is better for student performance, the empirical evidence is not as clear. While several international studies have found that small class sizes have a positive effect on student performance, others find no relationship between class size and performance, and a few even find a negative effect of small class size.[7] In Indonesia's case, Suryadarma et al. (2006) find that the ideal ratio to achieve optimal performance in mathematics at the primary level is 25 students per teacher.

Figure 8.8 shows that the average TIMSS score for schools with smaller class sizes is lower than the average score for those with larger class sizes. Schools with class sizes of 25–40 students appear to perform the best. However, when one takes into account the standard errors of the estimations, the difference in performance between these schools and those with 41 or more students is not statistically significant. In addition, given the large standard errors in the estimates for schools with small class sizes, a conservative estimate would make the performance of these schools quite similar to that of schools with larger class sizes. What is certain is that reducing class sizes would not necessarily improve the performance of Indonesian students, and might even be detrimental to performance.

---

6   This is not to imply that other differences between these countries do not matter for educational quality. This is only a partial analysis, without controlling for other differences.

7   Some studies, such as del Granado et al. (2007), make a distinction between the student/teacher ratio and the student/class ratio. In this chapter I make no such distinction and the terms are interchangeable. See Suryadarma et al. (2006: 405–8) for a short review of the literature on the effect of class size (and other factors) on student performance.

Figure 8.7   Number of students per teacher, selected countries, 2008

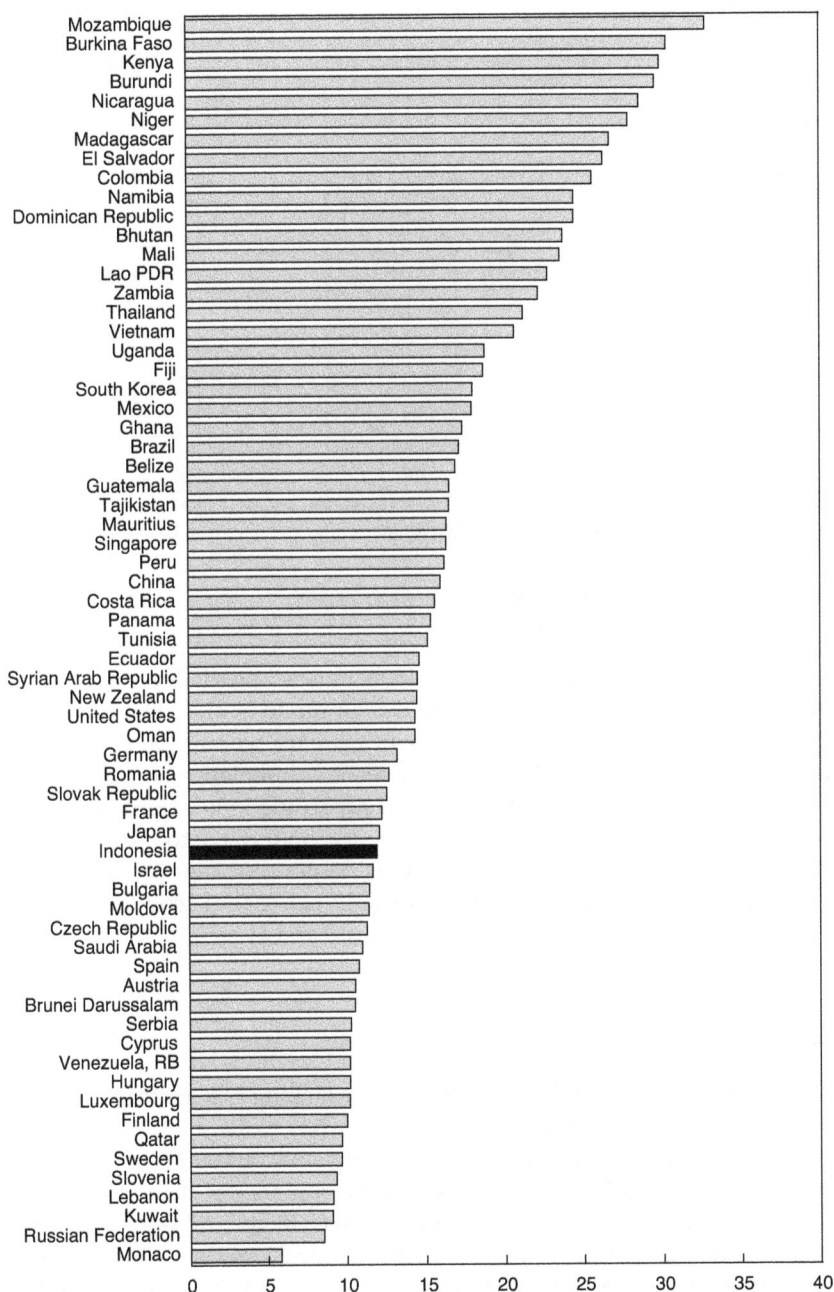

Source: Edstats, http://go.worldbank.org/47P3PLE940.

Figure 8.8   Correlation between score on mathematics component of TIMSS and class size, Indonesia, 2007

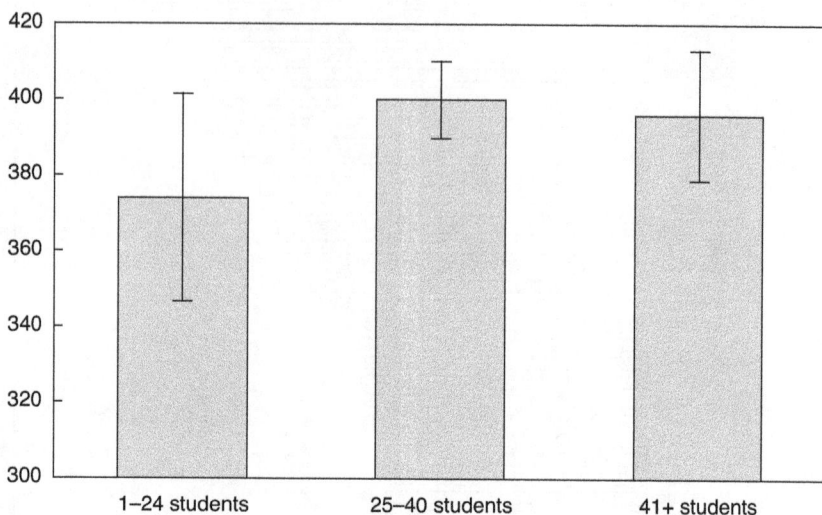

Source: Author's calculations based on Mullis et al. 2008.

The issue of the distribution of teachers is acknowledged to be a far more serous problem for Indonesia. Del Granado et al. (2007) have estimated that approximately 55 per cent of primary schools have too many teachers and 34 per cent too few. The teacher imbalance becomes more evident when schools are disaggregated according to location: urban, rural or remote. In urban areas, 68 per cent of schools have too many teachers and 21 per cent too few. In rural areas, 52 per cent have too many and 37 per cent too few. And in remote areas, 17 per cent of schools have too many teachers and 66 per cent too few. Rural and especially remote areas are clearly in dire need of teachers.

School facilities

It is generally accepted that schools that are lacking in teaching resources and facilities will produce students with lower skills. Figure 8.9 shows that while a more conducive school learning environment is only weakly correlated with Indonesian students' performance on the 2007 mathematics test, the availability of school resources in general is a strong predictor of good performance. Schools that have access to good resources have an average score of 458. In contrast, schools at the other end of the spectrum in terms of resources have an average score of just 380.

Figure 8.9   Correlation between TIMSS score and the availability of resources, and between score and teachers' perceptions of the school learning environment, Indonesia, 2007

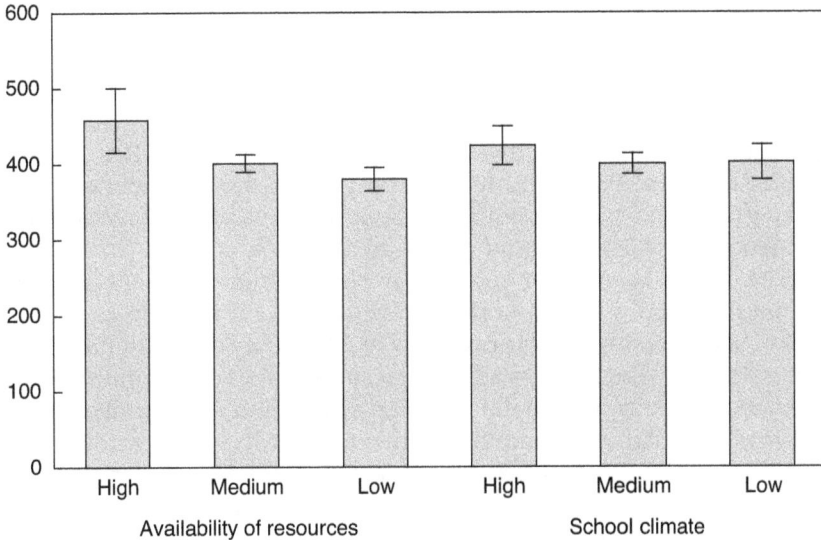

Source: Author's calculations based on Mullis et al. 2008.

Although this finding is not surprising, the main difficulty lies in determining exactly what types of resources are necessary for a school to function well and produce high-quality students. Given that virtually every school in Indonesia is already equipped with basic facilities such as chairs, desks and blackboards, one would have to investigate the importance of additional facilities beyond these basic facilities.

In a study of 110 primary schools situated across Indonesia, Suryadarma et al. (2006) examined the correlation between different types of facilities – school libraries, staffrooms, access to electricity, functioning toilets, maps, charts – and student performance in mathematics. They found that students at schools with at least one functioning toilet performed better on a mathematics test, although the effect was significant only for female students. Similarly, the World Bank (2001) has argued that girls in developing countries such as Bangladesh are more likely to attend school, and to do well at school, if toilet facilities are available.

Community participation

In its 2004 *World Development Report*, the World Bank (2003) argued that a bottom-up approach to service delivery, if designed properly, could be a valuable part of an overall plan for educational improvement. The improvement in learning occurred through two routes: an increase in community pressure on school management to improve student performance, and communities taking it on themselves to improve the quality of schooling by providing complementary services.

Analysts have come to differing conclusions about the efficacy of the bottom-up approach. In India, Banerjee et al. (2010) found that promoting community participation without a clear focus on the goals of the participation was not effective. In Mexico, however, Gertler, Patrinos and Rubio-Codina (2008) concluded that providing school committees with small grants and training improved their participation and reduced the incidence of grade failure and repetition of grades.

The official channel for community participation in school affairs in Indonesia is the school committee. Regulations on the role and structure of school committees became law in 2002. They establish the school committee's role as being to advise and support the school principal and teachers, to act as a mediator between school and community, and to improve parental and community involvement in school activities. In addition, a school committee can make recommendations pertaining to teaching programs, school budgets, performance benchmarks, teacher qualifications and school facilities.

To my knowledge, no study has been published on the effect of community participation on school quality in Indonesia. However, based on a survey of school committees in 2007, Pradhan et al. (2010) concluded that many of them remained weak and ineffective eight years after being established. The authors found examples of school committees that were under the full control of the school principal. As such, the committees had a closer relationship with school management than with parents and the community at large. Pradhan et al. found that only around half of the parents knew that a school committee even existed at the school their children were attending. Findings such as these have prompted the government to take action to promote the role of the school committee.

EFFORTS TO IMPROVE EDUCATIONAL QUALITY

In this section, I provide an overview of the efforts being made to improve the quality of schooling in Indonesia. The following list is by no means exhaustive, as I focus only on those initiatives that have a strong research methodology, that are carried out in cooperation with the national government or that directly address the concerns raised in the previous section.

Improving community participation

The Ministry of National Education, with assistance from the World Bank, undertook a randomised field experiment to strengthen school committees.[8] The experiment was implemented in six districts in Java between 2007 and 2009, and involved 520 rural public primary schools. It tested the effect on student learning outcomes of four interventions designed to strengthen school committees. These interventions were: (1) providing training to school committee members; (2) conducting elections of school committee members; (3) establishing linkages with other public institutions; and (4) giving school committees authority over a financial resource. The Ministry of Education/World Bank team designed these interventions during a series of field visits, taking into account lessons learned from previous projects. The ministry was particularly interested in interventions capable of being rolled out on a wider scale at relatively little cost.

Reporting the results, Pradhan et al. (2010) found the strongest positive effect for elections in combination with linkages, which increased scores in Indonesian language tests by 0.22 standard deviations, although there was no effect on mathematics.[9] The positive effects on learning were confirmed by the independent subjective assessments of teachers, who on average expressed higher opinions of their students' performance at the end of the survey period than they had at the start. There was also evidence of school committee elections increasing teacher hours by about 0.63 hours per day, although it appears that the intervention also increased teacher absence. These contradictory effects may explain the muted effect of elections on test scores. Instead, the effect of elections in combination with linkages seems to have occurred mainly through increased supervision of the principal and greater parental support for learning. The study also found that elections alone, while difficult to implement, raised the activity level of the school committee and increased the respect for the committee among teachers. Training was the most costly intervention but it had the smallest impact if implemented alone. Grants to school committees helped raise the level of attendance

---

8 In a randomised field experiment, researchers separate participants into two (or more) groups, a 'treatment' group that receives a specific development intervention or support (such as activities to improve student performance) and a control group that does not receive such support. The researchers then compare indicators of development achievement (such as test scores) for the two groups, controlling for individual, household and community differences between the groups.

9 An effect of 0.3 standard deviations or higher is generally considered large.

of parents at meetings, thus facilitating other interventions, but did not yield any results by itself.

Some of these interventions have already influenced national policy. A recent question and answer book on school committees issued by the Ministry of National Education states that all school committees should be democratically elected, using the election process tested during the study. The experiment suggests that, in addition, newly elected school committees should receive training, and that they should be guided through their initial meetings with village leaders. The study suggests this would have high payoffs in terms of students' learning outcomes.

Teacher certification program

The government introduced a teacher certification program in 2006 as one way to improve the overall level of teacher qualifications. The program is being implemented through portfolio assessment, where teachers who fail the assessment are required to undertake remedial training. Those who pass the assessment or who have finished the remedial course receive a monthly allowance equivalent to their monthly salary. The additional allowance can be considered a way of supplementing teachers' rather low salaries and attracting more individuals to the profession.

Hastuti et al. (2009) evaluated the impact of the certification program on the quality of education in six districts. They found some indications of deception in the preparation of portfolios, such as falsification and plagiarism, and a high degree of subjectivity in the assessment of portfolios. Virtually no teacher failed to receive the certification, although a large number were required to take a remedial course. The authors uncovered problems with the payment of the supplementary allowance for certified teachers. At the end of the evaluation in June 2008, only a small proportion of certified teachers had received the allowance, and even then they had received payment only for the first quarter of the school year.

Given the issues in the implementation of the program and the fact that virtually every teacher can expect to be certified, it is unclear whether the aim of the program is to improve teaching quality or just to increase teachers' incomes. Hastuti et al. (2009) did not find any strong evidence that the program had improved educational quality, although the program may have acted as a 'magnet' to attract better-qualified individuals into the teaching profession.

Remote area allowances

Indonesian policy makers are aware of the acute shortage of teachers in remote areas. This is a more pressing problem than the average student/teacher ratio, which is already lower than in many more developed countries. Policy makers are therefore focusing their attention on addressing the lack of balance in teacher distribution.

The government's remote area allowance for teachers constitutes a direct effort to overcome the shortage. It was envisaged that by providing an allowance for teachers working in remote areas, more teachers would be willing to teach in those areas. The program began in the 2007/2008 school year, with 20,000 primary school teachers in 199 districts selected to receive the remote area allowance (SMERU Research Institute 2009: 7). The schools were chosen by the Ministry of National Education from lists submitted by the district education offices. The selection of schools was based on two criteria: distance from the district capital and the availability of electricity in the village. All teachers in the selected schools were to receive the allowance if they had worked at the school for at least two years and were teaching full-time.

When evaluating the program, Toyamah et al. (2009) discovered that the allowance was actually subject to a quota, implying that not all eligible teachers would receive the allowance. The procedures and criteria for determining which teachers would receive the allowance were unclear, leading to friction between those who did and did not receive it. As with the teacher certification program, payment of the allowance proved to be unreliable. There was no clear timetable for distribution of the allowance and not every teacher received the same amount. Toyamah et al. found no effect of the allowance on rates of teacher absenteeism.

Other programs

I will briefly mention here two other programs that show promise for educational outcomes in Indonesia. The first is a program to provide performance pay for teachers, which essentially links teacher pay to how students perform on tests. Several studies have considered whether direct incentives for teachers lead to greater teacher effort and improved learning outcomes. Duflo, Hanna and Ryan (2007) found that, in a region in India, teacher absenteeism fell from 42 per cent to 21 per cent, and learning improved by 0.17 standard deviations, when teachers were asked to take daily, dated, pictures of themselves and their students in the classroom and were paid an incentive based on this recorded presence. Muralidharan and Sundararaman (2009) found that when direct financial rewards for teachers were linked to improved learning outcomes for students in Uttar Pradesh, India, the test scores of the students increased by around 0.17 standard deviations. It remains to be seen if such a program would have a similar effect in Indonesia.

The second program is a teacher training program slated to begin soon, with the first cohort to have around 50,000 participants. Teachers will be required to complete the program, to be delivered by accredited universities, in order to be certified. At this stage no further information on the program is publicly available.

CONCLUSION

This chapter has provided an overview of the current quality of education in Indonesia, the challenges that must be overcome to achieve higher quality, and the efforts that are being made to improve the state of education in Indonesia.

Using results from the mathematics component of the 2007 TIMSS, I find that the quality of education is poorer in Indonesia than in a group of neighbouring countries, and in a group of countries with similar economic and health conditions to Indonesia. While the gap with the latter group of countries is relatively narrow, the gap with the neighbouring countries is substantial and concerning. Indonesia is currently engaged in more open trade with these countries, so having a highly skilled workforce is a necessity. Therefore, policy makers must take immediate steps to improve the quality of education in Indonesia.

Policy makers face many challenges as they attempt to improve the quality of schooling in Indonesia. In this chapter, I have discussed problems related to course content and instructional hours, teacher absenteeism, teacher qualifications, the distribution of teachers across the country, basic facilities and community participation. A number of other issues are not discussed but are nevertheless important. They include corruption in the education sector and the gender imbalance in test scores favouring girls. Because all of these issues are important, it is admittedly difficult to determine which challenge should be addressed first.

I end this chapter by singling out three programs that are currently being rolled out in Indonesia: the program to improve community participation, the teacher certification program and the program to provide remote area allowances. All face difficulties and have had only limited success so far. Nevertheless, if the problems can be overcome, these programs are likely to make a real difference to the quality of education in Indonesian schools. Meanwhile, the lessons learned during the implementation of these programs are invaluable as policy makers and researchers continue to test ways to improve the quality of the education system.

In closing, it is worth noting the huge challenge posed by the large-scale decentralisation of education to the local level of government in 2001. The negative aspects of the decentralisation have indeed materialised – such as a lack of coordination between central and local education offices and an uneasy relationship between the Ministry of National

Education and local authorities as each stakeholder grapples with the new, post-decentralisation environment. Meanwhile, only a few positive aspects of decentralisation have materialised. They include free basic education in a number of districts and generous pay rises for teachers. The financial sustainability of these well-meaning policies has yet to be proven. In addition, no serious research has been undertaken to properly measure the effect of such policies on both the educational attainment and skills of school leavers.

REFERENCES

Banerjee, A., R. Banerji, E. Duflo, R. Glennerster and S. Khemani (2010) 'Pitfalls of participatory programs: evidence from a randomized evaluation in education in India', *American Economic Journal: Economic Policy*, 2(1): 1–30.

Barro, R.J. (1999) 'Determinants of democracy', *Journal of Political Economy*, 107(6): S158–83.

Behrman, J.R. and N. Birdsall (1983) 'The quality of schooling: quantity alone is misleading', *American Economic Review*, 73(5): 928–46.

Chaudhury, N., J. Hammer, M. Kremer, K. Muralidharan and F.H. Rogers (2006) 'Missing in action: teacher and health worker absence in developing countries', *Journal of Economic Perspectives*, 20(1): 91–116.

Dee, T. (2004) 'Are there civic returns to education?' *Journal of Public Economics*, 88(9–10): 1,697–720.

del Granado, F.J.A., W. Fengler, A. Ragatz and E. Yavuz (2007) 'Investing in Indonesia's education: allocation, equity, and efficiency of public expenditures', Policy Research Working Paper No. 4329, World Bank, Washington DC, August.

Duflo, E., R. Hanna and S. Ryan (2007) 'Monitoring works: getting teachers to come to school', unpublished paper, Massachusetts Institute of Technology, Cambridge MA.

Gertler, P., H. Patrinos and M. Rubio-Codina (2008) 'Empowering parents to improve education: evidence from rural Mexico', Policy Research Working Paper No. 3935, World Bank, Washington DC, May.

Hanushek, E.A. and L. Woessmann (2008) 'The role of cognitive skills in economic development', *Journal of Economic Literature*, 46(3): 607–68.

Hastuti, B.S., Akhmadi, M. Syukri, U. Sabainingrum and Ruhmaniyati (2009) 'Implementation of the 2007 certification program for practicing teachers: a case study of Jambi, West Java, and West Kalimantan provinces', research report, SMERU Research Institute, Jakarta, June.

Jamison, E., D. Jamison and E. Hanushek (2007) 'The effects of education quality on income growth and mortality decline', *Economics of Education Review*, 26(6): 771–88.

Mullis, I.V.S., M.O. Martin, P. Foy, J.F. Olson, C. Preuschoff, E. Erberber, A. Arora and J. Galia (2008) *TIMSS 2007 International Mathematics Report*, Lynch School of Education, Chestnut Hill MA.

Muralidharan, K. and V. Sundararaman (2009) 'Teacher performance pay: experimental evidence from India', NBER Working Paper No. 15323, National Bureau of Economic Research, Cambridge MA, September.

Pradhan, M., D. Suryadarma, A. Beatty, M. Wong, A. Gaduh and R.P. Artha (2010) 'Improving educational quality through enhancing community participation: results from a randomized field experiment in Indonesia', unpublished paper, Australian National University, Canberra.

SMERU Research Institute (2009) 'Teacher certification and remote area allowance programs: can they increase the quality of education?', SMERU Newsletter No. 28, SMERU Research Institute, Jakarta, January–April.

Suryadarma, D. (2010) 'The merits of ability in developing and developed countries', Discussion Paper No. 645, Centre for Economic Policy Research, Australian National University, Canberra, October.

Suryadarma, D., A. Suryahadi, S. Sumarto and F.H. Rogers (2006) 'Improving student performance in public primary schools in developing countries: evidence from Indonesia', *Education Economics*, 14(4): 401–29.

Suryahadi, A., D. Suryadarma and S. Sumarto (2009) 'The effects of location and sectoral components of economic growth on poverty: evidence from Indonesia', *Journal of Development Economics*, 89(1): 109–17.

Toyamah, N., B. Sulaksono, M. Rosfadhila, S. Devina, S. Arif, S.A. Hutagalung, E. Pakpahan and A. Yusrina (2009) *Survei Baseline Kehadiran Guru dan Bantuan Kesejahteraan untuk Guru di Daerah Terpencil* [Teacher Attendance and Remote Allowance Baseline Survey], SMERU Research Institute, Jakarta.

World Bank (2001) *Engendering Development through Gender Equality in Rights, Resources, and Voice*, World Bank, Washington DC.

World Bank (2003) *World Development Report 2004: Making Services Work for Poor People*, World Bank and Oxford University Press, New York NY.

9 EDUCATIONAL CHALLENGES WITH SPECIAL REFERENCE TO ISLAMIC SCHOOLING

Risti Permani

Indonesia has achieved impressive progress in certain human development outcomes. In 2007, the gross primary enrolment rate was above 90 per cent and junior secondary enrolment, at 75 per cent, had more than quadrupled since the early 1970s (Permani 2009). Yet income inequality remains a problem. Despite the rapid economic growth of the 1990s, between 1960 and 1996 the Gini coefficient measuring income inequality remained relatively constant, in the range 0.32–0.38 (Asra 2000). This persistent income imbalance has had serious effects for children born into severe poverty. In the absence of a mechanism to allow poor students to complete their education or to give parents access to credit to finance their children's education, some Indonesian children will remain trapped in poverty. Inequality in education breeds future income inequality. To avoid this, special attention should be paid to ensuring that children from low-income families get a good education.

This chapter is particularly interested in the Islamic education sector, for several reasons. First, despite its alleged links with terrorism, the Islamic sector is of great importance within the Indonesian education system. Although enrolments in both public and private Islamic schools (*madrasah*) are much smaller than enrolments in other types of schools (particularly the public non-religious schools), the sector nevertheless provides education to over 6 million students. Second, *madrasah* have a comparative advantage in reaching subgroups at risk of dropping out of school, such as school-aged married females and female students from poor families (ADB 2006). Third, in some rural areas the *madrasah* are the only schools that are able to deliver basic education to students from low-income families.

Unfortunately, Indonesia's Islamic schools have a reputation for being second-class schools. Given that most of their students come from low-income families, government policies to improve the quality of the education provided by the *madrasah* – that is, targeting the lower end of the population distribution – are likely to be an effective way of reducing income inequality. Such policies are likely to be especially effective for rural and female students.

Finding an appropriate method to deal with the reputational and other problems of *madrasah* requires an understanding of the underlying characteristics of the schools themselves, and of their students and the families from which they come. To complement policy reviews, this chapter uses data from the 2007 Indonesia Family Life Survey to find out whether parents' educational background, parents' religiosity, student's ability and student's prior attendance at a primary *madrasah* are related to the decision to attend a junior secondary *madrasah*.[1] In addition to revealing how *madrasah* students are placed relative to students from other types of schools, the results should provide a basis for making recommendations on policy options to deal with the problems faced by the *madrasah*.

More specifically, this chapter attempts to explain why *madrasah* students perform less well academically than students from other types of schools and to review the effectiveness of current government policies. The reasons for poor academic performance are manifold. Nevertheless, a few common features can be identified as key explanatory variables. Among the most prominent are school finances, school choice and student sorting, curriculum content and teacher quality. Each is discussed in turn below.

SCHOOL FINANCES

Madrasah schooling provides an alternative to secular public schooling for parents who want their children to obtain a religious education. The *madrasah* follow a curriculum set by the Ministry of Religious Affairs, while other schools essentially follow the curriculum of the Ministry

---

1   The junior secondary level has been chosen with current government policy in mind. With at least 90 per cent of students aged 6–12 enrolled in primary school, providing access to primary school education is no longer the main development challenge facing Indonesia. Although it remains important to get the other 10 per cent enrolled in primary school, the government is now focusing on junior secondary education as part of its initiative to promote nine years of basic education.

of National Education. The administrative difference between Islamic and non-Islamic schools is a crucial point in explaining the academic and other differences between *madrasah* and the mainstream schooling system.

Following the passage of the decentralisation laws in 1999, responsibility for the design and development of local curricula to supplement the national curriculum was delivered to the local government level. This did not affect the *madrasah*, however, because 'religion' was one of the areas to be retained by the central government under the decentralisation legislation.

The division of administrative responsibilities for the different types of schools has implications for school financing. It is widely accepted that the *madrasah* need more funding if they are to improve their performance. There has not been any quantitative research on the impact of changes in school finances on the academic performance of students attending *madrasah* in Indonesia, but the literature for other countries suggests that there is a significant link between school finance reform and student performance. In the United States, for example, equalisation of spending – where state governments supplement the amount of support available to poorer districts – led to a narrowing of test scores across groups of students with differing family backgrounds (Card and Payne 2002).

Although roughly 90 per cent of *madrasah* are privately operated, these schools still rely heavily on government support. The main form of support for all schools is the School Operational Assistance scheme (Bantuan Operasional Sekolah, or BOS). It was one of the programs introduced to offset the impact on the poor of a reduction in fuel subsidies in 2005. Under the scheme, schools receive block grants allocated on a per student basis in return for reducing or eliminating school fees. The funds can be used to cover the operational expenses of schools and to assist poor students; they cannot be invested in interest-earning investments or be used to construct new buildings. Parker and Raihani (2009: 7) find that BOS funds are sufficient to cover the basic operating costs of *madrasah*. However, the scheme has attracted some criticism. A team of researchers from the SMERU Research Institute reported a number of problems: a failure to communicate the goals and operational aspects of the program to school communities; an overly dominant role of the school principal in deciding where the money was spent; a lack of clarity about the stipulation concerning interest; the complexity of the procedures for paying tax on BOS funds; and the difficulty of preparing financial accountability reports (Suharyo et al. 2006).

There are also claims that the BOS scheme discriminates against Islamic schools. Given that the program is jointly administered by the

Ministry of National Education and the Ministry of Religious Affairs, *madrasah* should enjoy the same access to funding as other types of schools. However, the practice of allocating funding according to the number of students disadvantages some Islamic schools; the number of students at traditional Islamic boarding schools (*pesantren salafiyah*),[2] for example, fluctuates over time, making them difficult to fund on a per student basis (Suharyo et al. 2006). Islamic schools face the additional complication of having to prepare financial reports for both the Ministry of Religious Affairs and the regional educational offices (*kantor dinas pendidikan*). This leads to an inefficient use of resources. Moreover, it appears that the regional religious offices were not given the funding or the opportunity to meet with *madrasah* management and explain the BOS program before it started, leading to less than optimal access to and use of BOS funding (Suharyo et al. 2006).

In addition to these problems with the BOS program, the position of *madrasah* under the Ministry of Religious Affairs rather than the Ministry of National Education makes it difficult for them to access other sources of educational funding, particularly at the district government level. As noted earlier, under Indonesia's decentralisation legislation, religion is a central government responsibility. Therefore, the central government cannot require local governments to allocate funding for *madrasah* in their regional budgets. On 21 September 2005, the Ministry of Home Affairs issued a circular (903/2429/SJ) formally prohibiting local governments from funding 'vertical' institutions – that is, those under the jurisdiction of the central government, including *madrasah* and other types of Islamic educational institutions. In response to an outcry from the *madrasah* community, in 2006 the ministry issued a second circular (903/210/BAKD) exempting *madrasah* from the new rule under certain conditions. However, the regulation's complex administrative requirements discourage district governments from even attempting to comply with those conditions. The decentralisation legislation also prevents local governments from using the discretionary grants they receive from the Special Allocation Fund (Dana Alokasi Khusus, or DAK) to fund *madrasah*.[3]

---

2 A *pesantren salafiyah* teaches only the traditional Islamic texts rather than any formal curriculum.

3 See Law 33/2004 on Fiscal Balance between the Central Government and Regions, article 39. The central government makes two types of grant available to regional governments: specific purpose grants under the DAK to fund projects that are considered national priorities, and general purpose grants under the General Allocation Fund (Dana Alokasi Umum, or DAU) to fund general expenditure. The DAU provides the bulk of the revenue for most regional governments. The actual size of the transfers is set according to a range of criteria, including population size, land area, human development index

In short, whatever assistance is provided to schools by local governments, the level of funding provided to *madrasah* seems to be lower than that provided to general schools. Worse, the disadvantage experienced by the *madrasah* is not just a matter of funding; it is also a matter of professional status, morale and support for teachers (Parker and Raihani 2009). This situation is particularly serious given that the *madrasah* already have poorer academic performance than regular schools.

SCHOOL CHOICE AND STUDENT SORTING

In addition to inadequate financing, the poor academic performance of *madrasah* may be due to 'school sorting', where the academically more able students tend to go to the better schools. School sorting may reflect ability, neighbourhood or other types of sorting, or be the result of decisions made by parents about the type of school they want their children to attend. Educational choice as an investment decision can be seen where current income opportunities are given up in exchange for better income prospects in the future. If educational choice means that a higher degree of sorting by ability and peer effects matters, then the distribution of educational benefits is likely to be quite unequal (Epple and Romano 1998).[4] This could be the case with the Indonesian Islamic education sector, with better students choosing to go to public non-religious schools.

Despite the widely accepted view that education plays a positive role in economic growth, it is not clear that a religious education provides value added for the formation of human capital. Indeed, it is often argued that it plays only a minor role in human capital development, because the system of religious education is narrowly restricted to relaying religious doctrines and ethics (Zborovskii and Kostina 2004). Chiswick (2005: 1) defines the product of a religious education – namely religious human capital – as the 'knowledge, skill, experience and memories that enhance productivity in religious activities but have no effect on the productivity of resources allocated to other types of output'. The perception that a religious education does not enhance the productivity of non-religious resources leads parents to question the benefits of sending their children to religious schools. This in turn raises the issue of whether such

---

score, fiscal capacity and fiscal need (primarily calculated on the basis of civil service salaries).

4   According to Hoxby (2000), however, school choice may also lead to increased competition between schools and therefore better performance. But Cullen, Jacob and Levitt (2005) argue that the precise impact of school choice depends on which students take advantage of the choice, the types of options that these students have, and what happens to the students who are left behind.

decisions create school sorting, where parents of academically more able children send their children to non-religious schools.

Based on observation in the field, I am able to suggest at least two reasons why parents may choose not to send their children to *madrasah*. First, Islamic schools generally have poorer facilities than other types of schools. The opposite is the case in most Western countries, where privately run religious schools tend to offer better facilities than public schools. Based on national statistics published by the Ministry of Religious Affairs, only half of the 125,000 classrooms in primary *madrasah* (*madrasah ibtidaiyah*) were in good condition in the 2006/7 academic year. Public *madrasah* had better classrooms than the privately operated ones, with 67 per cent of all classrooms in good condition. The percentages for junior secondary *madrasah* (*madrasah tsanawiyah*) and senior secondary *madrasah* (*madrasah aliyah*) were 67 per cent and 74 per cent respectively.

Second, parents are not persuaded that their children will get an equivalent, or better, academic education at a *madrasah* than they would at a regular school. Again, this is in contrast to the situation in Western countries, where middle and upper-income families expect their children not only to receive a better education at private religious schools, but to receive a few extra hours of religious study each week on top of their regular subjects, to 'educate the mind' as well as 'nourish the spirit'. *Madrasah* devote much more than a few hours each week to religious studies; religious courses occupy at least 30 per cent of school hours. Compared with other types of schools, this implies a significant reduction in the hours spent on other subjects such as mathematics and science. As Hanushek and Kimko (2000) point out, the latter subjects are much more economically relevant to the future careers of students.

The above discussion suggests that parents who send their children to *madrasah* may not be academic performance maximisers, but rather education cost minimisers. Figure 9.1 suggests that, on average, *madrasah* students pay significantly less than non-*madrasah* students for school-related costs such as registration and tuition fees, books and uniforms. They also pay less for transport and accommodation.

The low cost of *madrasah* education is worrying. Recall that *madrasah* receive less financial support from the government than regular schools. To provide schooling that is equivalent in quality to that in regular schools, the Islamic sector should actually receive higher levels of financial contributions from parents. But the data suggest the opposite, indicating that the low cost of *madrasah* education comes at the expense of quality.

Drawing on previous studies, in this chapter I derive a simple econometric model to predict the determinants of a student attending a *madrasah*. Bedi and Garg (2000) found that gender, religion and parents' educational background were significant determinants of school

Figure 9.1   Average cost of education at madrasah and non-madrasah junior secondary schools, 2007 (Rp thousand)[a]

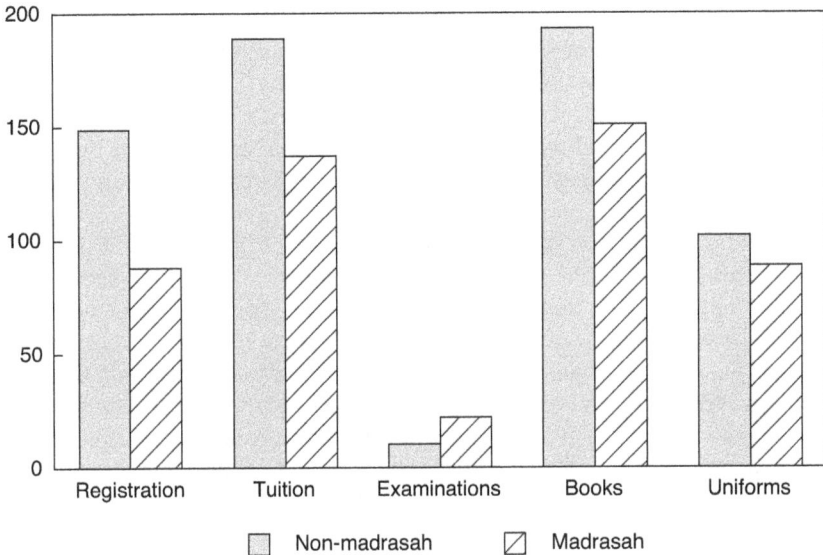

a   The data cover students who were at school during the survey year and enrolled in a junior secondary school between 2003/4 and 2006/7.

Source: Author's calculations based on Indonesia Family Life Survey, 2007.

choice. In particular, the probability that a child would attend a public school increased as the father's level of education increased. However, it is unclear what we can infer from this study about the probability of a child attending an Islamic school, because the authors classified public *madrasah* as public schools and put private *madrasah* into a separate category. In addition, they did not test for the degree of parental religiosity as a determinant of school choice, which turns out to be an important variable in the present estimation. A study using data from schools in New York also suggests that religious considerations are a very important factor in the choice of school: 62 per cent of private school parents but only 30 per cent of public school parents cited this as a factor (Lankford and Wyckoff 1992).

Parents can be expected to choose the school that provides the highest lifetime indirect utility for the child. This utility may reflect both economic and non-economic motives, which are themselves a function of student, household and school characteristics. Table A9.1 in the appendix presents data from the 2007 Indonesia Family Life Survey that shed light on the characteristics of *madrasah* versus non-*madrasah* students, households and schools. It shows that students enrolled in junior secondary *madrasah* had performed less well at primary school than students who had attended other schools, as indicated by lower scores on the national mathematics and science tests and higher rates of grade repetition. Nearly 30 per cent of the *madrasah* students in the sample had attended a primary *madrasah* before proceeding to junior secondary *madrasah*. The junior secondary *madrasah* students paid only half the registration fees paid by non-*madrasah* students. The data suggest that *madrasah* provide a poorer quality of education than non-*madrasah*, as indicated by lower pass rates on national examinations and lower educational qualifications among principals.

Based on data from the 2007 Indonesia Family Life Survey, this study uses a probit model to estimate the determinants of junior secondary *madrasah* attendance. Respondents are limited to those students enrolled in junior secondary school between 2003/4 and 2006/7. Parents make one of two choices: to send their children to a *madrasah* or to send them to a non-*madrasah*. The study focuses on three parental characteristics – educational background, economic background and religiosity – that reflect both the economic and non-economic motives for choosing a *madrasah*. To proxy household economic background, the study uses mother's and father's hourly earnings and the area of land owned by the family.[5]

School attributes and child characteristics may also affect school choice. Better schools may attract better students, reflecting school sorting. Indeed, this is a key aspect of the empirical analysis. The probit model includes only school variables that parents can predict easily before making a choice about schooling, such as the principal's background, the ratio of permanent to casual teachers, the existence of school committees, textbooks and facilities, and the level of financial assistance received by the school.

The student characteristics of interest are the type of primary school the student attended before going to junior secondary school and the student's level of accomplishment at primary school. The probit model also includes cost variables: the registration and tuition fees paid by the student in the previous academic year. Given the small range of years of enrolment at junior secondary school (2003/4–2006/7), information based on 2007 data should give a good prediction of the actual costs of registration in the respondents' year of enrolment.[6] Of a long list of vari-

---

5 I did not look closely at access to credit because most households in Indonesia face imperfect credit markets. Without a well-functioning credit market, it can be assumed that parents' decisions about schooling will be based on the current economic circumstances of the household (Glewwe and Jacoby 1994).

6 Table A9.2 includes subdistrict (*kecamatan*) fixed effects to control for any unobservable variation across subdistricts that may affect school choice.

ables included in the estimation, Table A9.2 displays only the significant determinants of *madrasah* attendance (see appendix).

Overall, the probit estimates suggest that a mother's level of religiosity, a student's prior attendance at a primary *madrasah* and disruption to a student's primary education (whether the student had ever left and then re-entered primary school) are the main determinants of a student attending a junior secondary *madrasah*.[7] Looking at some of the details, first, attending a primary *madrasah* increases the probability of a student attending a junior secondary *madrasah* by over 80 per cent. This may imply that students who had attended a primary *madrasah* were satisfied with their learning experience and preferred to continue to study at a *madrasah*. Alternatively, it might mean that they did not have the confidence to study at a (more demanding) non-*madrasah* school.

Second, repeating a grade at primary school was associated with a roughly 20 per cent increase in the probability of a student attending a junior secondary *madrasah*. This does seem to confirm the picture of *madrasah* being second-class schools for students who are not clever enough to go to public schools. However, no evidence was found that national examination scores at the primary level or school costs were significantly associated with *madrasah* attendance.

Third, having a more religious mother increased the probability of a child attending a *madrasah*, but there was no clear pattern for the effect of parental educational background on *madrasah* attendance. Similarly, household variables such as land ownership, hourly earnings and whether the household lived in an urban area were not significant.

Finally, the educational background of principals (whether a principal had completed postgraduate study), the number of years at the school as a principal and whether the school had access to electricity were significant. The first and second characteristics reflect the lower average level of education of *madrasah* principals and their longer average years of experience. More non-*madrasah* than *madrasah* schools had access to electricity, indicating a difference in the standard of facilities.

CURRICULUM CONTENT

As noted earlier, *madrasah* are required to devote 30 per cent of school hours to teaching religious courses. The time dedicated to religious subjects comes at the expense of hours given to regular subjects, making it

---

7 See Suryadarma, Suryahadi and Sumarto (2006) and Suryadarma (2009) regarding the probability of a student continuing to the secondary level. These studies point to a similar direction in parental choice and student sorting.

difficult for *madrasah* to compete with other types of schools in terms of the academic attainment and likely future earnings of students.

The 30 per cent requirement is based on a regulation originally introduced in the mid-1970s but implemented only in the late 1980s under Law 2/1989 on the National Education System. Analysing the impact of the requirement on the academic performance and future earnings of students requires us to consider two issues: first, whether *madrasah* students generally perform better or worse than students from other types of schools; and second, whether students attending *madrasah* before the change perform better or worse than students after the change, controlling for other factors.

Two influential studies shed light on the first issue, the first by Newhouse and Beegle (2006) and the second by Bedi and Garg (2000). Using data from three waves of the Indonesia Family Life Survey (1993, 1997 and 2000), Newhouse and Beegle concluded that students in public schools and non-Islamic private religious schools performed better academically than students in *madrasah* and private secular schools. Bedi and Garg found that the graduates of Islamic schools generally earned less than the graduates of public schools and non-Islamic private religious schools. Taken together, these findings suggest that Islamic schools are unable to compete with public schools and non-Islamic private religious schools in the areas of academic attainment and future earnings of students.

The second issue can be approached by examining the performance of *madrasah* graduates before and after the 30 per cent requirement was introduced in 1989. Using data from the 2000 Indonesia Family Life Survey, Permani (2010) found that, 11 years after the change, the educational outcomes and individual earnings of *madrasah* graduates remained much the same. She concluded that the reform had, however, contributed to the promotion of nine years of basic education in rural areas, reflected in an increase in the probability of rural students in primary and junior secondary *madrasah* completing their education. This was evident only one year after the reform, but a more significant increase was obvious by 1993 (five years after the reform).

The above results suggest that a reduction in the number of hours devoted to religious studies would not necessarily lead to an improvement in the academic and earnings performance of *madrasah* graduates. Neither can parents expect major changes in the *madrasah* curriculum as a result of the decentralisation of education, even though local governments now have more authority to design curricula.[8]

---

8 In 1994, the national Curriculum Development Centre transferred authority for 20 per cent of curriculum design and development to the provinces,

One solution to deal with the overcrowded *madrasah* curriculum would be to extend schooling hours to afford additional time for non-religious subjects. A *madrasah* principal interviewed by the author during fieldwork in early 2007 suggested that the only way to achieve this would be to introduce a boarding system for students, so that hours of study could be more tightly controlled. Such a system is already working well at As-salaam Pesantren, a junior secondary boarding school in Central Java. Students at the school are able to choose from over 40 subjects. In addition to its extensive curriculum, the school has gained a reputation for the quality of its courses, its good facilities and its highly qualified teachers. Unfortunately, this option does not come cheaply. In 2007, new students were required to pay over Rp 6 million in one-off entrance fees (*dana pangkal*). In addition, they would have had to pay for accommodation and many other items such as textbooks, uniforms, medical coverage and the use of computer laboratories.

TEACHER QUALITY

Principals and teachers are an important resource. Based on a study of six *madrasah* – four in West Sumatra and two in Yogyakarta – Parker and Raihani (2009) concluded that principals and teachers played a central role in school governance, even though parents, community leaders, supervisors and, in some cases, foundations were supposed to be involved as well. They singled out three leadership qualities possessed by the successful *madrasah* principals: they were visionary, democratic and able to lead by example. The authors found that parental and community participation in school decision making was generally low. This is not surprising considering the generally low level of academic attainment of the *madrasah* parent body. Only 50 per cent of such parents have completed at least junior secondary school (Table 9.1).

Despite their important role in promoting scholarship, the welfare of teachers has not received adequate attention from the Indonesian government. Teachers have long been revered as 'unsung heroes' (*pahlawan tanpa tanda jasa*) because they dedicate their life to educating the younger generation without expectation of generous monetary reward. This has

---

to allow them to incorporate subjects that were relevant to local conditions (Yeom, Acedo and Utomo 2002: 61–2). However, this did not much affect the delivery of religious subjects, which were part of the national curriculum. In the post-1999 decentralisation period as well, there was no significant change in the delivery of religious subjects.

Table 9.1   National statistics for madrasah, academic years 2003/4–2006/7

Category	2003/4	2004/5	2005/6	2006/7
Number of *madrasah*				
Primary	23,164	23,517	22,610	22,189
Junior secondary	11,706	12,054	12,498	12,619
Senior secondary	4,439	4,687	4,918	5,043
Gross enrolment ratio				
Primary	11.0	12.1	10.9	10.8
Junior secondary	14.3	15.9	15.8	16.3
Senior secondary	5.2	5.7	5.7	6.0
Share of private *madrasah* (%)				
Primary	93.6	93.4	93.1	92.9
Junior secondary	89.4	89.5	89.9	90.0
Senior secondary	87.0	86.5	86.9	87.2
Number of students				
Primary	3,124,153	3,152,665	2,996,375	2,957,900
Junior secondary	2,081,576	2,129,564	2,221,959	2,299,390
Senior secondary	726,893	744,736	777,627	817,920
Parents' educational attainment (%)				
Parent of primary student				
No schooling	6.67	7.34	7.36	8.81
Primary education	45.64	43.80	42.58	38.32
Junior secondary education	24.55	24.61	24.29	23.97
Senior secondary education	18.91	19.70	20.95	23.04
Tertiary education	4.23	4.55	4.82	5.86
Parent of junior secondary student				
No schooling	7.75	7.72	7.54	8.29
Primary education	41.62	41.44	39.76	38.65
Junior secondary education	24.98	25.05	26.22	26.05
Senior secondary education	19.90	19.89	20.54	20.97
Tertiary education	5.75	5.90	5.94	6.04
Parent of senior secondary student				
No schooling	6.05	6.14	6.68	8.86
Primary education	32.74	32.03	30.50	28.65
Junior secondary education	26.60	26.20	26.87	25.30
Senior secondary education	25.88	26.43	26.50	27.44
Tertiary education	8.73	9.20	9.45	9.75
Share of income from government (%)				
Primary	62.4	62.4	63.0	58.6
Junior secondary	51.5	51.3	53.1	56.3
Senior secondary	55.4	55.5	53.3	51.7

Source: Ministry of Religious Affairs (2004, 2005, 2006, 2007).

changed somewhat in the post-Suharto era, however, with teachers now demanding higher salaries and better working conditions.[9]

Madrasah teachers compare poorly with non-*madrasah* teachers on a number of indicators: they are less well qualified; they are more likely to be employed on a casual basis; and they earn less. However, concern over the limited capacity of primary *madrasah* teachers in particular is actually more about the quality of teaching than the number of teachers. As Table 9.2 indicates, the student/teacher ratio in *madrasah* is quite low: there are about 15 students per teacher at the primary level and only eight per teacher by the time students reach senior secondary level. Class size as indicated by the student/classroom ratio is 24 students per classroom at the primary level, 31 at the junior secondary level and 29 at the senior secondary level. But if one takes the quality of the classrooms into account (because many poor-quality classrooms are not in use), the ratio increases to 46–47 students per classroom at the primary and junior secondary levels and 39 per classroom at the senior secondary level. The explanation for these statistics is that the *madrasah* have large numbers of casual teachers who work short hours. Because they are employed on a casual basis, it is not surprising to find that *madrasah* teachers receive very low monthly salaries.

Of course, casual teachers are not necessarily poor-quality teachers. But they may have less incentive to perform optimally because they are paid less than permanent government teachers. Casual teachers receive only Rp 100,000 per month, compared with Rp 2 million per month for permanent government teachers (Sujatmiko 2010). Many are paid less than the regional minimum wage of Rp 0.8–1 million per month. It is therefore not surprising to hear that many of them have gone on strike to try and get their status changed to government employee. In 2007, only 44 per cent of primary *madrasah* teachers and 35 per cent of junior and secondary *madrasah* teachers had government employee status (Table 9.2). The issue of shifting casual teachers onto the government payroll is complicated from an administrative point of view, because most of them are employed by private schools (Asyhuri 2010). Improving the welfare of teachers in private schools therefore requires not only transparent recruitment procedures but also precise regulations on private school teachers' working conditions and employment status.

---

9   In 2008, the Indonesian Teachers Association (Persatuan Guru Republik Indo-nesia) announced that the expression used in the traditional teachers' hymn would be changed from 'unsung heroes' to 'heroes of the promotion of edu-cated people' (*pahlawan pembangun insan cendekia*), in order to focus attention on the need to improve teacher welfare.

Table 9.2   Characteristics of madrasah teachers and class size ratios, 2007

Category	Primary	Junior secondary	Senior secondary
Total number of teachers	197,954	217,253	97,986
Employment status (%)			
Government employee	44.3	34.9	35.0
Non-government employee	55.7	65.1	65.0
Educational qualifications (%)			
Secondary or below	23.6	10.6	4.9
Diploma I	1.7	1.5	0.7
Diploma II	36.5	7.4	2.3
Diploma III	4.1	11.7	7.5
Bachelor's degree	33.6	65.5	77.1
Master's degree	0.5	3.3	7.4
PhD	0.0	0.0	0.1
Terms of employment (%)			
Casual teacher (*guru honor*)	53.2	64.4	57.7
Class size ratios			
Student/teacher ratio	15	11	8
Classroom/teacher ratio	0.6	0.3	0.3
Student/classroom ratio	24	31	29
Student/good classroom ratio	46	47	39

Source: Ministry of Religious Affairs (2007).

In addition to the problem of employment status, *madrasah* teachers generally have a low level of educational attainment. Only a third have a bachelor's degree and around 24 per cent have no post-secondary education at all (Table 9.2). The government does of course offer numerous teacher development programs through the Ministry of Religious Affairs. But such programs reach only a limited number of teachers, most of them in the major cities.

Given the limited teacher capacity, it is especially important for *madrasah* to involve parents and the community in improving the capacity of schools. Pradhan, Suryadarma and Beatty (2010) give a hint of the approach that should be taken. They find that giving school committees grants that can be used to improve the learning experience at schools helps to improve parent attendance rates at committee meetings. However, it is the combination of links to local communities and the functioning of school committees that they believe is of most significance for improving academic outcomes.

Providing better facilities and teaching materials is also important. As previously noted, only half of all classrooms in primary *madrasah* are in good condition. National statistics published by the Ministry of Religious Affairs suggest that about 60 per cent of the total funding of *madrasah* is allocated to teachers' salaries and only 7 per cent to teaching materials such as books. No one would question the importance of teachers, but teaching materials and infrastructure are important as well.

Indonesia is likely to have more resources to devote to education in future thanks to higher government revenue, lower debt-service payments and reduced government subsidies. Since the reduction in fuel subsidies in 2005, Indonesia has freed up $10 billion to spend on various development projects, including education (del Granado et al. 2007). To make sure that the additional revenue is spent where it will be most effective, the government will need to select its priorities carefully. Thorough research on the religious education sector is therefore important. Unfortunately, this is an area where only a few quantitative studies are available.

CONCLUDING REMARKS

The Indonesian education sector has undergone remarkable development. While enormous challenges remain, it is important to acknowledge the achievements that have been made. In the early 1950s, about 80 per cent of the population was illiterate (Finkelstein 1951). By the early 1980s, the percentage had decreased to 27.1 per cent of the population (McMahon and Boediono 1992). By 2006, Indonesia had a 92 per cent literacy rate. Given the size of the population, this was an impressive achievement. The government has been equally successful in increasing junior secondary enrolment rates, from just 17 per cent in the early 1970s to 75 per cent in 2007. Getting the remaining 25 per cent into secondary school could be the most difficult task yet, however, given the persistence of income inequality. Educational policy will therefore need to address the issue of uneven educational quality across regions while finding ways to deliver financial support to students from low-income families. The strategy should be to develop *madrasah* schooling as part of broader government programs to reduce educational inequality, and therefore poverty, in Indonesia.

This chapter has identified several key problems with *madrasah*. Many of these could be addressed by making structural changes to the education system, to level the playing field between Islamic and regular schools. An extreme solution would be to remove the *madrasah* from the jurisdiction of the Ministry of Religious Affairs and place them under the jurisdiction of local governments. This would be a costly but effective solution. But no doubt many would object to this idea on the basis that it would lead to a reduction in the number of hours devoted to religious studies. Although the academic attainment of *madrasah* students might improve, demand for *madrasah* education, especially from religious households, might decrease, as implied by the probit model presented earlier.

A less radical solution would be to establish a mechanism such that local governments provide equal support to *madrasah* and other types of schools. Indeed, considering that the majority of *madrasah* students are from low-income families, local governments should already be providing additional funding to *madrasah* students from poor families. With such a diverse quality of education across provinces, it is of course challenging to oversee the delivery of education from the centre. But whatever legal processes the government must go through to get rid of the perception that the *madrasah* are the unloved 'step-child' of the Indonesian education system, religious education is still education. The Islamic schools should be administered by the Ministry of National Education to bring all types of education under one roof. Local governments should be required to make a greater contribution to *madrasah* development. And the *madrasah* themselves should be given more flexibility to design curricula that will allow them to continue to deliver more religious content than regular schools.

The question of how to improve the competitiveness of *madrasah* students in the workplace is obviously a non-trivial one. The empirical results suggest that a mother's religiosity, a student's attendance at a primary *madrasah* and disruption to a student's primary school education are key determinants of junior secondary *madrasah* attendance. Given the characteristics of students enrolled in *madrasah*, setting an overcrowded curriculum would only put them at a greater disadvantage. However, with many parents still valuing the kind of religious education the *madrasah* offer, a reduction in the number of religious courses would not seem to be a preferred solution either. It may be worth considering whether *madrasah* should extend their hours of schooling. Longer hours would probably 'save' the *madrasah*'s identity as religious schools while giving their students the same opportunity to study regular subjects as students from other types of schools. Although over 90 per cent of the *madrasah* are private schools, government support would be needed to facilitate such a major change. But longer hours would not necessarily imply a need for more classrooms, because religious courses could be taught in a more informal setting, such as in a *pesantren*. Indeed, Islamic education is rooted in such religious organisations.

Despite the manifold challenges, the *madrasah* system has shown its potential to give low-income families access to education, especially in rural areas. There is no reason why a *madrasah* education should not be a great preparation for a full range of jobs. In fact, given the size of the Indonesian population and a variable government track record in the provision of education, *madrasah* are probably the only schools that are able to deliver basic education in rural areas. Even primary school *madrasah* graduates are likely to be literate, placing them ahead of illiterate job seekers in the job market. But to improve the quality and sustainability of the *madrasah* system, more public–private partnerships in the provision of education will be a necessity.

REFERENCES

ADB (Asian Development Bank) (2006) 'Indonesia: madrasah education development project', ADB Technical Assistance Consultant's Report, Project No. 37475-01, prepared by SMEC Pty Ltd for the Ministry of National Education, Jakarta, May.

Asra, A. (2000) 'Poverty and inequality in Indonesia: estimates, decomposition, and key issues', *Journal of the Asia Pacific Economy*, 5(1–2): 91–111.

Asyhuri, R. (2010) 'Guru madrasah minta dijadikan PNS' [Madrasah teachers demand government employee status], *Berita*, 16 August.

Bedi, A.S. and A. Garg (2000) 'The effectiveness of private versus public schools: the case of Indonesia', *Journal of Development Economics*, 61(2): 463–94.

Card, D. and A.A. Payne (2002) 'School finance reform, the distribution of school spending, and the distribution of student test scores', *Journal of Public Economics*, 83(1): 49–82.

Chiswick, C.U. (2005) 'An economic perspective on religious education: complements and substitutes in a human capital portfolio', IZA Discussion Paper No. 1456, Institute for the Study of Labor (IZA), Bonn.

Cullen, J.B., B.A. Jacob and S. Levitt (2005) 'The impact of school choice on student outcomes: an analysis of the Chicago public schools', *Journal of Public Economics*, 89(5–6): 729–60.

del Granado, F.J.A., W. Fengler, A. Ragatz and E. Yavuz (2007) 'Investing in Indonesia's education: allocation, equity, and efficiency of public expenditures', Policy Research Working Paper No. 4329, World Bank, Washington DC, August.

Epple, D. and R.E. Romano (1998) 'Competition between private and public schools, vouchers, and peer-group effects', *American Economic Review*, 88(1): 33–62.

Finkelstein, L.S. (1951) 'Education in Indonesia', *Far Eastern Survey*, 20(15): 149–53.

Glewwe, P. and H. Jacoby (1994) 'Student achievement and schooling choice in low-income countries: evidence from Ghana', *Journal of Human Resources*, 29(3): 843–64.

Hanushek, E.A. and D.D. Kimko (2000) 'Schooling, labor-force quality, and the growth of nations', *American Economic Review*, 90(5): 1,184–208.

Hoxby, C.M. (2000) 'Does competition among public schools benefit students and taxpayers?', *American Economic Review*, 90(5): 1,209–38.

Lankford, H. and J. Wyckoff (1992) 'Primary and secondary school choice among public and religious alternatives', *Economics of Education Review*, 11(4): 317–37.

McMahon, W.W. and W.W. Boediono (1992) 'Universal basic education: an overall strategy of investment priorities for economic growth', *Economics of Education Review*, 11(2): 137–51.

Ministry of Religious Affairs (2004) *Buku Statistik Pendidikan Agama dan Keagamaan: Tahun Ajaran 2003/2004* [Book of Statistics on Religious Education and Religion: 2003/2004 Academic Year], Ministry of Religious Affairs, Jakarta.

Ministry of Religious Affairs (2005) *Buku Statistik Pendidikan Agama dan Keagamaan: Tahun Ajaran 2004/2005* [Book of Statistics on Religious Education and Religion: 2004/2005 Academic Year], Ministry of Religious Affairs, Jakarta.

Ministry of Religious Affairs (2006) *Buku Statistik Pendidikan Agama dan Keagamaan: Tahun Ajaran 2005/2006* [Book of Statistics on Religious Education and Religion: 2005/2006 Academic Year], Ministry of Religious Affairs, Jakarta.

Ministry of Religious Affairs (2007) *Buku Statistik Pendidikan Agama dan Keagamaan: Tahun Ajaran 2006/2007* [Book of Statistics on Religious Education and Religion: 2006/2007 Academic Year], Ministry of Religious Affairs, Jakarta.

Newhouse, D. and K. Beegle (2006) 'The effect of school type on academic achievement: evidence from Indonesia', *Journal of Human Resources*, 41(3): 529–57.

Parker, L. and Raihani (2009) 'Governing *madrasah*', Policy Brief No. 4, Australia Indonesia Governance Research Partnership, Crawford School of Economics and Government, Australian National University, Canberra.

Permani, R. (2009) 'The role of education in economic growth in East Asia: a survey', *Asian-Pacific Economic Literature*, 23(1): 1–20.

Permani, R. (2010) 'Can government regulation increase competitiveness of graduates of religious schools? Evidence from Indonesia', unpublished paper, University of Adelaide, Adelaide.

Pradhan, M., D. Suryadarma and A. Beatty (2010) 'Improving learning outcomes through enhancing community participation: evidence from a randomised field experiment in Indonesia', paper presented at the Sixth Australasian Development Economics Workshop (ADEW 2010), University of Western Sydney, Sydney, 10–11 June.

Suharyo, W.I. et al. (2006) 'A rapid appraisal of the PKPS-BBM education sector: School Operational Assistance (BOS)', research report, SMERU Research Institute, Jakarta, September.

Sujatmiko (2010) 'Guru madrasah di Bojonegoro protes ketimpangan kesejahteraan' [Madrasah teachers in Bojonegoro protest unequal welfare], *Tempointeraktif*, 24 August.

Suryadarma, D. (2009) 'Why are Muslims left behind in education? Evidence from Indonesia', unpublished paper, Australian National University, Canberra.

Suryadarma, D., A. Suryahadi and S. Sumarto (2006) 'Causes of low secondary school enrollment in Indonesia', working paper, SMERU Research Institute, Jakarta, August.

Yeom, M., C. Acedo and E. Utomo (2002) 'The reform of secondary education in Indonesia during the 1990s: basic education expansion and quality improvement through curriculum decentralization', *Asia Pacific Education Review*, 3(1): 56–68.

Zborovskii, G.E. and N.B. Kostina (2004) 'On the interaction between religious and secular education under current conditions', *Religious Education*, 46(9): 63–75.

Table A9.1   Summary statistics for respondents, 2007

Variable	Description	JS non-madrasah (N = 321)	JS madrasah (N = 32)	Differ-ence
Student characteristics				
MALE	Respondent is male	0.455	0.410	0.044
ATTENDMI	Respondent attended primary *madrasah* (1 = yes)	0.033	0.295	−0.262***
PUBLICPRI	Respondent attended public primary school (1 = yes)	0.924	0.769	0.154***
REPEATPRI	Respondent ever repeated a grade at primary school (1 = yes)	0.076	0.179	−0.103**
DISRUPTPRI	Respondent's primary school education was disrupted (1 = yes)	0.007	0.013	−0.006
MATHUAN	National examination test score at the primary level: mathematics (maximum = 10)	6.609	6.196	0.413*
SCIENCEUAN	National examination test score at the primary level: science (maximum = 10)	6.874	6.560	0.314*
REGCOST	Educational costs paid by the respondent per annum: registration (Rp thousand)	131.54	61.80	69.75*
TUITIONCOST	Educational costs paid by the respondent per annum: tuition (Rp thousand)	130.38	113.21	17.17
REDUCEDBP3	School reduced BP3 fee (1 = yes)	0.331	0.346	−0.015
Household characteristics				
FSIZE	Family size (no. of children under the age of 15)	2.375	2.282	0.092
MSCHOOLYR	Mother's years of schooling (no.)	8.815	8.250	0.565
FSCHOOLYR	Father's years of schooling (no.)	9.531	8.373	1.159*
FREL1	Father's religiosity: not religious (1 = yes)	0.015	0.013	0.002
FREL2	Father's religiosity: somewhat religious (1 = yes)	0.218	0.192	0.026
FREL3	Father's religiosity: religious (1 = yes)	0.662	0.731	−0.069
FREL4	Father's religiosity: very religious (1 = yes)	0.105	0.064	0.041

* = significant at the 10 per cent level; ** = significant at the 5 per cent level; ***= significant at the 1 per cent level. JS = junior secondary; BP3 = Badan Pembantu Penyelenggaraan Pendidikan (Educational Assistance Board, in charge of parental financial contributions);

Table A9.1 (continued)

Variable	Description	JS non-madrasah (N = 321)	JS madrasah (N = 32)	Differ-ence
MREL1	Mother's religiosity: not religious (1 = yes)	0.018	0.000	0.018
MREL2	Mother's religiosity: somewhat religious (1 = yes)	0.113	0.115	−0.003
MREL3	Mother's religiosity: religious (1 = yes)	0.789	0.833	−0.044
MREL4	Mother's religiosity: very religious (1 = yes)	0.080	0.051	0.029
FEARNINGS	Father's hourly earnings (Rp)	3,175.52	2,073.31	1,102.21
MEARNINGS	Mother's hourly earnings (Rp)	1,165.58	392.12	773.46
OWNLAND	Household owns land (1 = yes)	0.375	0.359	0.016
URBAN	Household lives in an urban area (1 = yes)	0.487	0.359	0.128*
PATTENDMTS	Respondents in same subdistrict (*kecamatan*) who attend junior secondary *madrasah* (% of total respondents)	0.193	0.271	−0.078***
School characteristics				
PMALE	Principal is male (1 = yes)	0.884	0.872	0.012
PPOSTGRAD	Principal has a postgraduate degree	0.385	0.115	0.270***
PEXP	Principal's years of experience in the current school	3.102	4.462	−1.360**
SCOMMITTEE	School has a school committee (1 = yes)	0.993	0.974	0.018
SSHAREBUILD	School shares building with other schools (1=yes)	0.131	0.154	−0.023
SSPECTEXTB	School has a special set of textbooks (1 = yes)	0.756	0.769	−0.013
GET_BOS	School receives BOS	1.087	1.256	−0.169**
GET_BKS	School receives BKS	2.855	2.821	0.034
PASSRATE	Average share of students who passed the national exam in the last two years (%)	93.721	89.719	4.003**
T_PERM_HON	Permanent/casual teacher ratio	6.912	4.036	2.876**
SELECTRICITY	School has access to electricity (1 = yes)	1.233	1.103	0.130

BOS = Bantuan Operasional Sekolah (School Operational Assistance); BKS = Bantuan Khusus Siswa (Special Assistance for Students).

Source: Indonesia Family Life Survey, 2007.

Table A9.2   Probit estimation of the determinants of junior secondary madrasah attendance, selected variables, academic year 2006/7[a]

Dependent variable: Are you currently attending junior secondary *madrasah*? (1 = yes)	Exclude earnings (1)	Exclude earnings & religiosity (2)	Include earnings & religiosity (3)
Student characteristics			
ATTENDMI=1	0.849**	0.810*	0.847**
	(2.755)	(2.513)	(2.729)
REPEATPRI	0.223**	0.190*	0.222**
	(2.815)	(2.444)	(2.819)
Household characteristics			
FEDUC=1	0.077	0.089	0.074
	(1.641)	(1.668)	(1.584)
FEDUC=2	−0.040	−0.032	−0.035
	(−0.681)	(−0.435)	(−0.577)
FEDUC=3	0.043	0.061	0.039
	(0.617)	(0.765)	(0.540)
FEDUC=4	0.044	0.077	0.071
	(0.397)	(0.596)	(0.599)
MEDUC=1	−0.110**	−0.114**	−0.108**
	(−2.955)	(−2.658)	(−2.882)
MEDUC=2	−0.053	−0.058	−0.052
	(−1.000)	(−0.910)	(−0.983)
MEDUC=3	−0.071	−0.077	−0.063
	(−1.273)	(−1.189)	(−1.080)
FRELIGIOSITY=1	0.059		0.070
	(0.650)		(0.745)
FRELIGIOSITY=2	0.100		0.104
	(1.490)		(1.547)
FRELIGIOSITY=3	−0.024		−0.017
	(−0.270)		(−0.176)
MRELIGIOSITY=1	0.974**		0.974**
	(2.919)		(2.846)
MRELIGIOSITY=2	0.438**		0.436**
	(3.115)		(3.057)
MRELIGIOSITY=3	0.957**		0.957**
	(2.912)		(2.873)

Table A9.2 (continued)

Dependent variable: Are you currently attending junior secondary *madrasah*? (1 = yes)	Exclude earnings (1)	Exclude earnings & religiosity (2)	Include earnings & religiosity (3)
Standardised values of (FEARNINGS/FSIZE)			-0.002 (-0.059)
Standardised values of (MEARNINGS/FSIZE)			-0.037 (-0.841)
School characteristics			
PMALE	-0.143* (-1.994)	-0.137 (-1.799)	-0.141* (-1.968)
PPOSTGRAD	-0.122** (-3.241)	-0.136** (-3.169)	-0.121** (-3.208)
SELECTRICITY	-0.070* (-2.220)	-0.086* (-2.192)	-0.070* (-2.225)
Subdistrict fixed effects	Yes	Yes	Yes
Pseudo-R^2	0.403	0.380	0.404
Log-likelihood	-186.428	-186.428	-186.428

* = significant at the 10 per cent level; ** = significant at the 5 per cent level; *** = significant at the 1 per cent level.

a   N = 353. Respondents are students who were attending a junior secondary school in the survey year. Robust standard errors are used. Refer to Table A9.1 for a definition of the variables. The following explanatory variables are not included in the table: MALE, PUBLICPRI, ATTENDMI*PUBLICPRI, DISRUPTPRI, MATHUAN, SCIENCEUAN, REGCOST, TUITIONCOST, FSIZE, OWLAND, URBAN, SCOMMITTEE, SSHARE-BUILD, SSPECTEXTB, GET_BOS, GET_BKS, PASSRATE and T_PERM_HONOR. None were significant at the 5 per cent level. The numbers in brackets refer to t-statistics. The full results can be obtained from the author upon request.

Source: Author's calculations based on Indonesia Family Life Survey, 2007.

10 WHAT IS AILING THE HEALTH SYSTEM? GOVERNANCE, NATIONAL POLICY AND THE POOR

*Adrian C. Hayes and Nida P. Harahap**

Like many developing countries Indonesia has made massive gains in population health since obtaining independence, and life expectancy at birth is now estimated to be just over 70 years compared with just under 40 half a century ago. In important areas of health, however, the rate of improvement has slowed since the mid-1990s. The secular decline in the infant mortality rate, for example, appears to have stalled in recent years at just over 30 deaths per 1,000 live births, and the proportion of underweight children (among those under five years old) has stagnated at around 25 per cent. According to a joint review by the Indonesian government and the World Bank, the Indonesian health system is 'underperforming' (World Bank 2008: 2), especially when it comes to serving the poor. The question is, why?

Several reasons have been suggested for the recent poor performance in the health sector. Some commentators point to the level of government funding. However, while still relatively low by international standards, public health expenditures have actually risen considerably since the mid-1990s: they increased more than fourfold during 1995–2007 (in constant 2000 rupiah prices), and from 0.5 per cent to 1.1 per cent as a proportion of GDP (World Bank 2008: 42).

* This chapter draws on an unpublished report prepared by the authors during 2009–10 for the World Bank in Jakarta. We are grateful to Claudia Rokx and others at the Bank, and to the many government officials who helped us with our study. We also thank Terry Hull, Chris Manning and Peter McDonald for their support. The views expressed in this chapter are our own.

Another explanation, popular with central government officials in Jakarta, is that the poor performance is a consequence of decentralisation. Responsibility for providing basic health services was transferred to the districts and municipalities at the beginning of 2001. Understandably there was a lot of confusion to begin with regarding the precise allocation of responsibilities across the three main levels of government (central, provincial and district) and it took time to build up the capacity of district-level governments so they could perform their new functions adequately (McLeod and MacIntyre 2006). These limitations are still far from fully resolved. In many areas local elites have taken advantage of the situation to 'capture' many public resources and consolidate their own power, further undermining the equity and effectiveness of service provision to local communities (Buehler 2010). However, 'decentralisation' in the context of the present discussion serves more as a characterisation of the problem than an objective explanation. After all, it was the central government that introduced decentralisation, arguing at the time that this would make services more responsive to local needs. Was there something more the central government could have done – or can still do – to make this happen?

We argue in this chapter that a dominant reason for health system underperformance is the failure of the central government to exercise its authority effectively to improve governance in the sector. Public health systems are poorly organised and poorly managed (and the private sector is poorly regulated). A striking indication of this is that when two health service delivery outcomes at the district level – routine immunisation rates for diphtheria, pertussis and tetanus (DPT3) and the level of attendance at deliveries of skilled health providers – are plotted against district health expenditures, there is at best only a very weak relation (World Bank 2008: 66–7). Findings like these confirm that the health system as currently organised is not effectively able to convert additional resources into improved health outcomes. The central government has admirable plans to introduce universal health coverage by 2014, but without a radical overhaul of the way the health system is organised most of the additional resources devoted to health are likely to be wasted. Further improvement in performance of the health system requires that the state, especially the central government, use its authority to improve health governance and change many of the 'rules of the game' in the sector.

Poor governance of public health systems affects everyone who uses them, but the health impacts are felt disproportionately by the poor because they cannot afford to access the more expensive services offered in the public system, or to switch to the private sector. Conversely, to understand why the services that the poor access are often so inadequate, we need to understand the system-wide shortcomings in health governance.

HEALTH GOVERNANCE

Governance is a broad topic and has been defined in many ways. According to the World Bank's Worldwide Governance Indicators Project:

> Governance consists of the traditions and institutions by which authority in a country is exercised. This includes the process by which governments are selected, monitored and replaced; the capacity of the government to effectively formulate and implement sound policies; and the respect of citizens and the state for the institutions that govern economic and social interactions among them (http://info.worldbank.org/governance/wgi/index.asp).

To document some of the shortcomings in health governance in Indonesia today, we focus our attention on the way central government authority has been exercised in three areas: establishing health performance standards for districts and municipalities; facilitating civil society participation in the planning and budgeting of local services, and in ensuring accountability; and relying on a particular 'style' of central government regulation.[1]

Minimum service standards

The English word 'governance' derives from the Greek verb 'to steer'. It is axiomatic in discussions of governance that clear goals should be established to give direction to the system in question, and performance standards to help assess whether or not there is satisfactory movement towards those goals. Following decentralisation, the central government devoted a lot of effort to establishing such performance standards for districts and municipalities. According to Government Regulation 38/2007, which clarifies how some of the articles in the 2004 decentralisation laws are to be implemented by regional governments, health is one of a number of 'mandatory' government affairs to be 'administered by provincial and district regional administrations' (articles 7.1 and 7.2) 'on the basis of minimum service standards established by the [Central] Government on a gradual basis' (article 8.1), and implemented according to 'norms, standards, procedures and criteria' established by the central government (article 9.1). The concept of minimum service standards (MSS) goes back to the original decentralisation laws of 1999, while the concept of norms, standards, procedures and criteria (NSPC) is relatively new and still not widely understood or adopted in everyday governance. We will therefore focus on MSS in this subsection. In truth neither con-

---

1 Of course, governance needs to be improved at all administrative levels (central, provincial and district), but the focus in this chapter is on the central level.

cept has been defined unambiguously, let alone the relationship between them.

According to Government Regulation 65/2005 (on guidelines for compiling and applying minimum service standards), MSS 'stipulate the type and quality of basic services that it is obligatory for the regions to provide and which every citizen has the right to access' (article 1.6); and 'MSS are developed as a tool for the Central and Regional Governments to guarantee equal access and quality of basic services to the community in connection with implementing obligatory functions' (article 3.1). In turn, 'A basic service is a type of public service that is basic and essential to meet the needs of the community in its social, economic and administrative life' (article 1.8). As well as the standards themselves, there are also MSS indicators, defined as the 'quantitative and qualitative achievement indicators used to describe the target level that should be met in achieving each MSS, namely inputs, processes, outcomes and benefits of the services' (article 1.7).

The Ministry of Health was one of the first ministries to formulate MSS for its sector. The initial list of standards proposed by the ministry included over 50 indicators. This was subsequently abridged, and the MSS currently in force are defined in Minister of Health Decree 741/2008 (on health sector MSS for districts and municipalities). Table 10.1 lists the MSS and their respective indicators. The decree makes clear that districts and municipalities have an obligation to provide basic health care and referral services for the poor. A separate decree (828/2008) provides operational definitions for the indicators, and another (317/2009) provides guidelines on how to calculate the cost of achieving the given targets.

A review of the MSS for health uncovers a number of difficulties. As we have seen, MSS are meant to represent a type of public service that is 'basic and essential' to meet community needs and that is therefore deemed an obligatory function of the local government. Decree 741/2008 lists four clusters of such services: basic health services; referral services; research and management of epidemics; and health promotion and community empowerment. It is clear from the MSS indicators listed in Table 10.1 that these clusters cover a wide range of public services, although the decree does not define any of them in detail. Instead, the reader must infer the kinds of services from the list of indicators. By inference, the mandated services appear to include maternal and child health, immunisation and nutrition for children, family planning for 'eligible' (that is, married) couples, primary and referral services for poor people, and level 1 emergency services in district hospitals. The difficulty with this approach is that the local community is not given a clear and unambiguous statement of which health services they can expect to access as a *right*. In fact, the services alluded to in the decree seem to reflect more

Table 10.1   Minimum service standards for the health sector

Type of service	MSS indicator	Target
Basic health services	Antenatal care coverage	95% by 2015
	Obstetric complications attended	80% by 2015
	Deliveries attended by skilled health providers with obstetric competencies	90% by 2015
	Post-partum visit coverage	90% by 2015
	Neonates with complications attended	80% by 2010
	Neonatal visit coverage	90% by 2010
	Villages with complete Universal Child Immunisation	100% by 2010
	Service coverage of under-5 children	90% by 2010
	Poor children aged 6–24 months receiving food supplements	100% by 2010
	Malnourished under-5 children receiving health care	100% by 2010
	Elementary school children receiving health examinations	100% by 2010
	Eligible couples practising family planning	70% by 2010
	Disease detection and treatment coverage	100% by 2010
	Coverage of basic health care for poor people	100% by 2015
Referral medical services	Coverage of referral services for poor people	100% by 2015
	Coverage of level 1 emergency services provided in district hospitals	100% by 2015
Epidemiological research & management of outbreaks	Epidemiological investigation conducted within 24 hours in villages where an outbreak occurs	100% of villages (where outbreak occurs) by 2015
Health promotion & community empowerment	Villages that are active in the government's Healthy Village (Desa Siaga) program	80% by 2015

Source: Minister of Health Decree 741/2008, article 2.

the list of ongoing programs at the Ministry of Health than an objective list of a local community's health needs. Thus, the items in Table 10.1 lean heavily towards communicable diseases, even though the leading cause of death in Indonesia today is cardiovascular disease (that is, a non-communicable disease). And there is no mention of a local government's obligation to meet those community health needs that are specific to certain regions rather than prevalent throughout the country, such as malaria, dengue and rabies.[2] Another difficulty is that, realistically, it would be very difficult to measure progress on some of the MSS indicators precisely enough to determine whether or not there had been improvement from one year to the next.

In short, the MSS for health currently mandated by the central government are not adequate to guarantee that district/municipal governments provide the basic public health services their local communities need; nor are the MSS indicators adequate for evaluating whether a local government is improving in providing the full range of health services its citizens need. The central government will need to promote a more robust, balanced and clearly defined list of MSS for health before it can claim that this policy instrument guarantees the health rights of local communities, especially the poor who are most at risk. At the same time, the government needs to provide a stronger basis for monitoring and evaluating how well district governments are performing in providing essential health services.

Civil society participation and accountability

The nineteenth-century English reformer, William Cobbett, tagged participation – the right to have a say in decisions affecting one's own life – the 'right of rights'. The 1978 Alma-Ata Declaration on Primary Health Care affirms that 'people have the right and duty to participate individually and collectively in the planning and implementation of their health care'. To be meaningful, such a right requires that people not only have a say in the matter but also that they can in some way hold those responsible for finalising and implementing the decisions accountable (Halabi 2009). What are the main avenues for citizens to exercise this right in Indonesia today? Are the poor able to exercise their 'right of rights' in matters of health?

Under the authoritarian New Order regime of President Suharto, the capacity of political parties and social movements to articulate

---

2 It is true that the list of indicators refers to 'disease detection and treatment', but this is so vague that it is not clear what diseases and conditions are covered (even though the target is 100 per cent by 2010).

community interests was severely constrained. During the past 12 years of *reformasi* and democratisation there has been a torrent of free speech, and now the president, governors, heads of districts and municipalities, as well as parliamentarians at all three levels of government, are all directly elected by their respective constituencies. A district head (*bupati*) or mayor (*walikota*) who does not provide public services responsive to the needs and aspirations of the people living in the district or municipality can be voted out of office. This is what the World Bank (2004) calls the 'long route' of accountability, where the 'voice' of clients is conveyed to those managing the health system through elected officials, who can then in turn convey the message to, and exercise some authority over, the state bureaucracy providing the services.

Being able to vote governments and the people's representatives in parliament out of office if they do not perform is an essential characteristic of democracy. But it is a blunt instrument at best for bringing about improvements in health services, since elected officials are responsible for many sectors and a voter's vote is in fact a weighted judgment on a range of issues. Moreover, even if the politicians want health services improved, that does not necessarily mean they will be able to achieve this. As we will see later, the control that a district head is able to exercise over civil servants working in the district is limited when it comes to improving efficiency and performance.

A second, more direct, kind of accountability is where clients are empowered to participate routinely in the planning and budgeting processes of services and to hold providers themselves (rather than politicians) accountable. This is what the World Bank (2004) calls the 'short route' of accountability. Districts have experimented with a variety of ad hoc mechanisms, such as district health councils (with civil society representation), community boards overseeing local health centres, complaints mechanisms, and working with local non-government organisations to monitor service quality. Prominently displayed mission statements and requests for feedback are now common in public health facilities. And the central government has introduced some relevant reforms. But the evidence to date suggests there is still a long way to go before public health services can be made more responsive to local needs and those of the poor, by virtue of Indonesians exercising effectively the short route of accountability.

A key question here is whether the planning and budgeting processes stipulated by the central government for local governments are sufficient to ensure that the annual local government budgets adequately reflect the needs and aspirations of the local people, especially the poor. During the New Order, planning and budgeting were highly centralised, top-down processes; planning was typically done first, and costings and budgets were added later. Since then the central government has introduced significant reforms, but the role of civil society in bottom-up planning and budgeting, and in holding local service providers accountable, is still not clearly defined.

One difficulty is to reconcile the relevant national laws. The main law regulating district planning is Law 25/2004 (on the national development planning system), which mandates a new process of 'development planning meetings' – *musyawarah perencanaan pembangunan*, or *musrenbang* – designed to foster responsiveness through public participation and the integration of bottom-up and top-down planning with political input. *Musrenbang* are held at the village, subdistrict, district, provincial and national levels, and are now part of the process for developing annual, five-year and 20-year plans. Meanwhile, the main law regulating district budgeting is Law 17/2003 (on state finance), which is part of a raft of reforms dealing with government finance, envisioning performance-based evaluation of budgetary outcomes.

A practical difficulty facing district-level officials is how to reconcile the two laws, since they appear to be rooted in different approaches. Law 17/2003 (in its elucidation) suggests, for example, that five-year development plans enshrined in law are not realistic in today's dynamic, globalised world; in contrast, Law 25/2004 clearly reaffirms the 'old' philosophy of long-term, medium-term and annual plans (Synnerstrom 2007; Sarosa, Hasan and Nurman 2008). This is not a trivial difference given that it affects how local government officials see their responsibilities for local planning and budgeting. An added difficulty is that neither law specifies in detail how planning and budgeting are to be integrated.

The Ministry of Home Affairs and the National Development Planning Agency (Badan Perencanaan Pembangunan Nasional, or Bappenas) have been active in advising districts and municipalities on how they should reconcile Laws 17/2003 and 25/2004. In practice, this amounts to little more than stringing together the steps required by each, sequencing the planning steps first and the budgeting steps last. As Sarosa, Hasan and Nurman (2008: 8) point out, the big question here is why the budget planning stage comes after the formulation of the regional government plan:

> Should not these 'budget planning' components ... be parts of the planning process and discussed by all stakeholders in the Musrenbang?

Since Law 25/2004 does not link *musrenbang* with budgeting, there is no guarantee that the needs and aspirations of local people expressed during the planning phase will not be over-ridden by bureaucrats in the subsequent budgeting phase, or indeed by members of the regional parliament (Dewan Perwakilan Rakyat Daerah, or DPRD), who have the final say on the regional budget.[3] In the final analysis, the manner in which planning and budgeting processes have been mandated at the district level by the central government represents neither a strong case of integrated planning and budgeting nor a strong case of civil society participation. Some districts and municipalities do better in these matters than the central government's laws and decrees might suggest. Some have opened up the *musrenbang* process so that community groups or their representatives can participate in or observe the budgeting process. But this is the result of local interest in democratic reform, while the central government's contribution to ensuring that local needs and aspirations are reflected in the local government budget is currently incomplete, fragmented and contradictory.[4]

There appears to be little coordination between the Ministry of Finance on the one hand and the Ministry of Home Affairs and Bappenas on the other. Ministries are often more focused on promoting their own political agendas than on serving the people. Some commentators see elite politics at work, especially with respect to opposition to state finance reform. As Synnerstrom (2007: 163) concludes:

> The government will eventually have to decide whether the law on state finance should prevail, or if the retrograde law on national planning should be allowed to continue to delay the introduction of a modern planning and budgeting process characterised by increased transparency and strengthened accountability.

There are yet other factors at work limiting the likelihood that regional budgets can adequately reflect the needs and aspirations of local populations. Sarosa, Hasan and Nurman (2008) found that non-government participation in the upper-level *musrenbang* tended to be limited to local elites so that the interests of the poor were under-represented. Moreover, local officials complained that the practical effectiveness of the process was limited because there were already too many regulations on

---

3 See Sarosa, Hasan and Nurman (2008) for a more detailed discussion, based on field studies.

4 During limited fieldwork in West Java and South Sulawesi in late 2009, we found that even where local officials reported that the *musrenbang* process was working well, they could recall no cases where civil society participation had contributed significantly to the planning and budgeting of health services. Local communities did mention the need for improved sanitation and more anti-mosquito 'fogging', but these were covered routinely by the non-health budget. We concluded that there was a need for much more health promotion and health education before Indonesia could expect to see more vocal client demand for better and more responsive health services. However, this conclusion would need to be tested through further, systematic research.

planning and budgeting in place. Before they could learn and apply one set of regulations, the central government had issued another. Also, the schedule to be followed every year was too tight.[5]

Modes and 'style' of government regulation

A close examination of regulations and guidelines issued by the Ministry of Health indicates that it is still struggling to find its new stewardship role in a decentralised health sector. It still drafts regulations in a style that reflects a 'command and control' mindset. That is, districts and municipalities are 'talked down to' and told in great detail what they can and cannot do; they are not addressed as partners in a broader collaborative enterprise (involving the private sector and community as well) where the Ministry of Health's role is to provide guidance, empower the districts, set limits, establish national standards and orchestrate resources to enable district health offices to be effective.[6] In a decentralised and democratic state, the central government needs to create a clearly defined space for policy decisions among autonomous units. The rules imposed by the central government should be aimed at establishing the boundaries and limits of such a space – within which local governments (with their non-government partners) can legitimately decide on their own 'rules of the game' – not at dictating to local government what it can do in specific detail. To borrow Braithwaite's (2008) terms, there is a need for regulation that is more 'responsive' and less 'ritualistic'.[7]

Government officials in Jakarta often talk about the need for a new mindset. What would this look like? Five key concepts presented by Salamon (2002: 9–16) provide a useful starting point. First is:

> a shift in the 'unit of analysis' in policy analysis and public administration from the public agency of the individual public program to the distinctive tools or instruments through which public purposes are pursued.

---

5 The central government is currently developing a new performance-based budgeting process aimed at better integration of planning and budgeting (using a common five-year perspective for both), to be implemented in financial year 2011. It will be important to monitor this, to see to what extent the problems discussed above are overcome.

6 See Lieberman and Marzoeki (2004) for more on what such a stewardship role might look like.

7 A good case study would be Ministerial Decree 922/2008, which divides areas of responsibility for health among the three main levels of government in great formal detail – almost like a ritual – with no reference to real issues on the ground or to the ways in which the health needs of the population are changing. This may not be 'rowing', but it is not 'steering' either. Rather, it reads like an exercise in cataloguing.

Second, the new governance mindset 'shifts the attention from hierarchic agencies to organizational networks', meaning government shares control over its programs with non-government partners (including both for-profit and non-profit organisations). Third, instead of a sharp division between the public and private spheres, the new paradigm tries to blend the two together so that 'collaboration replaces competition as the defining feature' of their relationship. Fourth, if traditional public administration relies on command and control and the 'privatisation school' downplays the need for public administration, the new governance mindset suggests a third way for achieving public goods in a world where central governments increasingly enlist a variety of third parties (that is, lower levels of government, banks, insurance companies, businesses, non-profit organisations and so on) to share the burden of implementing their programs:

> While stressing the continued need for an active public role ... negotiation and persuasion replace command and control. ... Instead of issuing orders, public managers must learn how to create incentives for the outcomes they desire from actors over whom they have only imperfect control (Salamon 2002: 15).

Fifth, in contrast to the emphasis on management skills in traditional public administration, the new governance shifts the emphasis to the enablement skills required to engage partners arrayed horizontally in networks.

Addressing governance issues such as those identified above would not solve all the problems in the health sector but it would help improve services for the poor and make the health system as a whole more responsive to the changing needs and aspirations of the population.

PLATFORMS FOR GOVERNANCE REFORM

Opportunities for governance reform within the health sector are constrained by factors outside the sector.

Government employment

One of the prerequisites for good governance is that government institutions be effective and reasonably efficient (Odugbemi 2008: 16). Modern, rational management of human resources is required, meaning among other things that civil servants:

- are hired because they are qualified, not because of nepotism or because they have paid to be appointed;

- are adequately paid for their services, and do not have to depend on sharing rents or other off-budget income;
- have clear job descriptions outlining specific duties, responsibilities and benefits, as well as explicit standards against which their performance will be monitored and evaluated;
- have well-defined opportunities for promotion based on merit and performance; and
- agree to be bound by a clear code of ethical conduct that defines acceptable and proscribed behaviour and that is backed by meaningful sanctions.

These conditions are not well satisfied in the Indonesian civil service today. Without such conditions, it is hard to expect civil servants to serve the public good.

Since independence, the Indonesian government bureaucracy has functioned more like a neo-patrimonial bureaucracy than a modern rational–legal bureaucracy. Early supporters of the post-Suharto reforms assumed that decentralisation and democratisation would quickly lead to civil service reform, allowing districts and municipalities to appoint and deploy government employees according to local needs. However, it soon became clear[8] that the central government intended to maintain both the status of civil servants as members of a single, unified, national civil service and its central control of this service. It is still virtually impossible for district heads and the heads of district sectoral offices to dismiss non-performing staff, even though they have more authority, following decentralisation, over the deployment of personnel. It is impossible to implement accountability for performance when staff are recruited at a young age and promoted based on seniority, completion of training and 'loyalty to the boss'. Practically speaking, good governance and civil service reform are inextricably intertwined in Indonesia.

Growth of the middle class and the private sector

The last two or three decades have seen a large growth in the provision of social services by the private sector in Indonesia. This is manifestly the case in the health sector. The expansion has been driven largely by the growth of the new middle class, but interestingly, it is not only the rich and the middle classes who now rely on the private sector for many of their health services; people from the poorest quintile do so as well. With

---

8 Especially after the initial 'crisis-ridden' period of reform had run its course by around 2004, and a 'politics-as-usual' environment had been established (Crouch 2010: 7–10).

the introduction of the government's new health insurance schemes (Askeskin and Jamkesmas), there has been a noticeable resurgence in the use of public sector services (World Bank 2008: 19–23). However, more analysis is needed before we can make a complete assessment of the impact of these schemes on the poor (see Chapter 9 of this volume by Sparrow).

The growth of the private sector has also been encouraged by a series of government policies, beginning with support for dual public–private practice soon after independence (whereby health professionals in public service were encouraged to supplement their incomes by opening private practices). More recently, since decentralisation, it has been advanced by abandoning compulsory service in rural areas for newly graduated medical doctors who have been trained at public expense, and by allowing the establishment of more private medical schools and training institutions for nurses and midwives. A precise analysis of the impact of recent reforms on the private health sector is difficult because the government collects little information on private facilities, services and practitioners (Heywood and Harahap 2009a, 2009b).

Some regional governments have announced 'free' health services, although invariably this turns out to cover some services (mostly primary health care services) and not others (such as conditions requiring hospitalisation or long-term care for chronic conditions).[9] The relatively low-risk but high-cost conditions (heart attack, stroke and so on) are generally not covered, even though these are the conditions most likely to reduce non-poor households to poverty. The incidence of chronic disease is on the rise in Indonesia. The near-poor are still at risk of being reduced to poverty because of the high cost of catastrophic illness in the family, even in districts that advertise 'free' public health services.

Good governance and public accountability – including regulation of the private sector – depends on a lively interest emerging among the public in improving health through deliberate interventions (Odugbemi 2008). Such interest is rare in Indonesia today: the elites go overseas for health care; the middle class relies on the private sector; and the poor expect and demand little of the public sector other than that it should be cheap, and preferably free. This could change quickly, however, with the introduction of government-supported, comprehensive health schemes (see Chapter 9 by Sparrow).

---

9 For example, the Bali Mandara health care program (Jaminan Kesehatan Bali Mandara, or JKBM), launched on 1 January 2010, appears not to cover emergency cases, including traffic accidents; it also excludes general check-ups, heart surgery, organ transplants and treatment of patients infected with HIV/ AIDS (*Jakarta Post*, 8 January 2010).

CONCLUSION

While Indonesia's health system has improved remarkably over the last four decades, it is still far from providing effective, efficient and accessible health care for all. Poor governance continues to thwart many of the best efforts at improving performance and serving the poor. Improved governance of the health system could lead to more prudent 'steering' of the system by the Ministry of Health and more efficient and effective 'rowing' by those actually providing services in the districts and municipalities. An improved regulatory framework could also foster greater transparency and accountability for all stakeholders and lead to a more productive partnership between public and private providers and facilities (and with the donor agencies).

Much depends on the Ministry of Health exercising new leadership. In our assessment, the most critical constraint is the absence of extensive civil service reform. Unless the government bureaucracy is liberated from what can only be described as neo-patrimonialism (and its New Order rituals) and reorganised as a modern meritocracy, it is hard to imagine how it can serve the people of Indonesia much more effectively and efficiently. Improved governance and civil service reform need to be pursued hand-in-hand. Without such an improvement, the close association between poverty and poor health is likely to endure.

Nevertheless, there is room for some optimism. The Indonesian people have initiated major democratic reforms during the last 12 years and there is wide and growing public support for the principles of good governance. As Indonesians like to point out, the reform process is still very much a work in progress. The key is to maintain forward momentum. One hope is that as the country moves towards universal social health insurance, both the middle class and the poor will realise that they have a vital stake in government health policy, and will demand more forcefully better governance in the sector.

REFERENCES

Braithwaite, J. (2008) *Regulatory Capitalism: How It Works, Ideas for Making It Work Better*, Edward Elgar, Cheltenham.

Buehler, M. (2010) 'Decentralisation and local democracy in Indonesia: the marginalisation of the public sphere', in E. Aspinall and M. Mietzner (eds) *Problems of Democratisation in Indonesia: Elections, Institutions and Society*, Institute of Southeast Asian Studies, Singapore.

Crouch, H. (2010) *Political Reform in Indonesia after Soeharto*, Institute of Southeast Asian Studies, Singapore.

Halabi, S.F. (2009) 'Participation and the right to health: lessons from Indonesia', *Health and Human Rights*, 11(1): 49–59.

Heywood, P. and N.P. Harahap (2009a) 'Human resources for health at the district level in Indonesia', *Human Resources for Health*, 7(6). Available at: http://www.human-resources-health.com/content/7/1/6.

Heywood, P. and N.P. Harahap (2009b) 'Health facilities at the district level in Indonesia', *Australian and New Zealand Health Policy*, 6(13). Available at: http://www.anzhealthpolicy.com/content/6/1/13.

Lieberman, S.S. and P. Marzoeki (2004) *Decentralization in Indonesia's Health Sector: The Central Government's Role*, World Bank, Jakarta.

McLeod, R.H. and A. MacIntyre (eds) (2006) *Indonesia: Democracy and the Promise of Good Governance*, Institute of Southeast Asian Studies, Singapore.

Odugbemi, S. (2008) 'Public opinion, the public sphere, and quality of governance: an exploration', in S. Odugbemi and T. Jacobson (eds) *Governance Reform under Real-world Conditions: Citizens, Stakeholders, and Voice*, World Bank, Washington DC.

Salamon, L.M. (2002) 'The new governance and the tools of public action', in L.M. Salamon (ed.) *The Tools of Government*, Oxford University Press, Oxford.

Sarosa, W., M. Hasan and A. Nurman (2008) *Making People's Voice Matter: An Analytical Study on District Planning and Budgeting*, Bappenas and Decentralization Support Facility, Jakarta.

Synnerstrom, S. (2007) 'The civil service: towards efficiency, effectiveness and honesty', in R.H. McLeod and A. MacIntyre (eds) *Indonesia: Democracy and the Promise of Good Governance*, Institute of Southeast Asian Studies, Singapore.

World Bank (2004) *World Development Report 2004: Making Services Work for Poor People*, World Bank, Washington DC.

World Bank (2008) *Investing in Indonesia's Health: Challenges and Opportunities for Future Public Spending*, World Bank, Jakarta.

11 SOCIAL HEALTH INSURANCE: TOWARDS UNIVERSAL COVERAGE FOR THE POOR?

Robert Sparrow

Indonesia is embarking on far-reaching health sector reform with the aim of achieving universal health insurance coverage by 2014. The ambition to provide universal coverage was formalised in 2004, followed in 2005 by the introduction of subsidised social health insurance targeted towards informal sector workers and the poor, who did not have access to social or private health insurance through formal sector employment. In addition to this national scheme, individual districts are undertaking their own health financing initiatives and reforms. The transition to universal coverage is far from complete, however, and the steps necessary to reform Indonesia's health system, and in particular health financing, are a subject of debate.[1]

With regard to the poor, these reforms need to attend to three key policy issues: equity in utilisation of public health care and overall health status; service delivery, in terms of providing access to care and a basic health care package; and social risk management, in terms of reducing the financial risk of health shocks for the poor. The current debate is focused largely on financial sustainability and efficient service delivery, which are crucial for successfully implementing universal coverage. However, the expected equity impacts of health financing reforms and subsequent demand-side responses have received relatively less attention and scrutiny.

Questions remain about the drivers of inequity and financial risk, the scope for public intervention and the ability of social health insurance

---

1 See, for example, Thabrany (2008), Gani et al. (2009) and Rokx et al. (2009).

to provide a remedy. For example, are the main barriers to health care access for the poor set by the direct costs of seeking care (for example, medical expenses), the indirect costs (forgone income, travel costs) or the poor quality of public health care? What financial risk from illness do households face, and what are the main sources of this risk (medical expenses, reduced labour supply, loss of income)? What are the main coping strategies employed by households (reduce savings, incur debt, sell assets, forgo health care), and to what extent are households able to deal with the financial consequences of health shocks? Finally, which of these cost barriers and sources of financial risk can be addressed by social health insurance?

This chapter aims to contribute to the debate by exploring policy lessons and future challenges for universal coverage and social risk management. It draws on recent experience with subsidised social health insurance and other health financing programs for the poor over the past decade. In particular, the chapter will (1) take stock of equity in health care utilisation and financial protection, and how Indonesia compares internationally; (2) provide an overview of health insurance and health financing programs for the poor over the last decade; (3) review the recently developed body of empirical evidence on the performance of these programs in enhancing financial protection and access to health services for the poor, as well as the blind spots of demand-side reforms; and (4) draw lessons and flag the main challenges for rolling out universal health insurance.

The outline of the chapter is as follows. The first section sets the context and discusses the policy relevance of health care access and financial protection in Indonesia, by briefly describing the Indonesian health system and trends in health care utilisation and financial protection. The second section describes formal health insurance schemes and health financing programs for the poor. The third section presents empirical evidence on the impact of demand-side interventions on reducing barriers to access and financial risk. The chapter concludes with a discussion of the lessons learned and the main challenges for universal coverage.

HEALTH SECTOR DEVELOPMENTS SINCE 2001

Both health spending as a share of GDP and health spending per capita are rather low in Indonesia compared with other countries in Southeast Asia (Rokx et al. 2009). In 2006 Indonesia spent 2.2 per cent of its GDP on health, of which public spending made up 50 per cent. In terms of the government budget, public health spending takes a 5.3 per cent budget share. About 33 per cent of total health expenditure consists of households' out-of-pocket health spending. Although this is a substantial share, out-of-pocket spending on health is relatively low in Indonesia, compared with other Asian countries (van Doorslaer et al. 2007).

The public health care system in Indonesia involves a wide network of public health care providers. These public facilities include hospitals (district, provincial and national), subdistrict health centres, auxiliary health centres and mobile health clinics. The public health centres offer primary health care services, implement a number of health programs and are able to refer patients to public hospitals. Family planning services and maternity care are available in almost all villages.

There is a considerable private health sector in Indonesia, covering more than half of all outpatient care utilisation and a third of all inpatient care. The private sector consists of private doctors, clinics, hospitals and paramedical services. It is not uncommon for doctors working in public centres also to maintain private practices.

The main problems with public health care delivery do not lie with the availability of public facilities, but with local infrastructure, lack of supply and the quality of health care. A particular pressing problem is the lack of doctors and specialists; Indonesia has low doctor-to-population ratios compared with other countries in the region that have comparable income levels (Thabrany 2005; Rokx et al. 2009).

Regional disparities are another concern. With decentralisation in 2001, local implementation of public health services and the bulk of administrative and budgetary responsibilities were transferred to district governments. Although equalising mechanisms were put in place, large differences between districts remain in financial, physical and human resources as well as institutional and fiscal capacity (Thabrany 2008; Kruse, Pradhan and Sparrow 2009; Rokx et al. 2009). The differences in financial revenue can be addressed by the central government through reallocation of the untied general grants (which constitute the lion's share of district revenue), earmarked grants or centrally operated programs such as social health insurance.

Health care utilisation and financial protection

Policy concerns about access to care and financial protection relate to 'horizontal equity' in health care,[2] the key constraints to health care access and the extent of financial risk and impoverishment due to illness.

This subsection investigates the scope for public intervention in Indonesia, by providing a descriptive analysis of trends and distributional

---

2 Horizontal equity here refers to a situation where those with equal health care needs enjoy equal (access to) health care.

patterns of utilisation and out-of-pocket health spending from 2001 to 2007, marking the period after the Asian financial crisis and the first seven years of decentralisation. Up to 2004, health financing for the poor was focused mainly on targeted fee waivers, with the transition to subsidised health insurance taking place in 2005–2006 (see below for details). The analysis is based on data from the National Socio-Economic Survey (Survei Sosio-Ekonomi Nasional, or Susenas). This is followed by a discussion of the empirical evidence on household vulnerability to financial risk from illness.

Health care utilisation

Inequality in health care utilisation was relatively high in Indonesia in 2001 compared with other Southeast Asian countries, particularly Malaysia, Thailand and Vietnam (O'Donnell et al. 2007). But from 2001 to 2007 we see a strong overall increase in health care utilisation and an improvement in horizontal equity. Nevertheless, inequities remain sizable, suggesting that barriers to health care access for the poor persist.

Outpatient utilisation, in terms of the average number of outpatient visits per person per month, increased from 0.15 visits in 2001 to 0.17 in 2004 and 2.3 in 2007 (Table 11.1). This increase was mainly due to increased utilisation of private care, although utilisation of public outpatient care also rose. Utilisation is clearly pro-rich, but this bias is gradually reducing over time. While the use of public care is slightly pro-poor, the difference between the poor and non-poor is dominated by private health care utilisation, which is highly skewed towards the non-poor. For example, in 2001 the utilisation rate of private care for the richest 20 per cent of the population was almost three times higher than for the poorest 20 per cent, although by 2007 this ratio had decreased to 2.

This trend is also reflected by the concentration curves depicted in Figures 11.1 and 11.2, which graph the cumulative proportion of the population ranked by per capita consumption (from the poor to the rich) against the cumulative proportion of health care utilisation. The 45-degree line reflects a hypothetical equal distribution, in which utilisation shares are equal to population shares. In other words, the concentration curve provides a graphical presentation of the distribution of health care utilisation: as the area between the concentration curve and the 45-degree line increases, the distribution becomes more unequal. The concentration curve for private outpatient care lies well below the 45-degree line, indicating that households at the upper end of the per capita consumption distribution have a more than proportionate share of private outpatient care. For public care the curve is slightly pro-poor but follows the 45-degree line closely.

Table 11.1   Outpatient and inpatient utilisation rates, 2001–2007[a]

	2001	2004	2007
OUTPATIENT CARE			
All modern outpatient care			
Utilisation rate	0.151	0.172	0.225
Poorest quintile	0.110	0.141	0.181
Richest quintile	0.190	0.208	0.247
Concentration index	0.113	0.077	0.064
Public outpatient care			
Utilisation rate	0.062	0.077	0.087
Poorest quintile	0.061	0.081	0.089
Richest quintile	0.058	0.070	0.073
Concentration index	–0.006	–0.025	–0.033
Private outpatient care			
Utilisation rate	0.085	0.084	0.124
Poorest quintile	0.047	0.051	0.079
Richest quintile	0.128	0.126	0.159
Concentration index	0.198	0.175	0.133
INPATIENT CARE			
All modern inpatient care			
Utilisation rate	0.061	0.068	0.141
Poorest quintile	0.019	0.027	0.069
Richest quintile	0.153	0.162	0.251
Concentration index	0.440	0.383	0.265
Public inpatient care			
Utilisation rate	0.035	0.040	0.084
Poorest quintile	0.010	0.021	0.053
Richest quintile	0.079	0.082	0.119
Concentration index	0.400	0.298	0.168
Private inpatient care			
Utilisation rate	0.023	0.025	0.051
Poorest quintile	0.005	0.005	0.013
Richest quintile	0.070	0.073	0.120
Concentration index	0.564	0.521	0.420

a   The outpatient utilisation rate refers to the average number of outpatient visits per person in the last month; the inpatient utilisation rate refers to the average number of inpatient days per person in the last year. Modern health care is defined here as public health care and formal private providers (hospitals, doctors, clinics and paramedical services); it excludes traditional health care and self-medication. The concentration index ranges from –1 (all health care is used by the poorest households) to +1 (all health care is used by the richest households). See the main text for the precise definition of the concentration index.

Source: Author's analysis based on Susenas household surveys (see description in text).

Figure 11.1   Concentration curves for outpatient and inpatient health care
utilisation in 2007

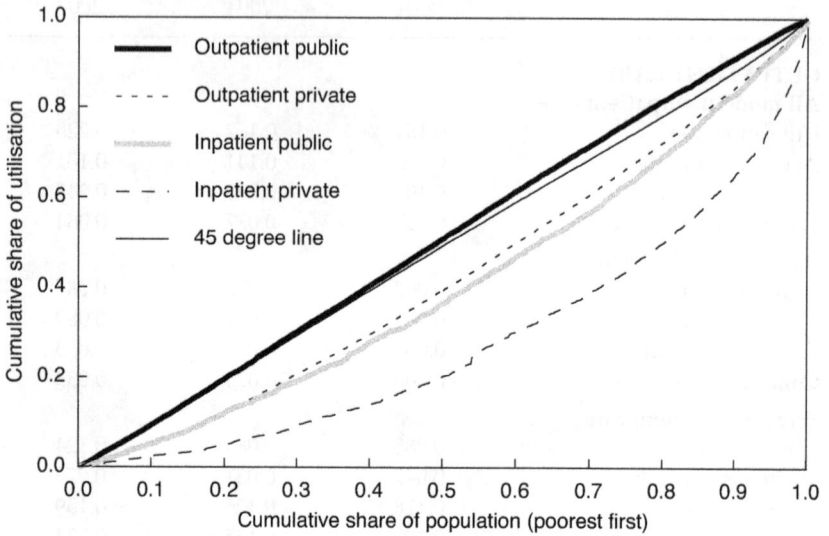

Source: Author.

Figure 11.2   Concentration curves for out-of-pocket health spending shares
in 2007

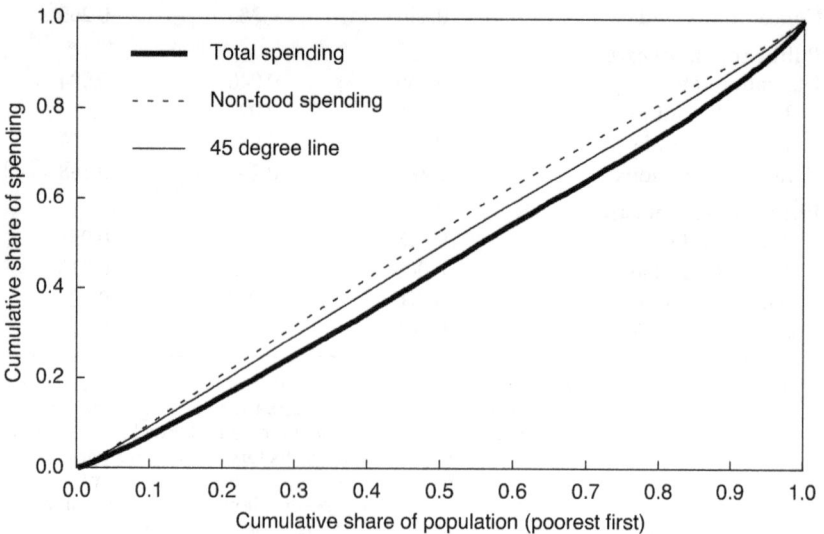

Source: Author.

The degree of inequality depicted by the concentration curve can also be expressed by a concentration index, which measures twice the area between the concentration curve and the 45-degree line. The concentration index ranges from –1 (all health care is used by the poorest households) to +1 (all health care is used by the richest households). An equal distribution of health care utilisation yields a concentration index of zero.

For outpatient utilisation the concentration index is positive but declines over time, from 0.113 in 2001 to 0.064 in 2007, suggesting that utilisation remains pro-rich, but has become more equally distributed over time (Table 11.1, upper half). This trend is driven by an increasingly pro-poor distribution of public care (a negative concentration index that increases in magnitude, from –0.006 to –0.033), as well as reduced inequality in private care utilisation (with a concentration index that is positive and large, but decreases strongly from 0.198 to 0.133).

Utilisation of inpatient care, in terms of the average number of inpatient days in the last year, increased for all quintiles but remains strongly pro-rich (Table 11.1, lower half). This increase is driven by a rise in public inpatient care, in particular after 2004 when it doubled. From 2001 to 2007, the poor seem to catch up, as the concentration index drops from 0.400 to 0.168 for public care and from 0.564 to 0.420 for private care.

Out-of-pocket health spending

Out-of-pocket health spending as a share of the total household budget is pro-rich, indicating that health care spending increases more than proportionally with total consumption (Table 11.2). We see that the average spending share is stable over time, at 2 per cent. However, this reflects countervailing underlying trends. For the poorest, the out-of-pocket health spending share increases slightly, while it decreases for the richest. This is also reflected by the concentration index, which is pro-rich but decreases over time. This pattern can be explained in part by the increase in health care utilisation over time by the poor.

But as noted by others, the out-of-pocket budget share is not a suitable indicator to capture health care needs and the financial risk of illness; it is more suitable for capturing differences in health care affordability and demand. The positive concentration indices are not unique to Indonesia, but are observed in many Asian countries (van Doorslaer et al. 2007). In practice, however, it is difficult to identify what determines this pattern of out-of-pocket health spending (Pradhan and Prescott 2002; O'Donnell et al. 2007). It could be explained by lower prices faced by the poor due to social policy (through subsidised social health insurance or price subsidies targeted to the poor under the social safety net health card program), but also by the poor not being able to afford medical care when they need it or opting for lower-quality care. A third, but unlikely,

Table 11.2   Households' out-of-pocket health spending shares and incidence of catastrophic payments for health care, 2001–2007[a]

	2001	2004	2007
Out-of-pocket spending			
Share of total budget	0.020	0.018	0.020
Poorest quintile	0.015	0.015	0.017
Richest quintile	0.029	0.024	0.024
Concentration index	0.134	0.104	0.074
Share of non-food budget	0.063	0.048	0.051
Poorest quintile	0.060	0.048	0.055
Richest quintile	0.065	0.047	0.044
Concentration index	0.016	−0.006	−0.045
Catastrophic payments			
25% share of total budget	0.008	0.006	0.006
Poorest quintile	0.001	0.001	0.001
Richest quintile	0.023	0.016	0.015
Concentration index	0.548	0.496	0.434
15% share of total budget	0.017	0.014	0.017
Poorest quintile	0.005	0.004	0.005
Richest quintile	0.042	0.030	0.032
Concentration index	0.422	0.382	0.308
25% share of non-food budget	0.038	0.024	0.029
Poorest quintile	0.024	0.016	0.023
Richest quintile	0.060	0.034	0.035
Concentration index	0.182	0.165	0.075
15% share of non-food budget	0.090	0.058	0.069
Poorest quintile	0.079	0.055	0.073
Richest quintile	0.102	0.064	0.063
Concentration index	0.049	0.033	−0.032

a   Catastrophic payments for health care refer to the incidence of health spending that exceeds an (arbitrary) budget share threshold. See the main text for further explanation, as well as for interpretation of the concentration index.

Source: Author's analysis based on Susenas household surveys (see description in text).

explanation would be that the poor enjoy a better general health status on average than the non-poor and thus need less medical care. Pradhan and Prescott (2002) therefore propose a method to estimate the out-of-pocket spending level that is expected to be required in order to meet health care needs, given households' demographic profiles. When Sparrow, Surya-hadi and Widyanti (2010) applied this method to 2005 household data, they found that the gradient reverses, with the poorest quintile requiring the largest out-of-pocket health spending share.

An alternative and more straightforward method is to use the out-of-pocket health spending share of non-food expenditure, since poor households are expected to spend a larger share of their income on food (Wagstaff and van Doorslaer 2003). Although this measure is not without problems, it controls for at least part of the difference in affordability by subtracting spending that most households have to make to meet minimum basic needs (non-discretional spending). Out-of-pocket health spending as a share of total non-food expenditure indeed shows a more pro-poor distribution that becomes stronger over time, indicating an increased financial burden for the poor (Table 11.2). Nevertheless, the shares remain small. In fact, the non-food out-of-pocket spending shares decrease, but faster for the non-poor.

While out-of-pocket budget shares are low on average, these averages may hide incidences of large health expenses that push households into poverty. Such shocks are relatively low-frequency events. It is nevertheless important to monitor them, as they can induce transient poverty by reducing disposable incomes, but may also have long-term income effects. Table 11.2 therefore shows the incidence of out-of-pocket budget shares greater than 15 and 25 per cent. Such extreme shares allocated to health care are often referred to as 'catastrophic' payments for health care.[3] The patterns for catastrophic payments for health care match those for out-of-pocket budget shares, in that they are distributed in favour of the poor. Less than 0.6 per cent of households allocated more than 25 per cent of their budgets to health care in 2007, and 1.7 per cent allocated more than 15 per cent; for non-food expenditure the shares were 2.9 per cent and 6.9 per cent respectively.

Indonesia's rates of catastrophic payments for health care are low compared with those in other Asian countries. For example, van Doorslaer et al. (2007) report that in Bangladesh the cost of health care exceeds 15 per cent of the total household budget for 9.9 per cent of households, while in China and India the shares are 7.0 per cent and 5.5 per cent respectively. Within Southeast Asia, Indonesia's rates of catastrophic payments for health care are similar to those in the Philippines, but higher than in Malaysia. When we look at changes over time, we find that concentration indices of catastrophic payments for health care decrease, mainly due to decreased catastrophic expenditure for the non-poor.

---

3   The threshold that determines a catastrophic payment is arbitrary, but a common choice is 10 per cent of total household expenditure or income (Pradhan and Prescott 2002; Wagstaff and van Doorslaer 2003). This analysis looks at 15 and 25 per cent thresholds, to provide results comparable to the cross-country analysis for Asia by van Doorslaer et al. (2007).

Table 11.3   Health care utilisation, out-of-pocket health spending and catastrophic health spending by insurance status, 2007[a]

	Social health insurance			Total popu-lation
	Subsidised public	Contributory public	Private	
Outpatient care utilisation				
Modern	0.294	0.236	0.213	0.225
Public	0.159	0.096	0.055	0.087
Private	0.119	0.125	0.149	0.124
Inpatient care utilisation				
Modern	0.225	0.275	0.237	0.141
Public	0.171	0.175	0.095	0.084
Private	0.042	0.091	0.137	0.051
Out-of-pocket spending				
Share of total budget	0.022	0.020	0.021	0.020
Share of non-food budget	0.062	0.040	0.043	0.051
Catastrophic payments				
25% share of total budget	0.007	0.007	0.005	0.006
15% share of total budget	0.019	0.020	0.019	0.017
25% share of non-food budget	0.041	0.023	0.024	0.029
15% share of non-food budget	0.094	0.052	0.057	0.069

a   The outpatient utilisation rate refers to the average number of outpatient visits per person in the last month; the inpatient utilisation rate refers to the average number of inpatient days per person in the last year. Modern health care is defined here as public health care and formal private providers (hospitals, doctors, clinics and para-medical services); it excludes traditional health care and self-medication. Catastrophic payments for health care refer to the incidence of health spending that exceeds an (arbitrary) budget share threshold. See the main text for further explanation.

Source: Author's analysis based on Susenas household surveys (see description in text).

The introduction of social health insurance does not imply that all financial risk for participants has been eliminated. Table 11.3 shows that for households with subsidised, public and private sector social health insurance, out-of-pocket health spending shares are not lower than for non-insured households. On the contrary, subsidised social health insurance is associated with relatively large out-of-pocket shares of both total and non-food consumption. For households that contribute to public and private sector social health insurance schemes, out-of-pocket shares are about average, while out-of-pocket shares of non-food consumption are below average. We observe a similar pattern for catastrophic payments. It is important to note that these results should not be interpreted as causal effects, as they could be driven by several factors.[4]

Health shocks, coping strategies and consumption smoothing

The financial risk of illness lies not just in the costs of health care, but also in the potential loss of income and indirect costs. In the absence of formal smoothing mechanisms to spread expenditure on health more evenly over time (through health insurance or credit), households rely on informal coping strategies, which can have severe implications for both short and long-term poverty. First, if health expenditure is financed out of current income, but consumption smoothing is imperfect, it may increase short-term poverty. Additionally, coping strategies such as depleting productive assets and buffer stocks, utilising social networks or incurring debt may have negative effects for future income-generating capacity and the ability to cope with future shocks. Finally, illness and hospitalisation may lead to forgone earnings through workdays lost or reduced labour productivity, with potential long-term consequences through reduced health and depreciation of human capital.

There is some evidence that Indonesian households are able to insure against small, idiosyncratic health shocks, but full insurance is generally not feasible. Moreover, when faced with covariate shocks and chronic illness, coping mechanisms are ineffective and informal insurance fails. The findings of three studies provide a picture of health shocks, coping strategies and smoothing in Indonesia, highlighting the negative effects of ill-health on income and consumption, and the potential benefit from access to formal or informal sources of credit.

First, Gertler and Gruber (2002) look at the effects of health shocks on household consumption, using a two-wave panel (for 1991 and 1993) of the Indonesian resource mobilisation survey for East Kalimantan and West Nusa Tenggara. They find that households are able to insure consumption against minor illness but not against major health shocks. Their health measures are self-reported symptoms and physical ability to perform what are referred to as Activities of Daily Living (ADL), meaning the physical activities that are customarily undertaken on a

---

4 It could be that social health insurance induces health spending, as households allocate more resources to health care in order to fully utilise subsidised health insurance; or because insurance shifts demand to relatively expensive hospitalised care, which is typically bulky and indivisible and the costs of which may not be fully covered by the insurance. Alternatively, the results may simply reflect the fact that households with relatively higher health care needs are more likely to enrol in social health insurance.

daily basis.[5] Changes in reported ADL are associated in particular with strong decreases in labour supply, wage income and non-medical consumption. Changes in ADL would indicate changes in physical mobility or disability. Since households seem to be able to insure against small health shocks, Gertler and Gruber argue that the main risks (or economic costs) of health shocks lie in the increased spending needs related to (infrequent) catastrophic spending events and loss of income. The policy implications for a universal social health insurance program would be to focus on high-cost illnesses and to introduce disability insurance.

Nguyen and Mangyo (2010) also find that a deterioration in ADL is associated with a decrease in labour supply, a fall in food and non-food consumption, and an increase in out-of-pocket health spending. They take a similar empirical approach to analyse the impact of health shocks, using data from the Indonesia Family Life Surveys for 1993, 1997 and 2000. However, the magnitudes of the impacts are smaller than those found by Gertler and Gruber (2002).[6]

Third, using data from the 1993 and 1997 Indonesia Family Life Surveys, Gertler, Levine and Moretti (2009) show that formal coping strategies through financial markets can be an effective means for households to deal with large health expenses. Their results are comparable to those of Gertler and Gruber (2002) in that they find that households are able to insure about 40 per cent of their medical expenses for major illness. In addition, they show that geographic proximity to microfinance institutions (in particular Bank Rakyat Indonesia) affects the ability of households to smooth consumption. Microfinance, or other sources of credit, may help households smooth consumption when faced with the direct costs (medical expenses) and indirect costs (reduced income) of major illness.

While informative, all these studies remain predominantly 'reduced form' analyses, and fail to pin down the transmission channels through which health shocks affect household living standards. It also remains unclear what informal coping mechanisms households employ to self-insure and deal with shocks, or the relative financial contributions from these strategies. Mapping these transmission channels and understanding coping behaviour are important for identifying the scope for public intervention, and for tailoring social policy responses to the main sources of financial risk of illness.

---

5 The ADL measure is based on questions regarding an individual's self-rated ability to undertake specific physical activities (for example, walking 5 kilometres or carrying 20 litres of water over 20 metres).

6 It is not clear what accounts for the difference between the studies, and whether the increased ability of households to insure consumption against health shocks is due to increased formal social protection or informal self-insurance.

HEALTH INSURANCE AND HEALTH FINANCING PROGRAMS FOR THE POOR

Social health insurance for the formal sector

Up to 2005, the health component of the social security system was limited to the formal sector through three schemes, two of which covered the public sector (Askes and Asabri) and one the private sector (Jamsostek).

The largest of the three is Health Insurance (Asuransi Kesehatan, or Askes), a mandatory health insurance scheme for civil servants. Participants' contributions are related to earnings, not benefits. Askes covered 15.6 million beneficiaries in 2007, including civil servants and their dependants. Employee contributions are matched by the government, and the insurance scheme is managed by a state-owned health insurance company, PT Askes.

Police and military are enrolled in the Armed Forces Social Insurance Plan (Asurasi Sosial Angkatan Bersenjata Republik Indonesia, or Asabri). It is very similar in design to Askes and covers about 2 million people. In addition, the military operates its own hospitals.

Employees in the formal private sector working at firms that have more than 10 workers, or payrolls of at least Rp 1 million per month, are eligible to join the Workers Social Security Program (Jaminan Social Tenaga Kerja, or Jamsostek). Although this scheme is mandatory, firms may opt out of Jamsostek by arranging alternative (private) health insurance that yields higher benefits for their employees. Under Jamsostek, firms pay health insurance premiums (as a percentage of basic salary) on behalf of their employees. In 2005 about 3.1 million individuals were enrolled in Jamsostek, out of a potential 20 million eligible private sector employees.

Health financing programs for the poor

A health care subsidy scheme was introduced in 1998. It was part of a larger social safety net put in place in response to the economic crisis that engulfed Indonesia in 1997. Under this program health cards were issued to the poor entitling all household members to free health care at public facilities, consisting of (1) outpatient and inpatient care, (2) contraceptives for women of childbearing age, (3) pre-natal care and (4) assistance at birth. Unlike the health insurance schemes, the health card program did not involve premium payments or the reimbursement of claims by health care providers. Instead, providers received subsidies based on the expected number of eligible poor households in the catchment area. These subsidies were not explicitly tied to services delivered to health card holders. Initially funded by the government and donors, the program continued after the economic crisis with funding from energy subsidy reductions, albeit under different names.

Social health insurance for the poor

Following the passage of Law 40/2004 on National Social Security, a new social health insurance scheme was introduced in 2005. Targeting the poor, it addressed the lack of access to social security in the informal sector, which accounted for 63 per cent of the total labour force in 2005.[7] The scheme was similar in design to Askes, except that the premium payments would be fully subsidised by the government on behalf of the beneficiaries and the benefit package differed slightly. The main objectives of the scheme were to reduce the burden of out-of-pocket health care payments, increase access to health care and improve the quality of health services for the poor. The insurance covered basic outpatient care, treatment in third-class hospitals, an obstetric service package, mobile health services, immunisation programs and medicines. In addition, supporting activities such as the provision of special health services to remote areas and isolated islands were initiated. Hospitals were reimbursed on a fee-for-service basis, while primary health centres received direct funding in the form of capitation payments, based on the estimated number of poor people in the respective catchment areas.

The target population was set at 60 million individuals in 2005, and was increased to 76 million in 2007. The initial monthly contribution per beneficiary was set at Rp 5,000, making the total annual expected government contribution Rp 3.6 trillion. In 2005 the government reserved Rp 3.9 trillion for the program (roughly $400 million), mainly financed through energy subsidy reductions (Aran 2007; ILO 2008).

The subsidised social health insurance scheme was initially called Health Insurance for the Poor (Asuransi Kesehatan Masyarakat Miskin, or Askeskin). From 2005 to 2007 it was managed by PT Askes, which issued social health insurance cards to beneficiaries containing a recipient's identification information and photograph. In 2008 the program was expanded and its name changed to Health Security for the Poor (Jaminan Kesehatan Masyarakat, or Jamkesmas). The Ministry of Health took over full management and operation of the scheme, with PT Askes remaining responsible for managing membership. Apart from the management changes, Jamkesmas differs from Askeskin in that it is aimed at a larger target population, eligibility is enforced more strictly and new procedures for claims handling and verification have been introduced.

---

7   This program was preceded by a number of pilot schemes, implemented in 25 districts across four provinces since 2002 (Arifianto et al. 2005).

The targeting of subsidised social health insurance follows a two-stage design. In the first stage, district quotas for insurance coverage are determined based on the estimated number of eligible citizens (that is, poor and near-poor). District poverty indicators are provided by the central statistics agency, Statistics Indonesia. These quotas also determine the maximum budget for compensating health care providers in a district, which is simply the number of beneficiaries times the insurance premium. In the second stage, districts are responsible for identifying eligible individuals and passing the relevant information to PT Askes. In some districts selection is based on the collection of census information using the Statistics Indonesia criteria for poverty. Other districts have chosen to use the census-based welfare indicator constructed by the Family Planning Agency, which is based on five criteria: (1) household food sufficiency; (2) type of housing (house with an earth floor); (3) level of access to modern care; (4) having separate clothing for leisure time and school/work; and (5) being able to practise one's faith.

Local implementation differs by district. In addition, districts have developed their own health financing reforms. Some districts chose not to participate, such as the greater Jakarta metropolis, which implemented its own social health insurance scheme. Other districts expanded the coverage of subsidised social health insurance using district budgets, or abandoned this approach altogether and instituted free public care financed from district public resources (Gani et al. 2009). Besides variation in health financing, there are also regional differences in social risk management, as benefit packages vary across districts.

The challenge now is to move from the current situation, with various parallel social health insurance schemes and almost half the population still without health insurance, to a universal system, within the context of decentralisation. Possible designs and scenarios have been discussed at length by others.[8] The remainder of this chapter will focus on demand-side and equity impacts, and lessons drawn from previous programs.

THE IMPACT OF PUBLIC HEALTH INTERVENTIONS

A number of studies have investigated the effect of public health policy interventions on reducing the barriers to using health services and the associated financial risks.[9] Estimating the impact of such policies,

---

8 See, for example, Hidayat et al. (2004), Thabrany (2005, 2008), ILO (2008), Gani et al. (2009), and Rokx et al. (2009).

9 For a review of the methods for evaluating the impact of development programs, see Ravallion (2008).

however, is not straightforward. A key empirical problem is the simultaneous nature of participation in public health programs and demand for health care. That is, observed differences in health care utilisation or spending between beneficiaries and non-beneficiaries of a public health program are not necessarily attributable to that program, but could be due to inherent characteristics that determine program participation. For example, enrolment in a social health insurance scheme is not random, but is determined by the targeting objectives and mechanisms of the program, as well as the decisions of individual households to participate. In addition, demand for health insurance may be driven partly by health status and demand for services. Some of these factors (such as targeting criteria) can be observed and registered, for example through a household survey. But others (such as health status) may not be observable. It can therefore be difficult to discern causal effects from the correlation between health insurance coverage and health care utilisation.

Over the last decade, several studies have attempted to overcome these empirical problems, and estimate the impact of the Indonesian health insurance and health financing programs mentioned in the previous section. The results of these studies may provide lessons for rolling out universal health insurance, by gauging the role of direct medical costs as a barrier to access to health care and by highlighting the implementation problems, pitfalls and bottlenecks.

Formal social health insurance

Starting with the established social health insurance programs in the formal sector, there is evidence that these schemes have increased health care utilisation. Using cross-sectional data from the 1997 and 1998 Indonesia Family Life Surveys, Hidayat et al. (2004) find a positive effect of mandatory health insurance on utilisation of outpatient care in the 1990s. They find that the Askes health insurance scheme for civil servants increased utilisation of public care, in particular for the non-poor, while mandatory health insurance for the private sector increased outpatient utilisation of both public and private care, with the effect larger for the poor. A simulation exercise suggests that expanding mandatory health insurance coverage to the full population would have mixed results for equity in access to health care, depending on the health insurance model. The overall equity impacts are driven by two underlying countervailing effects: expansion of either Askes or Jamsostek would increase access to public care in favour of the poor, while inequity in access to private care would increase strongly with increased Jamsostek coverage. This would suggest a divergence, pushing the poor to public and the non-poor to private care.

Using the same data but different econometric techniques, Hidayat and Pokhrel (2009) find somewhat similar impacts on health care utilisation: strong effects of Askes on public and Jamsostek on private care. They interpret this as evidence of a divergence in (perceived) quality of health care between public and private providers. Interestingly, the effect on private care is driven by an increase in the number of patients visiting a health care provider at least once, not in the total number of visits per patient. This would suggest an absence of supplier-induced demand. Hidayat (2008) further shows that the results are robust to conditioning on illness. Although these results are intuitively appealing, with interesting policy implications, the estimates need to be interpreted with caution because some empirical problems remain.[10]

Health financing programs for the poor

Turning to the health financing programs for the informal sector and the poor, empirical studies have investigated both the social safety net health card program and the subsidised social health insurance scheme for the poor. Results for the latter are likely to provide the best indication of the expected impact of universal health insurance, but the health card program can also provide useful lessons. Although the health card provides targeted price subsidies, not health insurance, it does provide insights into the effect of (removing) price barriers on access to health care for the poor.

Social safety net health card

The effects of the health card program have been evaluated for a variety of outcomes, using different data sets. In general, the empirical evidence finds positive effects on access to health care for the poor, but also problems hampering the effectiveness of the program. Pradhan, Saadah and Sparrow (2007) estimate the impact of the health card program on outpatient care and attempt to disentangle the effect of reduced prices for medical care induced by the user fee waiver of the health card (also

---

10 First, these papers take an instrumental variables approach to control and test for potential endogeneity, using unsuitable instruments for insurance coverage (employment status of household head and community involvement). Second, the data and econometric techniques that are employed do not lend themselves to simulation of the large changes induced by rolling out universal health insurance. Moreover, the financial implications for government (through the necessary subsidies), employers and households – and the subsequent effects on health care supply and demand – are not taken into account.

referred to as the direct price effect) and the effect of increased resources allocated to the public health sector (also referred to as supply or quality effects).[11] They find that the program helped to protect access to health care during the economic crisis of 1998–99, in that it prevented a further decline in public health care utilisation.

However, the study finds that the results differ strongly by wealth level. The effect of subsidised costs of care is large for the poor, with a particularly strong increase in public outpatient care. For the non-poor, the user fee waiver leads to a substitution effect from private to public care without a net effect on total utilisation. But the authors also argue that the bulk of the program's impact is due to the increased funding of public health facilities and that the non-poor capture most of these benefits. These results highlight the need for adequate incentive mechanisms for public health care facilities (such as public hospitals and village health centres), as public spending seems relatively ineffective in reaching the poor. Such incentives could be induced by tying compensation for providers to services delivered to health card beneficiaries on a fee-for-service or capitation basis, or by establishing explicit output-based contracts with providers (for example, payments for the number of health card patients treated).

Johar (2009) also looks at the effects of the health card on health care utilisation, but focusing on the period just after the economic crisis and using data from the 1994, 1997 and 2000 Indonesia Family Life Surveys.[12] Like Pradhan, Saadah and Sparrow (2007), she finds positive effects of the health card on utilisation of public care, although few of the estimates are statistically significant. The largest effects are observed for children. Another notable finding is a strong effect on contraceptive take-up. But the study does not control for cross-district variation in subsidies to health care providers, and therefore cannot distinguish between the price effect and the supply and quality effects. Nor does it look at differences for the poor and non-poor. With demand elasticity typically higher for the poor (the poor demonstrating greater responsiveness to price changes than the rich), this obscures the actual impact on the target group.

---

11 The analysis is based on propensity score matching methods for households and difference-in-difference estimation for districts, drawing on cross-sectional data from the 1999 Susenas, a district pseudo-panel for the period 1998–99 and administrative data for district budgets. A potential weakness with this approach would lie in the cross-sectional matching, which may leave scope for confounding unobservables (such as health status).

12 The analysis exploits the panel features of the data to control for non-random targeting, by combining propensity score matching and difference-in-difference estimation.

Two studies, Suci (2006) and Somanathan (2008), look specifically at the effect on health care utilisation by children. Suci (2006) finds a positive correlation between health card coverage and health care utilisation by children only during the initial phase of the program (early 1999), at the height of the economic crisis. By the end of 1999 no statistically significant effects were found, possibly because of the perceived temporary nature of the program. Suci also argues that other financial barriers need to be addressed, and that program participants need to be informed better about the program.[13] However, this study too does not control for the supply effect, or look at differences for the poor and non-poor.

Somanathan (2008) finds that the health card had a positive effect on public health care utilisation by children, by stemming the downward trend in utilisation observed during the crisis, in particular for children aged 0–5.[14] But most of the program's impact was captured by the non-poor, in line with the findings by Pradhan, Saadah and Sparrow (2007). In contrast, however, Somanathan finds no evidence of the health card program inducing a shift from private health care to subsidised public care. It could be that the substitution effects observed by Pradhan, Saadah and Sparrow were specific to the crisis, due to the increases in the prices of medicine and the general shortage of medicine at health care facilities. Such a substitution was generally not found for the longer term, as the non-poor prefer higher-quality private care. But this question is difficult to answer. Somanathan does not differentiate between the effect of the health card on demand (as a result of cheaper prices or costs of care) and its effect on supply through the greater provision of services.

In sum, the study by Somanathan (2008) emphasises that the effectiveness of price subsidies for the poor may be hindered by: (1) non-price barriers such as physical barriers, opportunity costs and poor distribution of health facilities and medical staff (concentrated in urban and semi-urban areas); (2) lack of awareness and knowledge of entitlements; and (3) provider incentives and responses.

These findings are supported by Sparrow (2008), who investigates the targeting of allocation and utilisation of the health card (based on the 1999 Susenas), and finds evidence of barriers to utilisation. Although the health card is clearly meant to be pro-poor, conditional on them having a

---

13 Suci (2006) uses two repeated cross-sections of a special social safety net household survey conducted in 1999, relying on bivariate analysis and logistic regressions. A problem with interpretation of these results is that the analysis does not control for simultaneity, and hence does not identify causal effects.

14 Somanathan (2008) combines propensity score matching and difference-in-difference analysis, using data from the Indonesia Family Life Surveys for 1997–2000.

health card, the poor are less likely than the non-poor to use the card to obtain health services. This pattern is explained mainly by educational level, physical access to health care providers, and opportunity costs or income forgone from seeking health care. This would suggest that the direct and indirect costs of using a health card are relatively higher in the more remote and rural villages, which have little access to public health care providers.

There is little evidence on the effectiveness of the health card program in reducing the impoverishing effects of health shocks during the crisis. The only study on this is by Sumarto, Suryahadi and Widyanti (2005), who find that the health card program did increase consumption, but not enough to reduce poverty incidence during the crisis.[15]

Subsidised social health insurance

Although the financing model for the social safety net health card scheme is different to that for the subsequent Askeskin and Jamkesmas subsidised social health insurance schemes, to some extent these programs provide similar benefits to patients, in the form of subsidised health care. Moreover, the schemes target the same population groups, although the scope of the social health insurance program is larger (covering 76 million people under Jamkesmas, compared with about 20 million beneficiaries for the health card program). The main difference between the schemes is that Askeskin and Jamkesmas explicitly tie the financial compensation given to public health care facilities to services provided to insured patients, whereas the health card program did not.

Sparrow, Suryahadi and Widyanti (2010) look at the impact of the Askeskin health card scheme on health care utilisation and out-of-pocket expenses during its first year of operation. Based on an analysis of Susenas household panel data for 2005–2006, they find that the scheme improved access to health care in that it increased outpatient utilisation among the poorest 25 per cent of the population. Most of this increase was observed at public health centres in rural areas, and public hospitals in urban areas. The scheme also increased the share of out-of-pocket health payments in household budgets in urban areas, possibly due to the increase in (relatively expensive) hospital care, the cost of which was not covered by Askeskin.

As argued earlier, health care is typically bulky and indivisible, and although health insurance may indeed improve the affordability of

---

15 Sumarto, Suryahadi and Widyanti (2005) use four rounds of the Unicef and Statistics Indonesia 100-village survey conducted between August 1998 and November 1999. They base their analysis on difference regressions and an instrumental variables approach.

health care and lower the threshold for households to utilise care, it may also lead to the counterintuitive result that out-of-pocket health payments rise. Wagstaff and Lindelow (2008) find similar results in China. This emphasises the importance of carefully assessing the benefit package of a universal social health insurance scheme and the provider payments system of a social health insurance scheme.

Although Sparrow, Suryahadi and Widyanti (2010) provide evidence that subsidised social health insurance can increase equity in health care access, one has to be careful in translating such short-term impacts into long-term effects. In addition, qualitative studies of the pilot schemes carried out before the introduction of Askeskin identified a number of potential weak points that could hinder the effectiveness of rolling out subsidised social health insurance. Arifianto et al. (2005) identify three problem areas. First, there may be indirect barriers to insurance uptake. For example, individuals without formal residence cards (not uncommon among the poor and internal migrants) were not eligible for the pilot schemes. In addition, some eligible households did not take up insurance for all members because of the indirect costs associated with enrolment. Second, anecdotal evidence suggests that there is a perception that not all services in the benefit package are actually delivered, and that subsidised care is of inferior quality to that received by self-paying patients (Thabrany 2005; Rokx et al. 2009). Similar problems of perception and stigma occurred with the earlier health card program.[16] Third, indirect costs unabridged by social health insurance remain a non-trivial obstacle to seeking health care. Such indirect costs can be due to the cost of travel in remote areas or areas where infrastructure is deficient, or the opportunity cost of health care treatment due to forgone earnings (Arifianto et al. 2005; Sparrow 2008).

Finally, a serious point of critique is that the premiums set for Askeskin and Jamkesmas, but also local programs, are too low compared with the actual costs of delivering services, and a comprehensive actuarial analysis is lacking (Gani et al. 2009; Rokx et al. 2009). This could lead to long-term problems with the quality of care, provider responses, cost control and financial sustainability of subsidised social health insurance.[17]

---

16 See Pradhan, Saadah and Sparrow (2007), Somanathan (2008) and Sparrow (2008).

17 There were also problems with the financing and management of the social health insurance schemes. In 2006 and 2007 budgetary shortages affected implementation, with the funds made available to PT Askes not sufficient to allow the schemes to operate at the desired scale (ILO 2008; Mukti 2008). Hospitals complained that payments were often delayed, that bureaucracy was excessive, and that communication between PT Askes, local and national governments and hospitals was lacking (Aran 2007; Widyanti and Suryahadi 2008).

LESSONS LEARNED AND THE MAIN CHALLENGES FOR UNIVERSAL COVERAGE

Indonesia has implemented comprehensive health financing reforms during the last decade, introducing subsidised social health insurance for the poor and taking large strides towards universal coverage. Nevertheless, many challenges lie ahead. A large part of the population is not yet covered by either social or private health insurance, and while health care access and equity have increased considerably, the poor still seem to underutilise health care, also reflected by relatively low health spending. Whether universal health insurance could close these gaps is unclear at this point.

On the one hand, there is strong evidence that reducing the cost of public care for the poor, through either targeted price subsidies or subsidised social health insurance, has increased demand for, and access to, public health care. Overall, the estimated effects are larger for the poor than the non-poor, due to greater responsiveness among the poor to increases in the prices of medicine and care, and binding resource constraints. The poor are more likely to respond to a lower cost of health care and have few alternatives compared with the better-off. While this is a positive finding in relation to both the health card scheme and other subsidised programs, it suggests that the direct costs of health care remain a sizable barrier for the poor, which could be addressed through universal social health insurance.

However, it is not evident that reducing the financial barriers to care would be sufficient to provide universal access, as there appear to be other binding constraints not addressed by health insurance: poor (perceived) quality of health care has led to a reluctance to utilise public care or to benefit from health financing programs for the poor; awareness and knowledge among households about services and programs are lacking; and the direct and indirect costs of using care and benefiting from these programs are relatively higher for the poor. In addition, social health insurance only covers financial barriers related to the direct costs of care. But the empirical evidence suggests that a substantial component of the financial risk of illness is due to the loss of income, particularly in cases of severe illness or injury, chronic disease or disability.

But even addressing financial risk due to direct health costs may not be straightforward, and benefit packages will need to be considered carefully. In designing and rolling out universal social health insurance, choices may have to be made about the benefit package. In several districts this is already observed. Due to uncertainty regarding the actual cost of services and adequate premium levels, it is currently not clear whether a comprehensive benefit package is feasible. It is therefore crucial to identify and address the main sources of out-of-pocket spending and financial risk. Since households seem to be able to partly self-insure against small shocks, social health insurance should focus on spreading the risk of catastrophic spending.

Future research would therefore need to address household coping behaviour and channels of financial risk from health shocks, provider payment mechanisms and the determinants of differential effects of health insurance for different population groups, in particular with regard to the role of (local) governance, the availability and proximity of health care providers and the quality of public health care.

REFERENCES

Aran, M. (2007) 'Pro-poor targeting and the effectiveness of Indonesia's fuel subsidy reallocation programs', unpublished paper, World Bank, Jakarta.

Arifianto, A., S. Budiyati, R. Marianti and E. Tan (2005) 'Making services work for the poor in Indonesia: a report on health financing mechanisms (JPK–Gakin) scheme in Kabupaten Purbalingga, East Sumba, and Tabanan', research report, SMERU Research Institute, Jakarta.

Gani, A. et al. (2009) 'Report on assessment of health financing system in selected districts and municipalities 2008', unpublished paper, Australian Agency for International Development (AusAID), Ministry of Health and University of Indonesia, Jakarta.

Gertler, P. and J. Gruber (2002) 'Insuring consumption against illness', *American Economic Review*, 92(1): 51–70.

Gertler, P., D. Levine and E. Moretti (2009) 'Do microfinance programs help families insure consumption against illness?', *Health Economics*, 18(3): 257–73.

Hidayat, B. (2008) 'Are there differences between unconditional and conditional demand estimates? Implications for future research and policy', *Cost Effectiveness and Resource Allocation*, 6(15): 1–11. Available at: http://www.resource-allocation.com/content/6/1/15.

Hidayat, B. and S. Pokhrel (2009) 'The selection of an appropriate count data model for modelling health insurance and health care demand: case of Indonesia', *International Journal of Environmental Research and Public Health*, 7(1): 9–27.

Hidayat, B., H. Thabrany, H. Dong and R. Sauerborn (2004) 'The effects of mandatory health insurance on equity in access to outpatient care in Indonesia', *Health Policy and Planning*, 19(5): 322–35.

ILO (International Labour Organization) (2008) *Social Security in Indonesia: Advancing the Development Agenda*, ILO, Jakarta.

Johar, M. (2009) 'The impact of the Indonesian health card program: a matching estimator approach', *Journal of Health Economics*, 28(1): 35–53.

Kruse, I., M. Pradhan and R. Sparrow (2009) 'Marginal benefit incidence of public health spending: evidence from Indonesian sub-national data', Working Paper No. 487, Institute of Social Studies, The Hague.

Mukti, A.G. (2008) 'Health insurance for the poor', paper presented at the Regional Conference on Revitalizing Primary Health Care, World Health Organization, Jakarta, 6–8 August.

Nguyen, T.N.N. and E. Mangyo (2010) 'Vulnerability of households to health shocks: an Indonesian study', *Bulletin of Indonesian Economic Studies*, 46(2): 213–35.

O'Donnell, O. et al. (2007) 'The incidence of public spending on healthcare: comparative evidence from Asia', *World Bank Economic Review*, 21(1): 93–123.

Pradhan, M. and N. Prescott (2002) 'Social risk management options for medical care in Indonesia', *Health Economics*, 11(5): 431–46.

Pradhan, M., F. Saadah and R. Sparrow (2007) 'Did the health card program ensure access to medical care for the poor during Indonesia's economic crisis?', *World Bank Economic Review*, 21(1): 125–50.

Ravallion, M. (2008) 'Evaluating anti-poverty programs', in T.P. Schultz and J. Strauss (eds) *Handbook of Development Economics*, Volume 4, North-Holland, Amsterdam.

Rokx, C., G. Schieber, P. Harimurti, A. Tandon and A. Somanathan (2009) *Health Financing in Indonesia: A Reform Road Map*, World Bank, Jakarta.

Somanathan, A. (2008) 'The impact of price subsidies on child health care use', Policy Research Working Paper No. 4622, World Bank, Washington DC, May.

Sparrow, R. (2008) 'Targeting the poor in times of crisis: the Indonesian health card', *Health Policy and Planning*, 23(3): 188–99.

Sparrow, R. A. Suryahadi and W. Widyanti (2010) 'Social health insurance for the poor: targeting and impact of Indonesia's Askeskin Program', working paper, SMERU Research Institute, Jakarta.

Suci, E. (2006) 'Child access to health services during the economic crisis: an Indonesian experience of the safety net program', *Social Science and Medicine*, 63(11): 2,912–25.

Sumarto, S., A. Suryahadi and W. Widyanti (2005) 'Assessing the impact of Indonesian social safety net programmes on household welfare and poverty dynamics', *European Journal of Development Research*, 17(1): 155–77.

Thabrany, H. (2005) '36 years experience of social health insurance in Indonesia', paper presented at the 5th World Congress of the International Health Economics Association, Barcelona, 10–13 July.

Thabrany, H. (2008) 'Politics of national health insurance of Indonesia: a new era of universal coverage', paper presented at the 7th European Conference on Health Economics, Rome, 23–26 July. Available at: http://staff.ui.ac.id/internal/140163956/material/NHIP-ProgramandPolitic-Indonesia.pdf.

van Doorslaer, E. et al. (2007) 'Catastrophic payments for health care in Asia', *Health Economics*, 16(11): 1,159–84.

Wagstaff, A. and M. Lindelow (2008) 'Can insurance increase financial risk? The curious case of health insurance in China', *Journal of Health Economics*, 27(4): 990–1,005.

Wagstaff, A. and E. van Doorslaer (2003) 'Catastrophe and impoverishment in paying for health care: with applications to Vietnam 1993–1998', *Health Economics*, 12(11): 921–34.

Widyanti, W. and A. Suryahadi (2008) 'The state of local governance and public services in the decentralized Indonesia in 2006: findings from the Governance and Decentralization Survey 2 (GDS2)', research report, SMERU Research Institute, Jakarta, February.

12 SANITATION AND HEALTH: THE PAST, THE FUTURE AND WORKING OUT WHAT WORKS

Lisa Cameron and Susan Olivia

Of the four most important causes of mortality among children under five years old in Indonesia, two (diarrhoea and typhoid) are faecal-borne illnesses directly linked to inadequate water supply, sanitation and hygiene (Ministry of Health 2002). It has been estimated that about 11 per cent of Indonesian children have diarrhoea in any two-week period, and that in excess of 33,000 children die each year from diarrhoea, and 11,000 from typhoid (Curtis 2004). Apart from the effect on health, inadequate sanitation is associated with significant economic losses. These losses accrue from households having to purchase expensive drinking water and from the time spent collecting safe water (often by women and children). Napitupulu and Hutton (2008) estimated the economic losses from inadequate sanitation, poor hygiene practices and lack of access to safe water at over 2.4 per cent of GDP, amounting to approximately $6.3 billion.[1] Women also often do not feel safe defecating in the open.

This chapter seeks to document the current sanitation situation in Indonesia and the extent to which it has improved over the last 16 years. Much remains to be done. On current estimates, Indonesia is unlikely to reach its Millennium Development Goal of halving the number of people without access to sanitation by 2015 (Napitupulu and Hutton 2008). Below, we provide a potted history of past and current policy attempts to

---

1 A four-country study by the World Bank's Water and Sanitation Project estimated the annual cost of poor sanitation at approximately $1.4 billion (1.5 per cent of GDP) in the Philippines, $780 million (1.3 per cent) in Vietnam and $450 million (7.2 per cent) in Cambodia (WSP 2008).

improve sanitation in Indonesia. We discuss the state of knowledge with regard to the relationship between health and sanitation, while noting that empirical evidence on the health impacts of sanitation infrastructure in developing countries – including Indonesia – is scarce.[2] Based on the data that are available, and our own work in East Java, we provide naive estimates of the relationship for Indonesia today. We then go on to discuss how understanding of the relationship between sanitation and health could be improved further, in particular through randomised program evaluations.

SANITATION IN INDONESIA

Table 12.1 presents information on the sanitation situation in Indonesia by province. The data are drawn from the 1993 and 2009 National Socio-Economic Surveys (Survei Sosio-Ekonomi Nasional, or Susenas). They show that approximately 23 per cent of households did not have access to a toilet in 2009. This is a poor result by international standards, with Indonesia failing to match the performance of neighbouring countries. Thailand and Malaysia have rural sanitation access figures close to 100 per cent, Myanmar around 67 per cent and the Philippines nearly 60 per cent (WHO and Unicef JMP 2010). Without access to a toilet, about 29 per cent of the Indonesian population, or approximately 68 million individuals, defecate in the open each day, in rivers, ponds or open fields. With 17 per cent of the population defecating in rivers (Figure 12.1), vast quantities of faecal matter are being washed down the river system. This water is also used for bathing, for washing clothes, for children to play in and, in some cases, as drinking water.[3] The lack of sanitation thus constitutes a severe health burden – one that falls disproportionately on young children, who are particularly susceptible to, and often die from, diarrhoeal disease.

Sanitation is worse in rural areas than in urban areas: 32 per cent of rural households did not have access to sanitation in 2009, compared with 7 per cent of urban households (Table 12.1). There is also great variability across provinces. Provinces that perform particularly poorly are the more remote regions, such as Maluku (41 per cent without access

---

2 Fewtrell and Colford (2004) conducted a meta-analysis of the impact of interventions to reduce illness through improvements in drinking water, sanitation facilities and hygiene practices. Of 336 published papers on this topic the authors examined, only two had studied the effect of improved sanitation on health at the household level.

3 According to the 2009 Susenas, 8 per cent of rural households obtain their drinking water from rivers.

Table 12.1   Proportion of households without access to a toilet, by province, 1993 and 2009 (% of households)

Province	1993			2009		
	Rural	Urban	Total	Rural	Urban	Total
Naggore Aceh Darussalam	60.0	12.8	51.0	30.9	6.5	24.7
North Sumatra	54.2	16.1	37.7	35.8	4.9	24.8
West Sumatra	72.1	18.2	55.1	38.7	9.2	29.5
Riau	55.7	10.7	37.3	18.3	3.4	11.8
Jambi	61.3	20.2	51.9	30.2	8.1	25.1
South Sumatra	67.0	17.5	51.0	33.8	7.3	24.6
Bengkulu	68.2	12.6	48.5	34.6	4.3	27.8
Lampung	43.8	21.1	38.5	17.1	4.3	14.2
DKI Jakarta	n.a.	4.0	4.0	n.a.	2.5	2.5
West Java	70.3	22.3	54.1	28.8	6.2	16.6
Central Java	56.9	30.5	48.4	26.2	11.9	19.8
DI Yogyakarta	25.9	21.9	24.1	3.4	5.5	4.6
East Java	58.5	28.7	49.1	26.5	8.7	18.6
Bali	55.2	18.3	46.6	27.3	7.2	17.9
West Nusa Tenggara	85.8	43.3	76.4	47.7	24.2	38.8
East Nusa Tenggara	39.5	10.2	36.4	30.9	2.0	26.8
West Kalimantan	75.0	7.4	61.2	39.1	4.6	30.8
Central Kalimantan	76.4	20.0	61.7	27.8	6.1	22.2
South Kalimantan	69.2	26.9	61.6	26.8	4.8	19.9
East Kalimantan	57.9	15.0	41.1	15.1	2.6	9.2
North Sulawesi	41.5	10.3	30.4	33.5	5.9	15.4
Central Sulawesi	64.3	26.7	54.7	41.6	9.3	35.7
South Sulawesi	63.2	23.6	55.8	36.8	9.2	28.2
Southeast Sulawesi	58.6	27.0	50.5	37.3	8.7	31.2
Maluku	72.1	21.1	56.9	50.8	8.7	41.3
Papua	67.5	13.5	57.6	43.0	2.7	41.1
Total	**60.9**	**20.5**	**48.6**	**31.9**	**7.0**	**23.1**

Source: Authors' calculations based on data from Susenas, 1993, 2009.

Figure 12.1   Place of excreta disposal among households that do not have access to a toilet, 1993 and 2009 (% of households)

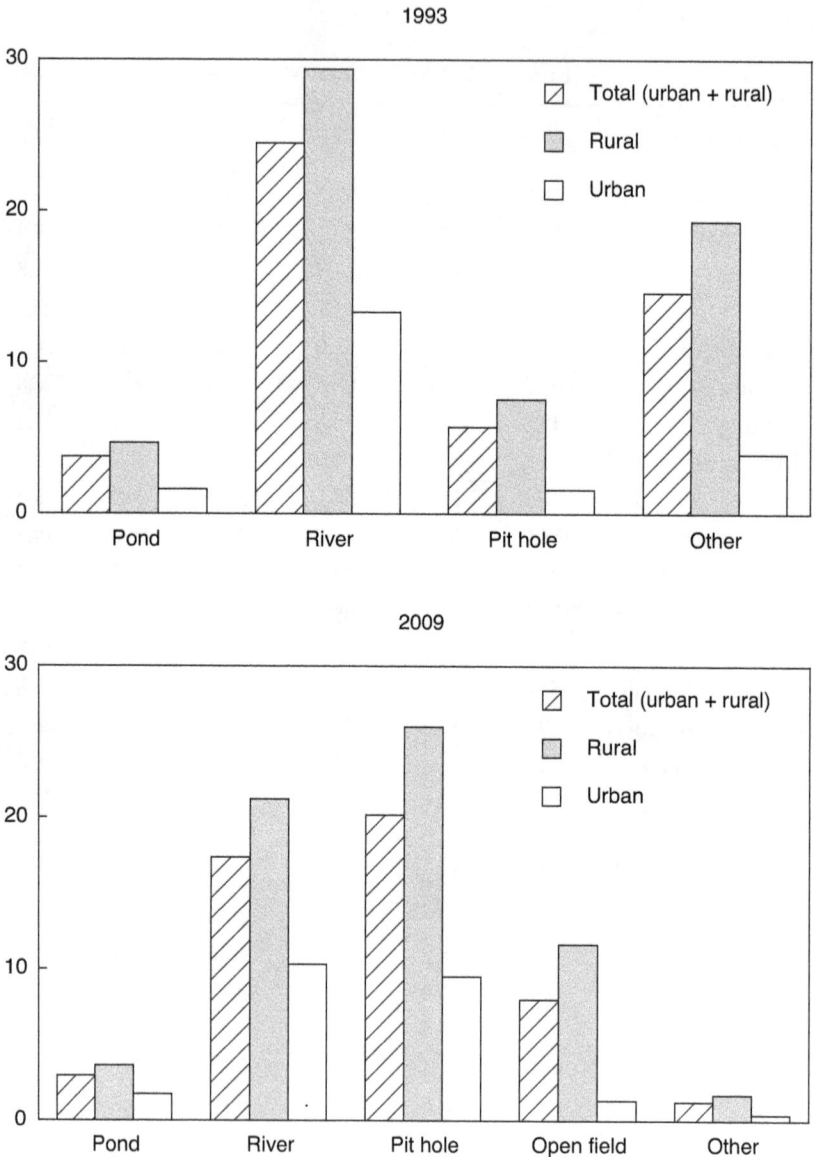

1993

2009

Source: Susenas, 1993, 2009.

to sanitation), Papua (41 per cent), West Nusa Tenggara (39 per cent), Central Sulawesi (36 per cent), Southeast Sulawesi (31 per cent) and West Kalimantan (31 per cent). However, some Sumatran provinces also perform poorly, such as West Sumatra (29 per cent) and Bengkulu (28 per cent). Even in densely populated Java, large numbers of people remain without sanitation in some areas. Figure 12.2 plots these figures at the district level on a map of Indonesia. It reveals that, even within Java, some areas have large proportions of the population that do not have access to sanitation. In the province of Banten (formerly part of West Java, and not disaggregated in Table 12.1), for instance, 31 per cent of households do not have access to a toilet.

Although much clearly remains to be done to improve sanitation in Indonesia, both Table 12.1 and Figure 12.1 also show that large gains have been made over the past 16 years. These gains may be attributable to rising incomes and increased urbanisation. Table 12.1 shows that the coverage of sanitation increased from 51 per cent in 1993 to 77 per cent in 2009. The proportion of households defecating in the open, meanwhile, fell from 42.8 per cent in 1993 to 29 per cent in 2009. Among households that do not have access to a toilet, a much larger proportion is now defecating in pits as opposed to rivers and fields. The decline in absolute numbers is less impressive, however, because the population has grown significantly over this period. The number of people defecating in rivers, for example, only declined from 46 million in 1993 to 41 million in 2009. Thus, a halving of the percentage of households without access to a toilet produced only an 11 per cent reduction in the faecal load in rivers.[4]

Open defecation, whether in rivers, fields or ponds, continues to be of fundamental importance to development because of the health hazard it poses to anyone living nearby. If some members of a community continue to defecate in the open, then the whole community is at greater risk of diarrheal diseases.

Access to sanitation is closely related to a household's socio-economic status. Figure 12.3 shows sanitation coverage by household per capita expenditure quintile. It indicates whether households have their own toilet, share a toilet, use a public toilet or do not have access to a toilet. Eighty-six per cent of households in the richest expenditure quintile have their own toilet, compared with 40 per cent in the poorest quintile. Households in the poorest quintile are much more likely to share a toilet, use a public toilet or have no toilet. The proportion of households sharing sanitation facilities (with neighbours or the public) is 15.4 per cent; the prevalence is higher among the poor (20.9 per cent) than the rich

---

4 See Tables A12.1 and A12.2 in the appendix for excreta disposal figures by province.

Figure 12.2   Sanitation situation in Indonesia, 1993 and 2009

1993

Legend:

Proportion of HHs with no toilet facility in 1993

- [ ] < 0.25
- 0.25 - 0.50
- 0.50 - 0.70
- > 0.70
- no data available

2009

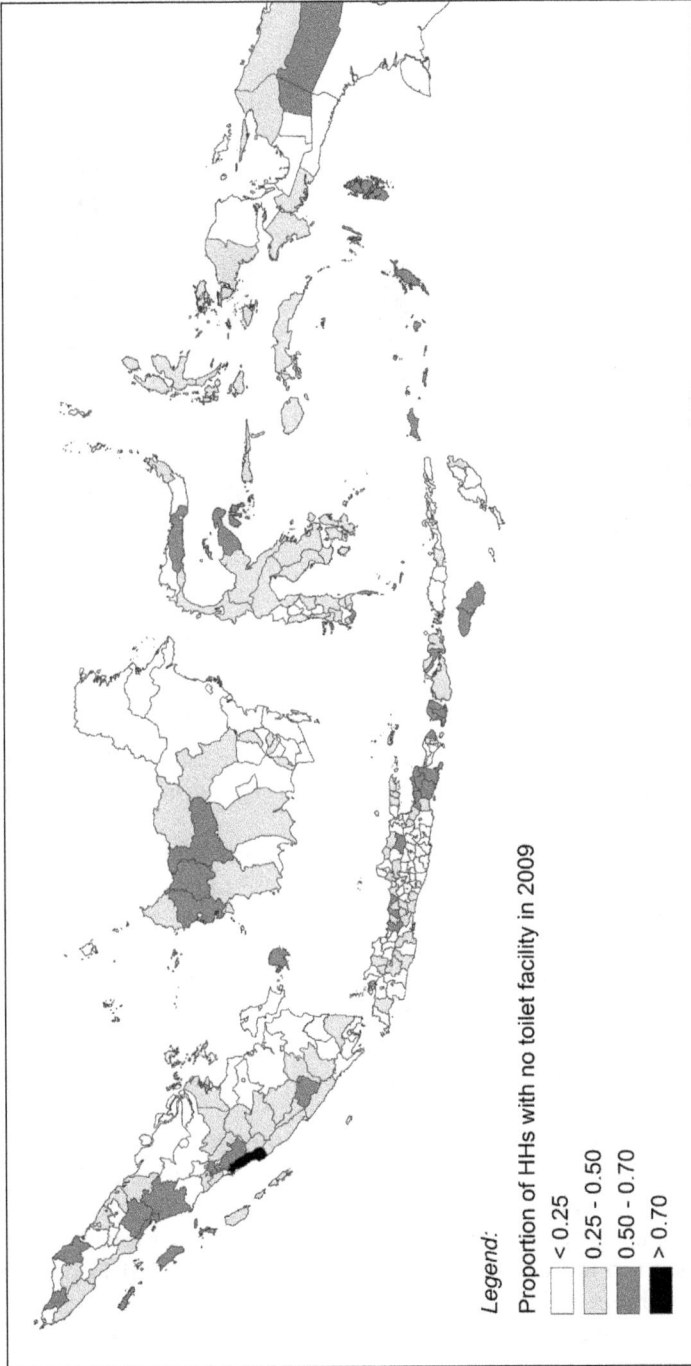

Legend:

Proportion of HHs with no toilet facility in 2009

- < 0.25
- 0.25 - 0.50
- 0.50 - 0.70
- > 0.70

Source: Author.

251

Figure 12.3   Access of households to sanitation facilities by per capita expenditure quintile, 2009 (% of households)

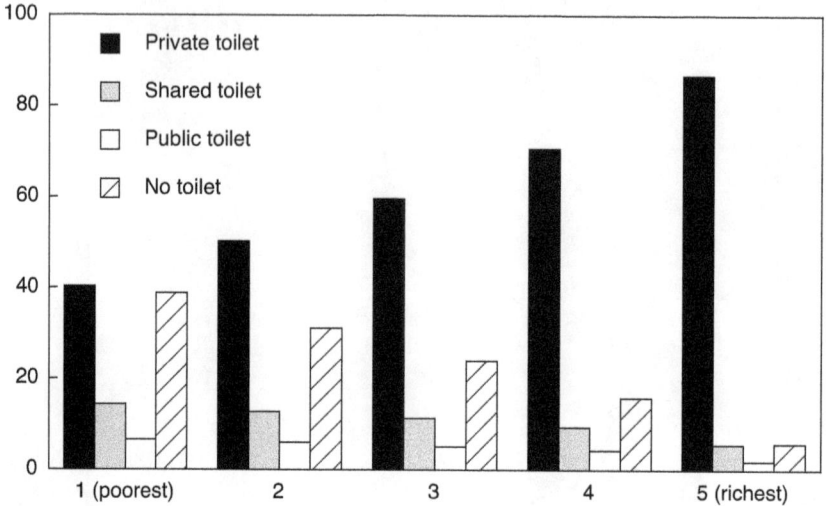

Source: Susenas, 2009.

(7.5 per cent). With household members having to go further to find a toilet, and then possibly having to 'wait their turn', the relatively high proportion of households using shared sanitation may lead to the loss of productive time for both adults (in terms of forgone income, for instance) and children.

Similarly, the quality of a toilet can also affect health. A water-sealed flush toilet is superior to a pit latrine, and a pit latrine with a slab is superior to one without a slab. Figure 12.4 shows how the characteristics of toilets vary with household per capita expenditure. Not only do more rich households have a toilet but, unsurprisingly, they also have better-quality toilets. Almost 83 per cent of the richest households have a flush toilet, but only 32 per cent of the poorest households. About 19 per cent of the poorest households, but only 4 per cent of the richest households, have a toilet that is just a pit in the ground.

In addition to the health costs of poor sanitation, there are costs in terms of lost time and feelings of insecurity. The Susenas data do not present data on these issues. Instead, we turn to data collected by the authors for an evaluation of a sanitation project in East Java (which will be discussed in more detail below). Table 12.2 shows that 14 per cent of the poorest households reported spending more than 10 minutes getting to their main sanitation facility (which could be a river), and that 18 per

Figure 12.4   *Type of sanitation infrastructure available to households by per capita expenditure quintile, 2009 (% of households)*

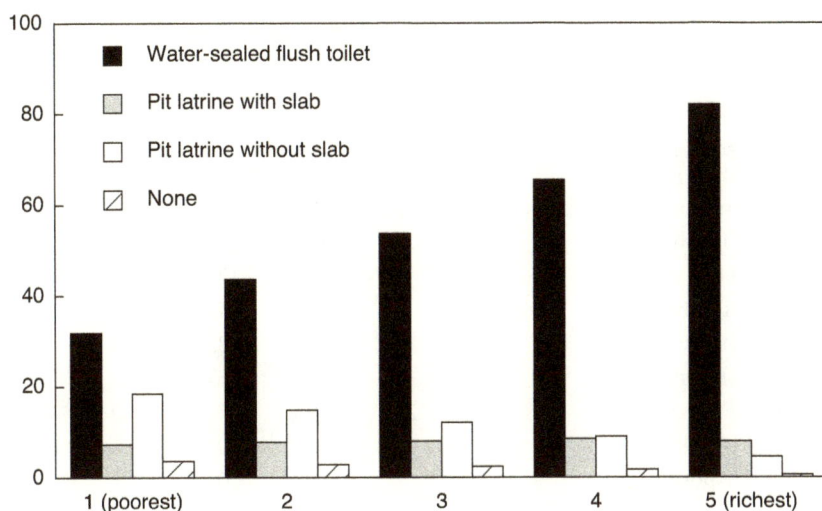

Source: Susenas, 2009.

Table 12.2   *Location of main toilet facility, use of a shared facility, and safety at night (% of households)*

Location	Income quartile				Total
	1	2	3	4	
Inside house	11.7	18.8	30.5	45.3	26.5
In yard	23.9	26.8	23.7	31.3	26.4
Less than 10 minutes walk away	48.9	42.2	36.1	19.8	36.8
More than 10 minutes walk away	13.6	9.5	7.9	1.9	8.2
Other or no specific location	1.9	2.7	1.7	1.7	2.0
Use a shared toilet facility	72.6	66.3	56.4	37.4	58.2
Proportion of women who report feeling safe when using a toilet facility at night (%)	81.6	84.6	83.0	89.8	84.8

Source: Authors' calculations based on TSSM data.

Table 12.3   Reasons for building or improving a toilet facility
(% of households)

	Income quartile				Total
	1	2	3	4	
Main reason to build or improve the toilet					
Convenience or location	33.3	33.1	31.6	23.3	30.6
Healthier for the family	19.7	18.8	16.4	24.4	19.7
Easier to keep clean	4.9	11.1	12.5	12.2	10.1
Privacy, dignity	3.6	3.5	4.6	5.2	4.2
Safety, security	6.1	4.1	8.9	4.8	6.0
To avoid sharing	5.2	5.4	5.6	5.9	5.5
Comfort	21.4	17.2	17.4	17.0	18.3
Prestige, pride	1.0	0.3	0.3	0.4	0.5
Sewage disposal is full	1.3	0.6	0.0	1.1	0.8
Other	3.6	5.7	2.6	5.6	4.3
Probability of future toilet installation					
High	8.0	11.9	6.3	19.4	10.5
Medium	19.3	18.6	25.2	26.4	21.8
Low	55.0	48.7	47.6	37.2	48.4
None	17.6	20.8	20.9	17.1	19.3
Constraints listed most frequently as obstacle to installing a toilet					
High cost	89.5	88.9	89.3	77.5	87.4
Competing expenditure priorities	18.2	18.9	16.8	15.0	17.5
Limited space	2.2	2.4	2.7	4.4	2.7

Source: Authors' calculations based on TSSM data.

cent of female respondents in this group felt unsafe when using such a facility at night.

Why don't people build toilets?

In the same survey, respondents who had a toilet were asked their reasons for building or improving the facility (Table 12.3). Convenience was the main reason given by respondents (31 per cent) followed by health considerations (20 per cent) and comfort (18 per cent). Respondents who did not have a private toilet at the time of the survey were asked whether they were likely to install one during the next 12 months. Nearly 20 per cent of households said they were not considering building or installing such a facility, and another 48 per cent reported a 'low' probability of building or installing a new facility.

But even if households *do* want to build or improve a sanitation facility, various obstacles stand in their way. The last few rows of Table 12.3 list the obstacles cited by respondents to the East Java study. More than 85 per cent of the households cited cost as the biggest constraint to installing a sanitation facility in the house. These findings underscore the difficulty of changing sanitation practices.

SANITATION INITIATIVES – PAST AND PRESENT

The previous section has documented the need for sanitation initiatives in Indonesia and discussed the obstacles to improvement, while noting that significant gains have been made. Some of these gains would reflect general improvements in living standards and household income, and some may be due to government initiatives aimed at improving access to sanitation. This section briefly outlines the major initiatives that have been implemented in Indonesia in the past.[5]

Presidential Instruction on Drinking Water and Family Toilets

Possibly the most ambitious undertaking to improve sanitation was the 1974 Presidential Instruction on Drinking Water and Family Toilets (Inpres Sarana Air Minum dan Jamban Keluarga). Part of the government's efforts to accelerate rural development through the construction of water supply and sanitation facilities, the program ran from 1974 until around 1990.

Documentation of this program is hard to come by. We understand that it involved the government providing both private toilets to households and public toilets for community use at zero cost. It is largely viewed as a failure. The approach taken was very top down. Communities were not consulted about the types of facilities they desired, and anecdotal reports abound of villagers not using the toilets as intended – for example, using them as seats at football grounds. An evaluation of the

5 Sanitation projects are an important aspect of the work of international development agencies in Indonesia. The Australian Agency for International Development (AusAID), for example, carries out sanitation projects in Lombok, Flores and other parts of eastern Indonesia (van der Eng 1998; AusAID 2009).

program conducted in the late 1980s found it to be underperforming and recommended it be stopped.

Although few data on the program are publicly available, the 1980 and 1983 censuses of village economic conditions (Potensi Desa, or Podes) administered by Statistics Indonesia, do report the proportion of villages in each province that received household toilets under the Inpres program. Table 12.4 reports those data. The results indicate that the program was concentrated in Java, Bali, West Nusa Tenggara and Sulawesi, with lower coverage in Sumatra and Kalimantan. Coverage was particularly high in Bali, where 70–80 per cent of villages reportedly benefited from the program. The lowest coverage was in Maluku (3–5 per cent), where sanitation continues to be poor today.

Water and Sanitation for Low Income Communities (WSLIC)

In the early 1990s the government of Indonesia, with assistance from the World Bank and the Australian Agency for International Development (AusAID), initiated a program called Water and Sanitation for Low Income Communities (WSLIC). The objectives were to provide safe, adequate and easily accessible water and sanitation services; to improve community health, awareness and behaviour; and to develop sustainability and effectiveness through public participation. Unlike the top-down Inpres program, WSLIC is an example of community-driven development. This approach seems to have been more successful, with the program generating high economic rates of return and having positive effects on the quality of life in recipient villages. The program has been implemented in three distinct phases – WSLIC-1, WSLIC-2 and WSLIC-3 – each differing in its geographic focus and scope.

Under the WSLIC programs, villages receive a block grant, to be supplemented by contributions from the beneficiary communities (largely in the form of labour and materials) and from the participating district governments. Under WSLIC-2, for example, each participating village was to receive a sum of Rp 195–280 million (about A$25,000–35,000), of which 20 per cent was to be contributed by the community (4 per cent in cash and 16 per cent in materials and labour) and 8 per cent by the district government. Villages were able to choose from a menu of sanitation and water options and received technical assistance.

WSLIC-1 spanned the six years from June 1993 to September 1999. It served about 2 million people in the villages of six provinces: Central Java, Maluku, East Nusa Tenggara, Southeast Sulawesi, Central Sulawesi and North Sulawesi. Officially, villages were to be selected from the 28,000 villages identified as being especially poor under the government's Neglected Villages Program (Inpres Desa Tertinggal) (World Bank 2006). However, the criteria for selecting villages for the program

*Table 12.4   Proportion of villages that received toilets under the 1974
Presidential Instruction on Drinking Water and Family Toilets,
1980 and 1983 (%)*

Province	1980	1983
DI Aceh	5.5	7.2
North Sumatra	10.4	11.0
West Sumatra	23.3	20.9
Riau	19.4	21.5
Jambi	12.7	17.4
South Sumatra	17.5	18.5
Bengkulu	12.8	17.8
Lampung	38.7	49.6
DKI Jakarta	38.7	30.1
West Java	38.5	37.7
Central Java	36.0	48.2
DI Yogyakarta	57.0	64.2
East Java	37.5	47.7
Bali	73.8	78.6
West Nusa Tenggara	36.1	51.5
East Nusa Tenggara	13.5	15.7
East Timor	n.a	9.7
West Kalimantan	4.4	4.7
Central Kalimantan	9.2	7.8
South Kalimantan	16.0	12.8
East Kalimantan	9.8	14.1
North Sulawesi	37.9	40.7
Central Sulawesi	20.2	32.8
South Sulawesi	52.2	52.4
Southeast Sulawesi	31.5	29.2
Maluku	3.1	4.5
Irian Jaya	4.5	5.0
Total	**23.7**	**27.9**

n.a. = not available.
Source: Authors' calculations from Podes 1980, 1983.

differed across provinces and districts, and political factors appear to have played a major role in the final selection (Robinson 2005).

WSLIC-2 began in November 2000 as a follow-on to WSLIC-1 and ran until 2007. The project targeted 32 districts and about 2,000 villages, home to 2 million people in eight provinces: South Sumatra, West Sumatra,

Bangka Belitung, East Java, West Java, South Sulawesi, West Sulawesi and West Nusa Tenggara.

According to the Institute of Economic and Social Research, Education and Information (LP3ES 2007) and the World Bank (2008), WSLIC-1 and WSLIC-2 led to the construction of 1,758 public bathing facilities, 1,379 public toilets, 639 school toilets and some 20,000 private family toilets. But as Robinson (2005) and Willetts, Wicken and Robinson (2008) point out, at the conclusion of WSLIC-2 and after more than 15 years, the coverage of the program remained relatively limited. In part this was because the period of operation coincided with the economic turmoil of the Asian financial crisis, unprecedented political change in Indonesia and the decentralisation of government. These factors made it difficult to implement the program on a wider scale.

The third phase of the program began in 2008. It is part of the government's National Strategy for Community-based Total Sanitation (Program Penyediaan Air Minum dan Sanitasi Berbasis Masyarakat, or Pamsimas). It retains many of the features of its predecessors but is more capable of achieving acceptance at the community level and therefore of being adopted on a wider scale. WSLIC-3 is designed to be a capacity-building initiative. In addition to providing a portion of the costs, as under WSLIC-2, districts are now obliged to cover all local operational costs and to replicate the program across an additional 500–1,000 communities (with the exact number depending on the district's fiscal capacity). Villages are selected on the basis of (1) poverty; (2) poor water supply and sanitation facilities; (3) a high incidence of diarrhoea; and (4) not being a recipient of similar assistance during the previous two years. The program is to be implemented in 5,000 of Indonesia's 70,000 villages. A further significant point of distinction with the previous programs is that WSLIC-3 is not purely an infrastructure-focused approach. It incorporates a Community-led Total Sanitation (CLTS) component that aims to change behaviour and generate demand for improved sanitation. This approach is discussed in detail below.

Total Sanitation and Sanitation Marketing

The Total Sanitation and Sanitation Marketing (TSSM)[6] program is currently being piloted on a large scale across East Java. It is intended to be a community-targeted and community-driven sanitation intervention. In contrast to previous approaches, no funding for infrastructure or subsidies of any kind are provided. Instead, the program aims to draw atten-

---

6   It is known in Indonesia as SToPs: Sanitasi Total dan Pemasaran Sanitasi.

tion to communities' sanitation problems and by doing so increase the demand for sanitation.

The method used to stimulate demand for better sanitation is the CLTS approach pioneered by Kamal Kar in Bangladesh in 1999 (Kar 2003). It is viewed anecdotally as having been very successful in reducing the incidence of open defecation, and has been introduced in more than 20 countries in Asia, Africa, the Middle East and Latin America (Chambers 2009). CLTS is based on the assumption that rapid and widespread behavioural change, and demand for household sanitation, can be triggered by exploiting the disgust associated with excreta. Facilitators are sent to communities to talk to people about the current sanitation situation and the consequences and implications of their practices. These discussions are held in public places and are open to all. They involve a 'walk of shame' where villagers take facilitators on a tour of the places where people defecate.

The facilitators help villagers understand how faecal contamination is spreading from the exposed excreta to their living environments and to their food and drinking water. A map of the village is drawn on the ground and villagers are asked to indicate where they live, where they defecate and the routes they take there and back. It soon becomes apparent – to people's horror and embarrassment – that everyone is ingesting small amounts of other people's faeces. This may lead to the community making a collective decision to get rid of the hazard by becoming an 'open defecation free' (ODF) community. The community must forge its own plan for making this happen, with only limited support and monitoring from the TSSM program. ODF status is verified by local government agencies. Communities achieving ODF status receive recognition and commendation from local and provincial governments.

The TSSM program pairs the CLTS approach with marketing to increase the supply of sanitation products and services available to communities. Extensive consumer and market research is first undertaken to find out what people want, the options already available to them in the market, and their attitudes towards and knowledge of sanitation-related issues. Targeted communication campaigns are then developed to make available a range of sanitation goods and services suited to the preferences and economic capacities of consumers. Local artisans are also trained to meet the increased demand for specific products generated by CLTS facilitation sessions.

Finally, like WSLIC-3, the TSSM program aims to build local government capacity. Districts are required to provide matching funding. Facilitators are hired using donor funds but implement the program in only a small number of villages in each district. The district learns from those events and then implements the program independently in as many other villages as it can given the funds it has available. The program thus aims to support the development of policies and institutional practices that facilitate the scaling up and sustainability of TSSM. While the low cost of the model contributes to the program's sustainability, weaning government officers off the expectation of subsidies and funding is a potential difficulty.

WHAT HAS WORKED, WHAT HASN'T AND WAYS FORWARD

Although the health costs of poor sanitation are well documented, there is still some debate about the mechanisms by which better sanitation improves health. For example, some believe that having a toilet is desirable only if it is kept clean. If it is not, then having a toilet on one's property may be worse than not having one. The materials used during construction are therefore important. For example, smooth porcelain is much easier to clean than a rough cement surface.

Here we explore the relationship between sanitation and health in Indonesia using a simple linear regression and data from the 2009 Susenas. The results are presented in Table 12.5.[7] The dependent variable is an indicator of whether the respondent had diarrhoea in the last month. There is a clear positive relationship between sanitation and health: having one's own toilet is associated with a 14 per cent lower prevalence of diarrhoea than if one does not. Having a flush toilet in particular begets a large benefit, in the form of a 25 per cent decrease in diarrhoea prevalence. In contrast, using a shared or public toilet is associated with an 11 per cent higher prevalence of diarrhoea than if one does not have a toilet at all. Our results are consistent with those of Esrey (1996), who examined data from the demographic and health surveys of eight countries: Burundi, Bolivia, Ghana, Guatemala, Morocco, Sri Lanka, Togo and Uganda. He found that having a flush toilet (latrine) was associated with a 13 per cent (8.5 per cent) reduction in diarrhoeal prevalence. After reviewing data from demographic and health surveys in more than 70 developing countries over the period 1986–2008, Günther and Fink (2010) also concluded that sanitation interventions were effective in reducing the incidence of diarrhoea. In particular, flush toilets lowered the odds of diarrhoea in children by about 13 per cent relative to defecation in the open.

Our own results suggest that having the household's water source within 10 metres of a place where people defecate increases the prevalence

---

7   The percentages presented here are calculated by dividing the coefficients in the table by the average diarrhoea prevalence in the sample of 0.0204.

Table 12.5   Relationship between sanitation and the incidence of diarrhoea[a]

Variable	Coefficient (t-statistic)
Sanitation facilities	
Private toilet (dummy = 1; 0 otherwise)	−0.003*** (3.24)
Shared toilet (dummy = 1; 0 otherwise)	0.002** (2.27)
Public toilet (dummy=1; 0 otherwise)	0.002* (1.69)
Water-sealed flush toilet (dummy = 1; 0 otherwise)	−0.002*** (3.22)
Pit latrine without slab (dummy = 1; 0 otherwise)	−0.0003 (0.35)
Water source within 10 metres of defecation site	0.003*** (3.63)
% of households in village that practise open defecation	0.003*** (3.12)
Demographic characteristics	
Age	−0.001*** (0.000)
Age-squared	0.000*** (0.000)
Educational level	−0.000*** (0.000)
Literate (dummy = 1; 0 otherwise)	−0.019*** (0.000)
Male (dummy = 1; 0 otherwise)	0.002*** (0.000)
Rural resident (dummy = 1; 0 otherwise)	0.002*** (0.000)
Housing area (in square metres)	−0.000*** (0.000)
Constant	0.046*** (27.20)
R-squared	0.01
Number of observations	1,155,566

*** = significant at the 1 per cent level; ** = significant at the 5 per cent level; * = significant at the 10 per cent level.
a   Provincial fixed effects were included. Standard errors are clustered at the village level. The omitted categories are: no toilet; pit toilet with slab.
Source: Authors' calculations based on Susenas, 1993, 2009.

of diarrhoea by 12 per cent. Also, we find that the greater the proportion of the village's population that defecates in the open (in fields, rivers or ponds, or on the beach), the higher the prevalence of diarrhoea – even if some households have quite good levels of sanitation. Thus, if 32 per cent of the village population defecates in the open (the average for rural areas), this increases the diarrhoea prevalence of households in the village by 5.3 per cent. Hence, households stand to benefit not only from having personal access to sanitation infrastructure, but also from improvements in their neighbours' practice of hygiene. In other words, if villages switch from open defecation to some form of improved sanitation technology, the health improvement for each individual is larger than the sum of the effects for individual households.

While the results presented above are strongly suggestive of a positive association between sanitation and health, a number of factors complicate their interpretation. The most obvious is that a household's socio-economic status is positively correlated with its access to sanitation. Unless we are able to control for every aspect of socio-economic status, the relationship we observe between sanitation and health will in part be a proxy for the effect on health of higher socio-economic status (better access to health facilities, better-educated parents and so forth), rather than the effect of having better sanitation. If this is the case, then building toilets without improving the socio-economic status of the household will have a more limited effect on health than is suggested by the associations in Table 12.5.[8]

Although there is a broad consensus that the infrastructure-oriented approaches used in most sanitation programs in Indonesia have failed to deliver results, we actually know very little about their effect on the outcome that matters most – health. Conventional sanitation programs that focus on the construction of facilities are often evaluated in terms of the number of households or regions covered. But what we really want to know is whether people's health has improved. Improvements in health will in turn depend on whether the new sanitation facilities are actually used, and whether people's behaviour has become more hygienic.

To obtain a reliable understanding of the effect of a sanitation program, one can use statistical techniques to control for as many factors as possible, in addition to sanitation, that may affect health. One can then be more certain that the remaining association between health and sanita-

---

8   In other words, a conventional regression (such as the one presented in Table 12.5) is in essence just a comparison of households with and without sanitation. To the extent that there are other differences between households that do and do not have access to sanitation, the results do not tell us the causal impact of improved sanitation on health.

tion is causal. However, the assessment of sanitation programs is complicated by the fact that participating and non-participating villages usually differ in several important respects – beyond their access to sanitation. Normally, governments select regions or households to participate in sanitation programs on the basis of pre-determined selection criteria. WSLIC is an obvious example: participating villages are chosen because they have high levels of poverty, high incidences of diarrhoea and poor sanitation. Comparing these villages with non-participating villages would not be comparing like with like: any differences found would be just as likely to reflect the different initial conditions in the villages as the impact of the program.

To resolve some of the above difficulties, the randomised evaluation approach is increasingly being used to assess the effectiveness of public programs.[9] This approach has the additional advantage of being more transparent for policy makers than the more complex statistical methods. It is analogous to a randomised medical trial in which a randomly selected target group receives treatment for a particular condition and a randomly selected control group does not. The authors of this chapter are involved in just such a randomised trial of TSSM in East Java.[10] Although there is anecdotal evidence that the program has led to reductions in the incidence of diarrhoea and in health expenditures (Chambers 2009), this is the first formal evaluation of TSSM in any country of which we are aware.

East Java was chosen as the site of the study because it has a progressive government that is interested in learning more about improving sanitation, and because a large proportion of rural households continue to practise open defecation despite a succession of large-scale water and sanitation projects. The incidence of diarrhoea and related diseases is high (WSP 2010). With the permission of the national government and the eight participating district governments, 80 communities were chosen at random to participate in the program and another 80 were randomly chosen as 'control' or 'comparison' communities. Each community represented one *dusun* (a subunit of the village), and only one *dusun* in each village was selected to participate in the TSSM program. A baseline survey was conducted in September 2008 in all 160 communities – covering a total of 2,087 households – before the implementation of the program. It provides detailed information on the demographic background and socio-economic status (income, employment, education) of households;

---

9   For a discussion of this approach, see Duflo, Glennerster and Kremer (2008).

10   The trial is being conducted by the Water and Sanitation Project of the World Bank. Professor Lisa Cameron (Monash University) and Dr Manisha Shah (University of California (Irvine)) are leading the evaluation.

the health (including diarrhoea prevalence), nutritional status, and physical and cognitive development of young children; and householders' knowledge of and attitudes towards hygiene, including their sanitation-related practices. Respondents were also questioned about household amenities, especially the household's toilet and water facilities.

To supplement the questionnaire, children's height, weight, and arm and head circumferences were measured and they were tested for anaemia. Village heads, community leaders (*kepala dusun*) and health cadres were also interviewed to obtain information on community access to sanitation, transport, markets, health and other relevant infrastructure, and to establish their level of knowledge about, and attitudes towards, sanitation interventions.

Analysis of the baseline survey data shows that, as hoped, the participating and comparison communities are very similar in the attributes one would expect to affect health, and also in their initial health status (WSP 2010).

The TSSM program was scheduled to start in participating villages within six months of the baseline survey being conducted. At the conclusion of the program in late 2011, an endline survey will be conducted. It will be similar to the baseline survey, but communities will also be asked to comment on various aspects of the implementation of the program.

In the two years between the baseline and endline surveys, local health cadres will conduct an additional short survey at least every two months to collect information on program implementation and diarrhoea prevalence among young children. When combined with the information from the main surveys, these are likely to yield a considerable store of data on children's health in all of the surveyed communities over the two years of the study. A comparison of changes in children's health in participating and control communities should allow an accurate estimate of the effectiveness of TSSM, and provide a basis for deciding whether a national roll-out of the program would be justified. Attention would then need to be paid to examining the extent to which conditions in other provinces differ from those in East Java – institutionally, geographically and culturally – and how those differences might affect program outcomes.

CONCLUSIONS

This chapter has documented how sanitation has improved over the past decade and a half in Indonesia. The availability of sanitation remains low by international standards, however, with 23 per cent of Indonesians still not having access to a toilet. Often in concert with international agencies, the Indonesian government has taken various approaches to address the sanitation problem. The top-down approach it initially used, based on the provision of infrastructure, is largely viewed as having failed. Community-driven development models are considered to have had more success, although rigorous evaluations are wanting.

Approaches such as WSLIC may have been successful but they are also very expensive and difficult to roll out at a national level. Programs to induce behavioural change are a lot cheaper, and anecdotal evidence from Bangladesh suggests that they can be very effective in reducing the incidence of open defecation.

Although it is well established that poor sanitation leads to poor health, the magnitude of the relationship and the route through which it operates is still surprisingly little understood. Simple comparisons of households and communities that have and do not have sanitation cannot shed light on this, as the two groups are likely to differ in a number of other ways. One way of overcoming this problem is to choose randomly who gets to participate in a sanitation program and who does not. The authors hope to be able to contribute to improving understanding of what does and does not work when the data from the large-scale randomised evaluation of TSSM they are currently undertaking in East Java become available in late 2011.

REFERENCES

AusAID (Australian Agency for International Development) (2009) *Australian Aid to Water Supply and Sanitation Services in East Timor and Indonesia: Evaluation Report*, Office of Development Effectiveness, AusAID, Canberra, December. Available at: http://www.ode.ausaid.gov.au/publications/pdf/ODEWatsanmainreport.pdf.

Chambers, R. (2009) 'Going to scale with Community-led Total Sanitation: reflections on experience, issues and way forward', IDS Practice Paper, Institute of Development Studies, Brighton.

Curtis, V. (2004) 'Hand-washing, hygiene and health: proposals for strengthening WSLIC-2's health component and a national hand-wash campaign', Hygiene Centre, London School of Hygiene and Tropical Medicine, London.

Duflo, E., R. Glennerster and M. Kremer (2008) 'Using randomization in development economics research: a toolkit', in T. Schultz and J. Strauss (eds) *Handbook of Development Economics*, Volume 4, Elsevier, Amsterdam.

Esrey, S. (1996) 'Water, waste and well-being: a multicountry study', *American Journal of Epidemiology*, 143(6): 608–23.

Fewtrell, L. and J. Colford (2004) 'Water, sanitation and hygiene: interventions and diarrhoea – a systematic review and meta-analysis', HNP Discussion Paper, World Bank, Washington DC.

Günther, I. and G. Fink (2010) 'Water, sanitation and children's health: evidence from 172 DHS surveys', Policy Research Working Paper No. 5275, World Bank, Washington DC, April.

Kar, K. (2003) 'Subsidy or self-respect? Participatory total community sanitation in Bangladesh', IDS Working Paper No. 184, Institute of Development Studies, Brighton.

LP3ES (Lembaga Penelitian, Pendidikan dan Penerangan Ekonomi dan Sosial) (2007) 'Laporan akhir kajian cepat terhadap program-program pengentasan kemiskinan pemerintah Indonesia: program WSLIC-2 dan Pamsimas' [Rapid evaluation of the government of Indonesia's poverty alleviation programs: WSLIC-2 and Pamsimas], LP3ES, Jakarta.

Ministry of Health (2002) *Indonesia Health Profile*, Ministry of Health, Jakarta.

Napitupulu, L. and G. Hutton (2008) 'Economic impacts of sanitation in Indonesia', Water and Sanitation Program Research Report, World Bank, Jakarta, August.

Robinson, A. (2005), 'Indonesia national program for community water supply and sanitation services: improving hygiene and sanitation behaviour and services', technical report, World Bank, Jakarta, December.

van der Eng, P. (1998) 'Indonesia: review of rural development information: volume 1. Report for the Australian Agency for International Development', Australian National University, Canberra.

Willetts, J., J. Wicken and A. Robinson (2009) 'Meeting the sanitation and water challenge in South-east Asia and the Pacific', International Water Centre, Brisbane, February.

WHO and Unicef JMP (World Health Organization and United Nations Children's Fund Joint Monitoring Programme for Water Supply and Sanitation) (2010), 'Estimates for the use of improved sanitation facilities', WHO and Unicef. Available at: http://www.wssinfo.org/data-estimates/table/.

World Bank (2006) 'Project appraisal document on a proposed credit to the Republic of Indonesia for a third water supply and sanitation for low income communities (Pamsimas) project', Report No. 35503-IND, World Bank, Jakarta, 1 June.

World Bank (2008) 'Water supply and sanitation for low income communities: Indonesia', World Bank, Washington DC.

WSP (Water and Sanitation Project) (2008) 'Economic impacts of sanitation in Southeast Asia: a four-country study conducted in Cambodia, Indonesia, the Philippines and Vietnam under the Economics of Sanitation Initiative', World Bank, Washington DC, February.

WSP (Water and Sanitation Project) (2010) 'Baseline report: impact evaluation of the total sanitation and sanitation marketing (TSSM) in Indonesia', World Bank, Jakarta, April.

Table A12.1 Place of excreta disposal among households that do not have access to a toilet, by province, 1993 (% of households)

Province	Total				Rural				Urban			
	Pond	River	Pit hole	Other	Pond	River	Pit hole	Other	Pond	River	Pit hole	Other
DI Aceh	1.0	23.2	6.8	20.0	1.1	26.8	8.0	24.0	0.6	7.6	1.4	3.1
North Sumatra	0.4	15.8	7.1	14.3	0.6	20.9	10.2	22.5	0.3	9.2	3.1	3.6
West Sumatra	21.2	27.9	1.7	4.4	26.7	37.7	2.2	5.6	9.2	6.5	0.6	1.9
Riau	1.2	19.2	5.9	11.0	1.4	29.8	9.3	15.3	0.8	4.0	1.0	4.9
Jambi	2.0	38.0	7.8	4.1	1.5	45.9	9.0	4.9	3.6	11.4	3.5	1.7
South Sumatra	1.5	27.8	9.3	12.4	2.0	37.2	12.2	15.6	0.5	8.1	3.4	5.5
Bengkulu	1.3	29.1	6.0	12.1	2.0	41.0	9.1	16.1	0.0	7.5	0.4	4.8
Lampung	2.0	15.6	16.0	5.0	2.3	17.1	19.3	5.2	1.2	10.6	5.0	4.3
DKI Jakarta	0.8	1.7	0.1	1.3	n.a.	n.a.	n.a.	n.a.	0.8	1.7	0.1	1.3
West Java	18.2	24.9	1.7	9.4	24.5	30.9	2.3	12.6	5.8	13.0	0.4	3.2
Central Java	4.4	34.8	6.2	3.0	5.6	39.5	8.4	3.5	2.0	24.9	1.7	2.0
DI Yogyakarta	1.5	19.2	2.3	1.1	1.9	18.7	3.6	1.7	1.1	19.9	0.5	0.4
East Java	0.8	34.8	6.1	7.5	1.0	39.3	8.3	9.9	0.3	24.7	1.4	2.3
Bali	0.3	10.8	1.3	34.2	0.2	11.2	1.7	42.1	0.4	9.6	0.0	8.3
West Nusa Tenggara	0.4	47.1	1.3	27.6	0.4	50.4	1.6	33.5	0.2	35.5	0.4	7.2
East Nusa Tenggara	0.1	0.2	9.4	26.7	0.1	0.2	10.2	29.1	0.1	0.4	2.6	7.0
East Timor	0.3	3.6	11.0	42.0	0.3	3.8	10.6	44.6	0.0	2.0	14.8	15.4
West Kalimantan	1.1	37.8	4.0	18.4	1.3	46.4	4.7	22.7	0.5	4.5	1.0	1.4
Central Kalimantan	0.2	52.7	2.9	5.9	0.2	64.3	3.9	7.9	0.3	19.6	0.0	0.1
South Kalimantan	0.5	50.6	4.2	6.4	0.5	56.8	4.9	7.0	0.5	22.2	0.9	3.4
East Kalimantan	0.4	28.4	5.0	7.3	0.4	40.6	6.9	10.1	0.4	9.4	2.1	3.1
North Sulawesi	0.2	13.1	0.6	16.5	0.2	16.5	0.8	24.0	0.1	7.1	0.2	3.1
Central Sulawesi	0.5	17.1	2.8	34.3	0.6	19.9	3.4	40.4	0.2	9.2	1.1	16.3
South Sulawesi	0.6	12.2	9.9	33.2	0.6	13.8	11.1	37.7	0.3	5.3	4.6	13.4
Southeast Sulawesi	0.2	4.3	14.1	31.9	0.3	4.2	17.9	36.3	0.0	4.7	3.3	19.1
Maluku	0.4	6.2	3.1	47.2	0.3	6.2	3.3	62.4	0.7	6.0	2.9	11.5
Irian Jaya	1.0	11.3	8.7	36.6	1.2	12.9	10.3	43.2	0.4	4.0	1.4	7.7
Total	3.8	24.5	5.7	14.6	4.7	29.4	7.6	19.3	1.6	13.3	1.6	4.0

Source: Authors' calculations from Susenas, 1993.

Table A12.2   Place of excreta disposal among households that do not have access to a toilet, by province, 2009 (% of households)

Province	Total					Rural					Urban				
	Pond	River	Pit hole	Open field	Other	Pond	River	Pit hole	Open field	Other	Pond	River	Pit hole	Open field	Other
Naggore Aceh Darussalam	2.5	21.4	18.6	6.1	1.2	3.0	26.6	22.4	7.4	1.5	1.3	6.2	7.6	2.2	0.4
North Sumatra	1.4	19.8	18.5	9.0	3.1	1.7	24.6	23.3	13.6	4.0	0.8	10.9	9.8	0.5	1.3
West Sumatra	13.4	29.8	12.7	2.0	1.5	16.4	37.3	14.6	2.4	1.5	6.9	13.2	8.5	0.9	1.4
Riau	1.1	11.9	34.3	3.4	0.5	1.2	15.6	43.8	4.6	0.7	1.0	3.8	14.1	0.8	0.1
Jambi	1.6	29.4	26.1	3.0	0.6	1.6	33.9	30.0	3.1	0.5	1.9	14.7	13.1	2.8	0.6
South Sumatra	3.3	26.6	25.3	1.7	0.4	3.9	34.8	30.9	2.2	0.5	1.9	7.8	12.4	0.3	0.2
Bengkulu	1.3	22.9	36.5	4.7	1.2	1.3	28.0	40.3	5.9	1.5	1.0	5.4	23.6	0.3	0.3
Lampung	2.6	10.4	40.8	1.3	1.2	2.9	11.3	46.8	1.6	1.4	1.5	7.5	20.9	0.3	0.6
Kepulauan Bangka Belitung	0.5	3.2	7.8	20.2	1.9	0.8	2.5	10.3	31.8	2.5	0.2	4.0	4.8	6.0	1.3
Kepulauan Riau	0.5	22.2	12.8	7.3	0.3	0.9	43.6	14.8	16.4	0.4	0.3	11.5	11.8	2.7	0.3
DKI Jakarta	0.7	5.6	3.0	0.2	0.1	n.a.	n.a.	n.a.	n.a.	n.a.	0.7	5.6	3.0	0.2	0.1
West Java	12.8	19.9	8.1	1.0	0.3	21.7	18.8	10.6	1.9	0.5	5.3	20.8	6.1	0.3	0.2
Central Java	5.1	18.4	16.2	1.5	0.4	7.4	21.4	22.2	2.3	0.5	2.1	14.5	8.6	0.5	0.3
DI Yogyakarta	0.9	4.5	18.1	0.2	0.1	1.8	2.6	35.9	0.5	0.2	0.1	6.2	3.0	0.0	0.1
East Java	0.8	16.7	23.5	3.1	0.3	1.0	21.0	34.1	5.2	0.4	0.5	11.2	9.9	0.4	0.1
Banten	6.5	10.6	9.4	16.8	0.2	7.9	17.9	11.2	30.0	0.2	5.3	3.6	7.6	4.2	0.3
Bali	0.2	5.6	5.1	12.3	0.2	0.2	7.0	7.5	20.1	0.2	0.2	4.1	2.3	3.4	0.2

Province	Total					Rural					Urban				
	Pond	River	Pit hole	Open field	Other	Pond	River	Pit hole	Open field	Other	Pond	River	Pit hole	Open field	Other
East Nusa Tenggara	0.4	0.7	53.7	20.8	5.5	0.4	0.7	53.5	24.1	6.4	0.7	0.6	55.1	1.4	0.4
West Kalimantan	1.7	24.5	21.9	9.0	2.0	2.0	30.4	26.0	11.4	2.6	0.9	5.7	9.0	1.5	0.3
Central Kalimantan	1.3	42.5	29.5	1.3	0.3	1.5	50.7	32.2	1.7	0.3	0.6	18.6	21.7	0.2	0.2
South Kalimantan	0.6	27.6	27.0	2.5	0.3	0.7	34.4	30.9	3.6	0.3	0.6	12.8	18.4	0.0	0.1
East Kalimantan	0.7	17.6	25.7	2.1	0.3	1.0	25.9	39.4	3.4	0.3	0.3	8.3	10.1	0.6	0.3
North Sulawesi	0.9	8.5	15.4	5.6	1.4	0.8	11.0	18.4	7.7	1.8	1.1	2.7	8.5	0.8	0.3
Central Sulawesi	0.9	19.2	13.2	16.0	1.9	0.9	21.6	15.2	18.9	2.2	0.6	8.9	4.3	3.3	0.8
South Sulawesi	2.2	10.7	11.4	14.7	0.7	2.7	12.7	13.6	19.0	0.8	1.0	4.8	5.1	2.7	0.4
Southeast Sulawesi	0.6	8.6	20.0	19.1	1.2	0.6	9.9	24.6	23.3	1.2	0.5	3.7	2.8	3.7	1.4
Gorontalo	0.7	18.5	5.9	23.6	1.8	0.8	22.3	6.3	28.9	2.1	0.4	6.0	4.6	5.9	0.6
West Sulawesi	1.3	24.3	16.0	14.1	0.6	1.5	25.9	18.7	15.5	0.7	0.4	15.0	1.0	6.7	0.2
Maluku	0.6	14.5	9.1	33.7	0.6	0.6	15.4	10.1	41.6	0.6	0.3	11.4	5.7	6.9	0.8
North Maluku	1.6	11.1	15.5	18.9	1.0	1.7	13.4	19.1	23.2	1.2	1.2	2.6	2.9	3.3	0.0
West Papua	1.0	14.0	24.6	8.8	0.4	1.2	17.3	30.8	11.0	0.5	0.3	3.7	5.3	2.1	0.2
Papua	1.4	10.6	30.3	22.8	7.6	1.4	11.2	34.2	27.2	9.2	1.3	7.6	11.4	1.7	0.2
Total	3.0	17.4	20.2	8.0	1.3	3.6	21.2	26.0	11.6	1.7	1.7	10.3	9.5	1.3	0.4

Source: Authors' calculations from Susenas, 2009.

PART 4

Connecting with the Poor: Government Policies and Programs

13 THE EVOLUTION OF POVERTY ALLEVIATION POLICIES: IDEAS, ISSUES AND ACTORS

Ari Perdana and John Maxwell

Effective poverty alleviation requires serious commitment and concerted action on the part of political leaders. Unfortunately, poverty alleviation has had few real champions among the Indonesian bureaucratic and political elites. Beyond the rhetoric of election campaigns, many prominent figures soon go missing in action – or their voices and their efforts are drowned out when more immediate and pressing political problems emerge. Programs and policies that might contribute to alleviating poverty now also require cooperation from political leaders and officials at many levels – and this is difficult to achieve in decentralised Indonesia where power and political authority are so diffuse and the capacity of central government agencies is limited.

Despite the political openness that has prevailed since the collapse of Suharto's New Order regime in 1998, serious debate about poverty alleviation policy has been rare in Indonesia and has not received the attention it deserves in a country where the majority of the population is either poor or at risk of becoming poor. Many other major political issues – constitutional change and the creation of a new national electoral system, the place of the military in politics, decentralisation, resolving the Aceh problem, dealing with outbreaks of communal violence – have taken precedence, dominating debate among politicians and party leaders.

In practice, poverty alleviation has largely been left to technical specialists and planners within agencies such as the National Development Planning Agency (Badan Perencanaan Pembangunan Nasional, or Bappenas), where particular directorates have assumed responsibility for designing and planning most of the programs that have thus far been implemented. Research institutions and some universities have also been involved in assisting the government to design and evaluate programs, and donor organisations have given strong support to anti-poverty programs.

In sharp contrast, until the most recent elections, poverty has not been a high-priority topic for discussion and debate among the major political parties. Parties have been slow to formulate and release carefully considered public policies in this area, and party leaders have demonstrated little understanding of the dimensions and the root causes of entrenched poverty or the complexities involved in attempting to arrive at appropriate strategies that might lead to sustained progress. As a result, many opposition politicians and party leaders in particular have fallen back on populist slogans and empty rhetoric during election campaigns.[1]

This chapter will look back at the policy and political context in which poverty alleviation programs have been formulated and implemented. It will cover some of the measures adopted to deal with poverty in the past, both during the New Order period and after the financial crisis when poverty levels rose alarmingly. The bulk of the discussion, however, will concentrate on the most recent period and present-day attempts by the government to tackle poverty.

APPROACHES TO POVERTY DURING THE NEW ORDER

From its foundation as an independent country in the late 1940s, Indonesia was a nation suffering from a serious poverty problem. Little was done to deal with the problems of absolute poverty during the 1950s and early 1960s. The scale and extent of poverty worsened dramatically during the final years of Sukarno's Guided Democracy as the national economy fell into a parlous state, ravaged by hyperinflation, a decline in the quality and reach of essential services, and the deterioration of basic infrastructure.[2]

The incoming New Order government, under the guidance of the technocrats, set about the task of rebuilding the economy through a range of macro stabilisation measures that were designed to reduce inflation,

---

1   One exception seems to have been the Prosperous Justice Party (Partai Keadilan Sejahtera, or PKS). At least in the beginning, its party cadres won a reputation for hard work and moral probity, and demonstrated their willingness to assist the poor, especially in areas where natural disasters had occurred.

2   In 1970 poverty was estimated at around 54 per cent in urban areas and 39 per cent in rural areas (Booth 2000: Table 3).

stabilise prices and achieve positive economic growth. At least initially, the New Order economic reforms were not aimed at reducing poverty through programs targeted directly at the poor. Nevertheless, the levels of sustained economic growth achieved over the next two decades, combined with a range of important general social welfare measures, certainly contributed to a significant decline in poverty. These measures led to greater food security (especially through the maintenance of generally low and stable rice prices, as well as the attainment of rice self-sufficiency and the provision of rural credit), a major increase in school enrolments, leading to a dramatic surge in literacy rates, and improved nutrition and living standards. They were underpinned by key social infrastructure projects – the construction of elementary schools, health centres, roads and communications infrastructure – funded by the national development budget and covering the entire country.

Although the poverty rate had been reduced significantly by the early 1990s, it was apparent that some Indonesians had not shared in the benefits of the New Order's development program and that many poor households, particularly in rural areas, were still trapped in poverty.[3] As a result, a program conceived by the economist Mubyarto and directed by Bappenas was put in place in 1994 to deliver assistance over the next three years to over 20,000 villages that had been classified as among the poorest or most 'neglected' in the country. The Neglected Villages Program (Inpres Desa Tertinggal) used geographic targeting to identify these villages, channelling block grants to each village to establish a system of small-scale revolving credit for use by the poor. Despite some positive outcomes, a number of studies have highlighted the inherent flaws in the program's targeting methods, suggesting that the poverty alleviation aims of the program were seriously compromised.[4] The difficulty of achieving accurate and effective targeting to identify and locate the poor was to be a recurring problem for government planners and agencies in the years that followed.

POVERTY POLICY AND THE ASIAN FINANCIAL CRISIS

The financial crisis that struck Indonesia so hard in late 1997 saw many of the gains in poverty alleviation of the previous three decades suddenly

---

3   By the early 1990s the number of Indonesians living in a state of absolute poverty had been reduced to about 27 million, or approximately 15 per cent of the population (Booth 2000: Table 3).

4   See Mubyarto (1966), Molyneaux and Gertler (1999) and Perdana and Maxwell (2005: 93–101).

eliminated.[5] Poverty increased dramatically as a direct result of the crisis: over 49 million Indonesians (nearly 24 per cent of the population) were judged by the central statistics agency, Statistics Indonesia, to be living below the official poverty line in 1998. As the capacity to earn an income in the modern and mostly urban sector contracted, many Indonesians were forced to seek alternative and reduced sources of income in the informal sector or in rural areas. The resulting hardship and social distress were evident in the data collected on declining levels of nutrition, especially among children from poor backgrounds. The ability of poor families to access health services and keep their children in school was now seriously threatened.

Despite the need for urgent action to assist the poor, the situation was compounded by the political crisis of early 1998 that eventually led to the end of the Suharto presidency and his New Order regime. A period of political uncertainty was followed by a period of extensive reform as the incoming Habibie administration was pressed to follow through with urgent macroeconomic measures to stabilise the country's economy and solve the problems caused by the collapse of the banking sector. Both domestic and foreign observers urged the government to take whatever steps were necessary to provide emergency relief for those most in need and arrest any further worsening of the incidence of poverty, since there had also been a substantial increase in the number of those most vulnerable to falling into poverty if further shocks eventuated.

Despite some delay and confusion about how to proceed, a raft of emergency social welfare measures were eventually put in place throughout 1998 in an attempt to cushion the poorest sections of society from the impact of the crisis. This set of reactive measures came to be known as the Social Safety Net (Jaring Pengaman Sosial, or JPS), funded almost entirely through budgetary support in the form of loans from multilateral and bilateral donor agencies.[6] The package of programs lumped under the JPS umbrella included measures to boost employment through job creation (various labour-intensive programs, block grants and small-scale revolving credit); a food security program to assist the poor to obtain sufficient basic foodstuffs; several measures to enable the poor to continue to access basic health services; and an education assistance package designed to provide a level of direct financial support so that the children of poor families could continue to attend school.[7]

---

5   On the impact of the financial crisis, see Booth (1999) and Feridhanusetyawan (2000).

6   Of particular importance was the World Bank's Social Safety Net Adjustment Loan.

7   For an overview, see Daley and Fane (2002).

It was the government's intention that these JPS programs would deliver emergency assistance to the poor, but in reality the targeting of most of the programs was to a greater or lesser extent seriously flawed. Poor targeting resulted in a degree of leakage of the benefits of the programs to those sections of the population that were not poor. At the same time, there were numerous instances of undercoverage, leading to many poor households missing out altogether on urgently needed assistance.[8] Ultimately, it was the government's macro-level economic stabilisation measures, especially the management of rice prices, that proved to be the key factor in reducing the poverty rate during the post-crisis period (World Bank 2006a: 20).

POST-CRISIS POLICY MEASURES

From fuel subsidies to the expansion of targeted assistance

One of the most important issues to emerge from the crisis was the need for the government to reduce energy subsidy expenditure (on fuel and electricity) and find ways to allocate more resources to targeted poverty alleviation measures and social welfare programs. Indonesia had maintained a general fuel subsidy applying to all petroleum products since the Sukarno era. Although in theory all Indonesians were able to benefit from such subsidies through lower prices for fuel, in practice this was an extremely regressive measure since it was the wealthy and the better-off within the community who benefited most – for example, those who owned motor vehicles and the big consumers of power. Since wealthier households consumed more fuel, in nominal terms the subsidy went disproportionately to the rich. Maintaining these subsidies was also a huge drain on the national budget during a period when the economy was still recovering from the financial crisis. This problem was compounded whenever a sharp increase in international petroleum prices occurred. Until 2005, fuel subsidies accounted for around a fifth of total government expenditure each year.

Ultimately the government was forced to take drastic action to reduce the subsidy and its negative impact on the budget. Aware that any increase in fuel costs would have an immediate flow-on effect to the community through higher charges and prices, including for essential items such as food, the government endeavoured to cushion the impact on the

---

8   For detailed analytical studies, see Cameron (2002), Sumarto, Suryahadi and Pritchett (2002, 2005) and Sparrow (2003). On targeting problems in the JPS program, see Perdana and Maxwell (2005: 92–130).

poor through a range of emergency measures funded by reallocating a proportion of the budgetary savings resulting from the subsidy cuts.[9]

After an initial minor cut in October 2000, the sharp increase in global oil prices in the mid-2000s forced the government to cut energy subsidies and increase the domestic prices of fuel and electricity. The most dramatic cut occurred in October 2005, when petrol prices were hiked by over 87 per cent and diesel by almost 105 per cent. Unfortunately rice prices also increased sharply at this time, the combined increase in fuel and basic foodstuff prices pushing inflation to 18 per cent. As a result, the official headcount poverty rate rose from 16.0 per cent in 2005 to 17.8 per cent in 2006.

To counter the adverse impact of the price rises, the government allocated some Rp 11 trillion to a direct cash transfer program, a rural infrastructure program and a set of compensatory programs in education and health. In mid-2005 it introduced a new education scheme, School Operational Assistance (Bantuan Operasional Sekolah, or BOS). Unlike the previous scholarships program, BOS provides block grants for schools, which can be used for any operational purpose excluding salaries and school construction.[10] In the health sector, the government launched a social insurance scheme for poor households, Health Insurance for the Poor (Asuransi Kesehatan Masyarakat Miskin, or Askeskin).[11]

In 2005 the government also introduced an emergency program of unconditional payments to poor households, known as Direct Cash Assistance (Bantuan Langsung Tunai, or BLT). Emergency cash payments of Rp 100,000 per month covering a 12-month period were made directly to over 15 million poor households through the national post-office network. Mindful of the targeting problems that had been so pervasive during the implementation of the post-crisis JPS programs, on this occasion Statistics Indonesia applied a different targeting methodology that appears to have produced a much better result. After another fuel price increase in May 2008, the program was repeated for a more limited period of time. Independent evaluations of the various phases of BLT – a complex measure implemented in great haste – suggest that the program

---

9   In addition, the government retained several crisis-related JPS programs: the 'cheap rice' program, now rebadged as Rice for Poor Families (Raskin), scholarships for primary and secondary school students, the health card entitling the poor to subsidised medical care and (later) a health insurance scheme for poor households.

10 Although intended to make education more affordable, especially for the poor, and while it may have improved the quality of schooling, the BOS program may not have improved access to schooling or increased enrolment rates. See World Bank (2006a: 141–2) and Suharyo et al. (2006).

11 Further details are given in Chapter 9 by Sparrow.

largely did succeed in providing many poor families with some relief, even though the poverty rate still increased slightly during this period.[12]

Politically, the BLT program proved to be a masterstroke for President Susilo Bambang Yudhoyono and his government. Up to this point opinion polls had been showing an erosion of support to the point where he and his party would have been unlikely to win the 2009 elections. But this decline was quickly arrested when BLT funds began to flow throughout the country. The widespread popularity of this program and the announcement of other social assistance measures were major contributing factors to Yudhoyono's re-election for a second term in 2009.

The introduction of conditional cash transfers

Direct cash transfers were designed to be a temporary measure for use during emergencies and could not provide a lasting solution to the problem of poverty, especially chronic poverty. Consequently, in 2007 the Yudhoyono government announced a major set of development initiatives to tackle poverty under an umbrella program called the National Program for Community Empowerment (Program Nasional Pemberdayaan Masyarakat, or PNPM). This program is discussed at some length elsewhere in this volume.[13] It covers an extremely complex and large set of community development measures divided between a core program and a support program, and has been designed for delivery to village communities throughout the entire country.

The guiding principle of PNPM is the active participation of village communities, drawing on local institutions, with the ultimate aim of community empowerment. The program is modelled directly on the World Bank's Kecamatan Development Program.[14] It applies the same system of competitive block grants for villages that submit proposals to a panel at the subdistrict (*kecamatan*) level, but only after a comprehensive village-level community consultation process has been conducted. A fundamental element of the World Bank program that is to be replicated in PNPM projects is the capacity to disburse program funds directly to local communities in a way that largely prevents the participation of profit-seeking contractors and attempts to avoid any meddling by officials from the various layers of the bureaucracy. Nevertheless, the dramatic 'scaling

---

12 See Hastuti et al. (2006), Hastuti et al. (2010: 18–19) and Sumarto and Surya-hadi (2010: 227–31).

13 See Chapter 14 in this volume by Yulaswati and Sumadi and the PNPM website, http://www.pnpm-mandiri.org, for additional details.

14 The Kecamatan Development Program was launched in 1998 and eventually funded activities in over 28,000 villages. For a fascinating insider's account, see Guggenheim (n.d.) and Guggenheim et al. (2004).

up' that has occurred and the government's claims of 'ownership' suggest that these principles may be difficult to maintain throughout the course of the program. Combating corruption – always a serious issue for the Kecamatan Development Program – will be a major challenge for PNPM, especially since many central government departments and local government actors are now eager to become more directly involved in the implementation of the program, bringing the risk that corrupt bureaucrats may seek a share of the spoils.[15]

Local community empowerment throughout Indonesia is a worthy aim, and the PNPM complex of programs is intended as a major transfer of funds from the centre to the grassroots level. If the experience with the Kecamatan Development Program is any guide, most villages will choose to use the grants for a variety of small-scale infrastructure projects or for the establishment of revolving funds to develop small-scale income-generating activities. But what contribution will these programs actually make to overcoming poverty? To what extent will PNPM become the poverty alleviation panacea that some national-level political leaders would like it to be?

Poverty alleviation features prominently in official press releases and publicity about PNPM. A degree of caution is nevertheless justified, since this program – like its forebear – does not set out to alleviate poverty by targeting poor households. Rather, it is a set of programs that targets geographic areas (villages) to deliver funding assistance for broader community development. Just what its actual impact will be on poverty – especially chronic poverty – at the household level is yet to be determined and must be the subject of careful monitoring and evaluation throughout the life of the program.

In addition to the PNPM core programs, and to accelerate the progress of poverty alleviation, in 2007 the government launched two other conditional cash transfers as pilot programs in seven provinces. Both focus on two critical areas intrinsic to poverty alleviation: maternal and child health, and elementary to lower secondary school education. While both programs have similar aims, they are operating under the auspices of different government agencies and have radically different approaches to the delivery of program benefits. The Family of Hope Program (Program Keluarga Harapan, or PKH) is being implemented by the Ministry of Social Affairs and directs the cash transfers to individual households (Hastuti et al. 2010: 19–21). PNPM for a Healthy and Clever Generation (PNPM Generasi Sehat dan Cerdas) is under the general direction of the

---

15 A certain level of corruption by officials and leakage of program benefits to the non-poor has continued to occur in the most recent anti-poverty programs despite serious efforts to improve their design and implementation.

Ministry of Home Affairs and focuses on dispersing cash transfers to entire village communities. Program participants – either participating poor households in the case of PKH or village communities in the case of PNPM Generasi – must commit to improvements on a specified list of health and education indicators as a means of securing program benefits.

Even if the PNPM program succeeds in empowering local communities, and thousands of valuable small-scale infrastructure projects are successfully completed all over Indonesia in the years that lie ahead – village roads, small bridges, simple irrigation systems, wells, clean water storage facilities and the like – the existence of such a program certainly does not free governments at the central, provincial and district levels from their responsibilities to plan, fund and implement specific poverty alleviation measures. There are many tasks that are beyond the experience, capacity and horizons of village communities. It therefore remains the responsibility of government to complement any progress made at the village level under programs such as PNPM.

POLITICS OF POVERTY TODAY: ISSUES AND CHALLENGES

How much is being allocated to social assistance?

While it is true that expenditure on non-energy subsidies and social assistance is increasing in nominal terms, overall these still account for less than 10 per cent of total government expenditure. The share of energy subsidies was cut from 20 per cent in 2005 to 10 per cent in 2009, providing greater fiscal space. Despite this, the combined allocation for non-energy subsidies and social assistance measures only increased from 8 per cent in 2005 to 14 per cent in 2009, and declined to 9 per cent in 2010 as the BLT program was phased out. By comparison, transfers to the regions account for around a third of total expenditure, while other central government spending has increased from 42 per cent in 2002 to 48 per cent in 2010 (Figure 13.1).[16]

This does not mean that the central government's performance should be evaluated only by the amount allocated in the national budget for social assistance. It may be more appropriate to evaluate performance in terms of the outcomes, that is, the extent to which existing programs

---

16 Some of this reflects an increase in education and social protection expenditure, including both targeted and non-targeted components. The education allocation (less personnel expenditure), however, accounted for only 13 per cent of the 2009 central government budget, and is expected to decline to 10 per cent in 2011. Social protection accounts for only 0.5 per cent of all central government spending.

Figure 13.1   Composition of central government spending (Rp trillion)

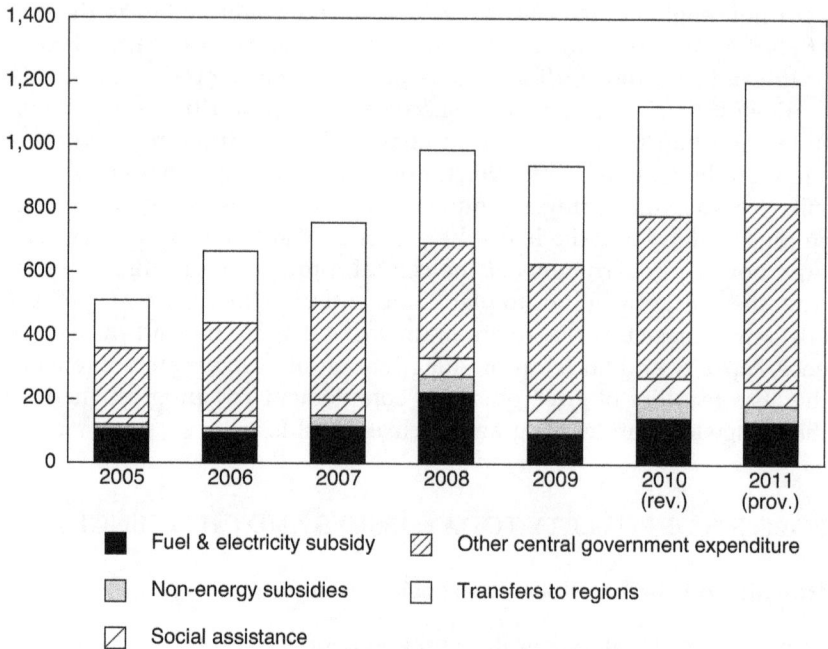

Source: Ministry of Finance.

have increased the welfare of the poor. Nevertheless, the composition of the budget reveals that a disproportionate amount of government expenditure is still being allocated to general subsidies and other expenditure, compared with support for activities aimed directly at assisting the poorest households.

More 'voice' and 'noise'

Greater political freedom for citizens and an expanded role for political parties and the legislative body (Dewan Perwakilan Rakyat, or DPR) are among the most significant achievements of the past decade. This means there are now more actors participating in the decision-making process. During the New Order, thorough and open public discussion of potentially controversial issues such as poverty was limited. Nowadays, not only is poverty discussed freely, but it has in some senses become a political commodity. Politicians often try to win popular support by attacking government policies on poverty, emphasising the negative aspects of poverty alleviation efforts and ignoring the fact that the poverty rate has generally been declining.

Such public debate has led to more open scrutiny, which may result in better policies. An improvement in the reporting of official poverty data is one example. In 2006 President Yudhoyono was widely criticised for using outdated poverty data in his annual Independence Day speech.[17] The government, particularly the staff who had drafted the speech, took responsibility, explaining that the most recent data had been unavailable at the time of the speech because Statistics Indonesia had only just conducted that year's National Socio-Economic Survey (Survei Sosio-Ekonomi Nasional, or Susenas). The government responded to the public criticism by asking the agency to improve the methodology and transparency of its poverty calculations, and to conduct the survey and release the poverty data earlier in the year so that the annual presidential speech would reflect the most up-to-date figures.

Poverty emerged as a central issue during the 2009 presidential election campaign. Debate about poverty had become more technical and data oriented, but Yudhoyono demonstrated a considerable understanding of the salient issues and a keen grasp of much of the detail during his public and media appearances. His opponents, on the other hand – particularly two of the vice-presidential candidates, the retired generals Wiranto and Prabowo – resorted to personal attacks and populist slogans, and used poverty numbers based on the international $2-a-day poverty line to question the government's achievements.[18] The latter produces a much larger number of poor than the official Statistics Indonesia poverty rate. There are various methods that can be applied to calculate a poverty rate and they all produce different results, but little effort was made to clarify these matters in a way that was readily comprehensible to the public. The 2009 election debate on poverty demonstrated the need for senior government leaders and also independent specialists to explain where the poverty figures come from and what they mean.

The growing 'voice' evident in public debate, with a greater number of participants, may lead to closer scrutiny of government poverty policies

---

17 The president's speech drew on poverty data from 1999 to 2005 showing that poverty had declined from 23 per cent to 16 per cent. Since the government had increased fuel prices in late 2005, it was widely believed that poverty had actually increased. This was confirmed when Statistics Indonesia data were eventually released.

18 Yudhoyono's vice-presidential running mate, Boediono, was attacked as a 'neo-liberal', while his opponent, Prabowo, proclaimed himself a supporter of 'the people's economy'. The international $2-a-day poverty line is based on the purchasing power parity (PPP) exchange rate and is not easily comparable with Statistics Indonesia's official poverty figures.

and demand for action, but there is also an increase in 'noise', which could drive poverty alleviation policies in a more populist direction. One obvious example is the difficulties the government has faced over the reduction in fuel subsidies. Senior political leaders have frequently failed to explain the government's decision in simple language so that ordinary people can understand why the dramatic cuts to the subsidy were necessary and what action the government was taking to assist those most in need. As a result, debate about the need for a rise in fuel prices has often resulted in scare campaigns, public protests and demonstrations – sometimes led by business pressure groups or even students and non-government activists supposedly representing the interests of the poor and needy. Consequently, political expediency has sometimes prevailed over sound policy. Consistent with Yudhoyono's reputation for hesitation and a reluctance to make tough or controversial political decisions – especially over pricing and general subsidies – in early and mid December 2008 the government announced two significant reductions in domestic fuel prices, realising that it would be facing an election in mid-2009.

The 2010 public controversy over the 'aspiration fund' (*dana aspirasi*) proposal is another example illustrating both the important role of the national parliament and the risks of populism. In mid-2010, Golkar – the second-largest party in the parliament – proposed that each electoral district should receive Rp 15 billion from the state budget to finance development projects that would be chosen on the basis of suggestions by individual members of parliament. The supporters of the idea claimed that the fund would promote regional development, and that members of parliament – the people most familiar with individual electorates – were in the best position to identify the projects most urgently needed by local constituents.

This proposal was widely criticised for the high probability that it would be prone to corruption.[19] Such a scheme would also create an overlapping role between the executive role of government and the legislative functions of the parliament, and in fact is not possible under current fiscal law. Following these criticisms, Golkar politicians quickly revised the proposal, calling instead for the government to allocate Rp 1 billion each year to every village in the country.

The government indicated that neither of the Golkar proposals was acceptable, although surprisingly it failed to remind proponents that the PNPM program was already delivering a significant and appropriate level of funding to villages in every district in the country, but accord-

---

19 The West Sumatra provincial parliament introduced a similar scheme some years ago. Almost every member of parliament was later jailed for corruption in connection with the scheme.

ing to a carefully planned and accountable process designed to minimise corruption and the misuse of government resources.

What led Golkar politicians to advocate this flawed scheme? Opposition politicians in the DPR faced a dilemma. Direct and conditional cash transfer programs such as BLT, PNPM and PKH had won wide support among the community, boosting the popularity of Yudhoyono and his government. This had made it difficult to attack those policies directly without risking a voter backlash.[20] It appears that the Golkar proposals were an attempt by opposition politicians to gain access to budgetary funds that they could distribute within their electorates for their own political purposes.

The expanded role of district governments

One of the most important characteristics of Indonesian poverty is the significant variation in the incidence of poverty across the archipelago.[21] Those regions where poverty rates are highest also tend to have lower levels of educational attainment, less access to clean water and sanitation, and the weakest public health outcomes, especially in the areas of maternal and child health and malnutrition incidence. There are also significant regional disparities in access to public facilities. As a result, those governments that have emerged as powerful entities at the regional level since decentralisation now have a critical role to play.

Under regional autonomy, significant levels of funding and political authority have been transferred to the regions, to provincial and especially to district governments. Each year around 30 per cent of central government expenditure is allocated to the regions (see Figure 13.1), to be supplemented by local sources of revenue. The progress of poverty reduction now depends to a greater extent than ever before on local government capacity to manage budgets, establish priorities and deliver sound policies.

Supporters of regional autonomy argued that it would improve the delivery of essential public services. District governments would be better informed about the specific challenges facing their areas than the central or even the provincial levels of government and could tailor service delivery to meet local needs. So far, however, the impact of decentralisation has been patchy, while the tendency to create ever more

---

20 In 2008 former president Megawati Sukarnoputri criticised the BLT program for making people dependent on government charity. She later retracted her comments, calling instead for improvements to the program's implementation.

21 See Chapter 11 by Suryahadi et al. and World Bank (2006a: xxiv).

new provinces and districts has the potential to exacerbate existing inequalities and reduce access to funding between regions. The success of any initiatives to tackle poverty alleviation at the district level is dependent to a large extent on the quality of those local political leaders who have emerged under regional autonomy.[22] While some promising local reforms and initiatives have been attempted, there have been numerous cases of corruption involving district leaders. There have also been many instances of failure on the part of local officials to deal adequately with poverty and welfare issues, such as the serious outbreaks of malnutrition that have occurred in eastern Indonesia.

One area that is crucial for poverty alleviation is infrastructure development. Within districts, there are a multitude of essential large-scale public infrastructure projects that cross village boundaries. These include a system of reliable district roads linking village communities – especially those in remote rural areas – to markets and essential services in larger centres, thus boosting local economic development; and the refurbishment or construction of vital district health and educational facilities. To meet the needs of local communities in the surrounding area, including the poor and needy, these schools and health centres should have adequate skilled staff and equipment to operate the facilities. In terms of public spending, education and to a lesser extent health expenditure has been increasing at all levels of government. But while central government spending on physical infrastructure (including roads, water, irrigation and electricity) has declined, provincial and district governments have been slow to commit funds in these areas. This has led to an overall decline in infrastructure spending.

The failure to allocate funds to rural road construction and maintenance is an especially glaring example of how decentralisation has so far failed to deliver public goods as expected. About four-fifths of Indonesia's total road system is now the responsibility of district governments. Less than 40 per cent of those roads are in acceptable condition, and more than a third are damaged or seriously damaged.[23] Unfortunately, most of the expenditure that has been allocated to road construction or refurbishment throughout Indonesia in recent years – including projects financed by foreign donors – has been biased towards building or upgrading 'national' roads.

22 See McCulloch and Sjahrir (2008: 26). For case studies of local reforms, see World Bank (2006b).
23 See World Bank (2006a: 107–12). These data are from the mid-2000s but the condition of district roads in the most underdeveloped provinces remains largely unchanged.

Agency and coordination

In decentralised Indonesia, many of the reforms and program activities that drive poverty alleviation must take place in the provinces and districts. However, there remain many important tasks that require effective coordination at the national level. These include such matters as comprehensive and nationally directed data collection processes; effective monitoring and evaluation drawing on a common pool of skilled personnel; and the allocation and pooling of financial resources to fund large-scale programs such as infrastructure projects. National-level coordination and decision making can reduce transaction costs and achieve economies of scale, and ensure that uniform national standards are being met so that all regions receive adequate attention.

Consequently, there is an important question about who is actually assuming responsibility for the effective coordination of poverty policies at the national level. Previously Bappenas played a central role in the design, planning and coordination of some of the most important anti-poverty programs, especially through the work of officials from its key directorates. Since the announcement of PNPM, it has become apparent that a number of central government ministries – not only health, education and social affairs, but also home affairs and several line ministries with no previous experience in this area – are now involved directly in poverty alleviation activities. This raises the problem of competing vested interests, and at the very least overlapping or conflicting responsibilities.

In early 2010 the president gave the difficult task of the oversight of poverty alleviation to his vice president, Boediono. A high-level task force has since been established within the vice president's office: the National Team for the Acceleration of Poverty Reduction (Tim Nasional Percepatan Penanggulangan Kemiskinan, or TNP2K).[24] This initiative has attracted financial support from at least one donor agency. A number of academic and technical specialists have been appointed to the team as specialist advisors, and work has begun to create a unified database of poor households to assist in the coordination of anti-poverty efforts across agencies and departments.

In many respects TNP2K is not an entirely new initiative. A poverty policy coordinating body was first established in 2001 during Megawati Sukarnoputri's presidency under the leadership of Jusuf Kalla as

---

24 For details of the taskforce, including its organisational structure and composition, and preliminary statements about general policy and proposed programs, see the TNP2K website: http://www.tnp2k.wapresri.go.id/.

coordinating minister for people's welfare,[25] and a similar body continued to exist throughout the first Yudhoyono presidency. These earlier
bodies achieved little as far as concrete policy and practical outcomes
were concerned. Nevertheless, after a lengthy process of consultation
with the donor community and non-government organisations, the
Kalla committee did release a draft interim poverty reduction strategy in
March 2003. This was passed on to the government for further development (ADB 2006: 81–4).

Without any substantial political resources or party backing, TNP2K
will have difficulty carrying out the essential task of coordinating policy
across central government agencies such as Bappenas and the various
key ministries that now have a stake in poverty alleviation policy. In addition, ways must be found to involve the regions in this process. It is
not clear, either, what role the present coordinating minister for people's
welfare will play. Agung Laksono, a former speaker of the DPR and a
senior Golkar figure, had chaired the previous coordinating body until
Boediono's appointment. His own party had promoted the flawed 'aspiration fund' scheme within the DPR, where it will be essential to gar-
ner support for any new initiatives or proposals that might emerge from
TNP2K deliberations.

CONCLUDING REMARKS

Poverty rates in Indonesia have been trending downward in recent years,
assisted by macroeconomic stability. For the first time in Indonesia's history, a government led by a popularly elected president has attempted
to put in place a number of important anti-poverty measures in health,
education and community development that offer some hope of tackling entrenched poverty, especially through the development of a longer-
term social assistance strategy.

Nevertheless, enormous challenges remain if Indonesia is to achieve
a further substantial reduction in the number of poor citizens, especially
in the chronically poor and very poor categories. Eliminating these particular pockets of poverty and reaching those who are not assisted by
broader development initiatives will require careful planning and the
implementation of a variety of special measures. It will also require political leaders who understand that there are no quick fixes or simple
solutions, and that poverty needs to be tackled on many levels using a
variety of approaches that reflect the needs of particular regions.

---

25 For details, see http://arsip.tkpkri.org/.

In this chapter we have noted the evolution of various approaches to tackling the problem. We have also highlighted some issues and challenges to poverty policies under a democratic and decentralised Indonesia. First, social assistance still accounts for only a small share of the central government's total spending. Second, democracy and openness provide various checks and balances, yet at the same time increase the risk that politicians will give in to pressure for populist solutions. Third, decentralisation is not yet operating to its full potential as a means of reducing poverty. And fourth, the central government must remain responsible for the effective coordination of poverty reduction strategies throughout the country.

REFERENCES

ADB (Asian Development Bank) (2006) *From Poverty to Prosperity: A Country Poverty Analysis for Indonesia*, ADB, Manila.

Booth, A. (1999) 'The impact of the crisis on poverty and equity', in H.W. Arndt and H. Hill (eds) *Southeast Asia's Economic Crisis: Origins, Lessons, and the Way Forward*, Institute for Southeast Asian Studies, Singapore.

Booth, A. (2000) 'Poverty and inequality in the Soeharto era: an assessment', *Bulletin of Indonesian Economic Studies*, 36(1): 73–104.

Cameron, L. (2002) 'Did social safety net scholarships reduce drop-out rates during the Indonesian economic crisis?', Policy Research Working Paper No. 2800, World Bank, Washington DC, March.

Daley, A. and G. Fane (2002) 'Anti-poverty programs in Indonesia', *Bulletin of Indonesian Economic Studies*, 38(3): 309–31.

Feridhanusetyawan, T. (2000) 'The social impact of the Indonesian economic crisis', in *Social Impacts of the Asian Economic Crisis*, Thailand Development Research Institute (TDRI), Bangkok.

Guggenheim, S. (n.d.) 'Crises and contradictions: understanding the origins of a community development project in Indonesia', unpublished paper, Yale University, New Haven CT. Available at: http://www.yale.edu/agrarian studies/colloqpapers/Crises.pdf.

Guggenheim, S., T. Wiranto, Y. Prasta and S. Wong (2004) 'Indonesia's Kecamatan Development Program: a large-scale use of community development to reduce poverty', Case Studies in Scaling Up Poverty Reduction, International Bank for Reconstruction and Development and World Bank, Jakarta.

Hastuti et al. (2006) 'A rapid appraisal of the implementation of the 2005 direct cash transfer program in Indonesia: a case study in five *kabupaten/kota*', research report, SMERU Research Institute, Jakarta, July.

Hastuti et al. (2010) 'The role of social protection programs in alleviating the impact of the global financial crisis 2008/2009', research report, SMERU Research Institute, Jakarta, July.

McCulloch, N. and B.S. Sjahrir (2008) 'Endowments, location or luck? Evaluating the determinants of sub-national growth in decentralized Indonesia', Policy Research Working Paper No. 4769, World Bank, Jakarta, November.

Molyneaux, J. and P. Gertler (1999) 'Applying a simple method to measure program impact: an evaluation of a large scale micro-credit/poverty alleviation program in Indonesia', Rand Corporation and University of California Berkeley Press, Berkeley CA.

Mubyarto (1966), *Ekonomi Rakyat dan Program IDT* [The People's Economy and the Neglected Villages Program], Aditya Media Press, Yogyakarta.

Perdana, A. and J. Maxwell (2005) 'Poverty targeting programs in Indonesia: problems and lessons learned', in J. Weiss (ed.) *Poverty Targeting in Asia*, Edward Elgar, Cheltenham.

Sparrow, R. (2003) 'Protecting education for the poor in times of crisis: an evaluation of the scholarships and grants program in Indonesia', unpublished paper, April.

Suharyo, W.I. et al. (2006) 'A rapid appraisal of the PKPS–BBM education sector: School Operational Assistance (BOS)', research report, SMERU Research Institute, Jakarta, September.

Sumarto, S. and A. Suryahadi (2010) 'Post-crisis social protection programs in Indonesia', in J. Hardjono, N. Akhmadi and S. Sumarto (eds) *Poverty and Social Protection in Indonesia*, Institute for Southeast Asian Studies and SMERU Research Institute, Singapore.

Sumarto, S., A. Suryahadi and L. Pritchett (2002) 'Design and implementation of the Indonesian social safety net programs', *Developing Economies*, 40(1): 3–31.

Sumarto, S., A. Suryahadi and L. Pritchett (2005) 'Assessing the impact of Indonesian social safety net programmes on household welfare and poverty dynamics', *European Journal of Development Research*, 17(1): 155–77.

Suryahadi, A., W. Widyanti, D. Perwira, S. Sumarto, C. Elbers and M. Pradhan (2003) 'Developing a poverty map for Indonesia: an initiatory work in three provinces', Parts 1–3, research report, SMERU Research Institute, Jakarta.

World Bank (2006a) *Making the New Indonesia Work for the Poor*, World Bank, Jakarta.

World Bank (2006b) 'Making services work for the poor in Indonesia: nine case studies from Indonesia', World Bank, Jakarta.

14 REDUCING POVERTY BY INCREASING COMMUNITY AND FEMALE PARTICIPATION

Vivi Yulaswati and Pungky Sumadi

The difficulty of resolving the problem of poverty immediately after the Asian financial crisis of 1997–98 gave rise to thoughts about the necessity for a stronger focus on results, and on broad community participation, when devising poverty alleviation strategies. In 2005, with analysis showing that blanket subsidies were mainly benefiting the non-poor, the Indonesian government took the tough political decision to reduce fuel subsidies. This policy resulted in an average rise in fuel prices of 138 per cent over the year. To protect poor households from the impact of these price increases, the government reallocated the savings from the fuel subsidy reduction to four major poverty alleviation programs: an unconditional cash transfer program (Bantuan Langsung Tunai, or BLT); a grants program to provide operational support for primary schools (Bantuan Operasional Sekolah, or BOS); a health insurance scheme for the poor (Asuransi Kesehatan Masyarakat Miskin, or Askeskin); and a program to deliver infrastructure to almost 13,000 poor villages.[1]

In 2007, the government redoubled its focus on poverty reduction by launching a *conditional* cash transfer program (Program Keluarga Harapan, or PKH) and integrating two community-driven development programs, the Kecamatan Development Program and the Urban Poverty Program, into the National Program for Community Empowerment

---

1 The Askeskin program was renamed Jaminan Kesehatan Masyarakat (Jamkesmas) in 2008. On the targeting of BLT and Jamkesmas, see Chapter 15 by Alatas, Purnamasari and Wai-Poi. The unconditional cash transfer is intended to be used only during crises.

(Program Nasional Pemberdayaan Masyarakat, or PNPM). Both PNPM and PKH involved the decentralisation of spending to the community level to increase the level of local participation and self-help.

Broadly speaking, the government's poverty reduction programs fall into three categories. The first is a cluster of programs targeting poor households and individuals. They include a subsidised rice scheme, a health insurance scheme and a scholarships scheme, as well as PKH. The second is a group of community-based programs for poor subdistricts and villages built around block grants and community facilitation. PNPM falls into this category. The third is a cluster of programs to support promising small and medium-sized enterprises by providing micro credit and other financial assistance.

This chapter focuses on the community empowerment program (PNPM) and the conditional cash transfer program (PKH). Both were designed to give communities the means to improve their own levels of welfare, in the belief that this would be a more effective way of identifying the vulnerable, tackling the lack of access to basic services and reducing disparities in poverty across regions. The next two sections will discuss each program in turn: their rationales, approaches and results. This will be followed by a discussion of some of the strategies that could be used to accelerate the pace of poverty reduction in Indonesia.

PNPM: A COMMUNITY-BASED ANTI-POVERTY PROGRAM

The decentralisation policy implemented in 2001 created an opportunity to focus more strongly on poverty. There was already a firm political will to shift the development paradigm from a top-down, state-centred, supply-driven process towards a more bottom-up approach driven by local demand. This approach was first used during the Asian financial crisis, when the government piloted several community-based projects to tackle unemployment and reduce poverty in both rural and urban areas. In addition to the Kecamatan Development Program and the Urban Poverty Program, these projects included grants for less developed villages, a rural infrastructure development program and a project to increase the incomes of farmers and fishermen. In most cases, however, the programs stopped when funding from donors came to an end.

Rationale

Aware that the decision to reduce fuel subsidies in 2005 was having a disproportionate effect on the poor, in 2007 President Susilo Bambang Yudhoyono launched PNPM as an umbrella program for community-driven development. Based on the lessons learned from earlier programs about effective poverty reduction instruments for rural and urban areas during crises, the government decided that the main objectives of PNPM should be job creation and community empowerment.

The structure of PNPM was designed to address four major problems identified with previous poverty programs. First, Indonesia's challenging geographic conditions and imperfect markets made it difficult to reach the poor in remote and isolated areas and assess their needs. The policy of providing block grants directly to villages and subdistricts would allow those best placed to assess local needs – the communities themselves – to design and implement programs. Second, the government wanted to reduce the bureaucratic complications associated with decentralisation by dealing with the lowest possible level of local government (villages and subdistricts). Third, by allowing community members to 'sit in the driver's seat', the program would increase the capacity of communities to identify areas of need and attack poverty. Evidence from participatory planning experiences also suggested that having a facilitated process to determine need would encourage the participation of non-elites. Finally, the creation of a single umbrella program was designed to eliminate the inefficiency and confusion caused by having a plethora of overlapping programs administered by many different ministries and institutions.

Main features

As an umbrella program for community-driven development, PNPM aimed to lay the foundation for community self-help through community-based organisations and capacity development. The program was expanded to cover all subdistricts in 2009, and now comprises two groups of programs. The first group of core programs targets particular regions: poor rural areas; poor urban areas; other poor and disadvantaged areas; regions in need of social and economic infrastructure; and rural regions in need of additional infrastructure. The second group of support programs is designed to strengthen certain sectors, such as agribusiness in agricultural areas, tourism-related activities in poor villages close to a tourism destination, and fishery and marine activities in poor coastal communities.[2]

From a management perspective, PNPM has several strengths. It has transformed the approach to community development from one based

---

2 In addition, there are several pilot projects to promote 'green' natural resource management practices and the use of renewable energy, and to achieve progress towards the three Millennium Development Goals in which Indonesia lags: maternal health, infant mortality and primary education.

Figure 14.1   The process of community empowerment

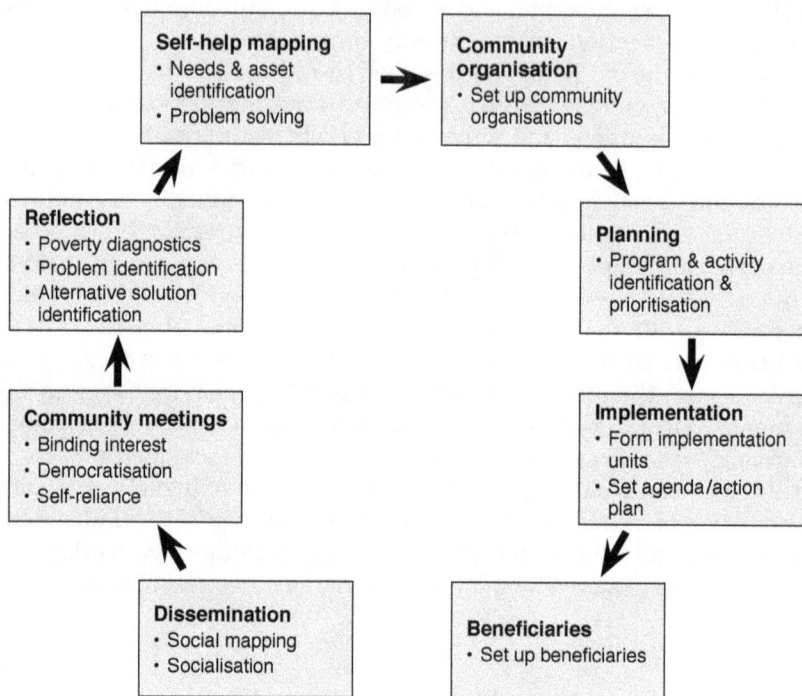

Source: Bappenas.

on *individual projects* to one based on *programs*, that is, from a partial to a more integrated and sustainable approach to poverty reduction. It sets uniform criteria for the allocation of block grants to avoid the problem of overlapping projects at the subdistrict level, and strengthens key mechanisms of community-driven development (such as village oversight, community procurement and complaint-handling systems). Other management innovations include its performance and results-based monitoring and evaluation system, its integrated database of program activities and community groups, and its alignment of community plans with regular development plans and budget mechanisms.

The conventional view in which the poor are viewed as subjects without information and choice so that there is no need to involve them in public policy decision making is not an effective way of tackling poverty. Through the idealised cycle of empowerment described in Figure 14.1, communities are encouraged to formulate their own problems, decide what to do about them and execute their decisions themselves. To facilitate this process, PNPM channels block grants directly to the community while providing technical assistance through community facilitators, who are the key agents of change. The capacity of each community determines the duration of the process and the quality of the result. The cycle may therefore take longer in the poorer communities.

PNPM involves a three-tiered mechanism for the coordination of programs and institutions, in which guidance on design and budgeting is provided by the National Development Planning Agency (Badan Perencanaan Pembangunan Nasional, or Bappenas); implementation and detailed technical supervision are the responsibility of the technical ministries; and policy coordination is managed by an inter-ministerial team chaired by the Coordinating Ministry for Social Welfare. In 2008, the Indonesian government and the World Bank established a PNPM Support Facility to coordinate international support for PNPM projects. A National Team for the Acceleration of Poverty Reduction (Tim Nasional Percepatan Penanggulangan Kemiskinan, or TNP2K) has also been established to speed up the roll-out of anti-poverty programs, to be coordinated by the vice president's office. Its role with regard to PNPM is somewhat unclear, however, as some programs have long lead times exceeding the usual decision-making timeframes of the vice president's office.

Evaluation

Given the rapid expansion and potential reach of PNPM, it is important to assess its performance and impact. The program was designed to have built-in evaluation, through baseline and follow-up surveys of target and control communities. A survey in 2007 tracking progress in rural areas under the preceding Kecamatan Development Program provided important baseline findings for PNPM. It found that, between 2002 and 2007, households in the poorest 20 per cent of the population reported a gain in per capita consumption of 11 per cent compared with control areas; households in poor subdistricts were 9 per cent more likely to move out of poverty than households in control areas; unemployment increased by 1.5 per cent less in poor subdistricts than in control areas; and household heads in poor subdistricts were 12 per cent more likely to enjoy expanded access to outpatient care (Voss 2008: v–vi).[3]

The block grants made available under PNPM are mainly used to provide or expand small-scale infrastructure. No complex services or

---

3 The preliminary results of a follow-up survey were released in early 2011. It showed less pronounced impacts, partly because the evaluation period was shorter. Improvements in welfare were found across all households, but the impacts were less evident for poor households and those in poor subdistricts.

materials are required, so the work can be performed by the communities themselves to create job opportunities. Most projects are completed within three to six months, providing welcome temporary employment for farm workers during the off-season or when harvests are poor. Rural infrastructure projects have been found to have high economic returns (an internal rate of return of 39–68 per cent) and low costs (56 per cent lower than equivalent projects built under government contracts) (Alatas 2005; Torrens 2005). The grants can have a significant impact on unemployment rates and the incidence of poverty.[4]

Increasing the size of the block grants might have an even greater impact on poverty, but this is offset by the limited capacity of communities to absorb and manage the funds effectively. There is also the problem of maintaining infrastructure once it has been built. Gaduh, Endarso and Herawati (forthcoming) find that voluntary contributions are inadequate to finance maintenance and may be prone to free-rider problems. Villagers are generally willing to supply unskilled labour for routine maintenance but do not have the resources to conduct periodic maintenance requiring a higher level of skills. Local governments could play a bigger role in this regard.

With its programs reaching 34,000 poor villages and 60–70 per cent of the poor, PNPM's poverty targeting at the subdistrict level can be considered successful (Alatas 2005). According to a study by Bappenas (2010), the majority of the household heads who are benefiting from PNPM have a primary school education, and the benefits are received chiefly by farmers and farm workers (Figure 14.2).[5] The most common form of community contribution is labour, especially in the case of infrastructure projects (Figure 14.3). This implies that PNPM could become an effective safety net for the rural poor, especially during the off-season when few jobs are available, or when drought, flood or other natural or economic disasters threaten livelihoods. However, PNPM also needs to have the flexibility to direct funds to projects that have not been identified as priorities during the planning process, if it becomes evident that they are urgently needed (Hastuti et al. 2010).

---

4 Papanek (2007) estimates that an average block grant of $160,000 per subdistrict across the country would create 14.4 million work-days per district, with the potential to lift almost 10 million poor people out of poverty nationwide.

5 This qualitative study assesses the effectiveness of PNPM's block grants in terms of size and utilisation. It examines community perceptions of the effectiveness of the grants in reducing poverty, and the quality of project delivery and output. The study is based on a survey of 960 poor, near-poor and non-poor respondents randomly selected from villages in subdistricts where the five core PNPM programs have been implemented.

Figure 14.2   Occupation of household head of PNPM beneficiaries by poverty status of village (%)

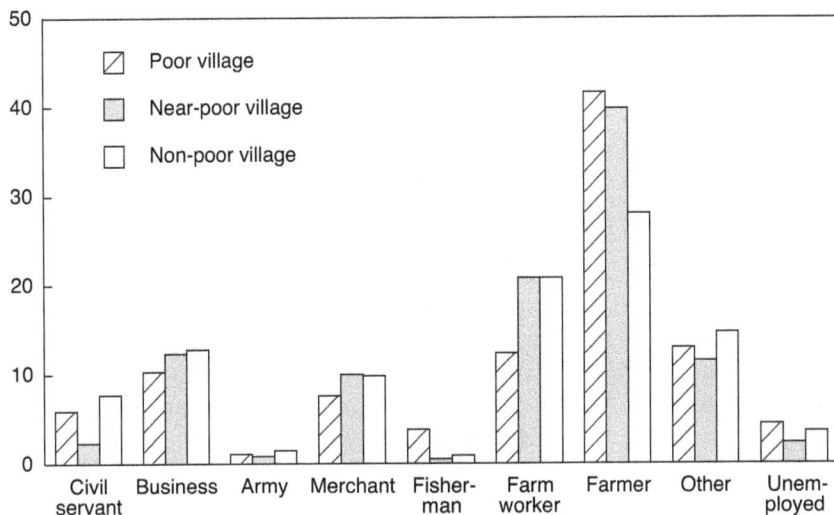

Source: Bappenas (2010).

Figure 14.3   Type of community contribution to PNPM infrastructure projects by poverty status of village (%)

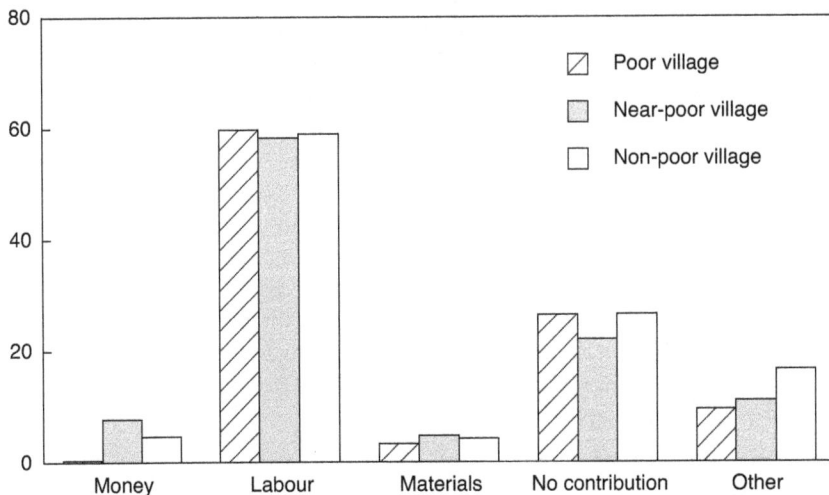

Source: Bappenas (2010).

With its extensive network across villages, PNPM has the potential to monitor and mitigate the effects of any crisis. Key design features include the ability to target specific areas that have high unemployment and poverty rates, a focus on the construction of much needed infrastructure and the potential to create assets that generate second-round employment benefits. It is important to set the level of wages slightly below the market wage for unskilled labour, and to make jobs open to all eligible participants.

So far, the level of community participation has been high. About 60 per cent of the adults who have attended planning meetings and 70 per cent of those who have provided labour for PNPM activities have come from the poorest section of the community. Women have also recorded high levels of participation, especially in local decision making on the use of block grants. In this respect, the organisers' approach of scheduling meetings at times when women are likely to be able to attend – in the late afternoon, for example, or around the time of Qur'an recitation or other informal meetings – has paid dividends. According to one study, female participation in PNPM meetings and other activities has ranged from 31 to 46 per cent (Barron, Diprose and Woolcock 2006). Such participation is thought to increase women's self-esteem, and their willingness to engage in productive activities financed by revolving funds.[6]

However, PNPM still faces challenges if it is to fulfil its potential to reduce poverty. Although it has had a positive effect on levels of consumption, access to health and education, and job creation, these benefits have been less evident among poor people living in the less poor subdistricts. A recent study of PNPM activities in urban areas found that they had had only a small impact on the household consumption levels of vulnerable groups such as widows and the elderly (Pradhan, Rao and Rosemberg, forthcoming). The bulk of the funding directed to improving drainage, paving and pathways in urban areas benefits the non-poor, and generally does not have a direct effect on the consumption levels of the poor.

PNPM is just one component of a much broader strategy of poverty alleviation. To foster further poverty reductions, the government will need to take action on several other fronts, including promoting growth in sectors where the poor are likely to benefit. In particular, it will need to focus on ways to use local resources and rural infrastructure to support the diversification of rural businesses, to encourage the development of micro and small enterprises, and to provide better access to productive resources and markets.

---

6 Revolving funds supplied through block grants are tending to replace informal sources of credit as a means of funding micro businesses. Mobilisation of other financial resources is also needed to support the productive activities of communities.

Figure 14.4 Road map for the PNPM

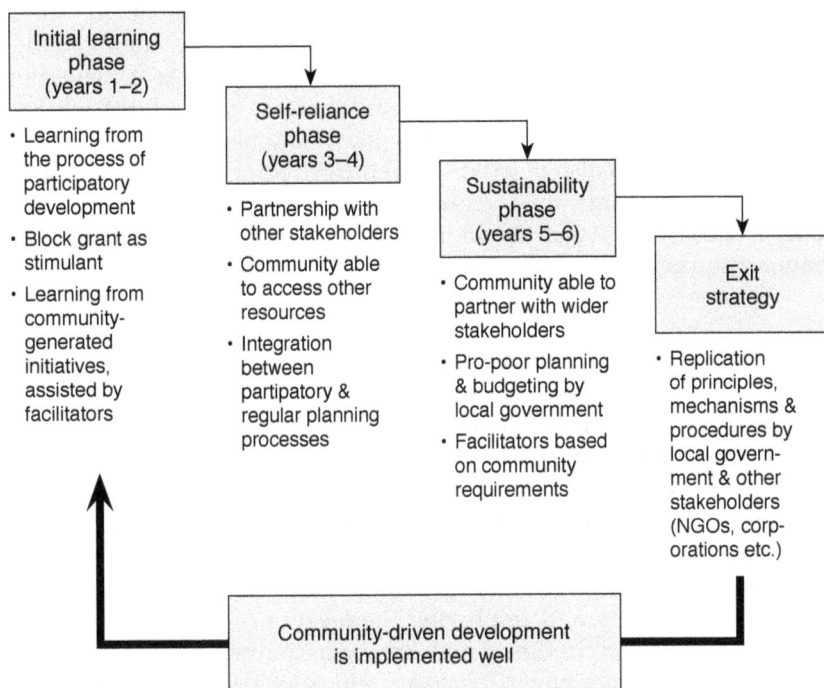

```
┌─────────────────┐
│ Initial learning│
│ phase           │
│ (years 1–2)     │
└─────────────────┘
        ┌──────────────────┐
        │ Self-reliance    │
        │ phase            │
        │ (years 3–4)      │
        └──────────────────┘
                  ┌──────────────────┐
                  │ Sustainability   │
                  │ phase            │
                  │ (years 5–6)      │
                  └──────────────────┘
                            ┌──────────────┐
                            │ Exit         │
                            │ strategy     │
                            └──────────────┘
```

- Learning from the process of participatory development
- Block grant as stimulant
- Learning from community-generated initiatives, assisted by facilitators

- Partnership with other stakeholders
- Community able to access other resources
- Integration between partipatory & regular planning processes

- Community able to partner with wider stakeholders
- Pro-poor planning & budgeting by local government
- Facilitators based on community requirements

- Replication of principles, mechanisms & procedures by local government & other stakeholders (NGOs, corporations etc.)

```
┌──────────────────────────────────────────┐
│     Community-driven development          │
│        is implemented well                │
└──────────────────────────────────────────┘
```

Source: Bappenas.

The future of PNPM

The road map for PNPM calls for two phases of implementation. The first was achieved when the program reached all subdistricts in 2009. The second phase entails making the program more self-sustaining by persuading local governments and other sectors to take greater responsibility for pro-poor targeting and financing. To become sustainable over the longer term, the concept of community empowerment needs to be strongly supported by local governments, non-government organisations and the private sector (Figure 14.4).

The success of the second phase of PNPM rests on the following elements. First, technical ministries, local governments and corporations (through their corporate social responsibility programs) need to become more involved in poverty targeting, particularly to identify pockets of poverty in non-poor subdistricts where the program has been in place for three years or more. Second, renewed attention should be paid to poor subdistricts, with specific interventions designed to benefit the most vulnerable. Until now, management has focused excessively on administration at the expense of the program's effectiveness for marginalised groups, especially when PNPM was expanded across the nation. Third, the capacity of local governments to undertake pro-poor planning, budgeting and management needs to be enhanced. This can be achieved by providing training and other support, especially in new subdistricts and districts formed by the redrawing of local administrative boundaries. Better management also depends on improved fiduciary and complaint-handling mechanisms, the integration of management information systems as a basis for robust monitoring and evaluation, and standardised training and certification for community facilitators.

PKH: INDONESIA'S CONDITIONAL CASH TRANSFER SCHEME

Conditional cash transfer programs are designed to provide cash assistance to families (especially mothers) who are willing to make long-term investments in the education and health of household members. First used in Brazil and Mexico in the 1990s, such programs have become an important element of social protection in many countries.

Conditional cash transfer programs appear to be a promising means of attacking poverty and improving the level of human development. Rigorous evaluations in some Latin American countries have shown that they are able to reduce poverty, increase educational attainment, improve the health of women and children, reduce the incidence of malnutrition and raise the status of women within the family.[7] Over the long run, the improvements in health and education are likely to give beneficiaries access to better-paying jobs, increasing their quality of life and assisting them to escape the intergenerational poverty trap.

Learning from the success of conditional cash transfer programs in Latin America in the 1990s, many other countries have since incorporated such programs into their social development policies. The Indonesian government has sought to develop a program that will allow it to work hand in hand with local governments to reduce poverty and, in a wider context, achieve the targets set by the Millennium Development Goals.

Rationale

There are many possible conditions for a conditional cash transfer program. The Indonesian government decided to focus on education and

---

7   See especially Gertler (2004), Hoddinott and Skoufias (2004), Schultz (2004), Grosh et al. (2008) and Syukri et al. (2010).

health because more than 25 per cent of the nation's budget is spent on these sectors, because of their importance for human development and because Indonesia has one of the lowest rankings on the human development index in Asia. Also, health, education and gender equality are key elements of the Millennium Development Goals.

Although Indonesia has made considerable progress in education, many children are still not attending school. In the poorest 20 per cent of the population, 15 per cent of around 10 million children aged 7–15 years did not attend school in 2005 (Table 14.1).[8] The proportion increased to 66 per cent among the 2.6 million children aged 16–18 years in the same quintile.

Lack of money was the main reason for not attending school, cited by 67 per cent of respondents to the 2003 Indonesia Demographic and Health Survey (Figure 14.5).[9] The need to work to supplement the family income was another common reason for absenteeism. Interestingly, cultural factors also seem to have played a role: some respondents said that they did not want (or were too shy) to go to school, were not attending because they had married or had left because they believed their current level of educational attainment was sufficient.

The reasons people gave for not attending health clinics were similar; the main ones were lack of money, distance and lack of transport (Figure 14.6). Cultural barriers again played a role, with some people not wanting to travel alone to a health centre or not allowed to by their spouses. In addition, the unreliability of the services provided by the centres contributed to a perception that medical professionals would not always be available when needed.

Given the poor record of attendance at health clinics, it is no surprise to find that the poorest 20 per cent of the population have the highest incidences of infant and child mortality and that the mothers in this income group are the least likely to have had a health professional present at the birth of their children (Table 14.2).

Indonesia also has a high proportion of underweight and severely underweight children among those aged 0–5 years, indicating compromised nutrition or malnutrition (Table 14.3). The proportion fell between 1989 and 2000 but then began to rise once again. This worsening situation was an important factor in the decision to include children aged 0–6 years among the beneficiaries of PKH, to capture all children from birth until they started school.

---

8 The 2007 Susenas indicates that the number fell by only 4,000 between 2005 and 2007.

9 According to the 2007 Susenas, this percentage fell to 59 per cent in 2007.

Table 14.1 School participation by age group and household income quintile, 2005

Age group	Quintile 1 (poorest)	Quintile 2	Quintile 3	Quintile 4	Quintile 5 (richest)	Total
7–12 years						
Attending school	6,289,968	5,595,414	5,130,838	4,665,460	3,855,791	25,537,471
Not attending school	526,191	307,371	212,146	143,229	82,865	1,271,802
Never go to school	341,040	186,888	127,208	92,381	47,778	795,295
Dropped out	185,151	120,483	84,938	50,848	35,087	476,507
Total	6,816,159	5,902,785	5,342,984	4,808,689	3,938,656	26,809,273
13–15 years						
Attending school	2,217,601	2,261,577	2,178,201	2,042,838	1,822,243	10,522,460
Not attending school	923,514	609,815	404,176	230,700	127,417	2,295,622
Never go to school	49,956	29,350	12,230	9,432	7,595	108,563
Dropped out	873,558	580,465	391,946	221,268	119,822	2,187,059
Total	3,141,115	2,871,392	2,582,377	2,273,538	1,949,660	12,818,082
16–18 years						
Attending school	891,118	1,092,855	1,249,396	1,432,246	1,582,917	6,248,532
Not attending school	1,733,156	1,429,640	1,125,616	877,001	636,448	5,801,861
Never go to school	56,215	28,597	20,196	13,395	6,766	125,169
Dropped out	1,676,941	1,401,043	1,105,420	863,606	629,682	5,676,692
Total	2,624,274	2,522,495	2,375,012	2,309,247	2,219,365	12,050,393

Source: Susenas, 2005.

302

Figure 14.5   Reasons for not attending school, children aged 7–18 years, 2003

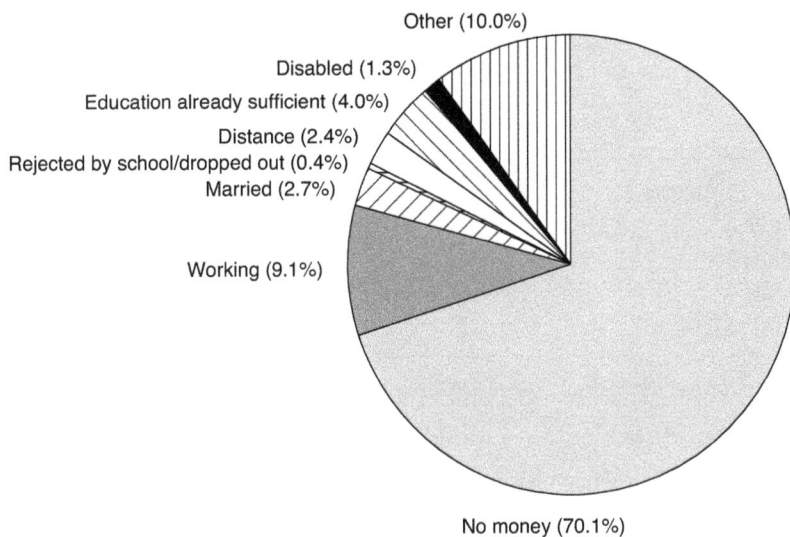

Other (10.0%)
Disabled (1.3%)
Education already sufficient (4.0%)
Distance (2.4%)
Rejected by school/dropped out (0.4%)
Married (2.7%)

Working (9.1%)

No money (70.1%)

Source: Indonesia Demographic and Health Survey, 2003.

Figure 14.6   Reasons for not attending a health centre, 2003

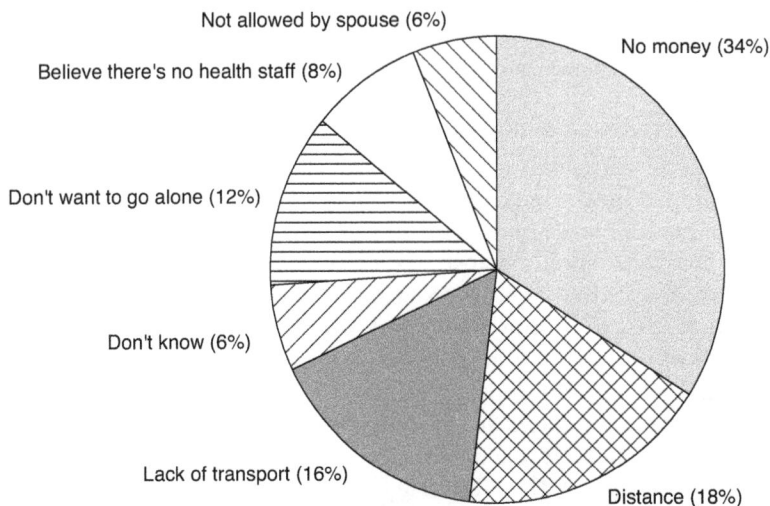

Not allowed by spouse (6%)
Believe there's no health staff (8%)
No money (34%)

Don't want to go alone (12%)

Don't know (6%)

Lack of transport (16%)

Distance (18%)

Source: Indonesia Demographic and Health Survey, 2003.

Table 14.2   Infant and child mortality rates and births attended by a medical professional, by household income quintile, 2003

Quintile	Infant mortality rate (deaths per 1,000 live births)	Under-5 mortality rate (deaths per 1,000 live births)	Births attended by health professional (%)
Quintile 1 (poorest)	61	77	21.3
Quintile 2	50	64	38.4
Quintile 3	44	56	48.1
Quintile 4	36	45	64.4
Quintile 5 (richest)	17	22	89.2

Source: Indonesia Demographic and Health Survey, 2003.

Table 14.3   Nutritional status of children aged 0–5 years, 1989–2005

Nutritional status	1989	1999	2000	2001	2002	2003	2005
Underweight	37.5	26.4	24.6	26.1	27.3	27.5	29.0
Severely underweight	6.3	8.1	7.5	6.3	8.0	8.3	n.a.

n.a. = not available.
Source: Tilden et al. (2006).

Features

Health and education indicators of the type described above, and the desire to accelerate progress towards the Millennium Development Goals, have shaped the design of Indonesia's conditional cash transfer program. Like Mexico's Oportunidades, PKH provides cash allowances to chronically poor households whose members include a pregnant or lactating woman or children aged 0–15 years. Pregnant women are required to attend at least four ante-natal check-ups and two post-natal check-ups. A medical professional must be present at the birth. Children aged 0–6 years are required to undergo routine check-ups and receive the immunisations recommended by the Ministry of Health. Children aged 6–15 must go to school and achieve an average attendance of at least 85 per cent. Households with children aged 16–18 years are also eligible for the benefit if those children have not yet completed junior secondary school. The performance indicators for the program are detailed in Box 14.1.

BOX 14.1 CONDITIONS FOR RECEIVING PKH BENEFITS

Education

- Enrolment of children aged 6–12 years in primary school.
- Attendance of children aged 6–12 years at primary school.
- Enrolment of children aged 13–15 years in junior secondary school.
- Attendance of children aged 13–15 years at junior secondary school.

Health

- Four pre-natal check-ups for pregnant women at a local health facility.
- Consumption of iron tablets during pregnancy.
- Delivery assisted by a trained medical professional.
- Two post-natal check-ups.
- Children aged 0–59 months to be immunised against tuberculosis (BCG); diphtheria, whooping cough and tetanus (DPT); polio; measles; hepatitis B; and other diseases according to the protocol set by the Ministry of Health.
- Infants to be weighed monthly to assess weight increases.
- Regular weighing for children aged 0–6 years.
- Vitamin A to be taken twice yearly by children aged 0–6 years.

Households that comply with the conditions set by the program receive an allowance that varies according to the structure of the family (Table 14.4). There are no restrictions on the use of the money but beneficiaries are encouraged to use it to improve the nutrition, health and education of family members. Demand from beneficiaries in turn is expected to place pressure on local governments to improve the supply of educational and health facilities. It would be difficult for PKH to achieve its objectives if, for example, a school did not have enough classrooms or teachers, or if a health clinic did not have a midwife or sufficient stocks of tetanus serum or vitamin A.

The program started in 2007 in seven provinces, covering around 388,000 households selected from the poorest 20 per cent of the population by income.[10] It is now operating in 20 provinces, covering around 798,000 households. Within those provinces, the program focuses on

---

10 The provinces of West Sumatra, East Java and Gorontalo volunteered to take part in the program. The administrators then selected three other poor provinces – North Sulawesi, West Java and East Nusa Tenggara – to participate, plus Jakarta in order to see how the program would work in an area with fewer infrastructural deficiencies.

Table 14.4   *Annual benefit per household for PKH beneficiaries (Rp)*

Household structure	Annual benefit per household
Fixed benefit	200,000
Benefit for a poor household that has:	
Child under 6 years old	800,000
Pregnant or lactating mother	800,000
Child of primary school age	400,000
Child of junior school age	800,000
Average benefit per poor household	1,390,000
Minimum benefit per poor household[a]	600,000
Maximum benefit per poor household[a]	2,200,000

a   The minimum benefit is set at 15 per cent the average annual income of a poor household; the maximum benefit is set at 25 per cent the average annual income of such a household.

Source: Bappenas.

subdistricts that would be able to cope with increased pressure on their educational and health facilities from students, mothers and young children. The government is keenly aware that cooperation with local governments is critical to the program's success. Under the country's decentralised system of government, they are responsible for ensuring that such facilities are present and functioning well. PKH would not work without their full support for local schools and health facilities.[11]

Given that PKH targets the poorest families in the country, the government decided that it would finance the program completely from its own budget. However, it has also invited interested international agencies to support the program and to collaborate with it in evaluating and improving certain aspects of PKH.

Preliminary evaluation

Bappenas made sure that a comprehensive method of evaluation was in place before PKH got under way. In collaboration with the World Bank, the agency conducted rapid assessments of the design within nine

---

11   Some district heads and local politicians were quick to see the political benefits of the program because it would allow them to demonstrate their concern for the poor. If local leaders supported PKH by making sure their areas had fully functioning health and education facilities, they would be able to claim that their policies were pro-poor.

months of the program commencing (Bappenas 2008; Castaneda 2008). Although no basic flaws in the design were found, Bappenas did identify shortcomings in the technical execution of some elements of the program, including socialisation (familiarising communities with the program), the placement and training of facilitators, and the procurement of equipment and consultants. Bappenas and the World Bank also collected quantitative and qualitative baseline data by which the performance of the program could be judged at a later date (World Bank 2008). The government was determined to carry out a rigorous process of evaluation that would allow it to address parliamentarians' concerns about the progress achieved under PKH.[12]

In response to the persistent requests of politicians during annual budget hearings, in early 2008 Bappenas carried out a preliminary evaluation of the impact of PKH in the seven provinces where it was first rolled out (Bappenas 2009).[13] The evaluation covered only nine months, but provided some tentative indications of progress in the participating villages. Table 14.5 shows some preliminary results for the education and health sectors based on a comparison of indicators in PKH and non-PKH locations before and after the program started.

There can be no doubt that the program increased the number of visits to local health facilities by mothers and children. The preliminary study showed a 36 per cent increase in the number of visits to health centres in PKH areas compared with a 30 per cent increase in control areas. However, the double difference statistical technique used in the study reduced the genuine contribution of the program to the increase in visits to just 3 per cent. The evaluation also found a 5 per cent increase in the weight of children aged 0–12 months and a 0.3 per cent increase in the number of immunised children in that age group in PKH areas (Bappenas 2009).[14]

---

12 PKH came under heavy criticism from the national parliament during its first two years of operation, with many members of parliament claiming it was a way of buying voters' support. Most of these politicians suddenly changed their position in 2009 – an election year – to support the program. Some asked for PHK to be implemented in the provinces in which their constituents lived. Others went so far as to ask for party cadres to be hired as program facilitators.

13 Given that the program had been in operation for only nine months (since July 2007), there was a risk that the results would not show significant progress. However, Bappenas believed that even small indications of success would suffice to satisfy the political demand for evidence-based progress. In this chapter, we present the main findings only.

14 No baseline data are available on the weight of children and the number of immunised children in non-PKH areas.

Table 14.5   Preliminary assessment of the impact of PKH, 2008 (%)

Indicator	PKH areas	Non-PKH areas	Differ-ence
Change in number of visits to local health centres	36	30	3[a]
Change in weight of children aged under 12 months	5	n.a	–
Change in number of immunised children aged under 12 months	0.3	n.a	–
Change in length of stay in school during school year	0.4	–0.4	0.8
Change in length of stay in class	1.79	1.76	0.03
Change in absence from class	–13.8	–9.3	–4.5
Change in number of teachers per school	0.7	0.4	0.3
Change in student/teacher ratio	4.9	1.6	3.3
Change in household expenditure on education (Rp per capita per month)	2,786	n.a	–
Change in household expenditure on health (Rp per capita per month)	4,271	n.a	–

n.a. = not available.
a   This is a calculation of the 'genuine impact' of the program, as explained in the text.
Source: Bappenas (2009).

The evaluation of education indicators revealed that the length of stay in school over a school year had increased only slightly, by 0.4 per cent compared with a drop of 0.4 per cent in non-PKH areas. The results for the absence from class indicator were more encouraging, with non-attendance dropping by 13.8 per cent in PKH areas compared with 9.3 per cent in non-PKH areas. So far, however, the gains in education have been relatively small, perhaps because the primary school enrolment rate is already above 95 per cent, making a 100 per cent enrolment rate progressively harder to achieve – but also because the evaluation period was simply too short to obtain a clear picture of the program's impact.

The study also identified improvements in the number of teachers per school and in the student/teacher ratio. This indicates that the start of the program has placed pressure on local governments to make sure that their education systems are performing well. The larger increase in the student/teacher ratio in PKH relative to non-PKH areas implies that more students are attending school because of the program. This means that there may be a need for additional teachers in those areas. Another interesting finding was that household expenditure on both education and health increased in PKH areas, by Rp 2,786 per person per month in the case of education and Rp 4,271 per person per month in the case of health.

Wider evaluation

Syukri et al. (2010: 90) conducted an in-depth study of how PKH beneficiaries were using their allowances. Although there were no restrictions on the use of the money, all recipients claimed that they had used it to cover the family's health and educational expenses, as recommended. The money was used to buy school uniforms, footwear, books and stationery; to pay for medical check-ups, medicine and nutritional supplements; and to cover the costs of transport to and from schools and health facilities.

In some cases, local facilitators placed restrictions on the use of funds when it became evident that the money was being spent on television sets and other luxury goods. Although contradictory to PKH guidelines, these interventions proved effective in helping the beneficiaries understand the importance of investing in the human development of family members. In certain cases, the study found that families had used the money to repair their homes, repay debt or purchase income-producing animals such as pigs, or had simply deposited the money in a savings account (Syukri et al. 2010: 91).

The authors were also keen to understand how decisions on spending were made within PKH families. In general, they found that it was the woman in the family who controlled the use of the funds. In households where women were in charge of the spending decisions, most of the money was used for small daily purchases to increase family welfare. In some cases, however, these women approved the use of the funds for strategic investments by their husbands.

The evaluation component of PKH is designed to provide an inventory of the program at a particular point in time, to uncover any systemic problems with its design or objectives. Thus, a spot check carried out by the Health Research Centre of the University of Indonesia found that the quality of education in some PKH locations was lacking, even though quantitative indicators of performance were satisfactory (Puslitkes 2010). Although school attendance had improved in the PKH areas that were sampled, only 85 per cent of the schools in those areas met the national standard for student/teacher ratios. In a surprising reversal of the national trend, the study found that 67 per cent of primary school teachers and 17 per cent of junior secondary school teachers had the minimum teaching qualification, an S1 degree (equivalent to a bachelor's degree).

However, only 6 per cent of primary schools and 89 per cent of junior secondary schools were equipped with a science laboratory.[15]

The Health Research Centre obtained similar results for health (Puslitkes 2010). Although mothers in the PKH areas sampled were assisted by skilled medical professionals, only 70 per cent of the health centres had at least a midwife on the staff. And of the pregnant women who had ante-natal check-ups, only 35 per cent were given a thorough medical examination.

These studies show that while there is scope to improve the implementation of PKH, the objectives of the program are attainable and the achievement of specific performance indicators may have spillover effects for the wider health and education sectors. The studies also provide some indication of how local governments (at the district level) may respond to the program. An agreement reached between the Ministry of Social Affairs and district heads before PKH was implemented specifically stated that local governments' health and education units would ensure that schools and health centres were functioning well, to make it possible for PKH beneficiaries to comply with the program's conditions. However, in many localities these units did not fulfil their obligations. Bappenas monitoring of PKH during 2008 and 2009 found that the reasons were various: the district head had not circulated the agreement to the local health and education units; program socialisation was lacking; or the local project implementation unit was weak and ineffective. The Health Research Centre found that some staff – even in the Ministry of Health in Jakarta – had not bothered to understand or fulfil their obligations, simply because the program 'belonged' to another ministry (Puslitkes 2010).

THE WAY FORWARD

PNPM and PKH are pillars of Indonesia's current poverty reduction strategy. The initiation of these programs has not been without challenges. Expanding the coverage of PNPM from a few thousand villages in 2005 to over 79,000 villages in 2009, for example, has brought into question the quality of the program. It is not easy to train an additional 34,000 facilitators and strengthen management in just a few years without compromising the quality of the services.

The distinguishing feature of both PNPM and PKH is their involvement of local communities, especially women, in the implementation of

---

15 The sample included Islamic boarding schools at both the primary and junior secondary school levels.

the programs. A wide body of literature confirms the importance and effectiveness of involving communities and women if a country is to achieve significant reductions in poverty. PNPM and PKH allow communities, and the women within them, to play a much more significant role in the nation's efforts to attack poverty.

But no matter how hard the government strives to promote the role of women, there will always be difficulties. When community councils meet to elect their leaders, for example, women tend not to put themselves forward as candidates. Nevertheless, women do play an important role in the PNPM context: whereas Barron, Diprose and Woolcock (2006) found that women's participation in public decision making ranged from 31 to 46 per cent, a more recent study indicates that it is now close to 60 per cent (Bappenas 2010).

At the household level, women dominate financial decision making, with positive results for the PKH program. As Syukri et al. (2010) showed, the program is effective in easing the financial burden on poor families. Consistent with similar anti-poverty projects around the world, PKH is finding that women are the key to achieving the nation's poverty reduction objectives.

Indonesia's strategy to promote the role of communities and women in reducing poverty seems promising. The government has based its anti-poverty strategy on a clear set of principles. The most significant challenge facing the nation is to maintain – and improve on – the results so far. In the future, the main task of the central government will be to persuade local governments to become more involved in – and take greater responsibility for – the operation of PNPM and PKH. This is especially pertinent given that political interest in the public decision-making process is increasing.

REFERENCES

Alatas, V. (2005) 'Economic analysis of KDP infrastructure', unpublished paper, World Bank, Jakarta.

Bappenas (Badan Perencanaan Pembangunan Nasional) (2008) 'Laporan perkembangan pelaksanaan Program Keluarga Harapan (PKH) TA-2007' [Progress report on Program Keluarga Harapan for fiscal year 2007], unpublished paper, Direktorat Perlindungan dan Kesejahteraan Masyarakat, Bappenas, Jakarta.

Bappenas (Badan Perencanaan Pembangunan Nasional) (2009) *Laporan Akhir Evaluasi Program Perlindungan Sosial: Program Keluarga Harapan 2009* [Final Report on the Evaluation of Social Protection Programs: Program Keluarga Harapan 2009], unpublished paper, Direktorat Perlindungan dan Kesejahteraan Masyarakat, Bappenas, Jakarta.

Bappenas (Badan Perencanaan Pembangunan Nasional) (2010) 'Draft laporan akhir studi evaluasi efektivitas Bantuan Langsung Masyarakat (BLM) PNPM

Mandiri' [Draft final report on the evaluation of the effectiveness of the community block grants of the National Program for Community Empowerment], Direktorat Penanggulangan Kemiskinan, Bappenas, Jakarta.

Barron, P., R. Diprose and M. Woolcock (2006) 'Local conflict and community development in Indonesia: assessing the impact of the Kecamatan Development Program', Indonesian Social Development Paper No. 10, World Bank, Jakarta.

Castaneda, T. (2008) 'Indonesia's pilot conditional cash transfer program – PKH: advances and challenges for the future', unpublished paper, World Bank, Jakarta.

Gaduh, A., G.K. Endarso and Y. Herawati (forthcoming) *Village Capacity in Maintaining Infrastructure: Evidence from Rural Indonesia*, World Bank, Jakarta.

Gertler, P. (2004) 'Do conditional cash transfers improve child health? Evidence from Progresa's control randomized experiment', *American Economic Review*, 94(2): 336–41.

Grosh, M., C. del Ninno, E. Tesliuc and A. Ouerghi (2008) *For Protection and Promotion: The Design and Implementation of Effective Safety Nets*, World Bank, Washington DC.

Hastuti, S. Usman, M.S. Mawardi, J. Sodo, D. Marbun and Ruhmaniyati (2010) 'The role of social protection programs in reducing the impact of the global financial crisis 2008/2009', SMERU Research Institute, Jakarta.

Hoddinott, J. and E. Skoufias (2004) 'The impact of Progresa on food consumption', *Economic Development and Cultural Change*, 53(1): 37–61.

Papanek, G. (2007) 'The employment and poverty impact of PNPM', World Bank, Washington DC.

Pradhan, M., V. Rao and C. Rosemberg (forthcoming), 'Urban Poverty Program (UPP)-2 quantitative evaluation study', World Bank, Jakarta.

Puslitkes (Pusat Penelitian Kesehatan Universitas Indonesia) (Health Research Centre, University of Indonesia) (2010) *Kajian (Spot-check) Pelaksanaan Program Keluarga Harapan 2007–2009* [Review (Spot-check) of the Implementation of the PKH Program 2007–2009], Puslitkes, Jakarta.

Schultz, T.P. (2004) 'School subsidies for the poor: evaluating the Mexican Progresa poverty program', *Journal of Development Economics*, 74(1): 199–250.

Syukri, M., S. Arif, M. Rosfadhila and W. Isdijoso (2010) 'Making the best of all resources: how Indonesian household recipients use the CCT allowance', *IDS Bulletin*, 41(4): 84–93.

Tilden, R., A. Gani, N.N. Noor, R.M. Widjajanto and J. Sonnemann (2006) 'The effect of decentralization on the health status and health care utilization patterns in Indonesia', Report of the Team Technical Assistance Decentralized Health Project I, School of Public Health, University of Indonesia, Jakarta.

Torrens, A. (2005) *Economic Impact Analysis of Kecamatan Development Program Infrastructure Projects*, World Bank, Jakarta.

Voss, J. (2008) 'Impact evaluation of the second phase of the Kecamatan Development Program in Indonesia', World Bank, Jakarta.

World Bank (2008) *Conditional Cash Transfers in Indonesia: Program Keluarga Harapan and PNPM-Generasi Baseline Survey Report*, World Bank, Jakarta, June. Available at: http://www.pnpm-perdesaan.or.id/downloads/CCT_Baseline_Survey(Quantitative).pdf.

15 TARGETING OF THE POOR AND VULNERABLE

Vivi Alatas, Ririn Purnamasari and Matthew Wai-Po

Economic growth does not always lift the poor out of poverty, or may not do so as quickly as either governments or the poor would like. Drawing on the *World Development Reports* for 1990, 1997 and 2000, Coady, Grosh and Hoddinott (2004) note the emerging consensus that elements beyond growth are required for poverty alleviation, such as more intensive growth in the sectors in which the poor predominate, and a building of their asset base. They also recognise that such strategies need to be complemented by shorter-term assistance for the poorest households.

A range of transfers and social assistance is now targeted towards the poor in many developing countries, as a means to provide short-term poverty alleviation. Social programs can be targeted broadly, where spending is directed not specifically at the poor but at the sectors where they are more likely to benefit, such as primary education, health care and rural development (van de Walle 1998). Programs may also target selected regions where pockets of poverty have been identified, or poor households or individuals by directly assessing their means (Coady, Grosh and Hoddinott 2004). How well these programs are targeted (and the costs involved) will have a large impact on how effectively they achieve their objective.

Particularly since the 1997–98 Asian financial crisis, Indonesia has implemented a range of social programs targeted both broadly[1] and

---

1 One such initiative was the Inpres program for primary schools (Sekolah Dasar Inpres), which saw more than 61,000 primary schools built between 1973 and 1978; see Duflo (2001).

narrowly, using a variety of targeting methods. At its peak in 2006, spending on programs directly targeting poor households represented 5 per cent of all public expenditures and 45 per cent of social spending.[2]

This chapter examines targeted social assistance and protection programs in Indonesia. We restrict ourselves to the more narrow targeting of poor households and individuals. We begin by briefly examining the evolution of targeted social programs. We then provide a quick overview of different approaches to targeting the poor, followed by an analysis of how effectively current programs are targeted. We outline some possibilities for future targeting in Indonesia before presenting our conclusions.

THE EVOLUTION OF TARGETED SOCIAL PROGRAMS

A brief history of social assistance in Indonesia

Targeted poverty reduction and social assistance programs have been in place in Indonesia for a number of years. Here we briefly examine major events in their history.[3] The first generation of social assistance programs targeted at households arose in response to the Asian financial crisis. The broad social safety net (Jaring Pengaman Sosial, or JPS) put in place at this time is summarised in Table 15.1.

These programs were initially designed as short-term interventions for the crisis period, but many of them remain in some form today. Until 2005, many of the continuing programs, including the rice subsidy, health card and scholarship programs, covered only a small number of the poor. They were designed and implemented by a wide array of government agencies, with limited budgetary resources and little coordination. Each of the programs relied on its own list of poor, maintained by a separate institution. Ultimately, these programs did not provide a sufficient safety net for most poor people.

With prices increasing steeply in 2005, the government was forced to reduce its substantial and untargeted fuel subsidies. The combined reductions left household gasoline and kerosene prices 150–185 per cent higher at the end of 2005 than in 2004.[4] To ameliorate the effects

---

2 Total public expenditure includes both central and local government spending. Social spending is total public expenditure less spending on defence, law and order, economic affairs and central government administration.

3 For international coverage of social protection and assistance programs, see Grosh et al. (2008) and the World Bank Social Safety Nets Primer series at www.worldbank.org/safetynets.

4 Prices paid by Indonesian households for kerosene, fuel and diesel remained roughly constant during 2003 and 2004 even though the international prices

Table 15.1   Indonesia's social safety net during the Asian financial crisis

Objective	Program
Food security	Special Market Operation (Operasi Pasar Khusus, OPK) (now known as Raskin): sale of subsidised rice to target households.
Employment creation	Padat Karya: uncoordinated collection of labour-intensive programs executed by various government departments.
Education	Scholarships for primary, junior secondary and senior secondary school students, and block grants to selected schools.
Health	Funding for: medical services; operational support for health centres; medicines and imported medical equipment; family planning services; nutrition; and midwifery services.
Community empowerment	Regional Empowerment Program to Overcome the Impact of the Economic Crisis (Program Pemberdayaan Daerah dalam Mengatasi Dampak Krisis Ekonomi, or PDM-DKE): block grants directly to villages for either public works or subsidised credit.

Source: Sumarto, Suryahadi and Widyanti (2005).

of such increases on the poor, two main programs for households were introduced as part of the petroleum-based fuel initiative (Bahan Bakar Minyak, or BBM).[5] The first was called Health Insurance for the Poor (Asuransi Kesehatan Masyarakat Miskin, or Askeskin). A continuation of the health card program, it aimed to give poor households access to a broader range of basic health services. Under the program, 16 million households received cards entitling them to free health care at local public health clinics and to in-patient treatment in third-class public hospital beds. In 2008 the program was expanded to cover around 30 per cent of the population and was renamed Health Security for the Poor (Jaminan Kesehatan Masyarakat, or Jamkesmas). The second program to provide unconditional cash transfers to the poor saw cash payments of Rp 100,000 per month made in four quarterly instalments directly to about

---

(crude oil and kerosene spot prices quoted in Singapore) had risen 80–125 per cent. See World Bank (2006) for more.

5 Two community programs were also introduced, a school block grant (Bantuan Operasional Sekolah, or BOS) and a village infrastructure program (Infrastruktur Pedesaan).

19 million households, or nearly one-third of the population. First implemented in 2005–2006, the Direct Cash Assistance program (Bantuan Langsung Tunai, or BLT) was repeated for nine months in 2008–2009 as food and fuel prices rose once again.

Meanwhile, the government continued to provide rice at subsidised prices under the Rice for Poor Families program (Beras untuk Keluarga Miskin, or Raskin). In addition, a pilot program of conditional cash transfers (Program Keluarga Harapan, or PKH) was introduced in 2007 and is currently being expanded.[6] It provides cash transfers to poor households with children aged 0–5 years, children of primary or junior secondary school age, and pregnant women, on condition that their children attend school and that they participate in preventative basic health and nutrition services. Unlike the unconditional cash transfer (BLT), which is intended to assist large numbers of poor and near-poor households during crises, the conditional cash transfer is designed to provide considerable financial support over the long term to a narrowly targeted group of very poor households, to help them build their human capital and lift themselves out of poverty.

The increasing importance of targeting

The pace of poverty reduction has been relatively slow in recent years despite strong economic growth. From 16.7 per cent in 2004, the poverty rate fell to 14.2 per cent in 2009, well above the target of 8.2 per cent set by the 2004–2009 Medium Term Development Plan.[7] Over this period, the number of poor people fell by 1.8 per cent per annum, while per capita GDP increased by 3.8 per cent.[8] Consequently, poverty reduction remains a central policy issue for Indonesia. It is a core pillar of the Medium Term Development Plan for 2010–2014, and President Susilo

---

6   The program is similar to Mexico's well-known Oportunidades, formerly known as Progresa.

7   The poverty rate is the proportion of people living below the national poverty line set by Statistics Indonesia (currently just over Rp 200,000 per person per month). It is based on consumption of 2,100 calories per day and a low level of basic necessities (housing, transport, health and education).

8   Improvements in key education and health indicators have also been slow. Despite primary enrolment of over 90 per cent, secondary enrolment rates have risen only slowly and senior secondary enrolment is under 50 per cent. Malnutrition prevalence (measured by low weight-for-age) exceeds 20 per cent and is not falling. Infant and child mortality rates have seen only modest decreases and remain high for the region. At 31 deaths per 1,000 live births, the infant mortality rate in Indonesia in 2008 was exceeded only by Cambodia (69) and Laos (48), with the Philippines (26), China (18), Vietnam (12), Thailand (13) and Malaysia (6) all lower (United Nations 2010).

Bambang Yudhoyono has declared it to be his government's highest development priority, with a stated objective of reducing the poverty rate to 8–10 per cent by 2014. A National Team for the Acceleration of Poverty Reduction (Tim Nasional Percepatan Penanggulangan Kemiskinan, or TNP2K) has been established to support this goal, but the likelihood of the target being achieved will depend in part on how effectively social assistance is targeted.

Targeting has increasingly become the focus of political and media attention. The start of the cash transfer program in 2005 triggered a fierce debate about whether targeted safety nets, especially cash transfers, would create dependency, with some suggesting that it would be 'better to give fishing rods to the poor, rather than fish'. There was also concern that the targeting of poor households could be used to buy votes. In addition, poor targeting has resulted from the decisions of some local governments to spread program benefits across entire communities rather than confining them to poor households, either for political reasons or to avoid conflict. Such practices have contributed to the subsidised rice program being spread too broadly and thinly.

HOW CAN SOCIAL PROGRAMS BE TARGETED?

Targeting in Indonesia occurs in a unique and complex context. The country has nearly 240 million people dispersed across 18,000 islands, making Indonesia the world's fourth-largest country by population and its largest archipelago. The central government has also decentralised considerable budgetary and operational control to the districts, of which there are now around 500. Moreover, targeting has to distinguish between the very poor, poor and near-poor, and – given the fluid nature of Indonesian poverty with high rates of entry and exit – between chronic and transient poverty. Indonesia's lower inequality of consumption relative to other countries, notably in Latin America, makes distinguishing between the poor and near-poor more difficult. The country's large population, geographic dispersion and decentralised structure, combined with lower inequality and the multiplicity of programs and objectives, amplifies the importance of choosing the right targeting methods.

Choice of targeting methods

A range of methods can be employed to define the beneficiaries of targeted programs. They include assessing individuals or households directly, targeting whole categories of people or pockets of poverty, and making program enrolment open to anyone who chooses to apply. All of

these distinctly different approaches have been employed to determine
social assistance beneficiaries in countries throughout the world. Coady,
Grosh and Hoddinott (2004) provide a comprehensive review of the advantages and disadvantages of each, and a bibliography of programs
and methods internationally (2002).

The two main methods used in developing countries to assess individuals or households directly are proxy means testing and community-
based targeting. Proxy means testing classifies a household as poor or
not poor based on easily observed household characteristics such as the
location and quality of the dwelling, asset ownership, household demo-
graphics and (sometimes) the education and occupation of adult members. Such indicators are correlated with a household's economic status
and can serve as a proxy for its actual consumption or income.[9] The information from the applicant is usually verified through a home visit by
a government official.

Proxy means tests have been applied widely, particularly in Latin
America, since originating in Chile in 1980. They have the advantage of
being much cheaper to carry out than a full consumption survey or verified means tests. They have also been found to be relatively accurate. In
Chile and Mexico, for example, Castañeda and Lindert (2005) estimated
that 80–90 per cent of the benefits of proxy means-tested programs were
received by the poorest 40 per cent of households. Nonetheless, the statistical errors of proxy means tests mean that such an approach will always result in some poor households being excluded from a program,
and some non-poor being included. Moreover, many developing countries cannot afford to survey all households, so further errors occur in
determining which households to visit. Most problematically, the Latin
American experience suggests that over time households learn to manipulate the proxy means test to 'improve' their scores, hiding assets or
reporting household characteristics incorrectly, and falsifying household
rosters. In 1987 this led Chile to no longer publish its scoring system
(Coady, Grosh and Hoddinott 2004).

Community targeting, on the other hand, relies on local knowledge to
identify the poor and vulnerable, with some element of the community
determining who the beneficiaries of a program should be. The entire
community, a representative subset or just community leaders may be involved in the selection process, which can be structured or unstructured

---

9 The indicators are weighted to construct a score. Where national socio-
economic household surveys are available, as in Indonesia, weights are derived from a statistical regression to give a direct estimate of household per
capita consumption. In other cases alternative statistical techniques, such as
principal component analysis, are used.

and have pre-defined or arbitrary criteria. Community targeting is less common (outside of Sub-Saharan Africa) than proxy means testing, and there are relatively few rigorously documented experiences. We discuss recent Indonesian experiments with community-based targeting later in this chapter.

Categorical targeting usually means classifying whole subgroups as eligible for a program. Examples include primary health care programs for children aged 0–5 years, educational support for school-aged children, programs to support the elderly, funds or services made universally available to regions with the highest poverty rates, or programs aimed at groups such as orphans or widows. However, the most common form of categorical targeting is geographical targeting, which was involved in nearly half the international examples surveyed by Coady, Grosh and Hoddinott (2004). Geographical targeting, or poverty mapping, uses data on regional poverty (or another outcome being targeted, such as nutrition status) as the basis for allocating resources or services. While associated with an increased share of benefits going to the poorest households, it generally needs to be used in conjunction with a second targeting method – usually proxy means testing – to determine which households will become beneficiaries within regions. In Indonesia, program quotas are often set at the district level using geographical poverty targeting, and combined with another targeting method below this level.

Finally, self-targeting allows anyone to apply for a program, but the application process or program benefits are designed so that the costs of participation are lower for the poor than for the non-poor. The most common example of self-targeting is public work schemes, where the wage is set below market labour wages, meaning that the income generated from participation is attractive only to the unemployed and underemployed.[10]

HOW EFFECTIVE IS TARGETING IN INDONESIA?

We now look at the effectiveness of targeting, by assessing the targeting performance of social assistance programs that use different combinations of proxy means testing, community-based targeting and geographical targeting. This section summarises the findings of a study by the World Bank (2010a), which assesses the performance of the major programs. It focuses on the three main household-targeted programs

---

10 Other costs of participation include the nature of the work (usually physically demanding for public work schemes), the social stigma attached to being officially classified as poor and the consumption of a subsidised commodity used predominantly by the poor (and thus presumably of lower quality).

mentioned earlier, namely the subsidised rice program (Raskin), the health card program (Jamkesmas) and the two rounds of the unconditional cash transfer program (BLT).

We first consider how much of the population is covered by each program. This is instructive, since all three programs have the same official target population: poor and near-poor households with per capita consumption below around Rp 240,000 per person per month. In 2009 this represented 13.5 million households, or 22 per cent of all households. Figure 15.1 shows the number of beneficiary households by program, broken down by poverty classification.[11] In 2008–2009, 16.1 million households (27 per cent of the total) received the unconditional cash transfer (BLT),[12] while 31.4 million households (52 per cent of the total) bought subsidised rice under Raskin. The coverage of the rice program was far greater than intended, and came at the cost of recipient households being able to buy considerably less than the intended monthly quota.[13]

Two estimates are presented for the Jamkesmas health care program. The first is coverage, with 16.9 million households (28 per cent of the total) saying they had a card entitling them to free health care. The second is usage, with 10.1 million households (17 per cent of the total) saying they had used the card to receive free health care. The distinction will be discussed shortly. As Figure 15.1 shows, all programs had both poor (target) and non-poor (non-target) beneficiaries.

Who then were these program beneficiaries? In Figure 15.2, program beneficiaries are divided into 10 groups by per capita consumption in

---

11 The near-poor line is 1.2 times the poverty line discussed in footnote 8. The poverty line for the very poor is approximately 0.8 times the poverty line. The three main programs discussed here are targeted at people below the near-poor line. The pilot program of conditional cash transfers (PKH) is targeted at the very poor. Official national poverty rates are based on the poverty line itself.

12 The number of BLT beneficiaries in 2008–2009 as assessed from the Susenas (13.5 million households) differs from the official figure provided by the Ministry of Social Affairs (18.5 million households). This is because household survey weights (from Statistics Indonesia population projections) are used to estimate population-level program coverage from the Susenas, whereas the official figure is from administrative data relating to benefits disbursed. This holds for all programs discussed in this section. It does not affect the consistency of the results, as the numbers of poor and near-poor being compared are based on the same survey weights. Thus, all program and poverty analysis is internally consistent. See World Bank (2010a) for more detailed discussion of this issue.

13 The World Bank (2010a) discusses a number of reasons for the low monthly purchases of rice. Among them, it finds that community-level sharing of rice meant beneficiaries received only 60 per cent of the amount they would have if distribution had been restricted to the intended recipients.

Figure 15.1   Beneficiaries of social assistance programs, 2009 (million households)[a]

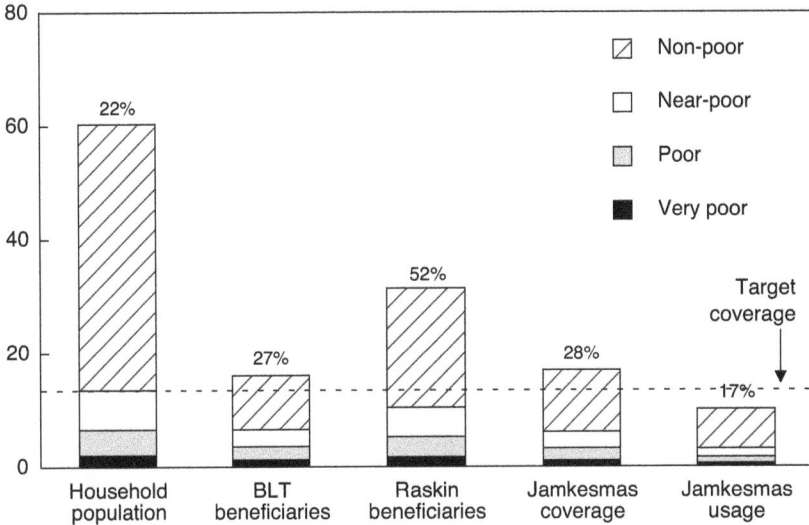

a   The percentages refer to the proportion of total households that benefited from the program. See footnote 13 on discrepancies with official data.

Source: Susenas, 2009.

2009, from the poorest 10 per cent (decile 1) to the richest 10 per cent (decile 10).[14] The unconditional cash transfer (BLT) was received by only 38–55 per cent of the three poorest groups of households (deciles 1–3, or the poorest 30 per cent of households). The proportion of non-target household groups receiving the transfer ranged from 4 per cent to 33 per cent; it was lowest among the two richest groups (deciles 9–10) and highest among those closest to the target (deciles 4–5). Thus, the program was pro-poor with low inclusion of the rich. However, it also resulted in many poor households being excluded, indicating considerable room for improvement in targeting performance.

Access to free health services under Jamkesmas, or program *coverage*, was enjoyed by a slightly lower percentage of the three poorest groups than received the unconditional cash transfer, at 38–50 per cent, and a slightly higher percentage of non-target groups, especially among the richest. However, *usage* of the program, that is, actual use of the health

14   Deciles are based on per capita consumption adjusted for spatial differentials in the pricing of poverty baskets, that is, regional purchasing power.

Figure 15.2   Distribution of benefits of social assistance programs by consumption decile, 2009 (% of decile receiving program)

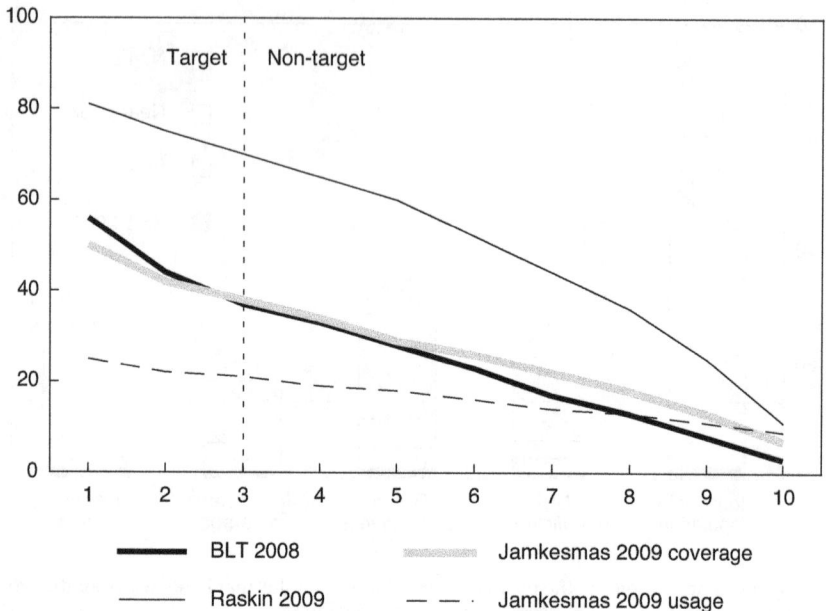

Source: Susenas, 2009.

card to receive free health care, was considerably lower. The three richest groups of card holders reported very high rates of use of the card to receive subsidised health care, whereas only half the three poorest groups of card holders did so. Since health problems are likely to be *more* prevalent among the poor, suggesting a greater need for them to use the card, the observed pattern could reflect higher levels of awareness of the program among the wealthier and a greater propensity for them to use preventative or remedial health care, or a lack of supply-side readiness in poor areas.

Next, 70–80 per cent of the poorest 30 per cent of targeted households bought subsidised rice under Raskin, but 44–65 per cent of the four next-richest groups did so as well, and even 25 per cent of the second-richest group (decile 9). That is, while not many target households missed out on the program, many non-target households, including some quite well-off ones, benefited from the program. This mistargeting of households came partly at the expense of poor people who were excluded from the program, but also, as previously mentioned, at the expense of the poor who benefited from the program. Most poor households received only a part of the rice they would have if distribution had been restricted to the intended poor households. This loss of benefit for households who were correctly targeted reduces the potential effectiveness of the program.

The analysis so far indicates that the current social programs are pro-poor. However, they all suffer from targeting deficiencies, with many poor excluded from benefits and many non-poor receiving them. A consequence of this is that *less than a third* of the targeted poor were beneficiaries of all three programs, while half the non-poor benefited from at least one program. Nearly half of all poor people were beneficiaries of just one program, or none at all, while a quarter of non-poor households were beneficiaries of two or more programs.

How should we compare the targeting performance of each program? Which programs could potentially benefit from adopting the targeting approach of another? A common approach is to examine the proportion of benefits received by the non-poor (leakage, or inclusion error) and the proportion of the poor who miss out (undercoverage, or exclusion error). One problem with these measures is that they cannot be compared consistently when programs have different target populations or different numbers of beneficiaries.

Here, we evaluate targeting performance, in addition, by determining the extent to which the poor have gained compared to random targeting (that is, where all households have an equal chance of receiving benefits), with the scores for pro-poor program targeting ranging from 0 per cent (the same performance as random targeting) to 100 per cent (perfect targeting, where all the benefits are received by the poor).[15]

Figure 15.3 shows the targeting performance of each major program in 2008–2009. The targeting of BLT was the most accurate; it performed 24 per cent better than random targeting, out of a possible 100 per cent for perfect targeting. Although perfect targeting is unachievable in practice, this relatively low score captures the extent to which non-poor beneficiaries have been included in the program (nearly 60 per cent of beneficiaries were non-poor) and poor households have missed out (around 50 per cent of all poor households). Jamkesmas had poorer targeting

---

15 Targeting accuracy can be assessed in various ways (Coady, Grosh and Hoddinott 2004), but none of the existing measures are satisfactory. Comparing targeting across programs, periods and places requires quantitative metrics with properties unavailable in a single measure. We are currently preparing a note on targeting metrics, outlining how the different elements of targeting performance and welfare impact can be assessed using different measures. The measure used here is a rescaling of the Coady–Grosh–Hoddinott (CGH) measure. CGH is the proportion of a program's benefits received by the target population divided by the proportion of the target population in the population as a whole.

Figure 15.3   Targeting performance of programs, 2009 (% of households)

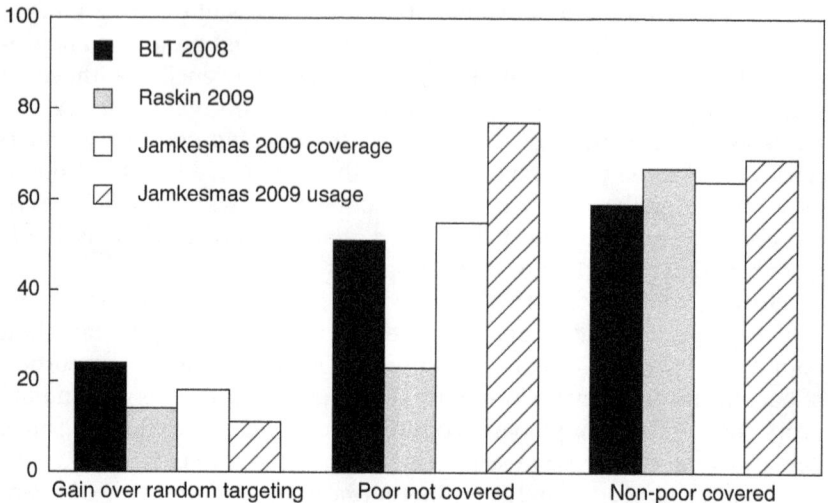

Legend:
- BLT 2008
- Raskin 2009
- Jamkesmas 2009 coverage
- Jamkesmas 2009 usage

Categories: Gain over random targeting, Poor not covered, Non-poor covered

Source: Susenas, 2009; World Bank calculations.

(18 per cent better than a program that was randomly distributed), with more non-poor households having access to the program than under BLT (higher inclusion error) and more poor households being excluded (higher exclusion error). The program *usage* was even less favourable for the poor. The Raskin program performed only 14 per cent better than random targeting. While it excluded fewer poor households than BLT, it included many more non-poor households. Moreover, the scores for the rice program did not capture the reduced quantity of rice enjoyed by beneficiaries due to the practice of spreading the benefits of the program across the community.

It is difficult to find proper comparisons overseas for targeting performance, since targeting measures are very sensitive to how they are calculated, and even when calculated in the same way can give different results depending on the coverage of the program and the proportion of the population being targeted. Moreover, even apparently similar programs may vary substantially in their design and implementation. With these strong caveats in mind, a comparison of the conditional and unconditional cash transfer programs in Coady, Grosh and Hoddinott (2004) suggests that Indonesia's BLT program has enjoyed less effective targeting than elsewhere (see World Bank 2010a: Table 3.4). However, the difficult targeting context of Indonesia, with its large and dispersed population, also needs to be considered.

A comprehensive analysis of the three programs' costs of targeting has not been conducted. Given that all three have the same target population, the list of beneficiaries for the unconditional cash transfer program could be used to determine the beneficiaries for the other two programs. This would seem a low-cost way of bringing their targeting performance up to the level of the BLT program (albeit one likely to meet political resistance). However, as we have seen, the targeting of BLT also leaves considerable scope for improvement, suggesting that the targeting of all programs could be improved through a comprehensive review.

Supporting this conclusion, the World Bank (2010a) has identified a number of common problems with targeting procedures, in particular poor program socialisation and inconsistent application of official procedures at the local level. Poor socialisation means that there is often confusion about who the program is for, leading to the wrong households being targeted, or to a sharing of benefits among the whole community, diluting those received by the poor. Targeting procedures are also often implemented inconsistently at the local level. Consultative community meetings are only sometimes held to verify beneficiaries, and local implementers do not always make use of the official indicators of poverty.[16] Socialisation and its effects on perceptions of programs and community satisfaction are discussed further in World Bank (2010b).

IMPROVING INDONESIA'S TARGETING PERFORMANCE

As we have seen, there is considerable room to include more poor people among the beneficiaries of Indonesia's social assistance programs, and to exclude more non-poor. This section looks at how such improvements might be made. We first highlight the key areas to be addressed, and outline the need for a national targeting system to be used by all targeted programs. We then look at the methods such a system might employ and how it might be developed from existing elements in Indonesia.

Key issues for improved targeting in Indonesia

Two issues must be addressed if targeting is to be improved. The first is to establish the most appropriate methodologies for different targeting objectives in the Indonesian context, and the best ways of implementing them. Different indicators are needed to capture chronic and transient poverty, and to identify areas of vulnerability among the non-poor. Some

---

16 See the qualitative studies by the SMERU Research Institute discussed in World Bank (2010a).

methods may be more appropriate for certain locations than others. For example, the approach might vary depending on a district's poverty rate or the extent of the existing targeting error.

Second, socialisation and commitment (or 'buy-in') to programs at all levels need to be improved. As the World Bank (2010b) observes, targeting receives little media attention, and lack of acceptance of targeting methods at all levels of government, and among communities, affects outcomes. To increase buy-in from line ministries, local governments and communities, the objectives and methods of targeting must be better communicated. Such buy-in is required for targeting procedures and outcomes to be adopted as intended.

Both of these issues could be addressed by establishing a national targeting system. Integrated targeting across programs would increase effectiveness and reduce costs. Such a system would allow the use of best-practice targeting methods across all programs, not least because separate systems often do not have the resources or capacity to implement such an approach. It would also facilitate the communication of a consistent message about targeting methods and objectives. At the heart of a national targeting system would be a unified database, or registry, of potential beneficiaries for all programs. Such a registry would ensure the use of consistent definitions of the poor across programs, reduce the costs of maintaining duplicate lists of beneficiaries, mitigate the risk of fraud and help to consolidate administrative costs. In addition to increasing coverage of the poor, it would allow greater policy coordination across programs, including socialisation.

However, any new system needs to be both politically and technically feasible, as well as affordable, and must have the required support functions. The relative costs of different methods of targeting must be determined, in addition to their effectiveness. Procedures for verification of household data must be established, administrative capacity to implement new approaches addressed, and an institutional framework agreed that outlines which agencies are to perform which functions. Monitoring and evaluation of procedures and outcomes must be conducted, and a complaints procedure established.

Evaluating targeting methods in an Indonesian context

The technical feasibility of implementing various targeting methods can be examined in the light of overseas experience. Coady, Grosh and Hoddinott (2004) collected numerous examples, synthesised the lessons from each and outlined the context in which they were most appropriately used. But local conditions matter, and there is no substitute for testing potential innovations in the field. We now discuss recent and continuing efforts to study the effectiveness of different approaches in Indonesia.

Indonesian programs use a combination of proxy means testing, geo-graphical targeting and community-based approaches to target benefici-aries. While each program has a different approach, they all generally set district-level quotas with geographical targeting, then use proxy means testing or community-based methods to allocate that quota within dis-tricts. In 2008–2009, Statistics Indonesia, the World Bank and the Abdul Latif Jameel Poverty Action Lab conducted a field experiment to evalu-ate proxy means testing and community-based methods of targeting (see Alatas et al. 2010). The experiment was designed to investigate two primary issues: targeting accuracy, and community satisfaction with the targeting outcomes.

With respect to accuracy, proxy means testing was found to be better at identifying poor households than the community approach. This was particularly the case for households close to the poverty line. However, the community approach was more accurate at identifying the house-holds at the very bottom of the distribution. Analysis suggested this was because the community rankings incorporated local knowledge not cap-tured by the indicators of the proxy means test.

Despite the greater accuracy of proxy means testing, surveys con-ducted after the experiment and other data suggested that the commu-nity approach resulted in higher satisfaction levels and greater perceived legitimacy, although proxy means testing did not perform poorly in this regard. It is unclear whether satisfaction was higher because outcomes more closely matched communities' perceptions of who was poor, or be-cause of their greater involvement in the process.

One conclusion from the experiment might be that the two meth-ods have different advantages and may be suited to different contexts. If proxy means testing is more accurate with respect to the entire con-sumption distribution, it could be a more accurate method for a large-scale social program targeting many poor people. On the other hand, a community-based approach better incorporating local knowledge about the very poor, and more closely matching local concepts of poverty, could be more accurate in identifying the poorest households for more tightly targeted programs. The experiment also underlines the importance of involving the community to achieve increased buy-in. With different ad-vantages, no single targeting method was clearly optimal.

Given this conclusion, the findings raise several interesting questions. First, can proxy means testing and community-based targeting be com-bined in a manner that exploits the strengths of each?[17] Second, while

---

17 Alatas et al. (2010) tested a very specific hybrid of the two but found that neither increased the accuracy relative to proxy means testing, nor the satis-faction with outcomes relative to community targeting.

no evidence was found of community elites manipulating the process to include non-poor family and friends among the beneficiaries of poverty alleviation programs,[18] it is possible that this might change over time as individuals learn to manipulate the system. As discussed, manipulation has been seen to occur over time with proxy means testing, but whether it would be more or less severe in community-based systems is an open question. In addition, 'elite capture' may be more likely when benefit levels are higher.[19] Finally, given how well community outcomes match individual self-assessments, an important question is whether some form of self-targeting system could provide a more cost-effective method of targeting the poor.

To address some of these issues, a second experiment was conducted in late 2010 in conjunction with the expansion of the conditional cash transfer program (PKH). Some villages were invited to self-target to a degree, with any household able to sign up for an interview at the village or neighbourhood office. During the interview, householders were asked to complete a proxy means test questionnaire, and those with qualifying scores had their responses verified through a home visit.[20] The experiment was designed to examine the effect of distance required to travel to the interview, and that of requiring either one spouse, or both, to attend. The objective was to test whether the non-poor decided the opportunity cost of time was too high to participate, while the poor decided otherwise. In other villages, the community was given a proxy means test-determined list of the very poor and allowed to add or substitute households, with certain restrictions. This approach was tested to see whether it would reduce both the number of very poor households excluded from proxy means-tested lists of beneficiaries, and the number of non-poor on such lists. The lessons of the field experiments will be important for the design of a national targeting system.

Developing a national targeting system in Indonesia

Developing a national targeting system completely afresh would require a heavy investment of financial and human resources, and could face

---

18 Community rankings were done in some villages by village elites and in others at meetings attended widely by the community, without significantly different results. Conducting meetings at different times of the day resulted in either more males or more females attending, but this too did not affect the results.

19 Beneficiaries each received Rp 30,000 (around $3) under the first experiment.

20 A qualifying score is one below the threshold determined by the community quota. The community quota in turn will be set by geographic targeting.

significant political obstacles. A more financially feasible and politically palatable approach would be to build on two existing elements: (1) available poverty data for geographical targeting; and (2) a planned 2011 update of the survey of the poor with an improved proxy means test.

First, additional poverty data are available to use for geographical targeting. The annual National Socio-Economic Survey (Survei Sosio-Ekonomi Nasional, or Susenas) allows the calculation of district-level poverty rates. In addition, information in the 2010 population census can be used to construct an updated poverty map at the subdistrict and village level. (The current map is based on 2000 data.) Using these data will ensure that beneficiary numbers at the district level and below are consistent with the poverty rates from the national socio-economic surveys. Currently many districts have too few registrants or too many.

Second, Statistics Indonesia is preparing to update its survey of the poor. This listing of approximately 19 million poor households evaluated through a proxy means test was first collated in 2005 and updated in 2008. Statistics Indonesia plans to update the list again in 2011 using a new proxy means test devised in 2008.

Analysis by the World Bank (2010a) suggests that the new methodology would significantly outperform current program targeting if applied to all households in Indonesia. Targeting performance under the new proxy means test would be nearly 50 per cent better than random targeting[21] and more than double that of the best-performing current program, the unconditional cash transfer (BLT). The share of the non-poor among beneficiaries (inclusion error) would be over 20 percentage points lower than under the BLT, Jamkesmas and Raskin programs. Similarly, the share of the poor who do not receive benefits (exclusion error) would be about 20 percentage points lower than under BLT and Jamkesmas.

The 2011 list could form the initial basis of a unified database of potential beneficiaries for all targeted programs, and would sit at the heart of a national targeting system. However, unless all households are surveyed – a proposition that is neither financially nor practically attractive – then selecting which households to interview is critical. Simply revisiting the 2008 households will not make the most of the new proxy means test, as the 2008 list excludes many poor households.

In Figure 15.4, we compare the targeting outcomes from using the 2005 proxy means test and the improved 2008 version. On the left-hand side ('All households'), the two tests are applied to every household; on the right-hand side ('2008 list only'), they are applied only to those

---

21 The result is out of 100 per cent, with 100 meaning perfect targeting, or that the poor receive all benefits.

Figure 15.4   Targeting (inclusion and exclusion) error of 2005 and 2008 proxy means tests when applied to two household samples (%)

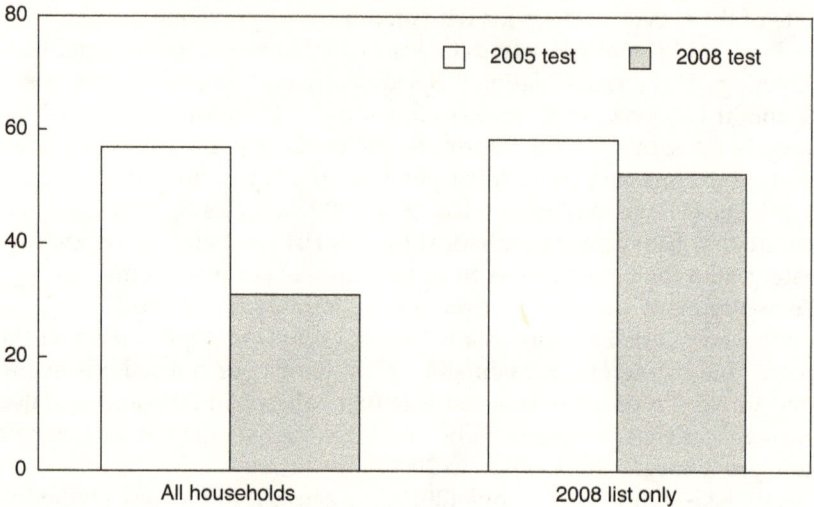

Source: Susenas, 2009; World Bank simulations.

households that were on the 2008 list of the poor. When applied to all households, the 2008 proxy means test results in much improved targeting error, with inclusion of the non-poor and exclusion of the poor being around 25 percentage points lower than with the 2005 test.[22] However, when the new proxy means test is applied only to households on the 2008 list, the improvement is much less pronounced. That is, merely revisiting the same households in 2011 will not reap the full improvement that the new proxy means test has to offer. Determining which households to survey is therefore critical, and will be an issue for detailed work in the 2011 implementation planning.

Finally, the results of the two targeting experiments can help to identify the optimal role for the community. As discussed earlier, community-based targeting can reduce exclusion error among the poorest households, while increasing satisfaction with targeting outcomes. The results of the two experiments can help to determine the best way to integrate community involvement in any new targeting process.

---

22 Inclusion and exclusion errors are the same when program coverage and target levels are the same.

CONCLUSION

A range of household-targeted programs initially introduced in response to the 1997–98 Asian financial crisis now forms the basis of Indonesia's social safety net. While these programs are pro-poor, they could be far better targeted. Each program is targeted in a different manner, with varying degrees of effectiveness. Improvements have been evident over time, in particular with respect to the formulation of the proxy means test. However, further improvements are possible. Involving communities in identifying the poor, determining which households to survey with the proxy means test and allowing self-selection by poor and non-poor households might further reduce targeting error.

A key step towards identifying and implementing advancements would be the establishment of a national targeting system based on a unified registry of potential beneficiaries. Such a system would ensure the use of the most effective targeting methods to suit different objectives and different locations. It would take time to establish but could be used for all current and future targeted assistance programs. It would allow better coordination of programs and lower the costs of targeting. The components of such a system are already in place, or soon will be. The design of the survey of the poor planned for 2011 could incorporate recent work on improved targeting methods, and the 2010 population census would allow an updating of the Indonesian poverty map.

However, for the system to be effective, implementation issues must first be addressed. These include the dataset (who collects it, who administers it, who has access to it, how it is shared, and how it is verified and recertified), the design of a national registry, the construction of logistical and institutional frameworks governing which agencies perform the required functions, the establishment of a complaints procedure, and of oversight and control mechanisms, and the development of adequate monitoring and evaluation processes.

REFERENCES

Alatas, V., A. Banerjee, R. Hanna, B. Olken and J. Tobias (2010) 'Targeting the poor: evidence from a field experiment in Indonesia', NBER Working Paper No. 15980, National Bureau of Economic Research, Cambridge MA, May.

Castañeda, T. and K. Lindert (2005) 'Designing and implementing household targeting systems: lessons from Latin America and the United States', Social Protection Discussion Paper 0532, World Bank, Washington DC.

Coady, D., M. Grosh and J. Hoddinott (2002) 'Targeted anti-poverty interventions: a selected annotated bibliography', unpublished paper, World Bank, Washington DC.

Coady, D., M. Grosh and J. Hoddinott (2004) *Targeting of Transfers in Developing Countries*, World Bank, Washington DC.

Duflo, E. (2001) 'Schooling and labor market consequences of school construction in Indonesia: evidence from an unusual policy experiment', *American Economic Review*, 91(4): 795–813.

Grosh, M., C. del Ninno, E. Tesliuc and A. Ouerghi (2008) *For Protection and Promotion: The Design and Implementation of Effective Safety Nets*, World Bank, Washington DC.

Sumarto, S., A. Suryahadi and W. Widyanti (2005) 'Assessing the impact of Indonesian social safety net programs on household welfare and poverty dynamics', *European Journal of Development Research*, 17(1): 155–77.

United Nations (2010) 'Millennium Development Goals Indicators', United Nations Statistical Division, http://unstats.un.org/unsd/mdg/SeriesDetail.aspx?srid=562 (accessed 20 December 2010).

van de Walle, D. (1998) 'Targeting revisited', *World Bank Research Observer*, 13(2): 231–48.

World Bank (1990) *World Development Report: Poverty*, Oxford University Press, New York NY.

World Bank (1997) *World Development Report: The Role of the State*, Oxford University Press, New York NY.

World Bank (2000) *World Development Report: Attacking Poverty*, Oxford University Press, New York NY.

World Bank (2006) *Making the New Indonesia Work for the Poor*, World Bank, Jakarta.

World Bank (2010a) 'Targeting effectiveness of current social assistance programs in Indonesia', Targeting in Indonesia Policy Paper No. 1, World Bank, Jakarta.

World Bank (2010b) 'Socialisation, perception and satisfaction of targeted social assistance programs in Indonesia', Targeting in Indonesia Policy Paper No. 4, World Bank, Jakarta.

16 SOCIAL ASSISTANCE: UNDERSTANDING THE GAPS

Lisa Hannigan

Over the past 10 years developing countries have been giving greater attention to social protection. It is seen as a necessary part of a country's efforts to address poverty effectively and to protect poor and vulnerable men, women and children from the impacts of shocks and stresses. The need for social protection in Indonesia was dramatically highlighted following the East Asian economic crisis of 1997–98. Before the crisis one-fifth of the population was categorised as vulnerable but this increased to more than a third after the crisis (Suryahadi and Sumarto 2003). This shock pushed people into chronic (persistent) poverty, which has severe intergenerational implications.

Indonesia has recognised the importance of social protection as a core part of its strategy to address poverty.[1] The government has introduced many measures, from cash transfer schemes to health insurance, and has indicated its intention to ensure the poor are 'covered' by social protection programs. But despite the many programs, there is no overarching social protection strategy. It is not surprising, then, that studies on social assistance[2] are finding significant gaps in coverage among the poor (World Bank 2010a).

---

1 There are a number of other types of government programs designed to address poverty and vulnerability. Discussion of these is outside the scope of this chapter. However, because they also provide cash infusions for poor families, they should be included in thinking about program mixes and financing.
2 Social assistance programs are a subset of social protection programs. They are non-contributory programs that involve transfers to the poor. Examples of social assistance programs operating in Indonesia are the government's cash transfer and rice subsidy schemes.

The current mix of social assistance programs in Indonesia and their respective targeting approaches and mechanisms mean that: (1) certain risks to poor people are not being covered; (2) certain groups of poor people are not being covered; and (3) some members of target groups do not have access to programs. What is not always so clear is what these gaps mean to poor people. This is the focus of this chapter. Research was undertaken in three locations in Indonesia to look more deeply at how these gaps are being experienced on the ground and whether there are other gaps that are not being recognised at the central level. The other key area of enquiry at the local level is what 'coverage' means for the people already deemed to be covered by social assistance programs, in terms of their ability to deal with shocks and stresses. What key vulnerabilities remain? Using qualitative methods, the research seeks insight into the appropriateness of current coverage.

This chapter examines the issue of appropriateness in the context of the current understanding of vulnerability in Indonesia and social assistance needs.[3] It looks at the planned government social assistance priorities and how well these align with the expressed needs and concerns of interviewed households. It pays particular attention to targeting issues given the high numbers of vulnerable people excluded from social assistance programs in the three locations. The chapter concludes by presenting the policy implications of the research findings.

METHODOLOGY

This study mainly uses a qualitative approach to analyse coverage and remaining areas of vulnerability in Indonesia. It uses the available quantitative data generated by the World Bank's ongoing public expenditure review of social assistance in Indonesia and its review of targeting. It also uses data from the government of Indonesia on current and planned coverage. The gaps identified through the quantitative analysis guided the focus of this qualitative research. The qualitative research work was undertaken in June and July 2010 in three locations: two remote rural villages – Oenai and Anin – in the district of Timur Tengah Selatan in East Nusa Tenggara; two villages – Langge and Uabanga – close to the urban centre of Gorontalo; and two *kelurahan* (the urban equivalent of a village) – Kali Baru and Semper Timur – in the Cilincing area of North Jakarta. The chief characteristics of the six villages in the case study locations are described in Table 16.1.

---

3 For further information on the appropriateness of targeting, see Slater and Farrington's (2010) social protection toolsheet.

Table 16.1   Characteristics of case study locations

	Oenai	Anin	Langge	Uabanga	Semper Timur	Kali Baru
District	Timur Tengah Selatan	Timur Tengah Selatan	Goron-talo	Goron-talo	DKI Jakarta	DKI Jakarta
District poverty rate (%)	33.6	33.6	22.7	22.7	6.0	6.0
Main livelihood	Subsistence farming	Subsistence farming	Farming	Farming/ fishing	Fishing industry/ construction	Fishing/ fishing industry
Main religion	Christianity	Christianity	Islam	Islam	Islam	Islam
District food insecurity[a]	Priority 1	Priority 1	Priority 4	Priority 4	No data	No data

a   Refers to the World Food Programme's composite index of vulnerability to chronic food insecurity. Districts are rated according to six levels of priority, with priority 1 districts being the most food insecure. Timur Tengah Selatan is ranked eighth in terms of food insecurity out of 492 districts.

Sources: Statistics Indonesia (2009); World Food Programme (2009); World Bank data.

These different environments were chosen to get a cross-section of people likely to have different constraints to exiting poverty and different experiences of vulnerability. The research involved focus group discussions with key informants, semi-structured interviews with households and life history interviews. The interviews were conducted with a mixture of poor beneficiaries and non-beneficiaries. Over 150 people were interviewed in the case study areas.

The qualitative analysis does not aim to be representative or able to be generalised in a quantitative sense. Further research into some of the findings will be required, but the qualitative analysis does illustrate particular points and dynamics. It deepens the understanding of how people experience (or do not experience) current social assistance mechanisms and the factors that affect people's vulnerability, and thus may assist in guiding policy advice. The strength of the qualitative method in this area of inquiry is that it can provide a nuanced understanding of an issue that could potentially be seen in the very black and white terms of 'covered' or 'not covered'.

The analysis does not cover all of the risks and stresses experienced in the case study areas; there is no mention of climate change risks, for example. Only issues raised by respondents themselves are described in this chapter, resulting in a number of issues being reported in areas such as health, for instance, but only one in education. Issues such as girls' access to secondary schooling and disabled children's access to education may be important in the case study areas but they were not raised by the respondents.

The interviews with households and key informants covered Indonesia's four major social assistance programs (see Box 16.1). They also focused on the constraints to exiting poverty and the areas of life about which people had the most concerns. This enabled an exploration of people's vulnerability to shocks and stresses. The research did not focus on the implementation problems of the various social assistance mechanisms.

CENTRAL LEVEL ASSESSMENT AND PLANS

To determine what the social assistance gaps are, there needs to be an understanding of what the government is trying to cover. One of the main difficulties in assessing gaps and solutions in Indonesia is the lack of clarity about what social assistance activities as a whole are trying to achieve. We understand the goals of individual programs and we know what their target populations are, but there is no overarching goal other than to 'cover the poor'.[4] In Indonesia, this could be understood as equating to covering the severely poor given that the poverty line is set very low; in March 2010 it equated to approximately Rp 211,000 per month, or around $0.80 per day (Statistics Indonesia 2010).

Government priorities and plans

While some in the Indonesian government remain unconvinced of the development benefits of cash transfers, social assistance has a reasonable level of political acceptance. With the stated goal of reducing poverty from 14.2 per cent in 2009 to 8–10 per cent by 2014 (Bappenas 2010), social assistance programs have received renewed attention. In February 2010, a presidential regulation was released establishing a new inter-ministerial National Team for the Acceleration of Poverty Reduction (Tim Nasional Percepatan Penanggulangan Kemiskinan, or TNP2K). TNP2K has three immediate priorities: to improve and expand the conditional cash transfer program (Program Keluarga Harapan, or PKH); to

---

4 Personal communication with government official.

BOX 16.1   MAIN SOCIAL ASSISTANCE PROGRAMS

Jaminan Kesehatan Masyarakat (Jamkesmas)

The Jamkesmas program was introduced in 2008 as a health insurance scheme for the poor. Jamkesmas card holders are entitled to free health care at local health clinics (*puskesmas*) and government hospitals. The cards have been distributed to over 76 million people but utilisation rates are low (approximately 10 million people).

Beras untuk Keluarga Miskin (Raskin)

The Raskin subsidised rice program is the longest running of Indonesia's social assistance programs. It was put in place in 1998 in response to the economic crisis. It entitles poor and near-poor households to buy a certain amount of rice, officially 15 kilograms per month, at a substantially subsidised price.

Bantuan Langsung Tunai (BLT)

BLT is a temporary unconditional cash transfer program used in response to covariate (shared) shocks. It was first used in 2005 in response to fuel price subsidy reductions, and was used again in 2008 in response to the food, fuel and financial crises. Over 19 million poor and near-poor households have received BLT benefits.

Program Keluarga Harapan (PKH)

PKH is a conditional cash transfer program aimed at the severely poor: approximately 3.5 million households (current coverage is 804,000 households). Households receive between Rp 0.6 million and Rp 2.2 million ($67–244) annually in quarterly payments on condition that they meet certain health and education requirements.

Source: Arif et al. (2010); World Bank (2010b).

---

overhaul the health insurance program (Jaminan Kesehatan Masyarakat, or Jamkesmas); and to improve program targeting.

Longer-term plans exist for a substantial expansion of the government's scholarship programs and the introduction of a cash-for-work scheme. These programs are not an immediate priority and detailed plans have not yet been developed. It is not clear, for example, what level of education the scholarship programs would focus on, or who the target population for the cash-for-work program would be.

To assist the government to develop a clearer picture of the state of social assistance in Indonesia, the World Bank has been undertaking a

Figure 16.1   Coverage of social assistance programs by income quintile

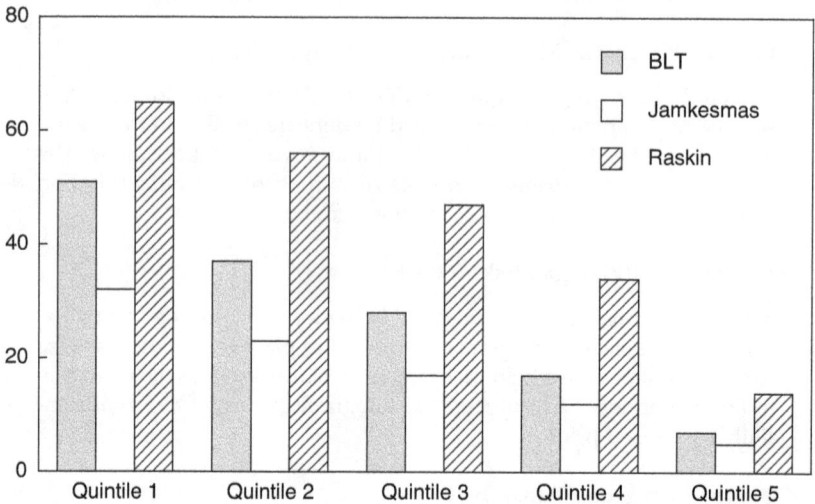

Source: Adapted from World Bank (2010a).

public expenditure review of social assistance programs and a review of targeting. This will allow the government to further develop its priorities for social assistance reform. Early results confirm fears about targeting performance. PKH is only just moving out of the pilot phase so analysis has focused on the coverage of BLT, Jamkesmas and the subsidised rice program, Raskin. As Figure 16.1 shows, Raskin does best at reaching the poor, with coverage of 65 per cent in the first (poorest) quintile. BLT and Jamkesmas cover only 51 per cent and 32 per cent of this group respectively (World Bank 2010a). Raskin does less well, however, at keeping benefits from the rich – 14 per cent of Raskin benefits are captured by the richest quintile. The main message from this analysis is that all of the major social assistance programs are currently poorly targeted.

As mentioned earlier, national social assistance programs have three obvious gaps in coverage of the vulnerable. First, we know that certain risks and stresses are not being covered, such as basic consumption needs and idiosyncratic (individual) shocks other than the health shocks covered by Jamkesmas. Second, certain groups (such as the disabled) are not being systematically covered by social assistance programs, either through dedicated programs specifically targeting them or through other programs. And third, from the World Bank's analysis, we know that there are some big gaps in coverage of intended recipients. Many poor households are not receiving the programs that are targeted towards them.

The important questions to develop a better understanding of these three gaps are the following. What are the implications of not being covered for an individual or household, especially when others in the community *are* covered? How are targeting errors perceived and experienced? Are there other gaps that are not being seen? And for those that are 'covered', what does 'coverage' actually look like on the ground and what are the key vulnerabilities that remain? The rest of the chapter looks into these issues more closely and discusses the potential policy implications of the findings.

GAPS AND VULNERABILITY IN CASE STUDY AREAS

The three gaps mentioned above were all very evident in the case study locations. Programs did not exist for vulnerable groups such as the elderly. Programs did not exist to cover idiosyncratic shocks such as small landslides that wiped out the crops of individual households. And many seemingly eligible households were not included in social assistance programs.

Other gaps

Two key areas of vulnerability that are not currently part of mainstream discussions on social assistance at the central level were mentioned by both beneficiary and non-beneficiary respondents. These gaps are described below, sometimes in the respondents' own words (although all names have been changed to protect the privacy of respondents).

Ageing households

In rural areas, some respondents with household heads over the age of 40 experienced a sense of unfairness about the government's social assistance programs. Over time they had worked very hard and managed to accumulate assets such as houses with wooden walls and cement floors. Their consumption shortfalls remained the same as everyone else's – they could not afford to feed their families all year round and they struggled to send their children to school – but they found themselves excluded from cash transfer programs because of the quality of their houses. Despite having relatively better houses, they felt they were actually in a worse position than many of their younger neighbours who, in Timur Tengah Selatan and Gorontalo, may have had houses with thatched roofs and dirt floors. With their earning ability declining, a number of older respondents who still had small children said they would not be able to afford to send them to school. Their accumulated assets were not easily convertible to cash.[5]

> 'Not all poor households were questioned. They only looked at the outside of the houses, but sometimes people with good houses are very poor. A few years ago they could work very hard, but now they can't.'
>
> *Rusni, Gorontalo*

It is important to note that respondents in urban areas also reported experiencing pressure on incomes as they grew older. Even some men in their thirties (or the wives of those men) said they had experienced a drop in income, although they did not attribute this entirely to age. Although healthy and capable of work, they said they were less preferred by employers both as daily labourers and factory workers. They said the competition for work had intensified and their earning potential had declined as they got older.

Health risks among the extended family

If a poor person has a Jamkesmas card, it might be assumed that their health risks are covered. But in Timur Tengah Selatan and, to a lesser extent, Gorontalo and Cilincing, family illnesses and deaths imposed a huge financial burden on respondents' families. That is, they remained exposed to the health risks of their relatives even if their own health risks were covered by Jamkesmas. This liability for the risks of others ate into people's accumulated assets. To cover the health or death-related costs of family members, respondents reported borrowing money or selling assets (such as pigs and chickens). They often had to borrow at very high interest rates and it could take months or longer for them to once again accumulate comparable assets. Death costs are not normally seen as a social protection issue, but because they affect the ability of households to cope with other adverse events, they are relevant.

> 'I have been trying to get some livestock to help improve my family's condition but it is hard to keep them. Just last week my uncle died and I had to give rice, coffee, a piece of cloth and a pig. Two years ago my husband's grandfather was sick and died and we had to borrow Rp 300,000 to contribute. We paid it back by selling our pig.'
>
> *Adrien, Timur Tengah Selatan*

---

5 An evaluation of Jamaica's PATH program showed a similar finding, with non-beneficiaries claiming they had acquired their assets during earlier times of prosperity (Mathematica 2007).

The extent to which these two gaps in social assistance coverage are experienced across Indonesia is a subject for further analysis. They are key issues for many respondents in the case study areas and therefore may be a problem more widely.

Key remaining areas of vulnerability

In addition to the gaps in coverage, there are gaps for groups and risks that are 'covered'. It is logical that beneficiaries would still experience vulnerability; none of the government's social assistance programs are intended to cover all of a household's needs. But when trying to strengthen existing social assistance programs and plan new ones, having an understanding of people's own assessments of vulnerability is useful to determine what is most important to them. This subsection looks at remaining areas of vulnerability in the areas of health, education and basic needs.

Health

Without health insurance, poor families risk catastrophic liability and emotional trauma.[6] Respondents provided numerous examples of how Jamkesmas had protected their assets from health shocks (or would have done so if they had had a card), but having a Jamkesmas card did not protect them from all of the negative impacts of health shocks.

The cost of transport to and from a health clinic (*puskesmas*) was a serious issue in the rural villages of Gorontalo and in urban Cilincing. Respondents were sometimes prevented from accessing free *puskesmas* services because of the high cost of transport. In the village of Uabanga in Gorontalo, for example, it cost Rp 20,000 (around $2.20) to take a motorcycle taxi (*ojek*) to and from the *puskesmas*. With household incomes as low as Rp 10,000 per day in the village, this cost could be prohibitive, especially for people who needed repeat care (see Box 16.2).

Medicine is free for Jamkesmas card holders treated at a *puskesmas* but not at a hospital. A number of respondents referred to the high cost of medicine at hospitals. One respondent from Gorontalo who had suffered a stroke was required to pay Rp 900,000 ($100) for medicine.

'It's a myth that having a Jamkesmas card makes treatment free.'
*Mother of Ratna, who had a miscarriage then had to pay
Rp 600,000 ($67) for post-operative medicine, Gorontalo*

---

6   There have been a number of much publicised reports in Jakarta of poor families not being allowed to take their newborns home until they have paid their hospital bills (Haryanto and Kencana 2010; Osman 2010).

BOX 16.2   EXPERIENCES OF VULNERABILITY: HEALTH

Availability of health services

'When I arrived home she was dead.'
Oktavius, Timur Tengah Selatan

Oktavius's wife had a Jamkesmas card that allowed her to give birth at the *puskesmas* for free, a service she was planning to use. Her fourth child came early and she experienced difficulties while at home. Oktavius went quickly to the *puskesmas* in his village to get the midwife but discovered she was on holiday with no replacement. He rushed to the next village but that midwife was not available either, so he continued on to a third village where he located a midwife who agreed to go with him when he showed her the Jamkesmas card. They hurried back to his house but it was too late. The baby was alive but his wife had lost a great deal of blood and had died.

Difficulty accessing health services without Jamkesmas

'I don't want to use a *dukun*.'
Ani, Timur Tengah Selatan

Ani is pregnant and desperate to give birth in a *puskesmas*. Her first baby was delivered by a traditional birth attendant (*dukun*) and died during delivery. Pictures of the dead baby are hung on her mother-in-law's wall. She cannot hang them in her own house, where she and her husband cook, eat and sleep, because it does not yet have any walls. She and her husband are saving to complete the house but they can barely earn enough from farm production and small crafts to cover their food needs. Ani does not have a Jamkesmas card and does not know how to go about getting one. The cost of delivering at the *puskesmas* with a midwife is Rp 300,000 ($33), a sum she does not think she will be able to accumulate in the five months leading up to the delivery.

Difficulty accessing health services with Jamkesmas

'I know it's just going to get worse.'
Kusnia, Gorontalo

Kusnia has tuberculosis. When first diagnosed a year ago she started taking the required medication. The visit to the *puskesmas* and the medication were free, but the *puskesmas* would prescribe only two weeks' worth of medicine at a time. The fortnightly cost of a return trip by *ojek* to the *puskesmas* is Rp 20,000 ($2.20) – well out of the family's reach. The cost has proven prohibitive for Kusnia, who has barely made a dent in the six-month course of drugs she is required to take. She has four small children and is desperately worried about her health as her symptoms worsen.

The quality of the medicine available at the *puskesmas* was also raised as an issue by a number of respondents in all three areas. Some said that whenever they went the *puskesmas* they were prescribed the same thing – Antalgin, a common pain killer – regardless of their symptoms.

In parts of Cilincing, the transport issue, combined with the poor quality of the medicine available at the *puskesmas*, had led some respondents to prefer local private clinics. Respondents with a Gakin card (Jakarta's equivalent of a Jamkesmas card) were entitled to free services and medicine at a *puskesmas*. But they often chose to pay Rp 35,000 at a private clinic because they would not have to pay for transport and perceived the quality of the medicine to be better.

Senior secondary education

The desire of respondents to keep their children at school until they had completed their senior secondary education was affecting their vulnerability (see Box 16.3). PKH only covers families with children at primary and junior secondary school, but respondents across all case study areas saw senior secondary education as the pathway to a better life. The PKH program was extremely helpful in assisting some poor respondents to meet the costs of schooling. However, most recipients said they would be able to keep their children in school anyway, because primary and secondary education was generally free in Gorontalo and Timur Tengah Selatan. There were still costs associated with uniforms, books and transport, but most respondents thought they could cover those costs if the program were discontinued. The difficulty came with senior secondary education because of the high registration fees – often upward of Rp 1 million ($110) – and the ongoing fees of at least Rp 50,000 ($5.50) per month. Respondents ate into their assets to cover these costs. The livelihood strategies of most respondents with children were focused on meeting this goal.

There was an acceptance among respondents that, at least in the medium term, they were making themselves more vulnerable by focusing their resources on the single goal of education in the hope of making themselves less vulnerable in the future (through their children's future earnings).

Basic needs

In trying to explain why they were so vulnerable to stresses and shocks, most respondents referred to problems with livelihoods (see Box 16.4). Many said they were unable to find work that would allow them to meet what they considered to be basic needs (including education).

BOX 16.3   EXPERIENCES OF VULNERABILITY: EDUCATION

Cost of senior secondary education

'I feel like I was locked out of my future.'
Mira, Timur Tengah Selatan

When Mira was growing up there were no cash transfer programs to help keep children in school. Mira had big plans for her life. She was going to be a teacher. She studied hard, got good grades and was on track to reach her goal. But when she was 15 her parents pulled her out of school. They wanted her to continue studying but could not afford the fees. She remembers that time with great sadness. 'I feel like I was locked out of my future. I couldn't take any steps towards a better life.' She is now being assisted by the conditional cash transfer program (PKH) and is confident she will be able to send her three children to primary school. But senior secondary school costs Rp 50,000 per month and Mira expects the cost to rise to about Rp 100,000 per month by the time her children (currently aged nine, seven and two) reach senior secondary school age. This sum is well out of the family's reach.

A number of respondents in Cilincing said that formal sector jobs did not pay enough to cover a household's basic needs, with factory jobs paying just Rp 600,000 ($67) per month for a 66-hour week. Also, these formal sector jobs were not always predictable. Factory contracts, for example, were often given for a duration of only three months. The next contract usually did not begin immediately and bribes of around Rp 200,000 ($22) sometimes had to be paid to secure the next contract. Most respondents were not in formal sector jobs but earning money from things like selling fish or chickens, which might bring in as little as Rp 10,000 ($1.10) per day. Many respondents who were currently paying high interest rates for credit from informal sources expressed a need for cheaper access to credit so that they could improve their livelihoods.[7]

Many respondents indicated a willingness to pursue any livelihood that would help their families meet their basic needs, but they either did not know how to obtain such jobs or did not have access to the required capital. In the rural areas, most people tend to stay in their villages of birth. But those who had returned after seeking work elsewhere did

---

7   For example, a respondent in Anin who had borrowed Rp 50,000 from a wealthier neighbour was required to repay Rp 75,000 within one month.

BOX 16.4   EXPERIENCES OF VULNERABILITY: FOOD

Food insecurity

'It never happened before and it's never happened again.'
Yunus, Gorontalo

Ratna lives in a small house with a thatched roof and dirt floor. The materials for the house were provided through a provincial assistance program two years ago. The family eats only one meal a day, normally just bananas from its small landholding. The benefits from the PKH and Raskin programs do assist in providing some extra food occasionally.

Yunus lives in a relatively large house in another village in Gorontalo. The house has glass windows, ceramic tile floors and brick walls. Despite the appearance of relative wealth, the members of this household, too, eat just once a day. Yunus explains this paradoxical situation as coming down to three fish. Two years ago on a fishing trip he caught three tuna, a fish he had never caught before and has never seen since. He was able to sell the tuna for Rp 1 million each, enough to construct the house.

Yunus feels his poverty runs just as deeply as that of other families with poorer-quality houses. As well as being unable to afford food, he is even unable to afford the fuel to be able to fish. He is able to access Raskin but not PKH. Yunus would like to gain access to government programs that might help his family become more food secure. But he feels he has been unable to do so because, unlike visibly poor households like Ratna's, his family's living conditions appear to be relatively good.

---

not describe migration as an unfortunate necessity or a 'struggle to stay put', as Rogaly (2003) characterises it in his study of migration in eastern India. Rather, they generally described their return in terms of having failed in the outside world. This finding has implications for other poverty reduction programs, where support could be provided for people to move elsewhere if it meant greater livelihood security.

Regardless of the level of social assistance they were receiving, none of the households interviewed in Timur Tengah Selatan, and only a few in Gorontalo, were consistently able to meet their food needs (in terms of being able to afford *enough* food, not just the *preferred* amount of food). The majority of respondents ate twice a day but many of the very poor households across all study sites, even in Cilincing, ate just once a day. Even the better-off households who were able to eat three times a day usually consumed a very limited variety of foods. In Timur Tengah Selatan, many households ate corn at every meal, sometimes supplemented

by vegetables. Many of the households that benefited from the Jamkesmas, Raskin and PKH programs ate protein only about eight times a year
(twice after each PKH distribution). A worrying finding in rural areas
was that parents who purchased rice under the Raskin program gave
their children preferential access to the rice, thinking it was more nutri-
tious, while they ate locally grown foods that were likely to be healthier,
such as corn and other vegetables.

Overall, the 'covered' population's ability to deal with stresses was
improved by their access to social assistance programs. The implications
of coverage differed substantially, however; for some the impact on welfare was shallow and for others it was significant. For Jamkesmas beneficiaries, the effect of health shocks was softened substantially. For those
experiencing other types of idiosyncratic shocks, there was little evidence
that the existing programs provided any protection. Some PKH beneficiaries reported saving some of the money to protect themselves from
future shocks but most said they needed to use it all for consumption.

PERCEPTIONS AND EXPERIENCES OF TARGETING

All of the government's key social assistance programs are targeted towards the poor – none are universal – and issues surrounding targeting
permeated the interviews. The research looked at respondents' perceptions of targeting and its implications. As described earlier, there is evidence of substantial mistargeting of the main social protection programs,
a conclusion supported by the discussions with beneficiaries and non-
beneficiaries. Across all areas, the analysis tried to stay away from issues
related purely to program implementation problems, but this proved
difficult for a subject like targeting. Even if targeting is improved, it will
never be perfect and may always struggle to deal with certain types of
risks and stresses.

'We are all poor here'

In the remote rural villages of Timur Tengah Selatan, where poverty is
reasonably homogenous, there was very much an attitude of 'we are all
poor here' – similar to that found by Ellis (2008) in Sub-Saharan Africa. In
Anin, 59 of 340 households were benefiting from PKH, but the facilitators
estimated that another 250 households had comparable or lower levels
of welfare. According to them, it was only the government employees in
the village who could meet basic consumption needs.

In Gorontalo there was not as pronounced a sense of 'we are all poor
here', but according to village officials and facilitators there were again

huge exclusion errors. In Uabanga, only 18 of the 85 households assessed by village officials as being eligible for PKH benefits were actually enrolled in the program. The village authorities and facilitators were very vocal about the exclusion error problem in Uabanga. They felt they could have prevented many of the errors if they had been consulted. They reported being completely excluded from the selection process; hence, many families living in reasonable quality houses, but who were actually very poor, were not receiving PKH benefits. Poverty in Cilincing was not as homogenous as in the rural districts, but there were again many cases where the poor had missed out with regard to social assistance (exclusion errors), as reported by facilitators.

The perception of large exclusion errors was causing tension and unrest in Timur Tengah Selatan. The first distribution of PKH benefits in a village in the district saw the burning of a building and stones being thrown at the distribution point. The facilitators viewed their job as being very dangerous. In Cilincing, people had protested outside the facilitators' houses. In Uabanga, Gorontalo, the police had been called to the village to quell protests over PKH targeting.

Because of the clustering of poor and near-poor around the same welfare level, community members who were not beneficiaries saw others with comparable levels of poverty, but who were beneficiaries, becoming visibly better off. PKH and BLT beneficiaries often had better-quality houses and could buy better clothes for their children.

'We used to be the same but I didn't have children when PKH beneficiaries were being selected. Now the people who receive PKH have much better houses than I do.'
Focus group discussion participant, Timor Tengah Selatan

'We bought the roof with BLT and the walls with PKH.'
Husband of PKH beneficiary, Timor Tengah Selatan

This phenomenon has been seen in parts of Africa as well, where the bottom 10 per cent of the population is often targeted for social assistance programs. In his study of social assistance in Sub-Saharan Africa, Ellis (2008) found that in areas where poverty was widespread in the community, destitution reduction goals could not be met without some proportion of 'leapfrogging' – that is, recipients' consumption exceeding non-recipients' consumption in adjacent deciles (where the standard of living differed by only a small amount). While not officially targeting any set percentage of the poor, Indonesia's targeting system appears to be acting like Ellis's leapfrogging model in the high-poverty-density areas of Timur Tengah Selatan. This has serious implications for how the programs are perceived in terms of fairness and accuracy. With no system for 'recertification' within any of the major social assistance programs,[8] many poor but excluded respondents report watching from the sidelines as the gap between them and their beneficiary neighbours grows wider.

Problems with proxies

Some respondents in Timur Tengah Selatan expressed the view that assessments of people's houses should not be used to judge current poverty levels. Proxy means testing, which is used to differing extents to determine the beneficiaries of Jamkesmas, BLT and PKH, uses proxies such as floor and wall type to approximate household welfare.[9] Two of the key issues raised by respondents in relation to housing were in-kind payments and spikes in income.

To cope with difficult periods or events, respondents in Timur Tengah Selatan often worked on other people's farms and were usually paid in-kind for their work. The in-kind payments were generally in the form of corn or rice but could include assets such as wood with which to build houses. Respondents would have preferred payment in a form more easily converted to cash but they had to take what was offered. Because of this, they were often sensitive about the condition of their houses being used as an indicator of wealth, since they felt this did not accurately reflect their income status.

The complications of targeting households that move in and out of poverty – a very common phenomenon in Indonesia – were evident in the case study locations. The respondents who had experienced a spike in income, often through one good harvest, usually invested it immediately in improving their houses. Houses were a valued asset for households but not one easily converted to cash. Again, the respondents expressed concerns about judgements being made about their current level of welfare on the basis of an assessment of their houses.

Other effects of poor targeting

Traditional village community work systems based on the principle of mutual cooperation (*gotong royong*) were being disturbed in the rural

---

8   Recertification allows people to be assessed as eligible for a program at times other than when bulk eligibility assessments are being made.

9   Proxy means testing is a method by which a range of indicators (including housing conditions) are used to identify a household's poverty status, in the absence of more detailed data on income or consumption. This method is adopted because the collection of income data is expensive, time consuming and difficult to do on a large scale. See Chapter 15 of this volume by Alatas et al. for more detailed discussion of proxy means testing.

case study areas. People who did not receive government transfers were staying home on *gotong royong* days, saying it was only fair that the recipients of welfare did more work. When non-beneficiaries did participate, their sense of unfairness was heightened. In most of the villages visited, the village head spread the Raskin rice subsidy evenly among all households to address this issue and to reduce tension in the village.

The research was not carried out in areas known for migration, but there were examples of people being excluded from programs because they were not present at the time of the survey to determine entry. In Gorontalo, for example, a respondent and her large family went to North Sulawesi to pursue work for eight months. When they returned to their permanent home in Gorontalo, they found that the statistics office had completed its survey and that the family was not included in the PKH program. They were told there was no way they could be assessed to determine their eligibility.

It is important that the system to determine program eligibility does not open itself up to double counting, but measures should also exist to ensure that households whose residential arrangements are not static can be assessed for inclusion in government programs.

POLICY IMPLICATIONS

The case study findings do not contradict the government's planned reforms to improve the coverage of social assistance programs. Current government plans to introduce programs focusing on vulnerable groups and to improve targeting are very relevant, as is the focus on Jamkesmas and a potential new scholarship program, given respondents' concerns about health and education costs. But while not contradicting the government's plans, the findings from the case study sites do point to the necessity for caution and perhaps further analysis in relation to a number of important areas. The research is particularly illustrative in the area of targeting, and in highlighting some of the real risks and stresses households face and the impact these have on their welfare.

Targeting

The extent of exclusion errors indicates either that the PKH program is underfunded in some areas or that there is a problem with the targeting approach, not just the targeting mechanism. The targeting approach refers to who is eligible to receive benefits; the mechanism refers to how to reach those who are eligible (Slater and Farrington 2009). The government is very committed to focusing on the targeting mechanism. But without a reassessment of the approach, at least in areas with a high density of poverty such as Timur Tengah Selatan, the leapfrogging phenomenon could escalate. The government is scaling up PKH but the talk is more about moving to new areas than deepening existing coverage. Given the level of exclusion errors in the quantitative and qualitative data, looking at whether the current coverage is appropriate, and assessing the appetite for program expansion, should be a priority for policy discussions.

The analysis has highlighted the importance of any new targeting mechanism being able to deal with a number of issues that have exacerbated exclusion error in the past. They include the following.

1   *Transitory poverty.* Occasional spikes in income and people's tendency to invest the proceeds in housing signal caution when using methods such as proxy means testing. Housing conditions do not necessarily indicate the current level of wealth of a family or its ability to accumulate wealth in the future.

2   *Attention to how people are paid.* When using proxy means testing in areas with very limited cash economies, attention needs to be given to the issue of people being paid in-kind for work.

3   *Recertification.* None of the four main social assistance programs has a functioning system for recertification. If people are not on the list from the initial survey, there is no mechanism in place for them to gain access to government programs.

All of these issues need to be incorporated into discussions about targeting mechanisms to ensure that targeting is appropriate – that is, that it captures the households it seeks to cover.

Recognition of real risks and stresses

The analysis revealed a number of risks and stresses among respondents that were not being adequately discussed at the central level in relation to the appropriate coverage of social assistance programs. Depending on the chosen targeting approach, the government may or may not want to cover those risks and stresses. But they should at least be discussed so that the implications of any decision not to cover them are understood.

Across all three case study areas, one of the main stresses reported by respondents was the difficulty of meeting senior secondary education costs. The pursuit of this level of education made poor families more vulnerable, at least in the short to medium term. This should be considered when determining how best to expand the scholarship programs, or as part of modifications to PKH. It might also be addressed as part of a loans program. Because it is such a common area of stress for nearly all poor households with children, the problem seems to warrant immediate discussion and action.

There also needs to be a broader emphasis within social assistance programs and targeting mechanisms on the effect of age on earnings potential – one that goes beyond just a focus on the elderly. The government has indicated its desire to focus on programs for the elderly, but in the case study areas the problems people experienced because they were getting older manifested themselves long before they would usually be considered 'elderly'. More attention should be paid to this issue given that it was observed in all three case study areas.

In both rural districts, people had difficulty meeting their daily needs, including the need for food. But there is no transfer mechanism covering the times when people cannot meet their basic consumption needs during 'normal' times, or when shocks are specific to individual households. This issue should be part of the targeting approach analysis. The question is to what extent the government is willing and able to cover these risks. There is potential here for the slated cash-for-work program. When asked about this proposed program, nearly all poor respondents in the survey regions, regardless of age, indicated a desire to participate, although whether they would do so in practice might depend on the level of wages.

Social assistance programs cannot address all of the factors that exacerbate vulnerability. Most respondents were constrained from exiting their current vulnerable state by the inadequacy of the earning potential of their current livelihood and the absence of alternatives. People in rural areas were often willing to work elsewhere but did not have the necessary means or connections. Social assistance programs can do little about this, but policy makers can ensure that social assistance programs are more closely linked to other government programs, such as microfinance, skills training and migration assistance programs.

Finally, policy makers need to be careful with the word 'coverage'. The depth of coverage can vary greatly, and caution is needed to ensure that there is a clear understanding of exactly what people are covered for and how this affects their vulnerability. In the case study areas in Timur Tengah Selatan, having access to PKH meant the difference between eating or not eating any protein during the year, while for some families in the urban areas of Cilincing, coverage by the Raskin program resulted in only two or three days worth of rice per month. Policy makers also need to have a good understanding of the limitations of the coverage – for example, the prohibitive nature of transport costs that inhibits access to the *puskesmas* in some areas – and the issues surrounding the cost and quality of medicine. Complementary measures may be required to assist in achieving the intended outcomes. For example, in areas far from a *puskesmas*, transport costs could be reimbursed if this can be done efficiently and equitably.

REFERENCES

Arif, S., M. Syukri, R. Holmes and V. Febriany (2010) 'Gendered risks and social protection: a case study of food subsidy program in Indonesia', research report, SMERU Research Institute, Jakarta.
Bappenas (Badan Perencanaan Pembangunan Nasional) (2010) *Rencana Pembangunan Jangka Menengah Nasional: Tahun 2010–2014* [Medium-term National Development Plan for 2010–2014], Bappenas, Jakarta.
Ellis, F. (2008) '"We are all poor here": economic difference, social divisiveness, and targeting cash transfers in Sub-Saharan Africa', paper presented at a conference on Social Protection in Africa: Learning from Experience, Kampala, 8–10 September. Available at: http://www.uea.ac.uk/polopoly_fs/1.87456!/fe-paper-sp-sept2008.pdf.
Haryanto, U. and M.A. Kencana (2010) 'Broken health care drives women to sell babies', *Jakarta Globe*, 13 July.
Mathematica (2007) *Evaluation of Jamaica's PATH program: Final Report*, Mathematica Policy Research, Inc., Washington DC.
Osman, N. (2010) 'In the dark about insurance, mothers give up newborns to pay hospital bills', *Jakarta Globe*, 9 July 2010.
Rogaly, B. (2003) 'Who goes? Who stays back? Seasonal migration and staying put among rural manual workers in eastern India', *Journal of International Development*, 15(5): 623–32.
Slater, R. and J. Farrington (2009) 'Targeting of social transfers: a review for DFID. Final report', Overseas Development Institute, London, September. Available at: http://www.odi.org.uk/resources/download/4521.pdf.
Slater, R. and J. Farrington (2010) 'Appropriate, achievable, acceptable: a practical tool for good targeting', Social Protection Toolsheet Targeting Social Transfers, Overseas Development Institute, London. Available at: http://www.odi.org.uk/resources/download/4697.pdf.
Statistics Indonesia (2009) *Trends of the Selected Socio-economic Indicators of Indonesia*, Statistics Indonesia, Jakarta, March.
Statistics Indonesia (2010) *Profil Kemiskinan di Indonesia Maret 2010* [Poverty Profile of Indonesia March 2010], Berita Resmi Statistik, No. 45/07/Th. XIII, Statistics Indonesia, Jakarta, 1 July.
Suryahadi, A. and S. Sumarto (2003) 'Poverty and vulnerability in Indonesia before and after the economic crisis', *Asian Economic Journal*, 17(1): 45–64.
World Bank (2010a) 'Targeting effectiveness of current social assistance programs in Indonesia', Targeting in Indonesia Policy Paper No. 1, World Bank, Jakarta.
World Bank (2010b) *Social Safety Nets Indonesia: Bantuan Langsung Tunai (BLT) – Temporary Unconditional Cash Transfer*, Poverty Group, World Bank, Jakarta.
World Food Programme (2009) *A Food Security and Vulnerability Atlas of Indonesia*, World Food Programme, Jakarta.

INDEX

district governments
see local governments
Dominican Republic, 34, 45, 173
DPR (Dewan Perwakilan Rakyat), 282,
285, 288
DRPD (Dewan Perwakilan Rakyat
Daerah), 213

E

economic growth, 3, 4, 6, 7, 23, 39, 40,
69, 76–7, 81, 82, 92–3, 96, 106, 114,
118, 138, 139, 145, 162, 275, 316n
during democratic transitions, 24–37
poverty incidence and, 5, 28, 57–64,
92–3
see also GDP
economic pie, size of, 51, 57–8
Ecuador, 45, 46, 170
education, 5, 6, 8–10, 14, 69, 71, 78, 83,
96, 107, 130
affordability, 9, 83, 188, 276, 278n,
339–40, 343, 344, 350–1
class sizes, 172–3
decentralisation, 180–1, 186, 192,
192–3n, 286
effect of parental, 127, 150, 151, 153,
154, 155, 156, 188–9, 191, 194
effect on occupational mobility of
migrants, 152, 154, 155
enrolment rates, 68, 83, 183, 194, 197,
301
expenditure, 9, 281, 281n
financial assistance, 276, 316
free schooling, 181, 343
funding, 9, 10, 185, 186, 187, 197
household head, 9, 71, 296
inequality, 183, 197
infrastructure, 83
Islamic system, 10, 183–99
junior secondary, 5, 10, 83, 97, 99,
100, 101, 102, 105, 183, 184, 184n,
189–90, 190, 191, 194, 280, 343
literacy rates, 197, 275
mathematics skills, 162–7
participation, 276, 301, 302, 303, 308
primary, 9, 69, 161, 170, 175, 177, 179,
183, 184n, 194, 296, 313n, 343
quality, 1–2, 9, 167–81, 188, 309
religion and, 186, 192n, 242
rural areas, 183, 199
scholarship schemes, 9, 337, 349, 350
secondary, 161, 164n
senior secondary, 9, 83, 194, 343–4,
350
vocational, 10n

women, 72–3, 74, 75
see also schools; teachers
elderly, 78, 298, 319, 339, 351
elections, national, 26, 27, 29, 37, 273,
274, 279, 284, 307n
presidential, 283
employment, 5–6, 6–8, 14, 82–3, 114,
344–5
agriculture, 1, 6, 7, 58, 59, 82–3, 94,
95, 116, 117, 118, 130, 142, 143, 144,
150, 153, 154, 155
casual, 6, 6n, 8, 195, 296
construction, 7n, 116, 117, 118, 138
determinants of occupation, 135–7
emergency job creation, 276
formal sector, 3, 6, 41, 115, 126, 129,
136, 221, 233, 236, 344
government, 216–17
growth, 115–20
human capital theory, 137, 153
indicators by gender, 74
informal sector, 6, 41, 113, 126, 136,
138, 221, 234, 237, 276
job creation, 6, 8, 14, 76, 276, 293, 298
manufacturing, 3, 6n, 7, 70, 114, 116,
117, 118, 119, 122, 129, 138, 143, 145,
145n
migration study, 140–56
mining sector, 94, 116, 117, 118, 143
rates, 74
self-employment, 136, 142, 150
services, 1, 3, 7n, 67, 82, 118, 130,
131, 136, 143, 145
temporary, 296
urban dualism, 136
utilities, 116, 117, 118
women, 73, 74
see also labour force; labour markets;
rural–urban migration
exchange rate, 77, 114, 116, 117, 123, 129,
130, 283n
exports, 60, 62, 70, 77, 114, 117, 127, 131,
145
export-oriented firms, 59, 77, 113,
114, 123, 129, 138, 139

F

Family of Hope (PKH)
see conditional cash transfer
program (PKH)
farmers/farming, 60, 62, 142, 144, 151,
292, 296, 335, 348
see also agriculture
females, 72–3
agricultural employment, 153, 155

TIMSS
  see Trends in International
  Mathematics and Science Study
TNP2K
  see National Team for the
  Acceleration of Poverty Reduction
Total Sanitation and Sanitation
  Marketing (TSSM), 258–60, 263–4
tourism, 105, 131, 293
trade liberalisation, 76–7
transport, 9, 95, 96–7, 104, 105, 264, 286,
  301, 303, 316n
  costs, 84, 95, 97, 188, 309, 341, 342,
  343, 351, 352
  paved roads, 97, 101–3
  sector, 116, 117, 118, 124r, 127, 142,
  143
Trends in International Mathematics
  and Science Study (TIMSS), 162–175
TSSM
  see Total Sanitation and Sanitation
  Marketing
tsunami, 2n
  Aceh, 80
Tunisia, 9, 164

U

Uganda, 170, 173
unconditional cash transfer program
  (BLT), 12–13, 14, 16, 17, 278–9, 285,
  291, 315–16, 320, 320n, 323, 324, 325,
  338, 347, 348, 350, 351
unemployment, 1, 6, 7, 10, 73, 107, 131,
  295, 296
  rate, 74
United States Agency for International
  Development (USAID), 64, 79
United States of America, 80, 134, 135,
  136, 172, 173, 185
urban areas, 4, 8, 49, 53, 54, 55, 56, 62, 66,
  67, 70–2, 84, 90, 293, 298
  labour market, 136, 139, 153, 340
  poverty incidence, 274n
  rural–urban migration, 8, 55, 56–7,
  59, 134–56
  sanitation, 246, 247, 248
  teachers, 174
Urban Poverty Program, 291, 292
Uruguay, 34, 45
utilities sector, 116, 117, 118

V

Vietnam, 3, 4, 8, 28, 29, 43, 51, 69, 80,
  129, 173, 245n, 316n

W

wages and wage employment, 5, 8, 9,
  41, 83, 90, 113, 118, 119, 123, 136, 138,
  232, 351
  below-market, 298, 319
  employment response to changes in,
  126–8, 129
  index of regular, 6, 7
  minimum, 83, 128, 195
  real, 6, 7
  see also incomes
Water and Sanitation for Low Income
  Communities (WSLIC) program,
  256–8, 259, 265
  effect of, 258
wholesale trade, 117
Wiranto, retired general, 283
wood products, 124, 125, 126, 127, 131,
  133
workforce
  see labour force
World Bank, 64, 177, 206, 256, 295, 306,
  327
  review of social assistance targeting,
  334, 337–8
  Social Safety Net Adjustment Loan,
  276n
  Water and Sanitation Project, 245n,
  263n
  Worldwide Governance Indicators
  Project, 208
  see also Kecamatan Development
  Program
World Development Indicators, 41, 42
WSLIC
  see Water and Sanitation for Low
  Income Communities

Y

Yudhoyono, President Susilo Bambang,
  279, 283, 288, 292–3
  effect on polity rating, 29
  election, 1, 29, 279
  fuel price policy, 12, 12n, 277, 283n,
  284, 292
  Independence Day speech, 283
  popularity, 279, 285
  statement on poverty, 2, 283, 317

Z

Zambia, 46, 173

INDONESIA UPDATE SERIES

Indonesia Assessment 1988 (Regional Development)
edited by Hal Hill and Jamie Mackie

Indonesia Assessment 1990 (Ownership)
edited by Hal Hill and Terry Hull

Indonesia Assessment 1991 (Education)
edited by Hal Hill

Indonesia Assessment 1992 (Political Perspectives)
edited by Harold Crouch

Indonesia Assessment 1993 (Labour)
edited by Chris Manning and Joan Hardjono

Finance as a Key Sector in Indonesia's Development (1994)
edited by Ross McLeod

Development in Eastern Indonesia (1995)
edited by Colin Barlow and Joan Hardjono

Population and Human Resources (1996)
edited by Gavin W. Jones and Terence H. Hull

Indonesia's Technological Challenge (1997)
edited by Hal Hill and Thee Kian Wie

Post-Soeharto Indonesia: Renewal or Chaos? (1998)
edited by Geoff Forrester

Indonesia in Transition: Social Aspects of Reformasi and Crisis (1999)
edited by Chris Manning and Peter van Diermen

Indonesia Today: Challenges of History (2000)
edited by Grayson J. Lloyd and Shannon L. Smith

Women in Indonesia: Gender, Equity and Development (2001)
edited by Kathryn Robinson and Sharon Bessell

Local Power and Politics in Indonesia: Decentralisation and Democratisation (2002)
edited by Edward Aspinall and Greg Fealy

Business in Indonesia: New Challenges, Old Problems (2003)
edited by M. Chatib Basri and Pierre van der Eng

The Politics and Economics of Indonesia's Natural Resources (2004)
edited by Budy P. Resosudarmo

Different Societies, Shared Futures: Australia, Indonesia and the Region (2005)
edited by John Monfries

Indonesia: Democracy and the Promise of Good Governance (2006)
edited by Ross H. McLeod and Andrew MacIntyre

Expressing Islam: Religious Life and Politics in Indonesia (2007)
edited by Greg Fealy and Sally White

Indonesia beyond the Water's Edge: Managing an Archipelagic State (2008)
edited by Robert Cribb and Michele Ford

Problems of Democratisation in Indonesia: Elections, Institutions and Society (2009)
edited by Edward Aspinall and Marcus Mietzner

Employment, Living Standards and Poverty in Contemporary Indonesia (2010)
edited by Chris Manning and Sudarno Sumarto